The
Immoral Landscape

THE IMMORAL LANDSCAPE

*Female Prostitution
In Western Societies*

Richard Symanski

BUTTERWORTHS Toronto

The Immoral Landscape: Female Prostitution in Western Societies
© 1981 Butterworth & Co. (Canada) Ltd.

Printed and bound in Canada

The Butterworth Group of Companies

Canada:
Butterworth & Co. (Canada) Ltd., Toronto and Vancouver

United Kingdom:
Butterworth & Co. (Publishers) Ltd., London

Australia:
Butterworths Pty. Ltd., Sydney

New Zealand:
Butterworths of New Zealand Ltd., Wellington

South Africa:
Butterworth & Co. (South Africa) Ltd., Durban

United States:
Butterworth (Publishers) Inc., Boston
Butterworth (Legal Publishers) Inc., Seattle
Mason Publishing Company, St. Paul

Canadian Cataloguing in Publication Data

Symanski, Richard.
  The immoral landscape

Bibliography: p.
Includes index.
ISBN 0-409-87130-3

1. Prostitution. I. Title.
HQ117.S95   306.7'4   C81-094075-2

For my Mother and Father

Contents

"*The Moralist tells us;* In medio sita est Virtus; *that is, He is the most vertuous man, who preserving himself indifferently between the two extreams of good and evil, knows how to apply himself to one or the other, with equal spirit and equal success, as the design in hand may seem to require: If we look into the practice of the Antients, or those of later times, we shall ever find this trade receiving all possible encouragement. The best governed, and the most Catholick Cities now in the World, do grant it, if not a publick toleration, yet at least a civil and sufficient connivence.*"

Ferrante Pallavicino, The Whore's
Rhetorick, *1683.*

Landscapes and Peoples

Time: 11:30 P.M., June 17, 1976. Place: San Francisco, Powell Street between Geary and Post. At mid-block the imposing St. Francis Hotel opens its majestic doors to greenbacks, conventioneers, salesmen away from home. The hotel and the nearby streetscape are places to pick up a trick, run a game, do a double, make the nightly nut to keep daddy happy.

What defines this streetscape? Halftones, the mumble of the masses, clanging cable car bells, a young man kissing his date for the first time, an ambience of toughness, suspicion, indifference, confidence, lonely men seeking animated ways to fulfill a stone-age imperative.

Here and elsewhere in the Tenderloin there are streetwalkers in numbers not seen in Baghdad by the Bay in more than ten years. The mayor and district attorney ran—and won—on a non-violent crime platform. A liberalism that said scarce resources ought to be used to chase murderers, rapists and armed robbers was an open invitation to pimps and prostitutes to invade the city. They happily obliged. They came from Alaska and even from the Big Apple—the "main switchboard."

Misty and Jo saunter boldly along their Powell Street stroll. One swings a purse high and low, the other moves her body to some inner tune. The twosome appears to be marking a territory with the assurance of rats urinating rings around reproductive resources in the slumscape.

A male, seemingly oblivious to the moment and the place, passes Misty and Jo and is gone from their minds forever. Another nears, looks to Misty's satin legs, stares at her thick red lips and makeup face. She returns a solicitous smile and says, "Hi, honey. Want a little company?" The stranger applies his brakes and a millenium-old negotation begins.

A pimpmobile, a customized baby blue El Dorado, rolls slowly up Powell Street. The large black face behind the wheel appears solemn. Eddie—no popcorn pimp this man—is in the tradition of other Tenderloin luminaries of recent years: Fillmore Slim, Tommy Shaw, Marshall Johnson, Sweet Jesus. Eddie wears a wide-brimmed hat with a single peacock feather. The hat looks like it might have belonged to Scaramouch. His diamond pinkie throws reflected light onto the pavement and into the eyes of cops, ripoff artists, bottom women, outlaws. Inaudible remarks are exchanged. The Pimp Bible says it would be undignified for Eddie to look for his women, to take any notice of the activity that feeds his coke habit, builds his wardrobe, makes him a bigger hero in the black ghetto than Reggie Jackson.

The undercover cop sits across the street on a small retaining wall, one of the long edges of Union Square. His beard is heavy, his blue jeans old and tattered, he doesn't wear an earring. The inhabitants of the streetscape know who he is. "You can smell him, honey. And if you can't just give him a big french and watch him run."

They continue hustling, they flag down taxis for two people, they return from trick pads and laugh derisively about their tricks. Some are aggressive, some are cautious. They have the eyes of owls. They worry—from experience.

He came out of nowhere, threw Misty to the ground as he grabbed her purse and ran like the Fourth of July had been celebrated in his asshole. He nearly ran over the cop who grabbed him, choked him, hit him repeatedly in the face in retaliation for a single blow. A crowd gathered and waited for a victor to emerge. The crowd watched, sensing an impending knockout.

Jo helped Misty to her feet and like two shoplifters at the exit, bags full, they quickly disappeared around the corner on Geary.

"Where's the girl? Somebody grab that fuckin' girl. Where'd she go?" The cop was puffing the words, barely atop the thief, still cuffing him. I thought of giving the cop false directions on Misty's flight path, but decided Misty didn't need my help. She knew the streets better than I could hope to.

The small group stood mutely, then began to disperse.

Less than an hour later the thief, who resembled a college kid of the early '60s, strolled nonchalantly past the St. Francis. No complainant, no booking. No one paid him any attention.

The appetites of the night began to die. I headed for home in the quiet chill, wondering how much trick money in Misty's purse could have induced her to submit to another round of indignities at the local precinct. I decided the issue didn't concern dollars, that Misty simply returned to her pimp and said, "Sorry, daddy. I'll double the nut tomorrow."

A number of years ago in Elko, Nevada, I met a young woman by the name of Kitty. Kitty was her house name. She was bright, articulate, well-educated, beautiful. She loves her younger brother and her husband, she visits her parents periodically (to this day they don't know about her job), she votes Republican, she believes in nuclear power, likes to backpack and is full of zest about life. When I first met her and in years to follow when I saw her we talked about politics, biology, her interests in Shakespeare and hard rock. Occasionally we chatted about what we did for a living. Kitty said she liked her job as a "working girl," a Nevada prostitute's way of describing her occupation. Mostly, she said she liked the money: often $1,000 a week after the house takes a 50 percent cut off the top.

The first time I met Kitty she said that after she graduated from the University of Michigan she had difficulty getting a decently paying or challenging job. She couldn't believe that a degree in business had prepared her for little more than a secretarial position. Her father, a professor at the University of Michigan, wanted to help. He just didn't have his hands on strings that mattered. "Find a job and work your way up," he had said. She could have gotten married as there was no shortage of suitors. But she found the prospect unappealing. Nor was she taken by the discovery that, to use her words, "most of the guys were primarily interested in chasing my ass around the table. Or demanding it after a night of dinner and dancing."

Through a friend Kitty heard about the brothels on Cherry Street in Terre Haute, Indiana. She was told that a young, attractive girl could make a sizeable income. All she had to do was put a price on what she had been giving away free; and close her eyes. Kitty decided to give it a try. She prospered on Cherry Street until even bribery money couldn't prevent the city's vice squad from closing all the houses. Out of work and unwilling to hit the streets she drifted for a few months, enjoying the money she had saved. She bought a sports car, she added to her wardrobe, she traveled. Then disaster struck.

In a head-on collision she received multiple injuries and had to spend several months in a hospital. The driver of the other car had no insurance. Her accumulated savings were not enough to begin to cover the huge bill. Kitty's parents didn't have much money, and she did not feel she could ask her father for assistance.

Another friend, a prostitute, told Kitty that brothels were legal in Nevada. The pay was good and the houses were always looking for new faces. There wasn't much to do in the desert towns of Wells or Elko or Winnemucca, especially since prostitutes were only allowed out of the brothels for a few hours in the afternoon, and even then they couldn't go into casinos or bars. But knowing this did not affect Kitty's decision at the time. The medical bill insured that. Even now that she has experienced enforced isolation as one cost of her earnings it doesn't seem to bother her.

The last time I saw Kitty in the summer of 1979 she had been working for nearly three straight months, seven days a week without a break. Without a break from cantankerous competitors, innumerable beauty contests called lineups, a dictatorial madam, superficial bar conversations. Without a break from days of chess, backgammon and reading. Without a break from nights of numerous trips to her second-floor bedroom with scared men, half-drunk men, old men and young boys, aggressive and impolite men who pay for fifteen minutes or half an hour of her time to fulfill fantasies.

The last time I saw Kitty she was happy, optimistic. Her bankroll was multiplying and she and her husband Ted will have the opportunity they have been planning for years. Ted was a heroin addict and former resident of Folsom prison. He has a difficult time getting jobs and when he does he often gets bumped because of low seniority. Kitty and Ted will soon be moving to the Southwest to open up a restaurant. They would like to have an adjoining bar, if she can get a liquor license. Because she has never been arrested no one will ever know that Kitty was a working girl in the perdurable immoral landscape.

These sketches of real events and real people are presented to suggest some of the themes I attempt to systematically explore in the chapters that follow. That I will not deal more with the particulars of individuals like Misty, Eddie and Kitty or with the emotive content of the immoral landscape—socially defined—is dictated by my desire to address general issues and generalities.

Any inquiry into prostitution encounters problems found elsewhere in scholarly inquiry, but in dramatic relief. With a few notable exceptions the topic has not been seen as one for serious intellectual inquiry until relatively recent times. For all the touted liberalism one is supposed to find in universities, academics have been amazingly provincial toward the topic. Sociology, of course, has always had something to say about prostitutes, often as part of a more general inquiry into "social deviance." Historians left the topic virtually untouched until the last decade or so; the 1970s saw the appearance of a dozen or so doctoral dissertations on prostitution, more than the number produced during the previous 100 years. Anthropologists, excepting a few in the 1970s and what ethnographers have had to say about prostitution in their field reports, have also been slow to give prostitution any attention. But the award for being an intellectual and emotional laggard, particularly in view of the discipline's expressed concern for cities and for social oppression and crime, belongs to geography. To my knowledge, no master's thesis, doctoral dissertation, monograph or book has ever been written on the topic by a geographer, and as of 1980 only a single article had appeared in a major geographical journal. None of this would matter if prostitution had nothing to do with geography. But, as I argue in the chapters that follow, much of the social problem of prostitution and its solution are eminently geographic.

The "prostitution problem" is intimately related to visibility or landscape appearance; the appearance of landscapes is a venerable geographic theme. For two thousand years one of the state's primary methods of coping with the visible manifestations of an immoral landscape—socially defined—has been zoning. A concern with the geometry of human relationships, the ordering of people in space, is at the core of geographic inquiry. The principal means that prostitutes have used to fight repression and oppression is mobility. Mobility is one of several processes that most interest the geographer, because mobility is behind the definition of places, the formation of landscapes, the nature of perceived landscape appearances, all human earthbound geometries. Finally, to come full circle, it would appear that any workable solution to the prostitution problem involves issues of visibility and zoning.

There are other problems. Prostitution is a topic easily exploited by hack writers writing for huge audiences that outwardly cling to puritanical values but privately lap up lascivious descriptions. Short of personal experience or a good deal of reading on the topic it is difficult to separate the sensational from the plausible, truth from untruth. For all kinds of reasons prostitutes withhold information from investigators; often they lie. On issues such as numbers of prostitutes and their locational coordinates, statistics are almost always suspect. Where prostitution has been regulated by government registration, arrest figures have grossly underestimated numbers of women while overestimating the occurrence of prostitution among lower-class women. In illegal environments, as in North America, some prostitutes are arrested numerous times, others, especially call girls, not at all. Again, there is a class bias in the data. In any event, arrests vary considerably from one time period to the next, depending on public outcry, public resources and public opinion.

Cognizant of these and other difficulties I have adopted several strategies. Like others I have relied on conventional arrest statistics but advise that readers not interpret them too closely. I have drawn from as many sources as possible: newspapers, unpublished manuscripts, master's theses, doctoral dissertations and commission reports, journal articles, autobiographies and other books, and fieldwork. I have used my personal knowledge of prostitution in the Americas more as a check of reasonableness on what others have said than as direct statements of fact or finding. Another approach has been the use of numerous examples. This, I feel, has the virtue of lending credence to the claim that certain patterns, despite their peculiarities, are not unique. Examples also provide a kind of documentary record, a record of the range in time and place of injustices committed against prostitutes, and the varieties of strategies they have employed in coping with oppression and repression.

The organization of the book is rather straightforward. Chapters 1 through 3 introduce the book's argument and the social and urban contexts of prostitution: where it occurs, how people feel about it, whether or not their perceptions and attitudes are accurate, how much it costs to be moral and ignorant. Chapters 4 through 8 address the issues of who benefits from prostitution and how men and the state use prostitutes to advantage. In particular, Chapter 4 begins with an examination of female exploitation and how this leads women into prostitution and then turns to male demand, particularly its roots in biology. Male demand, in conjunction with the control that males have over social systems, leads to unjust prostitution laws and discriminatory application of them—Chapter 5; and exploitation of prostitutes by the state and others—Chapters 6 and 7. The filtering of social prejudices pertaining to race and class into the subculture of prostitution and the geographic expression of these prejudices is the subject of Chapter 8.

Chapter 9 is a bridge of sorts. It explores ways in which prostitutes are simultaneously exploited by pimps and others and yet are profoundly dependent on them, issues that arise largely from the illegality of prostitution. Chapters 10 through 13 examine adaptive strategies, their rationale and their effectiveness. Chapter 10 focuses on the streetscape because this is where being a prostitute is most difficult and demanding. Chapter 11 draws attention to the fundamental importance of mobility. The next chapter describes adaptive strategies as they unfold in Chicago and London at two different time periods; both illustrate how difficult it is to effectively repress prostitution. Chapter 13 looks at the contemporary landscape of massage parlors, escort services and other fronts for prostitution, arguing that the very nature of illegality causes problems that the state wishes to avoid. Finally, Chapter 14 discusses solutions: the principal arguments for decriminalization, modifications that would—perhaps—solve long-standing problems and tactics to increase the rate of change in laws.

Nancy Burley and I have written an Appendix complementary to the text, especially Chapter 4. Through an evolutionary and cross-cultural examination of prostitution in scores of societies we examine the biology and culture behind the supply and demand sides of prostitution: why and when it is an evolutionarily good strategy for females to become prostitutes and for men to seek them out. Because the evolutionary arguments for women turning to prostitution are rather involved and not directly germane to the thesis of the book I have, in Chapter 4, confined the discussion of why women become prostitutes to "proximate" as opposed to "ultimate-level" (evolutionary) explanations. On the other hand, in Chapter 4 I do discuss the evolutionary reasons for male promiscuity, because ultimately it is male demand that drives the system of prostitution. The argument for male promiscuity serves another purpose, namely to counter the long-standing received opinion in the social sciences that prostitution primarily serves a social function. I argue that this is fundamentally not so, that such an argument is group selectionist and confuses the function of prostitutes to individual males with a social effect. The Appendix, then, more securely anchors one argument of the book: that while the forms that prostitution takes reflect a dialectical interplay between social norms and individual self-interest, a correct reading of prostitution must begin with the individual. There remains a widespread tendency in the social sciences to give too much attention to the concepts of culture and society, and with Marxists, to class, as forces that have their own existence and explain individual behavior. The result is that analyses are often confused and incompatible with an evolutionary perspective on the species.

I wish to thank those who made the writing of this book easier: James Root for helping me with the early phases of field work in Nevada in 1973; courthouse clerks throughout Nevada who made available local ordinances on prostitution; Margaret Day and Roxanne Price for drafting preliminary maps of prostitution in Nevada; John Fraser Hart who gave the topic a chance; Margo St. James of COYOTE, a national organization of prostitutes based in San Francisco for giving me access to files of newspaper clippings and unpublished reports; John Vanucchi of the Bureau of Special Services, San Francisco Police Department, who talked with me about prostitution in that city and gave me permission to examine arrest records; Debbie Mercier, Karen Larkin and Tom Knight who taught me about prostitution in Montreal; undergraduate students at the University of Texas at Austin and McGill University who gave me a platform on which to refine some of my ideas; John Jakle who offered criticisms on an early draft of eight chapters; Jim Bier who provided design suggestions on the graphs and maps and did the cartography; Carol Coopersmith who helped compile the list of references in the bibliography for the Appendix; and Peter Horowitz at Butterworths who gave me a significant say in the final format of the book and did not flinch when I gave him a manuscript more than twice the length of that I contracted for.

Many people kindly sent me unpublished doctoral dissertations and manuscripts, newspaper articles, reprints, bibliographies and leads to sources (my apologies to those I have forgotten): Jacqueline Barnhart, Jacqueline Boles, Mary Bulmahn, Paul Goldstein, Marion Goldman, John Fraser Hart, Kingsley Haynes, Barbara Heyl, Hal Hoverland, Jennifer James, Robbie Johnson, Rob Kent, Monique Layton, Carol Leonard, David Ley, Edward Lorenzen, John Lowman, Barbara Milman, Janet Morelli, James Newman, James Parsons, Dudley Poston, Leroy Schultz, Neil Shumsky, Robert South, James Vorenberg, Isidor Walliman and David Ward.

I owe particular thanks to streetwalkers and brothel and massage parlor prostitutes in San Francisco, Oakland, New York City, Austin, Nevada, Montreal, Mexico, Costa Rica, Colombia and Peru for patiently talking with me about their lives and environments.

Most of all I owe a deep and affectionate thanks to Nancy Burley. She is my wife, but never questioned my interest in prostitution or my motives for wanting to know prostitutes. While others often were unnerved and judgmental about the probity of my research, she never lost her aplomb. Nancy is, of course, an evolutionary biologist *par excellence*, whose principal research interest is sexual selection. Without Nancy I might not have seen so clearly why males in most species are promiscuous, nor would I have come to appreciate one of the great insights of all time—evolution by natural selection. But Nancy did more. She read every draft, forced me to abandon some, caught flaws in my logic and grammar and found time in her busy schedule for the tedious task of proofing galleys. Finally, she gave me writing space in her aviary and introduced me to a new and great kind of friend, parrots all—Dakwa Waza Garou, Gamin and Erasmus W. W. Smack. Hail, hail birds of the world!

Elko, Nevada, 1980

Chapter
1

Biology, Geopolitics and Landscape Morality

Prostitution persists as a social problem or, more properly, a biosocial problem for at least six reasons: (1) Sex is not freely available in the same way that fresh air and clean water once were. (2) Women have long been socially and economically discriminated against, because (3) men control social systems. (4) Men are more promiscuous than women, a difference based both in culture and the biology of the sexes. (5) Sex as a commercial service—prostitution—is deemed immoral by men who (6) make it illegal but nevertheless patronize prostitutes.

Several of these reasons dovetail in the concept of the double standard. Through their control of social systems men proscribe the sexual behavior of females and support an essentially monogamous mating system, yet they often behave promiscuously. Female prostitutes constitute one of several outlets for such behavior. From an evolutionary point of view it serves the male's best interest to write rules and support a system that keep his wife faithful, while at the same time behaving promiscuously.

Prostitution poses another kind of social problem. People have less concern about the perpetration of an immoral act than about the visual suggestion of its occurrence. Appearances matter most. But prostitutes who occupy public spaces symbolize more than women who have simply broken a respected taboo. They embody history, myth, prejudice, ill-conceived and misconceived attitudes and perceptions. For centuries the public mind has linked them inextricably with venereal disease and crime. They are still believed to be major sources of "social disease," and they are thought to be criminals, even part of organized crime. In an age of drugs, prostitutes find themselves more tainted by the image of drug usage than others. That the visible presence of a woman who rents access to her body bothers people is evidenced in many ways, not the least being the fact that almost all arrests are of prostitutes who walk the streets. In so far then as people catch sight of prostitutes and regard them as the personification of base values, they try to circumscribe and, if possible, erase them from the landscape.

Because the state continually concerns itself with the visible presence and location of prostitution, its laws and unofficial ways of handling the institution are geopolitical. To be sure, society cares about a good deal more than geography: venereal disease, the impact of prostitution on children and the family, reforming waywardness. But these matters notwithstanding, geopolitical issues remain central and perduring because prostitution cannot be reformed away or wished away. And it will not simply go away so long as men go to prostitutes for reasons as much biological as cultural, so long as men control social systems, so long as women are exploited and see advantage in turning to prostitution.

Since adjudicating or socially condemning behavior does not eliminate it, and proves ineffective when those in control of the system create the demand for the circumscribed behavior, the state attempts to cope by reducing visibility to acceptable levels. Acceptable levels of visibility are determined by the existing moral climate, available resources and the behavior of those who define the immoral landscape. The principal means of reducing public visibility are repression and spatial and temporal containment. Repression takes the form of harassments, abridgment of constitutional rights, arrests and incarceration. Containment or segregation is accomplished by encouraging, through differential repression or accommodation, prostitutes to work in some areas and not in others. Besides segregation prostitutes are also required to reduce their visibility by altering their appearance or that of the places where they work, and by requirements that they only labor at particular times of the day or night.

Geopolitical solutions to prostitution are founded on several propositions. One involves the belief that few societies are free of prostitution, particularly urban societies. Another is grounded in the historical experience that attempts to suppress prostitution always prove costly and are only rarely successful. Given these kinds of propositions it has usually been felt better to have an undesirable population isolated and in one or a few places rather than everywhere. A segregated group eases the tasks of identification and control, and impact primarily remains localized. Innocent folk will not be contaminated by disease, by crime, by examples of ignoble behavior. Men's passions will be loosened less often, and they will, so some have contended, less frequently corrupt their wives with base sexual appetites. Thomas Aquinas in his *Summa theologica*, probably the most widely quoted in this regard, said that prostitution in the towns corresponds to a cesspool in the palace. Do away with the cesspool and the palace will become an unclean and stinking place.

Men have gone further in implementing their geopolitical thinking. They make effective use of the simple axiom that power determines all things important. Power decides not just the nature of laws that repress, and not just general rules to contain or disperse undesirable elements, but also specifically where prostitutes will live and work. Visibility varies by location, the location of particular peoples. Prostitutes appear least noteworthy, or matter least, among those without political power and those deemed socially disorganized—minorities, the disenfranchised, those black, brown, or yellow, and the poor. Like other unacceptable peoples throughout history—immigrants, Jews, blacks—prostitutes consistently have been forced to live and labor among those with minimal social and political clout. This is the geopolitical sink principle.

The geopolitical sink principle derives from the social tenet that geographic spaces that define society's principal social relationships should reflect prevailing moral norms. In a broad sense, the moral code of a society represents the sacred, its transgression the profane. So long as a breach of social rules is sufficiently widespread, relatively inconsequential or engaged in by privileged segments of society (men, rulers, rule makers), a violation of the moral code does not require a special geographical interpretation. A social space, a place defined by the social interactions of individuals, is like a social norm in being plastic and accommodating. But when behavior does not fall within acceptable categories, or when the proscription is absolute rather than relative—as with adultery by females in many societies—then moral norm decodes into geography. Transgressors must live in a space apart from others who ascribe to and generally obey the prevailing system of social values. Violators must work, sometimes live, in social sinks, sinks that are geopolitical if created by the state. Sinks take two basic forms. One is a space beyond or apart from that which defines the core of society and its norms—at the fringe of settlement or in another place. Another kind of sink, represented by the containment of prostitutes within ghettos or slums, exists within the space occupied by moral society but has roughly the same relationship to the rest of society that a hole has to a doughnut.

Since males who control the state may wish to consort with prostitutes they resolve the moral dilemma by writing laws that apply only to females or, when legislation applies to both parties, having them enforced against prostitutes but not their customers. This differential system of justice satisfies social demands that arise from visibility and the image of prostitutes, is consistent with the general pattern of sexism by males and permits access to what is ostensibly denied as morally accessible. To meet requirements that tangible results bear a relationship to professed norm, cops and courts concentrate harassments, arrests and incarcerations on blacks, low-class prostitutes and those unable or unwilling to pay for the right to work.

Just as males perceive problems and seek workable solutions within their own frame of reference, so women do the same. While there are often social and personal reasons that make certain women likely candidates for prostitution, many simply discover that working in an illegal or immoral market makes good economic sense. Throughout history prostitution has provided a solution to the problem of economic hardship. Simply put, men are willing to pay more for sexual access than for almost all other forms of female labor.

When a woman works as a prostitute in a society that strongly condemns prostitutes and labels them criminals she encounters a multitude of difficulties. She is treated as an outcast, victimized by social labeling and self-fulfilling prophecies and preyed upon by the rich and the respectable, her customers and many others. Seen as a criminal and forced to associate with them, she finds advantage in behaving as expected and treated.

The prostitute seeks solace in whomever will provide it, often seemingly without regard to financial cost or personal health. For the streetwalker, and even other prostitutes, the pimp has proven to be the axial pillar in the search for solutions to insolvable dilemmas. Assistance, of course, is needed in a great many ways beyond what a pimp can provide. Cabdrivers, bellhops, lawyers and bartenders also make the job of prostituting easier. But as do pimps, they charge high fees. The sharper and more profound the moral cleavage and the laws supporting it, the greater the leverage outsiders have in exploiting prostitutes. The women become enmeshed in a quandary. Once criminalized they find it difficult to return to the "straight" world. Yet, to survive in an illegal environment they must actively seek the support of people who exploit them.

Prostitutes adapt in other ways to repression and maltreatment, especially through mobility. Most of the Western world governments at all levels have laws that attempt to preclude or control commercial sex. But governments employ different policies for streetwalkers and indoor prostitutes; they have widely differing approaches to respecting human rights and handing out jail and parole sentences; and where prostitution is legal or controlled, laws and their enforcement are seldom similar from one city to another. Prostitutes respond to these geographical inconsistencies by applying a deceptively simple strategy. They move to places or into niches where laws or their application are most favorable. It might be said that prostitutes have learned an old Chinese proverb that, "Of thirty-six ways to escape danger . . . running is the best."

Mobility is the complement to confinement, place-fixedness. In a sense the history of prostitution is a dialectic without a synthesis. Society attempts to confine prostitutes to this or that area, treating them unfairly both in the process and in the aftermath. Despite strong concepts of territoriality and predictability that come from knowing a place, prostitutes react to repression by moving. Their mobility prompts the thesis to reassert itself. One immoral landscape is obliterated, temporarily, and another is created or modified. The dialectic continues.

A strategy often complementary to mobility involves changes in the form of doing business: from being a house prostitute to a streetwalker, or vice versa; from soliciting in the street to soliciting through newspapers; by altering the name of a brothel without substantially changing the nature of the business.

Prostitution as an adaptive system reflects a well-known ecological principle, namely that the stability of a system resides in the diversity of its component parts or adaptations. Individuals within prostitution do not seek to make the system diverse and thereby stable; rather, they seek their own best interests. But because interests and options differ, as do the perceived means of achieving them, different strategies are used, to the benefit of the system as a whole and the detriment of those who wish to repress or eliminate it.

Most social solutions to prostitution, particularly those in North America, have been the wrong ones because they have involved widespread injustices and contradictions which have created secondary problems. Non-criminals become criminals because of illegality, social labeling and forced associations with criminals. Once in prostitution, the nature of the system makes it difficult for the women to leave. The state worries about pimps, the ways they exploit and sometimes brutalize prostitutes, and harsh laws are enacted to curtail the activities of pimps. Yet, illegality not only helps create the need for pimps, but it makes a pimp of the state. Illegality provides a mechanism for cops to demand graft, information and other "accommodations" from prostitutes, lest they be arrested.

Visibility is not reduced by concentrating prostitutes. To the contrary, visibility is density-dependent: the greater the density the higher the visibility. This widely utilized solution is self-defeating, for the problem that results is worse than if nothing had been done.

Because the adaptive strategies of prostitutes work so well and because existing geopolitical solutions are so ineffective, very scarce public resources chase poorly allocated resources. The pure monetary costs of repression are high, to say nothing of the fact that people often do not pay income taxes on criminal activities. Social costs add to the bill. Instead of the police focusing on violent crimes they deploy vice squads to chase prostitutes through a seemingly infinite number of adaptive exits. Prostitutes lose, the public loses, and the criminal justice system suffers because it loses credibility to no avail.

Landscape Morality

The United States has some of the most moralistic criminal laws in history, possibly surpassed only by those found in John Calvin's sixteenth century Geneva. Two students of crime writing a decade ago claimed that the sex laws in the United States "provide an enormous legislative chastity belt encompassing the whole population and proscribing everything but solitary and joyless masturbation and 'normal coitus' inside wedlock."[1]

It took until 1978 for the New York Family Court to make a decision and a declaration justly counter to prevailing opinion in the state and most other places in North America. After extensive research the court declared that the state's prostitution laws were invalid because they infringed upon the right to equal protection and privacy. The family court concluded that:

> If it is paternalism that prompts the legislature to protect women by proscribing prostitution, that motive is ill-served by the prostitution laws since women

are not protected, but rather are penally punished. . . . However offensive it may be, recreational commercial sex threatens no harm to public health, safety or welfare and therefore may not be proscribed.[2]

In 1979 a superior court in Washington D.C. did not agree that the city's solicitation statute, the primary vehicle in the United States for arresting prostitutes, conflicts with the First Amendment right of free speech.[3] Despite some recognition in the 1970s that prostitutes are humans with rights protected by the Constitution the majority of states have not advanced much further than the nation's capital.

Morality has two meanings. To those who live, toil, even die in a place, morality is a matter of individual self-esteem in that place. It concerns the question of how streetwalkers treat one another on Lexington Avenue, how young girls from the "Minnesota Strip" are manipulated by their pimps, and how store merchants, bartenders and cops on the streets of San Francisco's Tenderloin carry on. More particularly and weightily, these internal moral questions at these quite-specific places concern Ann and Rosalind, the night bartender at Mac's and the cop on the beat. The view emanates from within and is often individual- and grievance-specific. While molded and continually reshaped by matters external, the internal morality of a landscape has its own norms and ways of adjudicating differences.

External morality refers to the social, the aggregate, the anonymous opinions and prejudices of what a landscape is or ought to be. Mostly, the labeled and unlabeled judgmental depictions have no single spokesperson, usually no one who even cares that much about what happens in a place tomorrow or two weeks hence. For this reason the distal morality almost always contains distortions, lies and specious misrepresentations.

The external morality involves dubious, often erroneous assumptions. One is that immoral conduct has harmful social effects. In fact, such effects are either difficult to identify or when pinpointed, as with venereal disease and the claim that prostitutes are thieves and drug addicts, they prove to be nonexistent, unproven or less than assumed. Prostitutes pose less of a venereal disease threat to society than college coeds. The involvement by many prostitutes in larceny and hard drug usage arises, as much as anything, from their treatment by the state.

Many legislators assume that prostitution laws reflect social consensus. But do they? A 1971 poll of some 15,000 people conducted by a California assemblyman found that 50 percent of those questioned thought that legalized prostitution was a good idea.[4] A 1973 Harris survey revealed that only 46 percent of those polled thought that prostitution did "more harm than good." This compared with 78 percent who believed that military leaders who cover up secret bombing raids do "more harm than good," and 81 percent who disapproved of businessmen giving illegal contributions. A 1972 survey of Baltimore's population attempted to determine how people ranked the seriousness of 140 crimes.[5] This careful sociological study found that soliciting for prostitution ranked 108. People considered it more serious to underrepresent income on one's income tax return (it ranked 106), and slightly less serious to be overcharged for automobile repairs (it ranked 110).

Perhaps the most recent survey on attitudes toward prostitution in the United States was conducted by Barbara Milman at the Harvard Center for Criminal Justice. Her sample of 279 people, including a national survey of policemen in 57 cities, showed that only 40 percent thought prostitution immoral, 43 percent favored decriminalization of laws, except for those pertaining to pimping, and more than 75 percent believed that there was at least one better alternative to the current treatment of prostitutes.[6]

In Great Britain, where street solicitation and brothels are illegal, there is no apparent social consensus on the gravity of the problem. A 1965 Gallup Public Opinion Poll discovered that 29 percent of the people questioned believed that prostitution was a "very serious social problem." But the comparable figures for heavy smoking and gambling were 27 and 31 percent respectively.[7]

None of these findings makes a distinction between male and female attitudes, and one can only speculate how much the sexes vary in how they feel about prostitution. Bits of information suggest, however, what might be expected: that males are less critical of the institution than females. When the Italian Senator, Angelina Merlin, who had fought for years to have her country's brothels closed, finally succeeded in 1958, her indignant male constituency voted her out of office.[8] Two decades ago the British Wolfenden Report on homosexuality and prostitution proposed two years of incarceration for pimping. Three female members of the committee wanted a five year prison sentence.[9]

Internal and external landscape moralities frequently intersect. A beat cop treats street women differently because of what he has learned in the larger society, because of what he has cunningly experienced in working with them, and because of what he has been repeatedly told to do by bosses who live and think the exterior morality. Streetwalkers and massage parlor prostitutes have their notions of right and wrong continually shaped by their past, and by the treatment they daily receive from judges, journalists, passersby and businessmen who know where to go when their wives are physically or psychologically unobliging.

The external or social morality is heavily textured with hypocrisy. North Americans make a strong distinction between private sins and public crimes, between what average people do in bedrooms and what prostitutes do for a living.

> The sex laws of the United States today reflect a formidable mass schizophrenia. The split between our society's permissive—even obsessive—sexual behavior and attitudes, and our punitive, puritanical statutes is indeed scarcely credible.[10]

North Americans have never been very good at reconciling liberalism and Puritanism.

Recently in Minnesota, a district judge, a state senator, a United States Attorney General, several vice squad members and the chief lobbyist for the Minnesota Catholic Conference, all of whom have either argued for legislation against prostitution or enforced the laws, publicly admitted making use of prostitutes. Neither these officials nor their wives saw a contradiction in their behavior. Nor, apparently, did much of the public. The state senator claimed that of over one hundred letters received, "almost all were supportive."[11]

The cry, "Decriminalize prostitution," calling for the absence of state control over the matter, can be heard across the Western world. It is voiced by feminists and prostitutes and lawyers and the National Organization of Women, and from all kinds of people who have no particular predatory or personal sexual interest in the women. Scores of nations have decriminalized prostitution. Yet when the United Nations passed a resolution in 1958 calling for decriminalization the press in the United States all but ignored it.[12]

In recent years one might say that progress of a sort has been made. By 1979, 22 states—none in the South—had decriminalized private sexual acts between consenting adults (Figure 1-1). Of course, legislators must know that acts of prostitution are privately consummated between consenting

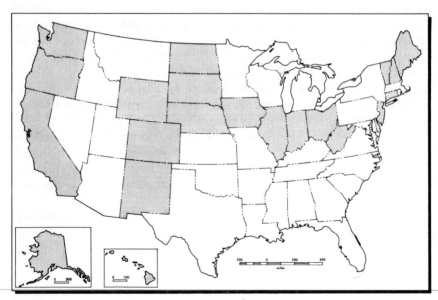

Figure 1-1 States (shaded areas) Which Have Decriminalized Non-Commercial Sex Between Consenting Adults as of 1979
Data from "Private Sex Decriminalized in Vermont" 1979:9.

people—the great majority of whom are adults. Yet, prostitution laws have not been decriminalized in the United States, in Canada or in Great Britain.

In Canada and Great Britain soliciting for prostitution is against the law but the act itself is not. In these countries a double moral standard encoded in law is a difference between social status and behavior, between those who do and do not have easy access to private spaces.[13] The prostitute who solicits in the streetscape is penalized for her poverty, her race, her lack of opportunities in getting business in private places. The call girl is of a different class in no small way because most of her trade is not obviously initiated in the public domain. The private confines of the bedroom are an equalizer of sorts. There, in Canada, Great Britain and a few states the streetwalker and her client can proceed without worry of prosecution because the behavior of both can hardly be distinguished.

Duplicity in North America is exemplified by the use of decoys, currently the most common means of enforcing prostitution laws. Decoys encourage an advance, lie when asked about their job and generally pretend to be males seeking the services of a prostitute.[14] Sometimes they even accompany the woman to the bedroom where they undress so that district attorneys can have a stronger case. Whatever the actual street or room behavior cops will perjure themselves to meet legal technicalities.[15] One Montreal defense lawyer claims that 75 percent of the city's police lie to get women convicted for soliciting.[16]

Decoys are used because of strong pressures to do something about street crime. The general rationale is reinforced by a variety of specific pressures: to meet arrest quotas, to earn overtime pay, to satisfy one's personal zeal toward crime fighting. Occasionally the crime report results are truly impressive. In Los Angeles on one weekend two police decoys posing as streetwalkers arrested 91 people.[17] The results are less dramatic for the numbers caught than the fact that men, not women, were arrested.

Some cops regard decoy activities as no more obnoxious than driving to and from work; lying and sneaky ruses are part of the job. But many dislike what they are doing.[18] Not only do they dislike the personal compromises, the degrading identification with a prostitute—in the case of female cops—but they come to appreciate their role in larger issues. The dilemma is vividly illustrated by the case of a San Francisco vice squad cop who, after thirty years on the force, opened the city's newspaper and found the chief of police posing with the city's most famous prostitute at the Annual Hooker's Ball.[19] Some cops believe that decoys might be justifiable if a felony were involved or if the complainant were other than the state. But such is not the case: they are usually dealing with a misdemeanor, with consenting adults and with laws that do not make sense.

Contemporary North Americans need not be singled out when it comes to hypocrisy and unjust treatment of prostitutes. Some West German cities segregate their prostitutes because they are an eyesore and a moral problem, yet many Germans take their girlfriends and wives to a kind of "genteel slumming party" up and down the infamous Reeperbahn in Hamburg's St. Pauli district.[20] Prostitution is legal in West Germany and prostitutes pay taxes just like other citizens, but they are not eligible for unemployment compensation, social security benefits, nor are they covered by the country's national health insurance program.[21] In the 1970s Protestant churches in Hanover and Hamburg refused to take their share of taxes from prostitutes' earnings. But the Protestant church in Cologne had no compunction about the matter, saying, "the Church is a communion of sinners and no member is worse than any other."[22]

At the time of the 1972 Olympic Games in Munich the authorities were fearful that the rest of the world would equate open prostitution with German moral decline in heavily Catholic Bavaria. In reaction they closed parks and other likely hangouts of prostitutes, as well as regularly authorized places of doing business. Closings, of course, were only temporary and massage parlors with celebrated services quickly arose to satisfy demand.

Contradictions have been noted frequently by observers of the immoral landscape. Maryse Choisy in her innovative "lived-through" reporting, one example of which was a one-month study of Parisian prostitution in the late 1920s, noted that:

> The dance halls of the Street of the Virtues were all ultravirtuous. The family trade could object to nothing. The prohibitions swung from the rafters in large letters. The signs read:
>   LADIES—NO SMOKING ALLOWED.
>   GENTLEMEN—DANCING TOGETHER IS NOT ALLOWED.
> What bourgeois morality among the professionally immoral![23]

Lest the impression be left that hypocrisy is solely a Western phenomenon, it should be noted that similar Victorian attitudes prevail in communist countries which also have prostitutes.[24] Indeed, the contradiction between professed attitudes and actual behavior may be more profound in countries that claim to have reordered the nature of social relationships than in the capitalist West.

An Exercise in Accounting

No one knows really how many prostitutes work in the United States at present, but estimates of the last decade range from 100,000 to 550,000.[25] A credible current figure is 250,000 to 350,000 full and part-time prostitutes.

The San Francisco Vice Squad in 1976 maintained that 250 women were soliciting on the city's streets on a given night, and that the total number of streetwalkers residing in the city was four times this number.[26] In the same year, Anchorage, Alaska was said to have 215 prostitutes: 150 in massage parlors, another 40 in hotels and 25 on the streets.[27] Figures for Detroit ranged from 5,000 to 15,000 in 1979.

Estimates for other countries and cities around the world are, if nothing else, suggestive. In 1957 Poland allegedly had 230,000 prostitutes, Budapest on the order of 10,000, and Tokyo more than 130,000, many of whom were working in more than 500 brothels. Ten years later some said Rome had 100,000 prostitutes. In the late 1970s between 5,000 and 7,000 women were seeking business in Hamburg's St. Pauli district.[28] But perhaps the most striking figure of all has been provided by a doctoral student who estimated that, in 1974, Addis Ababa, Ethiopia had 80,000 women in prostitution, roughly 25 percent of the adult female population of the city.[29] As interesting as these crude figures are, they only hint at the magnitude of a more important issue, namely, the amount of money generated by prostitution and, where the activity is illegal, the income that goes untaxed.

In the United States prostitution and closely related activities generate several billion dollars annually. Gail Sheehy in the early 1970s put the figure at between seven and nine billion, almost all of which is untaxed.[30] Though this may be a high estimate the amount greatly exceeds the annual budget of the United States Department of Justice, and is several times the yearly gross receipts from major league teams in baseball, basketball, football and hockey.[31]

The untaxed revenue coming from prostitution and associated enterprises in Montreal may exceed 70 million dollars.[32] In Sydney, Australia a three block area with 130 prostitutes was, at the peak of operations in the late 1960s, pulling in three million dollars a year.[33] Before Italy closed its brothels in 1958 it was receiving 20 million dollars a year in taxes from the houses.[34] West Germany admits to having 50,000 registered prostitutes, paying taxes on one billion Deutsch-marks a year, and another 150,000 women who work illegally.[35] Based on a recent study in West Germany, Barbara Yondorf stated that a single house of 100 women in Munich in the late 1970s paid $400,000 a year in taxes.[36] In Juarez, Mexico, in 1960, registered prostitutes were bringing in $500,000 a year, plus a similar amount from related activities; this was over one-half the city's income.[37]

Suggestive as these figures may be they neither provide historical perspective nor draw attention to the predators and parasites that engulf prostitutes and share in their income. In 1913 the Philadelphia Vice Commission discovered that more than six million dollars was being spent for prostitution and operations that fed off it: 2.6 million of this came from the work of some 200 streetwalkers, over 2.4 million emerged through 156 known parlor houses, and 78 expensive call houses (places for making prostitution arrangements for business there or elsewhere) accounted for the remainder.[38] All this money went to pay for "exhorbitant rental charges to property owners . . . liquor interests, especially the brewers . . . the madams and owners of houses . . . furniture dealers . . . suppliers of clothes . . . pandering lawyers, doctors, jewelers . . . the city and county government in fines collected from the prostitutes and . . . the girls themselves."[39] Chicago at the same time had more spectacular figures. Its special city commission report of 1911 estimated 5,000 prostitutes, not including those who were casual and clandestine, and profits of between 15 and 16 million per annum.[40] Smaller cities disclosed smaller amounts; for Pittsburgh, 2 million; for Kansas City, 1.4 million; and for Atlanta and Lexington, .5 million.[41]

The commercialized prostitution which enjoyed quasi-legal status in San Francisco's Barbary Coast for more than 60 years was a financial pillar to the city and one of its main attractions. The Barbary Coast divekeeper could not have profited as he did without the prostitute: "whatever she did worked to his advantage, whether she labored as a streetwalker, as an inmate of the brothels, as a decoy in the deadfalls, or as a waiter girl and performer in the dance-halls, concert halls, melodeons, and peepshows."[42] When the red-light district was finally closed in 1917 scores of brothels, saloons and other dives were shut down and 1,000 prostitutes went into retirement or found other places to work.[43]

Al Rose has undertaken a detailed historical examination of Storyville, New Orleans, one of America's most infamous red-light districts in the early twentieth century. The number of people involved in prostitution in one sense or another was so large that he concluded that "a very large part of the New Orleans public was, directly or indirectly, a huge collective whore."[44]

In 1914, three years before Storyville was closed for all time, the area was "supporting as many as seven hundred fifty women, some three hundred pimps and "macs," two hundred musicians, about five hundred domestic workers, and a hundred fifty saloon employees."[45] Perhaps as many as 12,000 people were living off the income associated with the prostitution of Storyville, turning over about 12 million dollars per year. In more prosperous times the amounts were even more spectacular. During Storyville's heyday two thousand prostitutes were working regularly, taking in as much as $140,000 a week. The 40 top parlor houses each sold $350 of alcoholic beverages weekly at a 400 percent profit. Professional gamblers were hauling in about $15,000 weekly, "good weeks and bad, carnival season and Lent." Piano players were doing almost as well; thirty of them were making several thousand dollars each week in tips. Rose claims that as much as "fifteen million found its way into the stockings of the prostitutes, the cassocks of the clergymen who owned whorehouse property, the pockets of the politicians and policeman, and the swelling bank accounts of the landlords."[46] But these gross figures and slight descriptions only begin to hint at the range of predators and parasites involved.

Behind each prostitute was a small army of avaricious leeches living off her degradation, pressuring for more 'production,' and fighting off any possible social change that might remove the need for this blight. There was a pimp, functioning as a salesman and publicity agent, who sought to direct men to his own string of whores. There was the madam who operated the house and charged high rentals or 'cuts' in return for managerial duties. There was the policeman, then as now at the lowest level of cupidity of all, willing to overlook anything, if the price was right. There was the landlord, ever on the scene, his grasping hand outstretched as he turned a face of sober dignity to the 'respectable' world. (The landlord could be an uptown Creole aristocrat, who sneered at the madam's demands that the leaky roof be fixed because the rugs were being ruined, or that a rat catcher should be employed two or three times a year to keep the vermin under control. Or he might be a Rampart Street furniture dealer who felt justified in charging the lowest class of whore thirty times more rent than the property could normally bring.) There were the conscienceless doctors with fake venereal disease cures who grew rich off these poor creatures (and their customers). There were the lawyers who waxed fat off the estates of bigtime madams—shysters in and out of city government who clutched tenaciously at the negotiable remains of such as Kate Townsend and Hattie Hamilton, hoping to grab a handful of their tainted loot.

There were the obsequious representatives of out-of-town clothing and shoe firms who paid the madams for the privilege of displaying their wares to the inmates of the bordellos, to whom they grandly gave away tawdry little gifts as premiums for the purchase of enormously over-priced merchandise. There were the newsboys who hung about the entranceways of the houses hoping for a tip to fall from anywhere—from a whore for an errand, from a man for giving directions, or from a gambler for carrying cocaine to a game. There were the pitiful music-makers of questionable talents who demeaned themselves on redlight doorsteps, begging for coins tossed from bagnio windows. There were the unscrupulous druggists and laundrymen who supplied all and sundry with opium, cocaine, or any other drug at inflated prices.[47]

Correlates of Class and Exploitation

Illegality and discriminatory treatment encourage prostitutes to form dependency bonds with numerous predators and parasites. Pimps, madams, landlords, lawyers, taxi drivers and bellhops that feed off prostitutes are different from other individuals only in that they correctly perceive that rapacious behavior is possible, and even protected, because prostitutes are social outlaws. Were not prostitution illegal or controlled by the state and were the social status of prostitutes different than it is there would be little need for predators, or those that did exist could more easily be pursued and prosecuted.

Prostitutes vary in the nature and extent of their dependent ties. Broadly speaking, the need for assistance from others, and often its profundity, is related to the degree of injustice committed in the name of society. The number of dependency linkages and relative degree of exploitation also correlate rather well with landscape visibility and social status. By a variety of measures, then, call girls are better off than brothel or massage parlor prostitutes, and all are usually less exploited and troubled than streetwalkers (Table 1-1). These broad generalizations may also apply to finer gradations of the traditional three-fold category of prostitutes. Just as high class call girls who service politicians and other power brokers are less in need of help from bartenders and bellhops than their lower-class counterparts, so it is that higher-class streetwalkers—those white or who serve a higher-status client—need less assistance to avoid hassles and arrests than do black prostitutes, those on the way down, those who solicit in landscapes that are socially most offensive. That a variety of factors cluster in a description of prostitute types confirms such adages as: "the advantaged have the advantages," and "when at the bottom everything seems to work against you."

Table 1-1
Exploitation and Its Correlates

Type of Prostitute	Location of Business	Social Esteem in the "Life"	Degree of Visibility	Prices Charged	Number of Dependency Linkages	Relative Degree of Exploitation
Call Girl	Private apartment Hotel Client's apartment	High	Low	High	Few	Low
Brothel/ Massage Parlor Prostitute	Brothel Massage Parlor	Variable, generally higher than streetwalker	Low	Lower than call girls, variable vis-a-vis streetwalkers	Few	Moderate to high
Streetwalker	Street Hotel Car Park	Variable, usually low	High	Variable, often moderate to low	Many	Very high

One meaning that attaches to number and profundity of exploitative ties is that the fewer and less penetrating these are the better the psychic health of a prostitute. Streetwalkers are not hardened and embittered because they were born that way, not even necessarily because they learned such traits before entering prostitution, but rather because their treatment by the state and by others breeds and magnifies the worst kinds of behavior.

A recent study of the psychological characteristics of major types of prostitutes discovered that call girls and women who work in brothels or massage parlors are, on the whole, "as mature and well adjusted as demographically similar females engaging in other occupations."[48] When financial success is used as a criterion of effective adjustment, call girls and house prostitutes have a clear edge over non-prostitutes of similar age, education and socioeconomic background. As John Exner and his colleagues note, these women "illustrate the 'well put together' end of the prostitution spectrum; capable of handling themselves well, manifesting good emotional controls, being well aware of conventionality, and doing well in the occupation of their choice."[49] In addition, most of these prostitutes seemed to have realistic career goals; they came to prostitution because of the "opportunity for rapid financial gain."[50] It is even worth mentioning that those prostitutes least subject to predation and the continual harassments of the streetscape have orgasms as frequently as "normal" women in the general population. There is no particular reason to believe these results are anomalous. Paul Gebhard and his associates at the Institute for Sex Research at Indiana University found that prostitutes on the whole are more responsive in reaching orgasms than women in the general population. Case histories for 127 white prostitutes showed that under ten percent were anorgasmic and more than 40 percent experienced multiple orgasms, a percentage strikingly higher than Kinsey reported for married white females.[51]

Streetwalkers are another matter. Of those examined in the Exner study many turned to prostitution because of personal traumas in their lives—a bad marriage, parents or a father they could not cope with, an offspring of the "wrong" color out of wedlock, a problem with drugs. Some have trouble correctly perceiving reality, their motivation for being in prostitution is confused, and their future goals are unrealistic or diffuse. They are the most jaded. They see life and their job as a "ripoff." And they are not very interested in sexuality. They have the hardest time reaching orgasm, regardless of whether or not they have been paid for intercourse.

The psychic condition of prostitutes is mirrored in class-conscious labeling. Because society measures and labels prostitutes with class terms such as whores, harlots, fallen women, prostitutes become acutely aware of rank. Call girls see themselves as high-class, the "top of the profession."[52] Massage parlor women feel they are better than streetwalkers, and the latter make all kinds of distinctions among themselves.[53] A "whore" among many is lower-class, a pejorative label, because she will supposedly take on anyone.[54] A "hustler" is better than both a whore and a prostitute because she is "smarter" and makes more money for her time and effort.[55] Other discriminations reflect the social geography of a city and its temporal rhythms. New York City's Lexington Avenue is high-class compared to Times Square, which is a cut above the Bowery, Harlem and Needle Park. Vancouver's "sleazies" and "fleabags"—terms of the street—ply their business on Skid Row and take their customers to the cheapest of hotels.[56] London's "four-to-sixers" enter the streets and the dank pubs just before dawn to solicit drunk clients who do not know or care what they are buying.[57] All these low-class streetwalkers have the worst working conditions, earn the least money and, in addition to all else, must cope with contempt from their own kind all the way up the judgmental ladder. Thus, by social norm and invidious comparisons drawn among habitués of the streetscape, these women are society's excreta. Worse, they are psychologically and physically damaged in ways that can only be imagined.

The Public Ledger

Prostitutes burden the prison system, the courts and the taxpayer. They account for as much as 30 percent of the population in women's jails. Seventy percent of women in American prisons were first arrested for prostitution.[58] The expense to cities appears astronomical considering the nature of the crime, the rate of successful prosecutions, rates of recidivism among prostitutes and alternative uses of taxpayers' money.

In 1967 San Francisco spent more than $270,000 to process 2,116 prostitutes. Jail costs in San Francisco for those convicted added another $100,000 to the ledger, bringing the total bill to nearly $375,000. This amounted to more than $175 per arrest.[59] The figures take on added significance when it is realized that 75 percent of those in jail for prostitution in San Francisco have no accompanying theft, drug, assault or other charges against them.[60] Furthermore, for all the money spent, only about 15 percent of those prostitutes arrested in the city spent time in jail, and only for periods of one to four months.[61] A different angle on the city's cost of repressing prostitution is provided by examining the yearly budget for the Bureau of Special Services, commonly known as the vice squad. While the vice squad has responsibility for handling gambling, liquor laws, pornography and prostitution, the majority of its time and its one million dollar budget is spent chasing and apprehending prostitutes.[62] Clearly, the money could be put to better use. In a given year, San Francisco solves no more than 15 to 20 percent of its killings, forcible rapes, robberies, aggravated assaults, burglaries and auto thefts.[63]

Seattle disburses about a million dollars a year to arrest, prosecute and jail prostitutes.[64] Anchorage, Alaska in 1975, spent over 1,500 hours and nearly half a million dollars to control and incarcerate its estimated 215 prostitutes.[65] In Toronto each arrest costs over $165 and each court case an additional $1,000. If convicted a woman receives either a $500 fine or a month in jail. Los Angeles has 275 vice officers (not all devoted to prostitution), yet from time to time the chief of police complains he does not have enough men to control violent crimes.[66]

A comparison of the numbers arrested and jailed sheds light of a different hue on the matter. In 1967 San Francisco and St. Louis each apprehended over 2,000 women for prostitution, Boston more than 500, Washington D.C. over 200. The number of women actually jailed in each of these cities was, respectively, 389, 176, 1 and 39.[67] The batting average for "sure-bet" convictions is not much better. San Francisco, in 1975, took just over 20 of its best cases to expensive jury trials; the District Attorney's office successfully prosecuted three of them.

Recidivism patterns accentuate the poor arrest and conviction ratios. During the first six months of 1967, 795 women were arrested for prostitution in New York City. Of this total, 525 had previously been apprehended for the same offense. Together, these women had a total of 5,568 prostitution arrests among them.[68] New York is not unique. For the period 1969-1972, recidivism among Seattle's prostitutes accounted for 29 percent of all such arrests. For this city, prostitution ranked second, only behind drunkenness, for recidivism.[69] In Honolulu, the rate among prostitutes is higher than that of any other female category.[70] The situation may be comparable in European countries. In the late 1940s, in London, arrested women not only had to pay fines but also had to post costly bonds, which were forfeited if rearrested. In spite of this, one out of every seven women had between 60 and 100 convictions.[71]

Prostitutes and their lawyers burden the court system by asking for continuances, and the problem would be worse were the stakes—for the prostitute—higher. As indicated by the number of court cases pending at year's end, San Francisco, like many cities, has hundreds of continuances yearly. In one case in San Francisco a woman was arrested four times within two months, and over the next 13 months she was granted 21 continuances. These permitted her and her lawyer to "shop" for a judge known to "go easy." If continuances are not granted a jury trial is requested. Not only are the courts clogged with more important cases, but a jury trial is very expensive, costing up to $2,000. Locating a dozen unbiased jurors can take three or more days and exhaust as many as four jury lists. Even then the process of deciding a case can be very time consuming. During 1969, in Montreal, 614 prostitution-related cases required 2,400 court appearances for judges, clerks, stenographers, prosecutors and bailiffs—at a cost of nearly $85,000.[72]

To obviate these kinds of problems prostitutes are frequently given short sentences or allowed to plea bargain, combining all of their arrests into a single package. Stiffer jail sentences are no solution for, as the San Francisco Committee on Crime has noted, "if mandatory penalties increase, there are more jury trial demands, more continuances and, following conviction, more appeals."[73] The last thing needed is more trials. In recent years, 25 to 35 percent of demands for jury trials in San Francisco were for prostitution cases.[74]

By such economic criteria as untaxed revenues and the costs of catching and convicting prostitutes, attention to prostitution in North America is simply irrational (Table 1-2).[75] Economic irrationality is compounded by the fact that prostitutes do not react as law enforcement officers and criminologists would prefer when penalties are increased. With intensified repression they simply search out new niches within which to sell their services. And like criminals and others who operate in illegal markets they conclude that, relative to the costs, crime pays.[76]

Table 1-2
Estimated Cost of Repressing Prostitution in Montreal in 1971

Income taxes lost	$26,000,000
Morality squad—25 full-time officers	398,200
Salaries, bonuses for the time spent in court, overtime, clothes allowances for under-cover police	
Cost of detention	12,100
Salaries for guards & matrons	
Medical center of the municipal court	1,600
Judiciary system	84,800
Prison upkeep	84,700
	26,581,400
Less: Municipal Court revenues	132,000
Estimated cost to city, province & federal government	$26,449,400

Data from Gemme 1971; Texier and Vézina 1978:287, 290.

Chapter 2	# The Urban Matrix

Prostitutes work in cities, especially large ones. The big city is a breeder of sorts because demand is there, because anonymity is possible—for both prostitute and client—and because of the absence of tight social controls often found in smaller places.

Geographical Origins

The geographical origins of prostitutes and their movements to cities have generally mirrored national patterns. According to William Sanger, during the mid-nineteenth century over 60 percent of 2,000 New York City prostitutes were foreign, and a third were from Ireland.[1] By 1912 only 28 percent of the city's prostitutes were from abroad, coming principally from Russia and Germany, secondarily from Austria, England, Hungary and Ireland.[2]

On the whole, prostitutes like other humans have adhered to a proximity principle. A large percentage of women entering prostitution have been born in the state where they worked, either in the same city in which born or nearby.[3] A significant fraction of the remainder come from nearby states. Sanger had data on 762 prostitutes born in the United States and working in New York City in the middle of the nineteenth century.[4] Fifty-two percent were from New York and another 33 percent came from four states—Pennsylvania, New Jersey, Connecticut and Massachusetts. Just over a score of women were from the South, and none was from the West. When a similar analysis was performed by George Kneeland more than a half century later he discovered that the same four states accounted for a like percentage of the whole but that those coming from New York State had increased by about 15 percent.[5] The majority were born in New York City. This is not surprising since the population of the metropolitan area had grown dramatically, particularly among impoverished migrant groups. But perhaps the most striking change was among black women born in the South, especially Virginia and North Carolina. Two percent of the 405 white prostitutes in Kneeland's sample were from this region, as compared to 45 percent of the blacks working in the city. From 1920 onward, blacks from the South played a major role in bloating the ranks of prostitution in New York City and other urban centers in the North.[6]

According to a number of reports that appeared during the 1970s, principal sources for New York City's prostitutes are Minnesota, Michigan,

Massachusetts and Ohio.[7] Of these the so-called "Minnesota Connection" appears to be the most important.[8] Minneapolis is a magnet for runaway girls in the upper-midwest. From there some go on their own initiative to New York City where they are easy prey for pimps. A pimp at the bus or train station offers the runaway sympathy and concern for her outcast status with family and friends, offers flattery in the form of appellations such as "Beauty Queen" and "Miss America" and money lavishly spent on dining and entertainment; that is, before the pimp pushes the naive initiate into the streets as a prostitute.

The Minnesota Connection, apparently unique among contemporary North American inter-city movements of women moving into prostitution, has another dimension. Compounded by Minneapolis' reputation as a good source of young girls and New York street demand for blond Scandinavians, pimps from New York City, Boston and New Orleans go to Minneapolis to actively recruit for the "Minnesota Strip," a stretch of Eighth Avenue streetscape below Times Square. There the "packages" between 14 and 17 ply their business as "flatbackers" (prostitutes who primarily engage in simple intercourse).[9]

In the past prostitutes have apparently come primarily from rural areas and very small towns.[10] And this still seems to be true in parts of the underdeveloped world.[11] But with the increasing urbanization of the twentieth century more and more women are born or raised in larger places. Among registered prostitutes working in towns bordering the United States, 61 percent of over 1,000 women were born in cities of 20,000 to 100,000.[12] They come from northern Mexico, moving in response both to lack of jobs in their places of origin and the financial rewards of border prostitution. Of 84 Vancouver prostitutes surveyed in the early 1970s the overwhelming majority were native to Canada's larger cities—Vancouver, Edmonton, Winnipeg, Regina and Toronto.[13]

The City in Historical Perspective

Prostitutes and the city have long gone together in the West and elsewhere.[14] Although prostitution was apparently not very important in colonial New England, several of the nascent cities had both streetwalkers and brothels.[15] Newport, Rhode Island is said to have had streetwalkers as early as 1744,[16] and Alexander Hamilton noted that prostitutes were commonly seen in New York City's Battery after sunset.[17] In the early nineteenth century the significance of prostitution in American cities is difficult to judge because most community leaders opposed discussion of the subject, believing that a public airing only swelled the ranks of prostitution.[18] Despite such sentiments moralists voiced their outrage at the behavior of prostitutes in New York City's theater district. At mid-century the city's prostitute population was estimated at between 6,000 and 10,000; prostitution was "open, public and widespread."[19] By the Civil War the number may have doubled, and fifty years later it reached 25,000.[20]

In the first half of the nineteenth century, when Paris and London were the only places with populations exceeding a half million, both cities were believed to have quite sizeable prostitute populations, and a problem of some magnitude.[21] London, it was maintained, had been in moral decline for at least a hundred years. Chroniclers in the early eighteenth century expressed concern for the "profligate state of Society in vulgar life" and for the "unrestrained license given to males and females, in the Walks of Prostitution where . . . in former times at places of public resort . . . there was at least an affectation of decency."[22] Another observer claimed that "the open and naked effrontery of the immoral transcends all description. They swarm round the streets of London at all hours of the day or night."[23] Though Paris at this time was thought to be a "sink of profligacy," London was worse, for London's prostitutes openly plied their business in theaters and entertainment centers.[24]

According to the police, by 1864 nearly 60 towns and cities in England and Wales had at least 50 prostitutes.[25] Besides London, with perhaps 8,000 to 10,000 women, the largest populations (between 1,000 and 2,000) were found in Portsmouth, Liverpool and Manchester. Port and peripatetic males were obvious reasons for numbers in Portsmouth and Liverpool being greater than for cities of comparable size. The large number of women in Manchester may have been related to a sizeable population of unmarried males, many of whom were employed in manufacturing.

One observer at this time contended that Edinburgh's prostitutes were distinguished from their English counterparts by "more decent conduct, and by manners less gross."[26] Yet, to the *Edinburgh Medical Journal* the city was in a class with Glasgow and London. One's eyes and ears would "tell him at once what a multitudinous amazonian army the devil keeps in constant field service, for advancing his own ends." In all these cities "the stones seem alive with lust and the very atmosphere is tainted."[27] Whether the problem was as bad as depicted, a hundred years later Edinburgh and Glasgow accounted for most of Scotland's prostitutes. Indeed, except for these two cities plus Aberdeen and Dundee, police statistics in the late 1950s showed no prosecutions for prostitution elsewhere in the country.[28]

Nineteenth-century cities on the Continent were not exceptional. During the last decades of the century Amsterdam had some 200 brothels with over 1,000 women working in them, while Brussels and Liege had between 20 and 30 houses.[29] Paris, however, was in many respects the European capital of prostitution.

Prostitutes were an issue in Paris as early as the time of Charlemagne.[30] Then, and in the centuries that followed, the *filles debauchees*, only one of several names for the women, were banished from the city, brutally punished, stripped of their property and sentenced to hard labor. But they consistently defied the authorities and when expelled from the city invariably returned. By the thirteenth century the government began restricting them to certain streets, often outside the fortified walls of the city. At one time they were forced to work in a kind of hutch termed *clapier* and subsequently became associated with a section of Paris known as *Clapier*. By the latter part of the fifteenth century one observer believed that the city had between 5,000 and 6,000 prostitutes in a population of 100,000.[31] Three hundred years later the prostitute population had more than quadrupled. But more striking is the contention that by 1800 prostitution was the major source of female employment in Paris.[32] Not all women so employed were without other sources of income. Many combined prostitution with occasional work as a public mourner, shop assistant, street vendor or seamstress.

At the beginning of the nineteenth century Paris had a population of about 500,000. This figure grew to a million inhabitants within 50 years, most of it resulting from migration from the French countryside. Although it is claimed that French men and women in the early decades of the century did not move much beyond the departments of their birth,[33] this does not seem to be true for many of the women who became prostitutes. The origins of more than 12,000 Parisian prostitutes who moved to Paris between 1816 and 1831, all of whom were registered with the police, were primarily from the Paris basin and surrounding departments. Yet, many came from departments at some distance, and some were foreigners (Figure 2-1). The migration field of these women grew in subsequent decades, reflecting the more general national pattern.[34] It seems fair to say that Paris, not unlike other large nineteenth-century cities, proved to be a gigantic magnet, an economic force whose reputation and reach increased over time. By the last decades of the nineteenth century Paris may have contained more than 35 percent of France's prostitutes.[35]

Many of the women did not go to Paris as prostitutes but turned to prostitution out of necessity.[36] Females had the fewest opportunities amidst the extremely rapid urban growth, a hypertrophic condition characterized by crowding, shortages of food and water, unemployment and poverty. Destitution was so profound that between 1824 and 1847 four of five Parisians were buried in pauper's graves.[37]

The French physician Alexandre Jean Baptiste Parent-Duchatelet devoted eight years of his life to studying and accumulating numerical data on French prostitutes.[38] He found the women typically in their late teens and early twenties, illiterate, poor and often illegitimate or from broken families. For more than 5,200 registered prostitutes by far the most important reason for turning to the brothels or streets was lack of employment. The few jobs available were usurped by men. Even those women who could obtain jobs as servant, laundress, seamstress or milliner usually could not earn enough money to secure the basic necessities for themselves, much less for children and parents they might have to support. Without honor or a means of support, prostitution was a logical alternative.

If the human dimensions of the immoral cityscape of the nineteenth cen-

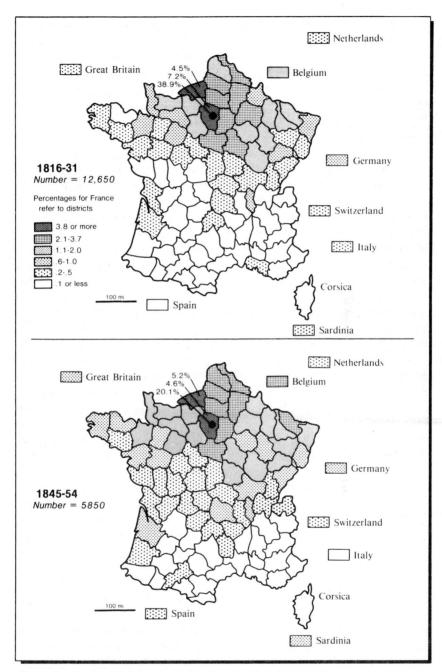

Figure 2-1 Geographical Origins of Prostitutes in Parisian Brothels
Data from Parent-Duchatelet 1836; 1857.

tury primarily reflected economic conditions and the outcome of a moral predicament for dishonored, impoverished women, the spatial order of the city measured in some imperfect way the growth of an urban mass from a core settlement to an expansive, sprawling metropolis. To be sure, the relationship between the geographical size of the immoral order and the city enveloping it was determined as much by the prevailing social climate as by the demands of a growing and spreading population. These relationships are suggested by data on Paris' tolerated brothels.

By 1778 French law prohibited prostitutes from working in the streets, squares, wharves and city boulevards. The law, however, said nothing about brothels and the police continued to license them as they had for some time. Heaviest concentrations of bordellos occurred near the Palais-Royal, an area known not only for its *femmes galantes*, but also for its gaming tables for the rich.[39] In the eighteenth century as many as 1,500 prostitutes purportedly gathered at the Palais-Royal daily.[40]

By 1824, when the city had 163 brothels, the Palais-Royal and surrounding districts harbored most of the city's house trade. Concentration was striking. Until the mid-1830s less than 10 percent of Paris contained more than 70 percent of the bordellos. The overwhelming majority were in or near the administrative core. By 1832 the number of brothels had climbed to 220. Most of the growth occurred in districts that already had the greatest number of houses. But a few new areas were invaded to the north and south, the same direction in which the city expanded in the first half of the century (Figure 2.2).

After 1832 virtually all major prostitution districts began losing brothels, even though the city's total rose slightly. A flight of houses to new areas beyond the walls of the city, evident by 1842, increased dramatically during the next decade (Figure 2-3). As in an earlier period the new locations mirrored the extending reach of city growth. By 1854 the most dramatic changes were occurring to the north, northwest and southeast of the city, and in the traditional core (Figure 2-3). From 1824 to 1854 the nine principal areas with bordellos decreased from 68 percent of the city's total to half this percentage. The period up to 1832 can be characterized as one of geographical intensification; the subsequent two decades were typified by deintensification.

During the Second Empire—1848 to 1870—clearing and construction of new buildings, new streets and new sewage systems began to alter the face of old Paris. At the same time municipalities, several of which were becoming industrial suburbs, were providing not only demand for prostitutes, but also a climate more conducive to the activity. Furthermore, by the beginning of the second half of the century the core of the city no longer permitted new brothels to open. Administrators had become increasingly concerned with the effects of prostitution on public welfare.[41] As in cities during the Middle Ages, public concern and laws dealing with prostitutes increased as the pace of urbanization intensified.[42]

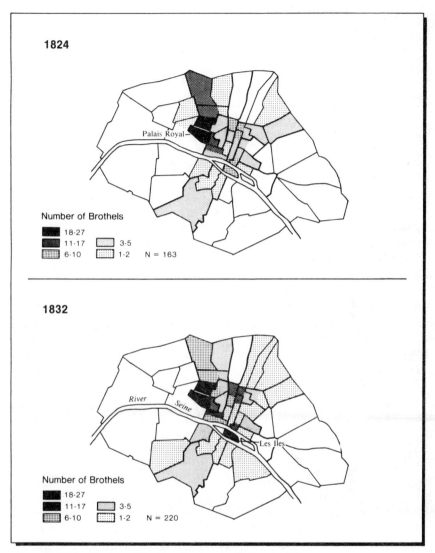

Figure 2-2 Distribution of Parisian Brothels in 1824 and 1832
Maps adapted from Parent-Duchatelet 1836:341.

The last half of the century was one of both further deintensification and an absolute decline in the number of bordellos in the greater city, despite the fact that midway through this period Paris approached two million inhabitants (Figure 2-4). The expanded city's brothel population dropped from a high of 229 in 1842 to 133 by 1880. In the next eight years there was a further decline to 75 houses. The sector known as the Palais-Royal had a mere four bordellos, down from 27 in 1832. While this change would seem to suggest the virtual demise of prostitution in what was, by the beginning

Figure 2-3 Distribution of Parisian Brothels in 1842 and 1854
Maps adapted from Parent-Duchatelet 1857:324-327.

of the twentieth century, one of the large and great cities of the Western world, in fact it represented a slow and long process of prostitutes moving into other business settings—bars, cafes, the streets and brothels beyond the clear purview of the law. At this century's end one estimate placed the Parisian prostitute population at 15,000 to 30,000.[43] Paris may presently have 35,000 of the country's estimated 100,000 prostitutes.[44]

Patterns established during the eighteenth and nineteenth centuries not only persisted into the twentieth century but often grew in magnitude and

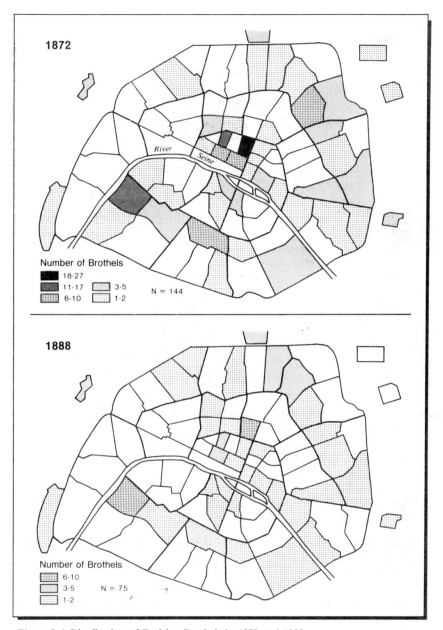

Figure 2-4 Distribution of Parisian Brothels in 1872 and 1888
Data from Reuss 1889.

proportionate significance. Near the beginning of the twentieth century, when Hamburg had more than a million inhabitants and Berlin more than two million, these cities contained an unusually large share of the 150,000 prostitutes in Germany.[45] While the problem was most severe in the biggest places, prostitution was also widespread in port cities, those with large trade areas, and places where industrialization was having a profound impact on the traditional order.[46]

City Size and Different Cities

No one knows precisely how prostitute populations vary with city size. Arrest statistics and the number of registered prostitutes in systems controlled by the state are the most common sources of data. The first measure suffers because many prostitutes are arrested several times, and many more, particularly call girls and those working in higher-class brothels, are seldom apprehended. Too, national arrest figures, such as those supplied by the Federal Bureau of Investigation, do not report on all places. Registration figures are no better since the majority of women usually find it to their advantage to work outside the system. These shortcomings in mind, different sources and settings nevertheless suggest that prostitution is minimal in small places, increases in cities up to about 100,000 and is most significant in very large places (Figures 2-5 and 2-6). Where a state lacks a city of any note or size this pattern is most apparent. West Virginia, one of the more rural states, has only about 100 to 150 prostitution arrests annually and perhaps contains no more than 350 prostitutes.[47]

The West German government plays a direct role in the relationship between prostitute populations and city size. It can require that cities of less than 20,000 not have prostitution and can actively repress those in defiance of the state mandate. In places between 20,000 and 50,000 the federal

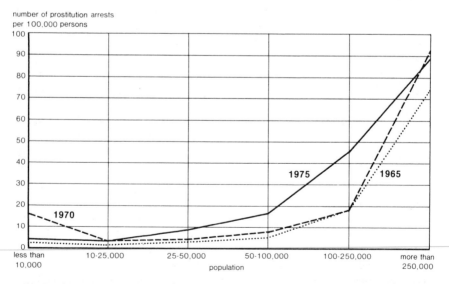

Figure 2-5 Prostitution Arrests by Size of Place in the United States
Data from Federal Bureau of Investigation 1965-1978.

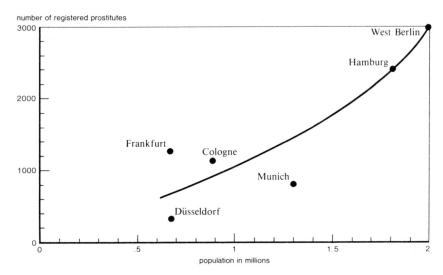

number of registered prostitutes

Figure 2-6 Registered Prostitutes in Select West German Cities in 1976 in Relation to City Size
Data from Yondorf 1979:422.

government has the right to prohibit prostitution in part or all of a city, while in larger urban centers it can require the women to work only in particular areas—though not on particular streets or in certain houses.[48]

Data on the historical incidence and location of brothels and road houses with prostitutes in Wisconsin also show the overwhelming significance of prostitution in large places (Figure 2-7). This portrayal suffers by way of omission, but has the advantage of suggesting some of the many exceptions to any simple generalization about the relationship between city size and incidence of prostitution. As was true in other American cities at the turn of this century, prostitutes in Wisconsin were found not only in brothels and road houses but also on the street, in assignation houses, hotels, rooming houses, cafes, chop suey restaurants, saloons and dance halls.[49]

As the cartographic rendition of Wisconsin prostitution shows, greater numbers of women than would be expected simply by looking at city size were found in places with geographical advantages (proximity to entertainment or resort centers or a state border). But geography itself is but a part of the story. For example, Superior, Wisconsin thrived as a "wide open" port and lumber town with gambling, drinking and prostitution. All were perceived by residents as major local services that were "good for business."[50] Furthermore, the local populace was quite permissive of these activities, while the city government was intolerant of outside interference in their handling of such matters. The demand for prostitutes in Superior was multiplied by the city's social and geographical pairing with Duluth, Minnesota, a city with a significant puritan element.

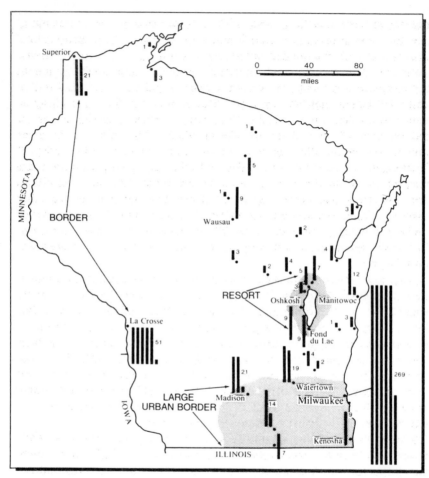

Figure 2-7 Brothels and Other Places of Prostitution in Wisconsin in 1914
Data from Wisconsin Legislative Committee 1914.

Examples that show variation in the relationship between city size and the prostitute population abound. In Illinois such Mississippi River towns as Rock Island, Alton and East St. Louis and the railroad and canal towns of Joliet and Peoria have been, in the vernacular, "wide open river towns."[51] With sizes ranging from 40,000 to 125,000 in 1970, their similarities, besides geography, have been transient populations, sometimes greater than average proportions of males, ethnic mixing and a certain social ferment. These characteristics occasionally have been combined with tie-ins between local governments and organized crime, promoting gambling and easy liquor laws, and apathy or acceptance of open prostitution. By contrast, such non-riverine Illinois towns as Moline, Rockford and Urbana have had relatively few prostitutes. In Moline and Rockford strong puritan traditions and police forces that have responded to local demands for repression of vice have been important factors in maintaining low levels of prostitution. Urbana has had like-minded police and a populace with strong anti-vice sentiments. However, Urbana's situation is slightly complicated because the city merges with Champaign to form a single population nucleus. Until at least 1940 Champaign had open prostitution and a policy particularly lenient toward vice among blacks. Champaign formed a service center for that segment of the Urbana population which either did not share the popular view about illicit activities or was comfortable with hypocrisy. If Champaign and Decatur, which also had relatively open prostitution, are exceptions to a rule that river and railroad towns have had more prostitutes than city size would predict, great disparities between riverine and other towns in Illinois are now largely a matter of history. With the appearance of a reform-minded government in the Illinois state house in the 1950s prostitution was repressed almost everywhere in the state, especially where it was most flagrant.

Large and very large cities also vary in the size of their prostitute populations. New York City, San Francisco, Amsterdam and Hamburg generate demand for prostitutes because of the size of their male populations. But the cities are also attractive to prostitutes because of sizeable numbers of seafaring transients, their preeminence as convention centers and their reputations as cultural and tourist attractions. Vancouver, British Columbia, falls into a similar category. During 1974, 624 women were arrested for soliciting there. Comparable figures for Calgary and Edmonton in the same year were 40 and 33 respectively.[52] Obvious advantages of Vancouver to prostitutes are its sailor population and male loggers.

Another Canadian city, Montreal, is the apparent polar extreme of Vancouver. This largest French-speaking metropolis outside Paris, a city much more populous than Vancouver, appears to have little if any prostitution. Even in that part of Montreal where one is supposed to find streetwalkers they are usually few in number. The reason for the undeniable streetscape anomaly is that a new administration in 1954 closed the city's brothels and chased women from the streets. To the present the city has had one of the most repressive prostitution programs in North America. Yet, appearances are deceiving. According to a recent study by two French-Canadian women, clandestine prostitution is thriving in Montreal.[53]

Like ordinary people in pursuit of all kinds of mundane social and economic goods and services, prostitutes and their clients, through their mobility, link cities into systems of cities. Because of demand, centrality, the nature of the city and historical advantage, cities—usually the largest ones—act as magnets in attracting prostitutes and clients from nearby smaller places. Within a large urban sprawl one or two cities may account for a disproportionate amount of trade. Prostitutes tend to work where others like them work. It requires no imagination for a new or old prostitute to realize that one or two women hustling in areas unfamiliar to men seeking services is self-defeating. Sufficient numbers are required to draw business and for an area to gain a reputation. Once a threshold is passed a landscape acquires its own inertia, often to the moral gain of nearby communities.

Men see advantage in going to large prostitution districts because they provide more choice. Also, anonymity for customers as well as prostitutes is distance related. Neither wants to be arrested or be seen by family and friends, possibilities that, in the mind at least, decrease the further one is from home turf. For clients much more than prostitutes there is an obvious cost to travel; if they frequently purchase prostitutes' services their geographical range may be that of the greater metropolis.

If one city is linked to others by the centripetal flow of prostitutes and clients from near places or those not too distant, they are also tied together by centrifugal forces. Secondary cities within an urban cluster have prostitution activity not just because of local demand and women who prefer a particular environment and its habitués, but also because prostitutes from elsewhere move in to capitalize on their novelty. Prostitutes new to an area usually have an advantage because of the premium males place on something they have not seen or previously experienced. Centrifugal forces also result from the fact of different jurisdictional statuses: cops, laws and attitudes toward repression invariably change from one city to another. When harassments and arrests intensify in one streetscape in one city a prostitute can temporarily solve her problems by moving across town or to another city. There she can "cool off" and go about her business until she wishes to return to favored terrain. If her new hustling address is not too distant she may be able to maintain her social network of friends and coworkers.

That these kinds of relationships have a basis in fact is suggested in a cartographic and graphic analysis of prostitution in California (Figures 2-8 and 2-9).[54] Five major systems of city-defined prostitution landscapes can be identified for California. The two principal ones are Los Angeles and one focused on the bay cities of San Francisco and Oakland. Lesser systems are San Diego and two in the Sacramento—San Joaquin Valley, one centered on Fresno, the other on Sacramento. The Los Angeles system illustrates the very considerable concentration of prostitution in a very large place, and the way its streetscapes draw off demand from the extended urban agglomeration. Orange County and even the somewhat distant cities of San Bernardino and Riverside have fewer prostitutes than might be expected, when compared with the valley systems. That San Diego is a rather separate system is attributable to its size and distance from Los Angeles and the presence of the navy.

In contrast are the systems of the Sacramento—San Joaquin Valley. Although there are notable population differences between the two major cities with prostitution and other cities in the valley, Fresno and Sacramento

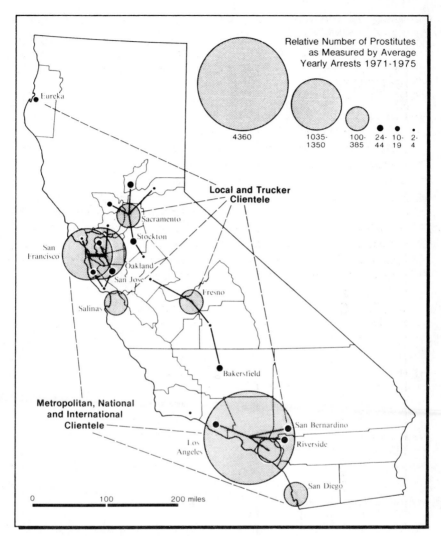

Figure 2-8 The Geography of Prostitution in California
Arrest data from California Bureau of Criminal Statistics 1976.

hardly compare in size with the major metropolitan centers in northern and southern California. This difference results in a steeper relationship between number of prostitutes and size of the county population (Figure 2-9). A notable feature of the Sacramento—San Joaquin Valley is the importance of trucking clientele, particularly in Fresno which is a major rest spot.[55] CB radios and extensive gossip networks undoubtedly carry a good bit of information about particular prostitutes and places worth trying. Herein may lie the principal sense in which the state's interior cities are prostitution systems.

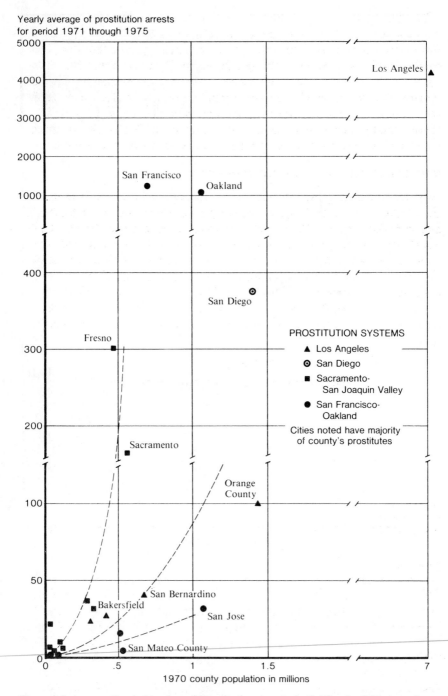

Figure 2-9 Average Yearly Number of Prostitution Arrests in California, 1971 through 1975

Arrest data from California Bureau of Criminal Statistics 1976; population data from United States, Bureau of Census 1973.

The San Francisco—Oakland area has some of the features of the Los Angeles region. These two cities both have significant streetwalking populations, whereas populous suburbs and nearby cities, such as San Jose, have smaller numbers of women. This system differs from its counterpart to the south in the rather equal prominence of two major cities. Like the Los Angeles area the national and international reputation of San Francisco attracts conventioneers and tourists—insignificant clientele in the state's interior. Finally, northern and southern California are linked by prostitutes who travel among major cities from San Diego to Anchorage, Alaska.

The Clustering of Immoral Behavior

Were prostitutes dispersed throughout a city they would pose little problem. But almost everywhere they have been highly concentrated by both official and unofficial design. The Parisian example is suggestive of how brothels have been grouped. This case is not unusual. As with such generalizations about any activity, degree of concentration depends on geographical scale. For example, almost all prostitution activity in Boston is confined to 2 of 15 police districts (Table 2-1).[56] But when these two areas are examined more closely, at the neighborhood level, soliciting activity appears much more dispersed (Table 2-2). If the scale of geographical analysis is refined further

Table 2-1
Concentration of Prostitution in Boston

	1975		1976		1977	
	No. of Arrests	%	No. of Arrests	%	No. of Arrests	%
District 1— Encompassing "Combat Zone"	944	70	941	62	495	47
District 4— Encompassing Back Bay	368	27	572	37	517	50
Remaining 13 Police Districts in City	32	3	15	1	31	3
Totals	1344	100	1528	100	1043	100

Data from Milman 1980.

such that individual blocks or cultural nodes such as parks, hotels and cafes are the focus of attention, then within neighborhoods activity is very highly concentrated (Figure 2-10).

Table 2-2
Concentration of Prostitution Within Two Boston Police Districts

Neighborhoods in Two Police Districts With Highest Arrests For Prostitution	1975		1976		1977	
	No. of Arrests	%	No. of Arrests	%	No. of Arrests	%
Back Bay	156	12	238	16	141	14
Combat Zone	380	29	591	39	235	23
Massachusetts Avenue	68	5	111	7	119	12
Park Square	419	32	245	16	170	17
Prudential	63	5	87	6	80	8
Fourteen Other Neighborhoods Combined	226	17	241	16	267	26
Totals	1312	100	1513	100	1012	100

Data from Milman 1980.

Of particular note in Boston is the rather dramatic changes from year to year in the percentage and number of women arrested within both police districts and neighborhoods (Tables 1 and 2). The neighborhood data show that in 1975 the Combat Zone and Park Square alone accounted for 61 percent of all arrests in the city's two major districts. Within two years it took four districts (Combat Zone, Park Square, Back Bay and Massachusetts Ave.) to tally a similar percentage of arrests (61 vs. 66 percent in 1977). To some extent the dispersion between 1975 and 1977 represents the willingness of streetwalkers to quickly move to new neighborhoods in response to repression. Often, however, dramatic fluctuations in arrests from one area to another index public and law enforcement concern over the high visibility

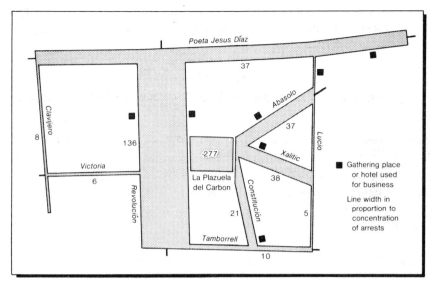

Figure 2-10 Concentration of Streetwalkers Around "La Plazuela del Carbon", Jalapa, Mexico
Note: The arrest figures are cumulative totals for the years 1957 through 1971.
Data from Barrera Caraza 1974:60.

of particular concentrations of prostitutes. The geography of these concerns may reflect nothing more than complaints from a half dozen citizens, an up-coming city election, a campaign by local businesses to reduce the amount of prostitution or a single incident brought to the attention of the public. The Combat Zone's higher arrest figures for 1975 and 1976 as compared to 1977 resulted from an increase in prostitutes in the zone during these years, aggressive street solicitation that offended Boston residents, robberies and muggings that were attributed to the women and their pimps, and finally, in late 1976, the killing of a Harvard football player in the zone by young men.

Streetwalking districts of consequence may contain anywhere from a half-dozen to scores of prostitutes and extend for a few blocks or a mile or more. Geometrically, locales are often strongly linear, extending along a main thoroughfare, with minor soliciting activity on intersecting streets. Major contemporary examples of strong linearity include New York City's Times Square district along Eighth Avenue and the higher-class strip to the east along Lexington Avenue. Some areas, such as San Francisco's Tenderloin District, are rectilinear, even compact.

Whether a locale is linear or compact it invariably possesses one or more core areas—places where solicitation is relatively intense. In the Times Square District and in San Francisco's Tenderloin during recent times, prin-cipal core areas have been the low- to mid-Forties along Eighth Avenue for the first mentioned and Powell and O'Farrell Streets for the second. De-pending on location and the nature and intensity of police repression, the geography of cores may shift dramatically over time. Boundaries are usually fuzzy and change more often than cores. Boundary shifts occur for a variety of reasons: turnover of prostitutes, women voluntarily changing the definition of their work areas within a city or moving to another city, the time of the year or day, and repression.

The specific locations of prostitution are determined and constrained by history and geopolitics: where it began and where people came to accept it; where prostitutes helped blight a neighborhood in establishing a niche; and where public opinion, financial interests and those who enforce laws have pushed prostitution or permitted it to remain. History, the inertia that follows upon locational precedence, is often as significant as matters geopolitical. For example, the guild system of medieval Germany established areas for the location of urban trades and prostitution. Initial siting and a process of inertia meant that 200 to 300 years later prostitution was in the oldest part of the city, the *Altstadt*—"dark, narrow, winding alleys, set well back from the new main thoroughfares and shopping streets which grew up in the course of the nineteenth century."[57] Parisian streets with brothels have been similarly used since medieval times.[58] San Francisco's present-day Tenderloin was in evidence three-quarters of a century ago. Cities once designated as centers of prostitution have kept that label for centuries.

But just as surely as history plays a hand in molding and maintaining the immoral streetscape, so there are temporal changes, perhaps unforeseen, that encourage prostitution where it was previously absent or change a minor soliciting locale into a major one. If the emergent district is compact and attracts a sizeable number of lower-class prostitutes it may receive unusual public attention and acquire a notorious reputation. Such a place is Oakland, California's "Meatrack," a three-quarter mile strip that became infamous in the 1970s (Figure 2-11).

On Friday and Saturday nights in 1976 as many as 50 to 75 streetwalkers traversed the locale, engaging in activities ranging from solicitation to quiet chats over coffee and pie with friends. One and all gathered at a restaurant near the intersection of Telegraph Avenue and West McArthur Boulevard, a hot spot for pimps to "flash" (show style) and, for young black males, a workshop for apprenticeship in the world of pimpdom. At 14, 15 and 16 they sat inside the restaurant against a wall and watched the entry, the exit, the ploys and the maneuverings of their real heroes.[59] The restaurant as a node for the district's prostitutes and pimps has parallels elsewhere. At LaBrea Avenue and Sunset Boulevard in Hollywood one restaurant is known to the police as "pimp command quarters."[60]

West McArthur Boulevard had once been an active and prosperous motel zone catering to tourists and salesmen. But when freeways were built over the area traffic bypassed a section of the boulevard, to the considerable

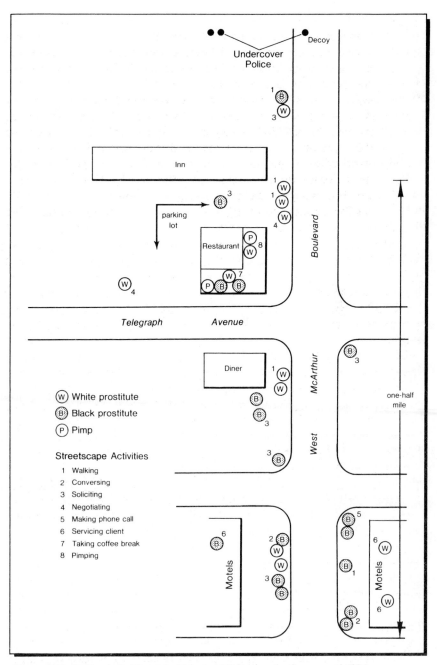

Figure 2-11 Oakland, California's "Meatrack" During the Summer of 1976
Note: The map depicts activity on one Saturday night at approximately 10:30 p.m. Based on author's fieldwork.

financial detriment of local businesses. Motel owners in this section—mostly older people who depended on their real estate holdings for retirement income—saw little alternative but to rent their rooms as "trick pads." Some found prostitutes disgusting and some were morally offended. For many these considerations gave way to the need for economic survival. Some joined forces with streetwalkers, asking a fee of $1.00 to $2.50 for each "trick" or "date," as the local hustlers referred to their clients. In return the women were assured they would be warned when the police were coming.[61] Those owners along West McArthur Boulevard who decided not to rent to prostitutes and their customers faced possible retaliation from pimps and prostitutes, quite possibly civil rights suits.[62] All residents of the area had to learn how to live with patrolling males, patrol cars, streetwalkers and the taint on one's identity that comes from living among prostitutes.

"Like attracts like" is a dictum that applies as much to places as it does to other matters. Because they are criminalized and outcast by society, prostitutes attract criminals, others who engage in businesses that thrive on the fuzzy border of illegality, and still others who profit from the very nature of prostitution. Rome's prostitutes gather at busy street corners near condom vending machines. Barcelona has *goma* shops that specialize in the sale of condoms. Some shops have as many as 50 varieties with names that describe male self-images and fantasies—"Conquistador," "El Cid," "Brave Bull"—fantasies that can be enacted with obliging prostitutes nearby.[63]

Common geographical associations have been burlesque shows, peep shows, "adult" movie theaters and book stores. During the early 1970s the Times Square area between 6th and 8th Avenues and 42nd and 49th Streets had more than 25 pornographic book stores.[64] Areas where streetwalkers solicit in New Orleans, Los Angeles and San Francisco have been invaded by alleged sex shops: rap studios, encounter houses, nude painting studios, dating services. They come into an area to prey on those who buy and sell commercialized sex.

To be sure, the prostitute profits from the geography of sex-related establishments. As Gaily Sheehy has noted, "the link between pornography and the infiltration of a new area by prostitutes is firmly established. One promises, the other delivers."[65] The prostitute knows that if a customer goes first to a "grindie" theater or a pornographic book store his pump is primed; a hesitant male becomes a decisive and easy mark. But the agglomeration advantages to the prostitute and to those who precede or follow her have an associated cost. One and all—prostitute, quasi-prostitute, criminal, parasite—increase the visibility of the place. High visibility promotes strong public reaction.

Chapter 3

Attitudes
and
Perceptions,
Real and Distorted

Visibility Matters

[People often ignore socially odious activities until visually or verbally confronted by them. Streetwalkers and places where prostitutes work have a way of stimulating moral condemnation and arresting one's sense of self and society. The constant visual reminder that a woman is a prostitute, nay a "whore," or a district a combat zone of debauchery, provides reason enough for discriminatory treatment by the public and its legislative representatives.)

Visibility in the cityscape is related to concentration. The greater the clustering, the more visible the phenomenon and the greater its impact on perceptions and attitudes. Visibility, concentration and threshold are kindred concepts. Small numbers of streetwalkers and massage parlors go unnoticed, but past some threshold people and police become sensitized to their presence. As one commissioned investigation of prostitution noted: "In reality it is not so much the conduct of any particular prostitute that causes the annoyance as the presence of numbers of prostitutes in the same place."[1]

Unacceptable visibility is registered by body counts, overhearing words believed to be a solicitation, an unusual style of dress or posturing. These images and realities are threatening. Wives complain to husbands. A few people complain to their ministers and a few phone calls are made to the district precinct. A minority speaks for a majority, proclaiming that a cityscape is profligate and something ought to be done about it, despite the fact that all helped to create the concentration in the first place. The immoral landscape was created to solve a problem, that of having prostitution everywhere or in too many places. But the solution created its own problem, that of having too many prostitutes in one place. The geographic dialectic is one of extremes, one without a synthesis. At one moment people say, "Keep the whores out of my neighborhood." At another moment the cry is, "Do something about the eyesore in Times Square."

In 1959 the British Parliament passed the Street Offenses Act, aimed at getting streetwalkers off the streets. Based on the now famous Wolfenden

Report, the Act was proof that the legalities of prostitution depend on land-scape appearances.[2] The Wolfenden Report had no concern for what people do in private; it cared only to address the question of public decency. While the committee members recognized that a prostitute on the street might not be any more obvious than a toyseller or street photographer, they never-theless concluded that "the right of the normal, decent citizen to go about the streets without affront to his or her sense of decency should be the prime consideration and should take precedence over the interests of the prostitute and her customers."[3] More telling is the comment of one member of the House of Lords who defended the Act on the grounds that "sweeping the dirt under the carpet" is justifiable because hidden dirt is healthier and less unsightly.[4]

From 1915 until the early 1950s the number of prosecutions for street soliciting and related sexual offenses in London never averaged more than 6,000 arrests annually for any cluster of three to five years. The average yearly figure jumped to nearly 11,000 for the period 1952-55 and then to 17,000 in 1958, the year before implementation of the Street Offenses Act. These numbers do not reflect an increase in the prostitute population, nor do they primarily register a change in soliciting practices. The dramatic rise in arrests indexes shifting citizen concern. The police admitted as much; they adjusted their arrest patterns to the intensity of public outcry.[5]

In a Gallup Poll taken after the Wolfenden Report was completed, 75 percent of those surveyed thought that prostitutes should be cleared from the streets, and a like percentage believed that heavy penalties, including im-prisonment, should be used if necessary.[6] Other findings suggest that visibility was a good part of the issue. Forty-three percent of those polled felt that brothels should be licensed; over a majority favored call girl prosti-tution.

Though Gallup Polls were not used in the nineteenth century there is reason to believe that similar attitudes have a long history in Great Britain and Western Europe. Victorian police in England had virtually no power to prosecute women working in brothels. Along with those who solicited in theaters and music halls they were considered a secondary problem com-pared to streetwalkers.[7] A student of the period claims that one of the reasons for introducing a vice squad into Victorian England was the belief that it would help clear the streets. The police professed that "swearing, drunkenness, and indecency were quite exceptional in controlled areas."[8] Parisian guardians of the moral order, the *police des moeurs*, thought similarly. By the second decade of the nineteenth century prostitutes were confined to licensed houses. Street solicitation was against the law.

Italy closed its houses of prostitution in 1958. Subsequent dissatisfaction with the decision involved not just the realization that the law eliminating brothels resulted in a proliferation of pimps, and may have increased the venereal disease rate among prostitutes, but also the fact that the greater number of streetwalkers that resulted was of public concern.[9] Overt immoral behavior is apparently so important an issue that Italian law states that if something shows under a woman's skirt she can be found guilty of enticement.[10]

During the first years of the twentieth century scores of North American cities favored segregation of prostitutes in red-light districts, and they did what they could to prevent streetwalking and open solicitation. Between 1910 and 1920 when all but a few of the districts were closed and it became evident that many of the women had turned to the streets, the number of states with statutes against solicitation increased dramatically—from 14 in 1917 to 33 by 1924.[11] The consistency of the American attitude is suggested by recent studies. In the mid-1970s, 81 percent of Anchorage's citizens thought that prostitutes should be confined to brothels.[12] The final conclusions and recommendations of a rather liberal San Francisco crime commission report in 1971 more or less concurred, stating that "the real question is how the City should go about developing a means of dealing with prostitution that limits its visibility."[13]

⌈ Cross-cultural comparisons do not seem to change the picture. In Japan in 1948 a National Public Opinion Survey found strikingly different attitudes toward various classes of prostitutes.[14] Seventy-seven percent of those questioned felt that streetwalking should be prohibited, yet 70 percent were *opposed* to the prohibition of brothels. Nearly 60 percent emphasized the "moral evil" of streetwalking; only 35 percent expressed similar attitudes about brothel activity. Approximately half of those interviewed lacked sympathy for the predicament of streetwalkers, while only a quarter held this opinion toward brothel women. Finally, over three times as many people opposed the punishment of those working in houses as against administering "justice" to streetwalkers (71 percent vs. 23 percent). All these statistics point to the same conclusion: a crucial variable in the Japanese position was the extent to which prostitutes' visibility disrupted the public's sense of decorum.⌋

Two noted sex researchers recently constructed a list of ten factors believed significant to Americans in their evaluation of offensive sexual activity.[15] Third on their list in order of importance behind force (such as rape) and sexual exploitation was public visibility. Although they cite copulation or fellatio committed in public parks, theaters, restrooms or other places where people are unwilling witnesses as germane examples, the presence of streetwalkers and the sight of open solicitation would also seem to fall within this category. Other investigators with decades of research behind them have also been cognizant of the issue of visibility, classifying prostitutes by this criterion.[16] At one end of a continuum are so-called flagrant prostitutes, those who "tap on a window with a nail file or ring or call loudly, or stand in a window or doorway, in order to attract the attention of potential customers."[17] At the opposite extreme are those identified as clandestine, primarily call girls. Vern Bullough, one of the world's outstanding contemporary sex historians, not only agrees that visibility is a major issue but has stated that the more overt forms of prostitution should be outlawed.[18]

Social concern with the immorality of the visible landscape has long been registered in shorthand labels, line and boundary markers which name, judge and condemn. In the Byzantine Empire a street in Constantinople that led to the theater was known as the "street of the harlots," because the occupation of actress was supposedly synonymous with that of prostitute.[19] Demeaning designations were used in fourteenth-century Southwark, near London. There, streets with brothels bore such vernacular names as "Slut's Hole" and "Whore's Nest." A century later in Paris one could find names in the prostitution quarters such as *rue Puits d'Amour* (Whore's Hole Lane) and *rue Poilecon* (Hairycunt Lane).[20]

Places in the Americas have clearly denoted moral and Christian disapproval. Nineteenth-century San Francisco and Reno were two cities famous for their "cowyards," large buildings consisting of more than a hundred cribs from which prostitutes sold their services. "Hog ranches" were prostitution quarters that serviced the men in nineteenth century frontier military outposts. Deadwood's red-light district was known as the "Bad Lands,"[21] while Abilene's counterpart was the "Devil's Addition."[22] Similar labels are to be found in Latin America. Jalapa, Mexico's zone of prostitution at the beginning of the twentieth century was called the *bolsa del diablo*.[23] In pre-Castro Havana a corner of the red-light district where streetwalkers congregated was referred to as *La Esquina del Pecado* (sin corner), and a three-block stretch of low-class houses was called *Calle de los Perros* (street of the dogs).[24] Contemporary American parallels are "Meatrack" (a district with either female or male homosexual prostitutes), "Sin Strip," "Skin Alley," "Erogenous Zone" and "Combat Zone."

⌈ Behavior and laws reflect attitudes. The F.B.I. Uniform Crime Reports show that streetwalkers make up a significant proportion of all women arrested, preceded only by charges for larceny, narcotics violations and drunkenness.[25] Among prostitutes streetwalkers constitute the vast majority arrested, now and in the past. Arrests for less overt forms of prostitution—those occurring in brothels, massage parlors and bars—account for less than five percent of the total. In spite of the unjust attention showered on street prostitutes a recent national survey of policemen found that almost 70 percent felt that their arrest rates should be increased.[26] ⌋

Cities in the United States arrest streetwalkers under a variety of vagrancy, loitering and solicitation laws. Forty-four states have solicitation statutes, more than the number that expressly prohibit a commercial sex act, and more than three times the number of states that make the status of being a prostitute illegal.[27] Until 1972 Canadians relied on vagrancy laws to keep the streets clear of prostitutes. Now they use solicitation statutes. Their concern with overt prostitution has escalated to the point where, in recent years, they have tried to define a private automobile as a public place.

If existing laws appear outdated or inadequate to concerns of the moment, states simply modify or introduce new laws. An anti-loitering ordinance was put into effect in New York City in 1976, just in time for the Democratic National Convention. It is worth noting what the ordinance contained.

> Any person [can be arrested] who remains or wanders about in a public place and repeatedly stops, or repeatedly attempts to stop, or attempts to engage passersby in conversation, or repeatedly stops or attempts to stop motor vehicles, or repeatedly interferes with the free passage of other persons, for the purpose of prostitution . . . .[28]

One can be certain that terms like "repeatedly" and "attempts to" were interpreted liberally by cops.

High visibility not only increases the likelihood of arrest, but also exploitation by predators and parasites. To forestall or prevent arrest the street woman gives out information to cops on street crimes and pays off cabbies, bellhops and bartenders. The British approach to prostitution vividly illustrates the contradiction between law and reality and the intimate links among visibility, illegality and exploitation. The Street Offenses Act was intended not only to remove soliciting activity from the view of decent people but also to protect prostitutes from exploitation by pimps and others. British laws, like those elsewhere, are particularly tough on men living off the earnings of prostitutes. While the Act was reasonably successful in the narrow sense of removing the women from the streets it was an utter failure in protecting them from predators. They were pushed into the welcoming clutches of pimps, and they were forced to find new places to hustle.[29] A long list of hungry landlords and entertainment establishments was waiting in the wings to provide flats and access to customers—at exhorbitant prices. As time and facts have demonstrated in London, the greater the repression, the greater the exploitation.

Prostitutes not only obviously differ in where they labor and the prices they command in the sexual marketplace, but also in how their skin color affects their treatment. The prostitution landscape mirrors the larger society. On the street, where survival is most difficult to negotiate, black prostitutes are disproportionately represented. Because of their color they receive the most hassles, they are the first to be arrested—traditionally have been arrested out of proportion to their numbers—and they have the fewest opportunities to solicit in alternative environments. Thus, even if visibility is held constant, meaning simply that the issue is not that of whether a woman is working on the street or in a house, the more a prostitute is a reflection of prejudices in society the more likely she is to be apprehended; because of this, one would expect her to be more victimized, more profoundly exploited. Being a certain color increases needs: the "wrong" color predisposes and increases particular kinds of behavior, and reduces others—one of which is working in environments less visible than the street.

By the preceding reasoning, the most pernicious aspects of prostitution—predation and parasitism—are reached by two different roads, one via visibility, the other through sexism and racism. But reality is always more complex than straight-forward reasoning suggests. In the present context this means that degrees and types of predation and parasitism are linked to both visibility *and* discrimination; where prostitutes are highly visible and also strongly discriminated against, accommodations, compromises, arrests, predation and parasitism and retaliatory behavior are more of a necessity and more commonplace.

Drugs in the Streetscape

The simple visual reminder of immoral sexual behavior has not been solely responsible for opinions, labels and laws discriminatory to streetwalkers and other prostitutes. A compounding contributor is the belief that prostitutes are malefactors under a more encompassing principle of immorality, one that associates them with drug use, venereal disease and felonies such as robbery and assault.[30] These alleged connections loom large not only in the public mind but also in law enforcement circles.

Many people believe that the immoral landscape of the prostitute is populated with drug addicts. This view is a half-truth at best. Not all prostitutes are on drugs and those that are vary in frequency of usage and type of drug. Further, one must ask whether it is profitable to be addicted, and whether addiction began before or after entering prostitution.

During 1967 the San Francisco vice squad arrested 140 "known prostitutes" for possession of narcotics or dangerous drugs. The city's total of arrests for drugs and narcotics during the same year was nearly 4,300.[31] More revealing is the vice squad's estimate that only 15 percent of the city's prostitutes are drug addicts.[32] A British study of 66 female narcotic addicts found no evidence of a causal connection between prostitution and addiction.[33] A recent examination of prostitution in a number of West German cities with legalized prostitution discovered that, with the exception of Frankfurt, the correlation between drug usage and prostitution was not significant.[34]

Monique Layton's study of 100 streetwalkers in Vancouver, British Columbia in the early 1970s ascertained that only 12 women reported using soft drugs—hashish and marijuana. Another 22 were regular users of heroin and LSD, speed and other amphetamines, whereas approximately twice this number used heroin occasionally. Layton discovered that hard drug usage was much more common among older prostitutes, but that all women were caught in a bind. On the street taking drugs was expected, "the thing to do." For some 16 prostitutes this problem was compounded by husbands or pimps who were heroin addicts or hard drug users. On the other hand, pimps generally did not like their women to be addicted because the prostitutes could not simultaneously keep up their habits, which cost perhaps $200 a day, and also meet daily pimp quotas, about the same amount as the cost of their habits. The pressure was clearly on filling the money box. Those who did not could expect a beating.[35]

Studies of prostitution in the same city sometimes do not agree on the incidence of drug use. Charles Winick claims that a substantial number of New York City prostitutes are addicts,[36] while Gail Sheehy has said that most are not.

> A persistent myth about prostitution is that most girls are addicts. This is not only untrue, it is impossible for a girl working at the competitive speed—running five miles a night, six nights a week, and turning six to twelve tricks daily *despite* rotations through jail cells and courts—to keep up the pace demanded by the pimp.[37]

She also argues that those who persist in taking drugs lose status by being lowered to the bottom of the pimp "stable," or in some cases expelled from it, which results in a drop in street status. Francis Ianni, who has studied the black mafia in New York City, contends that pimps prefer "unhooked flatbackers" (flatbackers specialize in simple intercourse)—those not addicted or into shoplifting.[38]

Whatever the situation in New York City, or elsewhere in the West, distinctions need to be made among different classes of prostitutes. Equally important is the issue of causality, whether prostitution or drug addiction came first. The high cost of addiction, the good money to be made from prostitution and the nature of the job itself make drugs and commercial sex inevitable partners. As Jennifer James has noted: "prostitution provides support for drugs and drugs make it easier to prostitute."[39] The problem is commonly recognized by the women themselves. One who told her story to Kate Millett declared that "you need the shit to kill the pain of prostitution; you need the prostitution to kill the pain of needing the drug."[40]

One recent study of 60 prostitutes found that drug addiction tended to predate entry into prostitution among lower-class street women, who turned to prostitution to support their habit. That the use of heroin and depressants was dysfunctional to their job was of secondary concern. By contrast, higher-class women began using drugs after entering the life, primarily restricting themselves to alcohol and stimulants helpful in their work.[41] Type of drug usage and class of prostitute are also related in Vancouver, British Columbia. Those who smoke marijuana tend to be high-class; those on the bottom are into heroin; women in the middle prefer cocaine.[42]

That addicts often enter prostitution to support their habit is a finding reinforced by interviews with female drug addicts. One investigation discovered that 47 percent had prostitution experience, and 79 percent relied on prostitution as their source of income for drugs.[43]

Often locational and behavioral discriminations can be made between prostitutes not on drugs and those who are addicts.[44] In Seattle addict-prostitutes hang out in different areas than their non-addicted counterparts; they also have different values, goals and norms concerning acceptable behavior. They have dissimilar work habits. When an addict-prostitute goes to the streetscape she usually has a companion and her man watches nearby for her to score. She pays little attention to dress, uncautiously solicits cars openly at traffic lights, and lacks care in her choice of clients and in discriminating among those from whom she steals. Arrested frequently, she does not have the good sense to move to a new turf when she becomes known to the vice squad or when the threat of arrest increases.

The "professional" prostitute gives careful attention to her garments, shows up regularly and at a predictable hour on her stroll, considers it "low-class" to have her man present in the work area, and is careful not to take just any customer, steal from any male or pay no heed to the police. For these reasons her likelihood of being arrested is less than that of the addict-prostitute. She lowers the possibility further by transferring to a new streetscape when she feels "known" by the cops or the heat is on. And the professional woman of the street is less tied to place; unlike the addict-prostitute she does not have to fear losing her tie to place-defined drug connections.

Professional street women make a clear and sharp distinction between themselves and those on drugs. Their perceived individuality involves not just financial drain and lost street time when strung out, but status. They do not wish to socialize with addicts, they do not see them as professionals, they may not even see them as prostitutes. Language reflects self-image and the image of others. Those who "chippy" with narcotics are referred to as "hypes," "jive-asses," "flea bags," "flaky broads," "junkie chicks" and "junky broads."[45] Some terms describe an absence of street ascribed professionalism, others denote simple addiction, irrespective of whether the addicts prostitute themselves. Those who are most successful on the street simply do not have positive terms for addicts and addict-prostitutes. In short, addict-prostitutes are another subculture, an immoral landscape within the congeries of those similarly labeled.

Misconceptions About Venereal Disease

The public entertains a strong and erroneous misconception about venereal disease and its association with prostitution. In Barbara Milman's recent survey of 279 people, many of whom were in police departments across the United States, 70 percent agreed with the statement that "prostitution is a significant factor in the spread of venereal disease."[46] More than anything, the percentage demonstrates that a well-established historical fact dies slowly.

Historically, venereal disease among prostitutes was widespread. In a study of prostitutes in more than forty cities in the first decade of this century Howard Woolston contended that 60 to 75 percent of the prostitutes had the "social disease," and that 84 percent of the infections in the Navy at that time came from this source.[47] Not surprisingly, numerous nineteenth- and early twentieth-century governments in the West argued that containment of venereal disease was one of the principal reasons for segregating, supervising and medically examining prostitutes on a regular basis.[48] However, even if Woolston's percentages are not exaggerated the figures are less an indictment of prostitutes and their hygienic concerns than the fact that venereal disease was widespread before the discovery of penicillin. Near the turn of the century, in Germany, one male in five was believed to have had syphilis, and gonorrhea averaged more than one attack per male in the population.[49] In the nineteenth and early twentieth centuries, as in several that preceded, venereal disease was one of society's more serious concerns.

That the situation changed dramatically once penicillin and other cures became available is difficult to dispute. Prior to the Second World War prostitutes accounted for more than 75 percent of the venereal disease contacts reported by the military. By 1960 the rate was below 10 percent. More than half of this figure was being described as "pick-up, no fee."[50] Even though there were claims that the closing of licensed brothels, as in France in 1946 and Italy more than a decade later, led to a dramatic increase in venereal disease among prostitutes, more broadly based United Nations studies could find no increase when houses were closed.[51] Since the evidence seems mixed and inconclusive it only seems reasonable to suppose that when prostitutes find themselves working outside the law they are more likely to avoid the institutional structures that they associate with oppression and control.[52]

The Chief of the Center for Disease Control of HEW estimated that for 1970-71 less than 3 percent of 13,600 females who had infectious syphilis were prostitutes.[53] Recent estimates by United States public health officials indicate that heterosexual prostitutes account for no more than five percent of all venereal diseases.[54] The rates, of course, vary among types of prostitutes and among cities, states and countries. Ten percent of all women arrested a decade ago in Montreal were purportedly infected.[55] In Oakland and Sacramento, California the rate in 1975 was said to be something above 10 percent.[56] Despite a venereal disease rate among prostitutes lower than that in the general female population, Sacramento's women were being denied bail until they underwent a venereal disease examination. During 1971-72 less than three percent of some 13,000 Alaskan women diagnosed with infectious syphilis were prostitutes.[57] Of 2,300 prostitutes examined monthly throughout 1976 in Hamburg, West Germany, 30 to 40 had gonorrhea and one to five had syphilis.[58] From 1970 to 1972 only one case of syphilis was noted by public health authorities in Nevada's 33 brothels, which housed approximately 250 women servicing tens of thousands of men yearly.[59] Several women who have worked in Nevada's brothels for one to four years maintain they have never seen a case of syphilis. The significance of these rates, even when not adjusted for type of prostitute, becomes apparent when it is realized that the venereal disease rate among high school students, aged 15 to 19, may be 25 percent or higher,[60] several times the rate among average prostitutes.

Generalities on venereal disease transmission need to be qualified by type of prostitute, cultural setting and kind of venereal disease. Syphilis, for example, is not a serious problem among prostitutes, for no other reason than that there are only a few brief infectious periods. By contrast, gonorrhea is much more prevalent and is not so easy to detect in a female.[61] These differences in mind, data on gonorrhea in the United Kingdom during 1956 indicate differences between inland cities and so-called "quiet areas" on the one hand, and London and port cities on the other (Table 3-1). In urban areas with significant numbers of streetwalkers, many of whom are lower-class within the prostitution hierarchy, the rates are expectedly higher.[62] Port cities and war zones are similar.

Table 3-1
Female Gonorrhea in the United Kingdom in 1956

	London	Ports	"Quiet Areas"	Inland Cities	Totals
Prostitutes	114	89	4	8	215
Others	338	319	35	116	808
Totals	452	408	39	124	1023
Percentage Attributable To Prostitutes	25.2	21.8	10.3	6.5	21.0

Data from Chesser 1973:462.

Criminal Environments and Criminal Behavior

The role of organized crime in prostitution at present is minimal. In comparison to hard drugs and other illegal markets the returns relative to the costs are low. Although pronouncements to the effect that prostitution is tied up with organized crime occasionally surface, even from the desk of a major American city chief of police, little valid evidence can be produced.[63] The President's Crime Commission Report of 1967 concluded that prostitution plays "a small and declining role in organized crime's operations."[64]

Outside the United States the picture may be somewhat different. Allegedly organized crime is involved with prostitution in Montreal.[65] The same may be true for Australia.[66] And on the Continent the Central Office for the Suppression of Traffic in Human Beings maintained that in the mid-1970s a vice ring in France controlled more than 3,500 French prostitutes in Great Britain, Italy, Belgium and Luxembourg.[67] On the other hand, in West Germany, where the state regulates brothels and streetwalking activity, organized crime has stayed away from prostitution.[68]

If it makes any sense to talk about organized crime in prostitution in the United States today it would have to be in the context of black pimps. Some at the top of the social hierarchy, generally those who work in major cities, exchange notes on "fast tracks" and "slow tracks," easy cities and go-easy cities on crime.[69] Within major urban areas pimps occasionally agree to have their women solicit certain territories and not others and may exchange prostitutes and move them around on geographical circuits. But all this is small time stuff and rather loosely organized in comparison to the Mafia or similar groups.

To be sure, the role of organized crime in prostitution has been substantial in the past. Al Capone controlled one of the largest syndicates of brothels in North America in this century.[70] "Motzie" Di Nicola had a chain of vice resorts in Connecticut in the 1930s that produced 2.5 million dollars a year.[71] Lucky Luciano, who attempted to monopolize the brothel trade of Manhattan in the 1930s, is another example.[72] But since pre-World War II days tighter law enforcement, concerted and continuing efforts to break up the brothel trade, the increased significance of call girls and the greater and often safer returns in narcotics and labor unions have resulted in organized crime playing a lesser role in prostitution.

Though organized crime may no longer be an issue in prostitution in the United States there is strikingly strong public belief that prostitution and crime of some sort are inextricably linked. Eighty-five percent of those recently polled in a survey conducted under the auspices of the Harvard Center for Criminal Justice thought that prostitution in an area leads to an influx of crime.[73] A similarly high percentage (77 percent) felt that the activity is often accompanied by muggings and crimes of violence. These kinds of attitudes have been prevalent in the West for well over a century.[74] Such attitudes contain an element of truth, but require elaboration and qualification.

In the first instance there is no causal connection between prostitution and crime. Some areas of cities have high crime rates and no prostitution, while others have large numbers of prostitutes and high crime rates. In Boston, for example, two police districts in the city have considerable crime and no prostitution. On the other hand, in the Combat Zone and in Back

Bay prostitutes are numerous and crime is high—larceny, muggings, more violent offenses. Much of it would probably be there without prostitutes, but much is attributable to their presence. In the Combat Zone so-called "rat packs" have been responsible for thievery and muggings. Although the rat packs were thought by some to be prostitutes, there is reason to believe (a belief even held by some of the zone's cops) that they were composed primarily of women posing as prostitutes.

The most significant crimes in the immoral landscape often go unrecorded because criminal brutality is meted out, by clients and cops, against prostitutes. When a husband cannot beat his wife, when a lover does not want to molest his female companion, when the lone male has nowhere to turn, frustrations and angers that come from the social interactions of an ill-ordered society are taken out on a despised street creature, someone institutionalized in law, in the social moral code, in accepted mistaken conceptions and perceptions of social class. The vent may occur in a London flat, a New York City "trick pad" or on any street or dark alley in any city in the world.

> Another time I was up in a hotel with one of them tricks and he choked me and choked me so bad I passed out. All he wanted was sex. He wanted to have intercourse but he didn't know how to approach me about it. Like I ask him, "What do you want done? What do you want done?" He kept telling me he didn't know. So I say, "Hey, if you can't tell me what you want, I'm going to go with the money and all." And he grabbed me and choked me so bad that I was unconscious . . . the hotel man found me and dressed me and put cold rags on me later on.[75]

Unlike the brothel boarder the streetwalker usually has few defenses against the male who wishes to harm her. Some women go to the room or bed prepared, maybe even clasping a small, open knife inside the fist during intercourse.[76] The best defenses include working with another woman, frequenting local hotels where a savvy manager remains alert for trouble, using cabs for transportation rather than the client's car, and intuition. Intuition, of course, that comes from experience.

Statistics and raw numbers on beatings of prostitutes by clients, cops and lunatics confirm that these women are often easy marks for abusive scenarios. Between 1962 and 1972, 20 prostitutes in Munich were victims of violent deaths. In 1973, in that city, 30 such women were subjected to armed robbery, 801 to theft.[77] A two-year study in Seattle found that 64 percent of a sample of 76 prostitutes had been assaulted at least once by a customer, and that a significant number of prostitutes had also been physically maltreated by policemen.[78]

The rape rate among women with previous arrest records and "bad reputations" is significantly higher than for other classes of women.[79] Occasionally prostitutes go to hospital wards and police precincts to complain they have been raped. Whether this means the male did not pay as promised, forced the prostitute to do something she does not practice, robbed or beat her or treated her exactly like any other rape victim is seldom clear. But no one, least of all cops, cares. The fact that most prostitutes are treated as criminals, and are unofficially segregated into high crime areas, makes them easy prey for rapists.

Streetwalkers often fear they will be robbed by street parasites who know they occasionally carry considerable sums of money. They also know that their vulnerability parallels that of clients: neither can afford to report a theft. Fear of robbery is not confined to such obvious settings as dark streets or the early hours of the morning in rundown streetwalking districts. Petty thieves or drug addicts may snatch a prostitute's purse in a heavily trafficked and relatively well-policed area.

The problematic issue facing many a streetwalker is: where do I hide my "take?" The best place to conceal earnings can be a major concern, as illustrated by Parisian prostitutes four decades ago.

> Handbags? Too vulnerable. Some girls hid a small purse in some intimate part of their bodies, stuck between their buttocks or onto their upper thighs with adhesive tape. Others hid the big bills carefully folded in their flowered garters, in their garter belts, in the lining of their skirts, or between their breasts.[80]

For a time in London streetwalkers hid paper money inside their shoes and put silver in their gloves.[81] Some New York City streetwomen used to hide their money in wigs, but dissatisfied customers learned to look there.[82] Some women started to deposit their cash with the hotel desk clerk.

The prostitute is one of the victims in her own environment but she also behaves criminally, apart from being labeled as a criminal for being a vendor of sex. But, as with drugs and venereal disease, differences need to be noted among prostitutes. In Boston, Barbara Milman discovered that the later a prostitute is arrested in her career the less likely she is to engage in criminal activity. Those who begin first as prostitutes rather than as criminals are less likely to get involved in a violent offense. She also found that women who first engaged in criminal activity or prostitution as a juvenile are more likely than others to be involved in a serious crime. Finally, prostitutes arrested for robbery tended to be a member of a minority group.[83]

A study of English prostitutes several decades ago noted that while many women had records of shoplifting and petty larceny only a very small percentage had been party to a serious or violent crime.[84] Of 72 prostitutes interviewed in Seattle only 20 percent had ever been apprehended for other than loitering or prostitution.[85] Based on these studies and others in Boston, plus her own, Milman has concluded that:

> There is a substantial group of professional prostitutes who do not otherwise engage in criminal behavior; there is a sizeable group of prostitutes who

engage in larceny and other non-violent crimes; and there is a smaller group of prostitutes who are also violent offenders.

Women with regular clients, those who work on a referral basis and those who hustle in brothels almost never steal from customers. They would lose business, be evicted from the house or, in regulated systems in Europe, be reported to the police. In so far as these kinds of distinctions are made the characterization that many prostitutes engage in larceny is probably valid. The historical record is supportive, as is the logic following from the prostitutes' predicament.

Strong moral circumscription and the illegality of prostitution promote criminal behavior by prostitutes. By defining a woman as criminal for selling access to her body society pushes her into contact with criminals. Through social labeling, self-image and the behavior and images of those with whom she associates the prostitute comes to appreciate the value of behaving outside the law. She sees that the payoffs from larceny are high and that chances of getting caught are relatively slim since clients are usually unwilling to complain to the police.[86] Her reasoning is buttressed by the attitude she develops towards customers, because of the way they treat her.

A working philosophy finds its way into everyday vocabulary, the argot of the street and the bedroom. It is evidenced in the frequency of certain words, the manner in which uttered, the extent to which others pick up on them.

"I say, fuck the bastards. I'll take anything I can get."
"Get as much as you can while you can."
"My motto is: don't get caught."

The contempt prostitutes have for most men and the perception of the service they perform is best expressed in the term "trick." Trick is a noun, the anonymous client who did not get what was promised; it is an action terminated (the customer has been tricked); and it is an unspecified number on a seemingly endless chain (another trick turned). To the prostitute a trick is also the "square" husband and the man who cheats on his wife. A client not described as a trick is a "John," the "innocent" John Doe of police blotter fame that appears alongside the prostitute's name when she is booked. Mr. Anybody on the books might just as well be Mr. Nobody in bed. Case histories of 127 white prostitutes revealed that slightly more than half of them said they never liked their customers, and only 5 percent liked a quarter or more.[87]

Streetwalkers use equally colorful argot to judge their peers on customer-related matters. A "flatbacker" offers only regular intercourse; to those on the street she is a "dumb broad" because she does not "run a game" (talk a lot, make minimal use of her body, get more than the going rate from her "trick").[88] Prostitutes who can satisfy "talk tricks" are "high game."[89]

They are into conning," as they say on the streets of Vancouver, British Columbia.[90] Other street women are known as "rip off artists,"[91] "boosters"[92] or "boosting broads."[93] Their speciality is stealing from customers rather than delivering on verbal contracts. All these distinctions have central meanings, for the most salient activity in "the life" is the "game," the pattern of exploitative interactions between those in the life and those who are seeking services.[94] In the hostile environment of the streetscape where injustice and maltreatment are the norm, trickery and duplicity are highly valued.

Slang used outside the subculture, sometimes within it, bears similar messages. "Hooker" may derive from the famous Union General Joseph Hooker who, as legend has it, permitted prostitution to flourish along the Potomac, liked to frequent the red-light district and gave his name to signify not only an "abandoned woman and a drink of whiskey,"[95] but also the district itself—Hooker's Division.[96] But, then, hooker may come from a recent English term for thief, or from Old English, *hok*, an implement for grabbing. This etymology suggests that the label was given to prostitutes because of the recognition that they often do more than deliver on sex.[97]

From one society or historical period to another the words vary but the meaning remains the same. A Swedish prostitute speaks of *blasa torsk* (to trick a cod); it summarizes her attitude toward a customer.[98] In the thieves' vernacular of two decades ago in London the name for a client was "mug" or "steamer," argot of derision which, like trick, characterizes the customer as a fool.[99] Mug has a Commonwealth flavor about it; Australian prostitutes frequently use the term to express the idea they are taking as much as they can get for minimum effort.[100]

Prostitutes in de Sade's time considered clever stealing a necessary requirement for obtaining one's "bachelor's degree" as a common prostitute. Women without it lacked importance among peers.[101] Equally institutionalized is the attitude inculcated in call girls who receive training in their business. They are taught they should be concerned primarily with "maximizing gains and minimizing effort, even if this requires transgressions of either a legal or moral nature."[102] Even argot for house of prostitution or business location may emphasize thievery and deception. "Gaff", from the French *gaff* (fish hook) or *gaffer* (a spear), has long meant an English prostitute's flat used for doing business. The term suggests the customer was hooked, or spent more money than he cares to remember.[103]

Street names can reveal prostitutes' attitudes and tactics. In the chief prostitution area of Amsterdam, centering around the *Ouderkerksplein* (Old Church Square), one of the more important side streets is *Bloedstraat*, or "Blood Street." If someone has the appearance of wealth and the opportunity presents itself, he is—or was in the mid-1960s—likely to be rolled or mugged.[104] Prostitutes consider military personnel notorious for carrying large amounts of money and being big spenders. One of the off-limit areas to the U.S. military in Colon, Panama is "cash alley," appropriately named because of the many muggings, robberies and other crimes carried out there by prostitutes and accomplices.[105]

In the 1860s one estimate placed the number of London streetwalkers at 7,000; as many as three-quarters of them may have been thieves.[106] Some of the women agreed to one price on the street and then demanded additional money in the bedroom. If the client did not come up with the new tariff a "bully" would enter and throw him out, barren of all his possessions and without the services he came for.[107]

Thievery by prostitutes and accomplices in the mining camps and towns of the nineteenth-century American West was also common.[108] Theft in the Denver cribs required the removal of a man's pants and sometimes his coat, and often involved the cooperation of men known as "panel workers," "creepers" and "hook artists." New arrivals to town were particularly vulnerable, while those who had been in Denver for some time knew which cribs to avoid lest they be caught in an all-too-common ploy. After a crib prostitute encouraged a man to remove his clothes she would hang them inside a closet and shut the door. One wall of the closet would have a sliding panel from which a friend, known as a panel worker, would emerge to steal valuables. In order to avoid detection only the wallet's contents or items of particular value were rifled. An advantage working in the prostitute's favor was the universal tradition that services were paid for in advance. Unless suspicious, a client was unlikely to check his wallet until after leaving the crib.

Denver's creepers required more skill in stealing from customers. Once a man's pants and coat were removed the prostitute set them at the foot of the bed. Her colleague in crime would then creep from behind a curtain or other cover, take what was deemed of value and then go to an unoccupied room at the rear of the crib. In some cases the creeper would leave the crib by a back door, thereby preventing discovery should the client become suspicious and wish to look around. The woman seldom had anything to worry about since most men did not imagine her stealing from them while engaged in sexual activity.

A third crib method involved the use of a light pole with a hook on the end of it. The prostitute's confederate would stand outside the window transom of the crib, skillfully hook the pants or coat (hence the name hook artist), draw them out through the window, loot the contents and then return the garments to their previous location. Again, upset as a client may have been at the discovered theft, it was difficult to prove that the crib woman was responsible. Of course, she was quick to deny any association with the "unfortunate incident" when approached by an angry customer.

"Panel houses" and "creep houses" for thievery were not exactly a rarity in such cities as Chicago and New York in the nineteenth century.[109] Manhattan in the early twentieth century had creep houses to which clients were taken by prostitutes for the sole purpose of robbery.[110] In this city and elsewhere the women looked for a particular kind of mark: one who was drunk and "flashed a lot of money."[111] For the client who knew about creep houses and thought he was being cautious the "paddy hustle" was an alternative. The male entrusted his money to a third party—perhaps a pimp—left with the woman and then returned to discover that money and "friend" had disappeared.

Prostitutes have often expressed that they "know" just when creepers or other accomplices should exit from their hiding place to roll a client. Through trial and error they have learned that a man is least aware of touch when sexually aroused. Even Las Vegas teenage girls have found, or been told, how to take best advantage of the vulnerability of an excited male. Some engage in "parking lot fellatio" behind the casinos, charging a meager five or ten dollars for their services. To make their efforts worthwhile, they reach for the man's wallet just as he has a climax.[112] This intuitive knowledge by old time and new time prostitutes seems to be well-grounded in human physiology. Kinsey noted that when erotically aroused senses become dulled and temporary anesthesia may even result. In extreme cases individuals lapse into a temporary state of unconsciousness when experiencing an orgasm.[113] To describe this condition the French coined the terms, *"la petite mort"* (the little death) and *"la mort douce"* (the sweet death).[114]

Simple extortion often has proved effective in emptying a client's pockets. One type engaged in by both low- and high-class prostitutes involves making the customer believe he is having an affair with another man's wife. Pimps have sometimes been a principal participant in such ruses. A pimp storms into a hotel room, acts enraged at the supposed infidelity of his "wife," and demands that the client either pay for his transgression on the spot or "suffer the consequences." This is the so-called "badger game." Variants of this strategem are found in a number of cultural settings. In South Africa, European prostitutes of forty years ago who worked such schemes were known as "gold diggers"; their special tactic entailed the perusal of social and personal columns in the local press, followed by conning to get introduced to the most promising marks.[115] Nineteenth-century New Orleans had its own variety of the badger game. During the winter husband and wife teams from the North would go South to spend a season extorting money from the rich. The wife would permit herself to be courted and seduced by a wealthy southern gentleman, accepted his many lavish gifts, and then when these ceased or slowed her husband would "happen" upon the scene and "discover" the infidelity. Extortion was the mutually agreed compromise. The more successful of the prostitute-extortion artists were able to handle several "affairs" simultaneously.[116]

The decision whether or not to rob a client may depend heavily on solicited geographical knowledge. Many prostitutes make it a practice to talk with customers as much as possible: on the street, on the way to the room, in the room. If they find that he lives in the immediate area they may not cheat him for they want his return business. If, however, he resides in another city, or better, another state or country, non-delivery of services becomes a real possibility. Conventioneers and salesmen are ideal targets. Why come across when an out-of-towner has enough trouble finding his way around a city without looking for a fleeing prostitute?

Some prostitutes limit themselves to a single theft per evening. They save it for the finale and then go home immediately after the caper. Others steal only when working with another prostitute. This reduces the risk of detection and, if caught, reprisals are less likely. Still others take the client to a hotel at some distance from their usual stroll. This decreases the possibility that he will return to look for them. Whatever the tactic, when a prostitute is able to pull a robbery without intercourse she rates high points among her colleagues.[117]

Pimp demands may force a prostitute to rob when she otherwise would not consider it. In combination with periodic police repression of street-walking activity, this pressure may result in a vicious circle. The number of street arrests increases, clients become more difficult to get, and the pimp pushes his women even harder as his income declines. Prostitutes now have little choice. They must work longer hours and must steal as well.

The money stolen from one or two clients can be quite substantial, and a prostitute who steals may have to work only part of an evening to meet personal or pimp quotas. The issue may be compounded by the knowledge that "flatbacking" is a lot of hard work.[118] Why work for $15 or $25 when a single ripoff may net $200 or more? And besides, good payoffs give days off to relax body and mind. In a recent year in San Francisco between 20 and 30 prostitution-related robberies were reported each week. Matters appear to have worsened since 1967 when nearly 600 robberies of this sort were reported, with a victim dollar loss approaching $150,000 a year.[119] Of course, the actual number of thefts and amounts stolen from clients may have been several times these figures.

Exploited Females and Male Interests

Chapter 4

The Material Conditions of Life

Historically, those attracted most to prostitution have been from the lower classes, especially minorities and social or moral outcasts—women who lost virginity outside the connubial bed, those with children but no husbands. In certain social milieus the renting of one's body in return for money or goods has been socially legitimatized.[1] One student of the poor in eighteenth-century France found that conditions were so bad that some prostitutes used the homes of their parents to service customers.[2] Conditions in nineteenth-century England were not much better.

> The prostitution system . . . with its obeisance to male sexual need, its protection of "modest" women, and its tolerance of cruel excess—was serviced by terrible poverty. For most women, the streets were an alternative to the treadmill of the factories, with incredibly long hours in awful conditions, or to domestic service—often working for a tyrant—which then employed almost as many people as industry.[3]

While seduction, socially disapproved sexual behavior and abandonment by one's family may have been necessary preconditions for entry into prostitution for many women, the material facts of life were almost never inconsequential. Emma Goldman, ardent activist and feminist who was deported from the United States in 1919, argued that it was economic and social exploitation together that forced women into prostitution.[4] Studies at the time backed up her assertions. In a book entitled *A New Conscience and an Ancient Evil*, the renowned Jane Addams reported that half of the women who came to Chicago from Illinois' small towns in the early twentieth century might have to spend several weeks looking for a job that paid mere subsistence wages.[5] During their search for employment men preyed on them, seduced them, married them, compromised their moral systems and enticed and pushed them into prostitution. Whatever the psychological disturbances that developed from working in brothels under slave-like conditions, the women could justify and rationalize their behavior by noting that they were earning three to four times as much as they could elsewhere in society. The same pattern prevailed in most North American cities.[6] Prostitutes in Newark, New Jersey in 1914 averaged just over $45 a week; the figure for women from similar socioeconomic backgrounds was $14.[7] A half dozen years later Howard Woolston maintained that almost half of more than 1,100 streetwalkers he came in contact with had no job before entering prostitution. And for those who could find employment many had to settle for a mere $5 to $7 a week, not a living wage.[8] The Annual Report of the Ontario Bureau of Industries for 1889 vividly showed just how difficult it was for females in Canadian cities, particularly those with dependents (Table 4-1). Once a woman became a prostitute she faced almost insurmountable social prejudice. She had to recognize that she was "not only being paid for her sexual services, but for a loss of social standing as well."[9]

Table 4-1

Average Household Income and Expenses for Female Workers in Ontario in 1889

Household Income	Female Workers Over 16 Years of Age	
	Without Dependents	With Dependents
Yearly earnings from regular employment	$216.71	$246.37
Other sources of income	—	23.05
Earnings of dependents	—	16.48
TOTAL INCOME	216.71	285.90
Household expenses—clothing, board and lodging:	214.28	300.13
SURPLUS (DEFICIT)	$ 2.43	(14.23)
Other Pertinent Statistics:		
Average number of hours worked per week	54	59
Average number of days worked per year	259	265
Average number of dependents	—	2.1

Adapted from Rotenberg 1974:48-49.

The instinct to survive by any means has been especially apparent in the worst of times.[10] A student of the history of London's brothels claims that when England experienced a notable population increase between 1550 and 1650, also a time when inflation was rampant, the bordellos, the streets, the taverns and the playhouses were packed with soliciting women. There were even children's brothels, full of girls from seven to fourteen.[11] The 1857 depression in America had a like effect; New York City's prostitute population rose by some 20 percent that year.[12] During the Great Depression in such cities as Chicago and New York the number of bordellos and street-walkers may have increased by 100 percent.[13] Black neighborhoods in Chicago reportedly had prostitutes "in every kitchenette apartment."[14] Those who knew the circumstances and the women claimed that if the women could have gotten any job they would not have become prostitutes.[15]

The ravages of war have highlighted the renting of young girls. Magnus Hirschfeld in his study of the sexual history of the Great War described the situation in a number of Belgian cities.

> One could observe little girls of twelve and fourteen garishly painted despite their rags, accosting soldiers and saying, *"Monsieur, pour une livre de pain?"* For a pound of sugar mothers offered their children, emphasizing their virginity; and little boys and girls of eight would tug at the soldier's coattails to drag him to their sister, while making the symbolic gesture of sexual intercourse.[16]

Economics has continued to play a major role in women entering prostitution. An intensive study of South African prostitutes between 1939 and 1941 found that more than 75 percent came from the lowest classes. Almost all of them were unskilled. When they found jobs, they were invariably paid substantially less than men. Most discovered, particularly if they had children, that they could not be self-supporting. Within three months of taking a low paying factory job the women drifted into prostitution.[17]

The material predicament of women remains particularly difficult in underdeveloped countries. Widespread unemployment and underemployment, low standards of living, striking social and economic disparities among classes, and the inferior social and economic status of women are thick threads that define the larger contextual syndrome. For specific individuals, lack of skills, loss of virginity in societies that value it before marriage, and personal and familial financial problems are recurrent themes in the lives of those who become prostitutes.[18] The statistics are seldom equivocal. Ninety percent of 1,000 Mexican prostitutes studied a decade ago lacked skills and alternative opportunities; most also had one or more children to support.[19]

Child prostitution is gravest where poverty is most profound. In Rio de Janeiro, for example, as many as 2,000 girls between the ages of 11 and 17 work in Carapebuce, a district outside the city. There, in a month, a girl of 12 can earn ten times as much as her factory-working father, enough to support two large Brazilian families. Brazilian law forbids the exploitation of women, but the authorities do little to change the poverty that feeds the ranks of prostitution.[20]

It might be argued that the situation for most women in the Western world at present no longer resembles the predicament of 50 or 100 years ago, and therefore monetary concerns cannot play the role they once did. The fact is that most women still do not have equal access to jobs, nor do they receive equal pay for similar work. According to the United States Bureau of the Census the median annual income of a full-time female civilian worker in 1977 was $8,618, while the comparable figure for males was $14,626.[21] For many black women, and for whites who come from poor subcultures,[22] such as Appalachians in cities of the Midwest, the situation is much worse.[23] It is not surprising to find that prostitution is more easily understood in these communities.

In the 1960s continuing studies at the Institute for Sex Research at Indiana University, where Kinsey did his pioneering work, found that in a white population of 127 prostitutes not a single woman turned to prostitution because she lost her virginity or was the victim of a broken marriage promise. A mere four percent contended they were forced into prostitution by husbands or someone else, and another four percent became prostitutes because they needed money for a morphine or heroin habit. Ninety percent of the women listed money as their reason for becoming prostitutes.[24] As Paul Gebhard puts it:

> Some prostitutes have asked a simple question which may be paraphrased thus. As an unskilled, poorly educated female why should I scrimp along in a badly paid tedious job and live in unpleasant surroundings when by prostituting a few days a week I can earn several hundred dollars, have a nice apartment, frequent the better hotels, often meet interesting men of a higher socioeconomic level, and lead a life full of novelty?[25]

The contemporary issue is not as simple as discrimination along sex or class lines. I have talked with numerous women who work in Nevada's brothels. Sometimes college-educated, they frequently talk about the good money they make—$500 to $1,000 a week after the madam takes her share—and what they cannot make elsewhere. Too, they talk of their savings, their clothes, their travels, the future that money will buy. The issue, then, is not as it was once, that of merely putting food on the table and clothes on children, but rather that of enjoying the same pleasures and material advantages that others have.

The difference between what individuals have and what they feel they ought to possess may lie behind the reasoning used by many prostitutes. In the early twentieth century department store employees in American cities were often recruited into prostitution. One study in New York City discovered that it was not impoverishment that led these women into brothels, but rather an environment of spending and accumulation that caused rising expectations. Ironically, it was the highest paid saleswomen who were likely to become prostitutes.[26] A student of female issues has asserted there are two kinds of prostitutes in present-day Toronto: those who work from need, and those who work from greed. The first are likely to be lower-class women, those in the second category have bought the myth of consumerism.[27]

The emphasis placed on the material basis of prostitution reflects the fact that economic considerations are the principal reason women have turned to prostitution. Be this as it may, there is rarely a single explanation for social phenomena, and prostitution is no exception. Not only need other factors be discussed, but a distinction must be made between precipitating and sustaining forces.

Participation in morally circumscribed behavior, either as willing participant or victim, has often been significant in the lives of prostitutes. Jennifer James and Jane Meyerding discovered that age at first intercourse, the experience of rape or incest and a lack of parental guidance in sexual matters have been prominent in the lives of prostitutes. Particularly striking is that over 50 percent of the women they studied were victims of some kind of sexual abuse.[28]

In the West women have long been sexual objects first and people who are intelligent and stimulating second. By social definition, then, women are unidimensional. Some women seek escape. A prostitute in Boston put it this way:

> For me prostitution is a way to achieve a little bit more freedom in an oppressive world. I don't enjoy pleasing men at all. So I face each new "assignment" with something less than joy. I have to concentrate on the mechanics of the task and the money I'm earning. I have to work especially hard to be nice to these men, because it does not come naturally.[29]

The Western emphasis on sexuality is tied up with another social fact: women who participate in any form of socially deviant behavior are assumed to be prostitutes. Not only has prostitution been the principal way that women have veered from the social norm, but it also follows that if women in general are seen in terms of sexuality then deviant women will be seen in the same light, whether or not such deviance has anything initially to do with prostitution.[30]

Increasingly women have realized they can use their sex for non-sexual ends, and that sex is a means of equalizing power and economic position. Combined with what may be some form of deviant behavior on their part and perhaps an understanding of what a deviant label implies, prostitution appears attractive. Yet, the move from "good girl" or deviant to prostitute is neither automatic nor immediate. There are various routes and stages through which women may pass on their way to full-time prostitution. Two models have been identified for those who become London prostitutes.[31] One stresses an initial period of rather vague and ill-defined promiscuity in which a woman becomes increasingly alienated from those in her environment. She simply stops relating to people. In stage two the woman moves to London (many London prostitutes allegedly come from provincial industrial cities) where she may enter into relationships with a few men, frequent drinking establishments or work as a club hostess. It is in this stage that the woman makes the decision whether or not to pass into full-time prostitution. The second model differs from the first in that stage two may take place in the small town or provincial capital where the woman grew up. There she may have been an "easy lay" in school, later she works as a waitress in a provincial hotel. After sleeping with a traveling salesman or two, perhaps receiving money or gifts, she makes the connection between sex and remuneration, and how much she can make by renting her body. Soon she leaves for London to become a full-time prostitute.

In a sample of 30 streetwalkers in Minnesota, Nanette Davis found that many of the women did not have an early commitment to prostitution, did not quickly move into the life, and economic deprivation was not their principal motive for turning to prostitution.[32] The easy money, of course, allowed them to rationalize what they were doing. Davis noticed that the women tended to go through three stages: a gradual drift, a period of transitional deviance and finally professionalization. The drift into promiscuity was a phase in which the women used their bodies as a status tool, a means of acquiring esteem and power among peers. Their promiscuity led to labeling. They were seen as "bad girls" and "easy marks." Stigmatization for some was magnified by confinement to a correctional institution. When the women finally became prostitutes they faced new problems. They had to learn to live with a more definite and intense form of social stigmatization and with the segregation and punishment that followed. They also had to learn how to respond to new peer group pressures, expectations, models: "everybody does it," "you gotta' have a pimp, honey," "ripoff your tricks, you won't get caught."

Promiscuous Males

The most important reason males give for going to prostitutes is diversity—in partners and sexual experiences. In a survey of 732 clients nearly twenty years ago, 73 percent gave diversity or variety as the reason for frequenting prostitutes.[33] That those surveyed were not simply deprived of sex is suggested by the fact that 575 of those sampled were married. Psychiatrists, marriage counselors and particularly prostitutes agree with these findings, the latter emphasizing that men visit them for a different experience, or for what they cannot get from their wives.[34]

Desire for fellatio may even exceed the demand for simple intercourse, particularly when combined with the latter (known among prostitutes as "half and half" as opposed to fellatio resulting in orgasm which is known as "french" or "full french"). One study of politicans and power brokers found that 85 percent asked for fellatio; only ten percent wanted straight intercourse.[35] Martha Stein's intensive, path-breaking analysis of more than 1,200 clients of 64 call girls showed that 83 percent enjoyed fellatio.[36] She also discovered that "the most common complaint about wives was that they would not stimulate their husbands orally."[37] This finding may echo a study in the 1930s that revealed that wives complained more often than husbands that their partners wanted to engage in "unnatural practices."[38] The disclosures of these studies are numerically close to what others have found in different environments and among different kinds of clients.[39] Again, prostitutes provide nonstatistical support; a commonplace cynical job description is "fucking and sucking."[40] None of this, of course, explains exactly why men ask for fellatio. While a desire for variety and lack of cooperation from one's wife may be primary reasons, some men believe they are less likely to get a venereal disease by oral copulation.[41] Aging males often find it easier to get an erection by fellatio.

The demand for fellatio is neither new nor culture-specific. Young children were used in Roman brothels and in the Japanese Yoshiwara (red-light district) for the purpose.[42] In the Yoshiwara small girls practiced "fluting" because full-fledged geishas refused to engage in sexual "deviations."[43] In New Orleans' red-light district at the beginning of the twentieth century oral copulation was so popular that there were special establishments called "French houses" in which fellatio might be the only service rendered.[44] Fellatio is usually more expensive than straight intercourse. In the New Orleans' French houses, reduced space needs and increased turnover permitted the service to be competitively priced with straight intercourse.[45] In the same district mothers and young daughters sometimes worked as teams, the latter behaving just like their Roman or Japanese counterparts.

Language and visible patterns in the contemporary landscape attest to the significance of fellatio. In North America and Europe street prostitutes perform fellatio in their own or their clients' automobiles. In London these women are known as "quickie tarts,"[46] and the service they perform while the driver circles streets slowly is, in New York City, referred to as a "block party." Besides the advantage of being able to perform fellatio in a car, many prostitutes prefer it to intercourse because it is faster and does not require undressing.[47]

English prostitutes who work in flats and advertise in tobacco shops and newspapers or above their glowing red doorbells often refer to themselves as "French models," or as someone giving French lessons. In Italy advertisements in *Il Messagero* for fellatio are common, appearing as euphemisms: *Bolognese* and *diplomate lingue*.[48] Not to be forgotten are the young Italian, Spanish and Latin American prostitutes who wish to preserve their "virginity" for marriage.[49] They are competitive both on the streets and in brothels in spite of performing only fellatio or anal intercourse. They can specialize in these services not just because demand is great but also because in many Latin American countries prostitutes claim they only practice straight intercourse, believing that cunnilingus, fellatio and anal intercourse are perversions.[50]

Fellatio, of course, is but one type of sexual diversity that men seek. Cunnilingus and various coital positions are also demanded. Morton Hunt in his examination of American sexual behavior in the 1970s found that while there was considerable change from the time of Kinsey's studies in the 1940s, the percentage of people who deviate from simple intercourse is not as high as many sexual libertarians might suppose (Table 4-2).

Table 4-2
Changing Sexual Preferences in the United States

Educational Attainment	Percentage of marriages in which fellatio used		Percentages of marriages in which cunnilingus used	
	Kinsey	Hunt	Kinsey	Hunt
High school males	15	54	15	56
College males	43	61	45	66
High school females	46	52	50	58
College females	52	72	58	72

Positions	Percentage of whites using variant positions in marital coitus		
	Age 18-24	Age 35-44	Age 55+
Female-above	37	29	17
On-the-side	21	15	15
Rear-entry (vaginal)	20	8	1
Sitting	4	2	1

Data from Hunt 1974:198-203.

The perceived need for diversity plays a not insignificant role in explaining why men frequent prostitutes of races other than their own.[51] In the 1880s a San Francisco madam with Chinese prostitutes allegedly ran her house exclusively for whites. Business became so good that she required clients to make appointments in advance.[52] Other nearby Chinese brothels at about the same time catered to presumed anatomical differences between the races. The inference that one difference implied others was a common source of bar conversation and betting. Entrepreneurs with Chinese women charged 25 cents or less for a "lookie."[53]

Black prostitutes have always been popular in red-light districts, their clientele being mainly white. Racism has not greatly dampened the demand. Instead, it led to the creation of districts just for black males, or the confinement of less desirable black women and their customers to inferior sections of white districts. Most districts of any size have had houses such as Black May's in Chicago's Levee, a brothel staffed entirely by blacks and servicing only whites.[54]

The streets of the Western world are populated by significant numbers of black prostitutes. From their relatively high numbers, their persistence on the landscape and the small proportion of black males arrested for soliciting, it is safe to infer that much of their trade is with white males. A black prostitute who worked the streets of Harlem some decades ago described how she had a "sweet man" who had little trouble getting business for her. Frequenting New York City's downtown clubs, his approach was simple:

What does a hot-natured fellow like you want to be bothered with them anemic white chicks for, when you can come with me and get you some *dark meat*? You want real loving, then you got to get some *dark meat*, boy. Well, man, those downtown tricks come running. . . .[55]

Charles Winick and Paul Kinsie have noted that, until recently, prostitution has been the major source of interracial sex.[56]

To be sure, other variables besides diversity contribute to racial boundary-crossing in prostitution. The strength of demand for some types of prostitutes is frequency dependent; it matters little whether the desired trait is an abstract value called "beauty" or one directly tied to racial or ethnic origins. The scarcer a desired trait, the greater the demand for it and the higher the price the characteristic will command. It needs to be emphasized that the population constituting a scarce resource is not just the number of prostitutes available to males; rather it includes prostitutes plus other sexually available women. A single black in a large brothel may command relatively little attention if black women are abundant and sexually available in the larger society. In societies strongly conscious of racial differences and which attempt to maintain sharp racial lines, certain types of women may, with few exceptions, be sexually available only in prostitution. In such settings, disproportionate numbers of women of some racial or ethnic groups find a niche in prostitution. The concept of a scarce resource may assist in understanding a range of facts: the contemporary demand for black prostitutes among white men, why South African white prostitutes have found a market among native blacks and even why octoroon women (supposedly one-eighth black) occupied such relatively high social status in New Orleans' top parlor houses at the turn of the century.[57] The final case may illustrate better than many examples the interaction between a clearly defined racial trait (at least as advertised to gullible males), relative scarcity (a particular degree of blackness) and the premium placed on diversity or difference.

Diversity or variety forms a major component of promiscuity, and it might, therefore, be asked if males are more promiscuous than females. Lewis Terman's study of psychological factors in marital happiness in the 1930s, based on 341 middle- to upper-class married couples who had experienced premarital sex, showed that husbands consistently desired extramarital sex.[58] An investigation in the 1920s and another one in the early 1950s found a greater desire for sexual activity among men than among women.[59]

Historically, the female demand for male prostitutes has been practically nil. To be sure, in most societies women have not had the freedom to seek out male prostitutes; men would not permit it. But the so-called sexual revolution of recent times could have changed all this, and it has not. The opening of a heterosexual brothel for females is a unique and notable event,[60] and there is absolutely no evidence that the street's male prostitutes are anything but homosexual. Today in the capitalist societies of the West males would quickly meet a demand for their services as heterosexual prostitutes—were it there. That the supply greatly exceeds demand was suggested some years ago when 1,600 men and boys applied for positions in a Hamburg brothel for women.[61]

Students of prostitution and others, even including Friedrich Engels, have referred to the "virile male animal . . . essentially polygamous," or stated that "many males—if not, indeed, the overwhelming majority—have (like most animals) distinctly varietist or promiscuous sex urges."[62] Richard Lewinsohn, who has written a history of sexual customs through the ages, has argued that men have a basic need for a sexual relationship less complicated than marriage and concubinage. They would prefer a simple transaction in which "there remains only the sexual act . . . sole and undisguised . . . without either a long prologue or epilogue." He adds that "this extreme convenience, from the man's point of view, is the foundation of prostitution. It existed among very primitive peoples; it appears as a firmly-rooted institution in the oldest historical times."[63]

All these claims are male-generated, and they may well appear to be little more than examples of self-serving sexism. But are they? Propositions from biology and sociobiological theory would seem to suggest that men are indeed more promiscuous than women, a view not entertained among social scientists who begin with the premise that biology is of little or no relevance to an understanding of prostitution—or human behavior for that matter.[64]

Sociobiological theory states that evolution proceeds largely through natural selection (see Appendix). Those individuals that have produced the most offspring are those that are, ipso facto, most heavily represented in succeeding generations. By this reasoning it follows that those individuals able to get the largest number of successful copulations are the most successful biologically, or in evolutionary terms. Albeit, there need be no direct relationship between number and success, though on average there will be. And it is averages that matter. Because the physiological, energetic costs of reproduction are less to males than to females and because females must carry offspring for nine months while males remain unburdened, promiscuity has been a more important evolutionary strategy to males than to females. Or to put it differently, because females have had more to lose when they mate indiscriminately, they have tended to be more selective of their mates—choice permitting. Lack of selectivity and promiscuity are not the same, but the two overlap to a considerable degree. That this sociobiological argument may have validity apart from an exercise in theoretical reasoning and apart from evidence drawn from prostitution is suggested by studies of mating behavior in nonhuman populations.[65]

Cross-cultural evidence shows that males in most societies are encouraged to be promiscuous. And in the many cases where promiscuous behavior is disapproved males nevertheless often do not obey such norms. In the long run of evolutionary time, not the short-run of a couple of generations or a couple of hundred years, such behavior will prevail. It will prevail because it is adaptive. Once one begins to appreciate the inevitability of evolution by natural selection, and once one transcends the myopia of seeing human nature in terms of one's own lifetime or the brief history of a century or two, then the dictum that critical cultural norms reflect biological realities becomes obvious. If norms are critical to reproductive behavior and do not mirror such tendencies for any lengthy period of time, then societies with these norms will, of necessity, disappear.

On the evolutionary stage, prostitutes provide little apparent biological payoff to males. This is particularly true at present since prostitutes generally use effective contraceptive methods. But adaptations are to past environments, not to those of the present. Furthermore, a behavior displayed in one environment does not mean that it evolved in that setting. Male promiscuity that manifests itself in demand for prostitutes did not evolve to give rise to such a class of women. Rather promiscuity arose in the normal course of evolving reproductive interactions between the sexes. Promiscuity evolved because males who behaved in this manner were selected for. But because mating systems have been essentially monogamous, and many males in any mating system have not had access to copulations, prostitutes have been the human medium for the temporary fulfillment of a biological imperative.

It should be noted that a revolution in the use of contraceptives and changes in the status of women's sexual freedom do not alter the argument for greater promiscuity among males, even though they may have altered the relative degree of promiscuity between the sexes.[66] Nor does it matter that males may not have consciously thought about being promiscuous. Evolution does not depend on conscious behavior; evolution does not think. Certain social scientists have had a difficult time understanding this truth.[67]

One of the more obvious implications of this line of reasoning is that while social and particularly economic exploitation of the female histori- cally has probably been the most important reason for the entry of women into prostitution the demand side of the equation lies primarily elsewhere. Men have not exploited women economically in order to make use of them sexually, though exceptions can be cited, but rather the economic predica- ment of women has made it infinitely easier for the male to pursue cultural and biological directives. The argument here is that male promiscuity, not the economic position of women, drives prostitution. Social system struc- ture is not that serious a competitor as an explanation for prostitution. For example, Marxists have been shown to be wrong in believing that socialism would do away with what they believed to be a purely economic phenome- non.[68]

A popular sociological argument draws attention away from individual needs or circumstances by emphasizing that prostitution is a form of de- viance socially defined.[69] The institution, so the argument goes, derives its vitality from marriage and the family. Prostitution provides an outlet for the limited variety of satisfactions that can be had in marriage and the fam- ily. It is, in a sense, a "gap filler" that preserves the social order. The thesis implies that there are social forces that derive from these institutions and create prostitution. This kind of perspective, one that tends to emphasize social effects rather than factors generating actual demand for prostitutes, has been used to interpret a number of historical and contemporary expres- sions of prostitution. In her study of Toronto's prostitutes at the turn of the century, Lori Rotenberg applies this reasoning both to marriage and the virgin girl.

> It satisfied the male prerogative for pre-marital sex without threatening the in- stitution of marriage. Prostitution also safeguarded the virginity of the major- ity of society's single women. If single men could satisfy their sexual needs through association with prostitutes, then so-called respectable girls would be less likely to have sexual relations before marriage.[70]

This view goes back at least to the great moralists—Cato the Censor, Cicero and Seneca—and has also been expressed in one form or another by the likes of Emile Durkheim, Bertrand Russell and the 1908 Supreme Court.[71] The idea that prostitution like pornography serves as a safety valve for anti-social behavior,[72] or that it is a boundary-maintaining mechanism whose very viability derives from reminding society of its moralistic, nor- mative contours, may be seductive sociological theory but it comes dangerously close to confusing social effects and the function of individual actions. Reasoning based on benefits to society easily loses sight of the fact that male interest, whether seen as biological or cultural (properly as both), and female interest create the institution of prostitution and sustain its viability.

The double standard has been implicated as the structural basis for prostitution. The Bulloughs, who have written excellent histories of the institution, have argued that:

> The primary function of prostitution has been to uphold the double standard, since without prostitution the double standard could have been preserved only through slavery, homosexuality, and rape. Prostitution was regarded by society as a better alternative than these, and since the establishment, as represented by the church, the government, and the intellectual community, has adhered rather consistently to the double standard, prostitution has persisted.[73]

Freda Adler, a student of female crime, has taken a similar position.

> Given the sexual freedom men have reserved for themselves and the code of premarital chastity and post marital fidelity they have imposed on women, prostitution is the only mechanism which would permit the coexistence of these two mutually exclusive and contradictory ideals.[74]

These quotations point to a well-known social norm common to many societies. The widespread existence of prostitution and the concomitant demands placed on women for fidelity support the assertion that the double standard is a significant, functioning social norm. What seems questionable, however, is whether prostitution functions primarily to uphold the double standard or persists because of it, or, as already argued, merely expresses a male evolutionary strategy. The Bulloughs' reasoning, like that of sociologists, ignores individuals and evolutionary rationale. Adler also seems to slight male interest, and seems to see a contradiction where one may not exist. Cuckoldry is the great male bane, and for a good evolutionary reason. Unlike a female, a male can never be absolutely certain that he is the father of offspring he is supporting. The double standard, as social norm, simply expresses his attempt to look out for his evolutionary interests. Male insistence, then, that the female remain chaste while he be permitted his promiscuous ways is hardly a contradiction—from the male point of view.

Class and Class Perceptions

Though the promiscuous male thesis may explain much of the demand for prostitutes, there are other reasons men make use of these women, some of which have little or nothing to do with promiscuity per se. Throughout history many men have lived or worked in environments with pronounced sex ratio imbalances: in the immigrant ghettos of industrializing cities, in settlement frontiers and in war zones. Others have gone to prostitutes because of physical defects,[75] or have required a "second wife"—someone to listen to family or personal problems.[76] Important as these reasons have been at particular times and places, it is more germane in the present context to focus on factors related to perceived differences in class. For it is through class lenses, legitimized in law and social norms, that individuals judge and debase others, treating them as if they were mere property to which the right is inalienable.[77] Whereas the concepts of class and the double standard may not provide insight into the ultimate forces that drive prostitution, they are fundamental in other ways because they lead to inequalities based on sex.

One of the significant ways societies distinguish class membership is through the use of labels. Those of inferior status often are given pejorative tags, slang designations that arise in jokes and invidious comparisons of family background, occupation and the adjudged morality of behavior. Male-generated slang has consistently suggested that prostitutes are subhuman, mere "stock,"[78] or that they are nonhuman, anatomical parts that connote degradation, deviant receptors for a kind of uncontrollable male excretion. Since at least the seventeenth century the prostitute has been a "buttock," a "buttock broker," or simply a "butt" or "ass peddler." She has been engaged in "buttock banqueting" and has worked in "buttocking shops."[79] Today, when the prostitute does not bring in enough money to satisfy the insatiable demands of her pimp she is called a lowly "poop butt," "jive ass," or a "nothin' ass bitch."[80] Other derogations have included *le chat*, French slang for vagina; "pussy," a Second World War synonym for prostitute; and "chippie," which may have meant "piece."[81] At one time the prostitute was known as "pig meat."[82] The nineteenth-century Victorian journalist preferred the euphemism, "pretty horsebreaker."[83] In the frontier American West the women were "soiled doves," "calico queens" and "painted cats."[84] Many worked in "cathouses"—a term that still has currency. Others in the West were called "squab" and "chicken";[85] prostitutes who solicit in Canton and other Chinese cities are known as "roadside chickens" and "wild pheasants."[86] On the Western front in the Great War soldiers referred to prostitutes as "cows" and "pieces."[87] "Bitch" and its variations, all of which evoke the image of a female dog in heat, have a long history. "Bitch heaven" has been hobo and underworld slang for the belief that Boston has had more cheap prostitutes than any other large city in America. One-time black slang for a prostitute was simply "dog."[88] Surprisingly, perhaps, "bitch" as now used by black pimps carries no particular malice; indeed, "bad bitch" refers to a good or exciting prostitute.[89]

A perceived difference in class between client and prostitute may protect the customer—in his own mind—from deleterious social labeling and legal hassles.[90] Imagined inferiority may also be the basis for sexual satisfaction, deriving from a belief that lower-class status and "deviance" go together. If the woman, a prostitute, is deviant, then the man, a client, must be normal—or such is the logic.[91] Although the perception that prostitutes come from the lower-class has had a basis in historical fact,[92] the situation appears to have changed dramatically. A 1976 study by Jennifer James and Jane Meyerding found that 64 percent of 136 Seattle prostitutes reported their childhood family incomes as middle or upper class.[93]

Who are the men who frequent prostitutes? What classes do they come from? Kinsey found that it was mostly lower-class males who frequented prostitutes. Seventy-four percent of those who had been to one had not gone beyond grade school, whereas only 28 percent of males with a college education had a similar experience.[94] Today it appears that the patterns have changed. Contemporary evidence points to the use of prostitutes by the middle classes and others, who, if not upper class, make important decisions affecting society. A customer profile of 47 clients in Seattle revealed that the overwhelming majority were white, married and from the suburbs. As many as half were businessmen or members of professions[95] (Table 4-3). Larger samples suggest the generality of the Seattle findings.[96] Almost all of the 637 men arrested in Detroit in 1978 for soliciting prostitutes were white and from the suburbs; most were married.[97]

Table 4-3

A Profile of 47 Streetwalker Customers in Seattle During the Mid-1970s

Race	
White	95.8 per cent
Black	2.1 per cent
Asian	2.1 per cent
Occupation	
Businessman	35.0 per cent
Aircraft/factory	13.8 per cent
Lawyer/accountant	11.4 per cent
Unidentified	11.4 per cent
Salesman	10.6 per cent
Other	17.8 per cent
Married	
Yes	88.6 per cent
No	11.4 per cent
Residence	
Urban	23.8 per cent
Suburban	76.2 per cent
Age	
Range	17-51 years
Mean	41.4 years

Data from James and Meyerding 1977b.

Thousands of Anglo-American men yearly visit the "Boys' Towns" (red-light districts) along the United States—Mexican border. One student of the phenomenon has noted that some clients are higher-class "business types," who, in the Lower Rio Grande Valley, form regular liaisons with the Mexican prostitutes.[98] Italy is alleged to have some one million prostitutes. However inflated the figure may be, the busiest work time for a prostitute, the *bella de giorno* (beauty of the day), is the three-hour lunch break. The reluctance of businessmen to institute an eight-hour work day comparable to that of other Western countries has been attributed in part to their demand for commercial sex at this time.[99]

Customers of call girls, of course, are from the higher socioeconomic classes.[100] One study showed that over half the trade of these prostitutes involved state and federal politicians and executives of public monopolies.[101] About half of the public officials visit the women two or three times a week. "Call houses" (brothels) for executives and entertainment people, usually married men above 45, can be found in a number of present-day American cities.[102]

Men of power and influence and money have long had a special vested interest in maintaining prostitution.[103] For centuries throughout Western Europe and North America "sporting guides" catered to the middle and upper classes.[104] In 1790 Paris had a directory, *Les Bordels de Paris*, which contained special sections on expensive houses: the *Bordel des Pucelles*, noted for its virgins, and the *Bordel des Elegantes*.[105] The *Pretty Women of Paris*, published in 1883, had an alphabetical listing of select prostitutes in Paris, including descriptions of their "charming features," where they came from, their color, their titles (real or bogus) and particular sexual proclivities. One description of a prostitute said that she "looks well when dressed as a man; but undressed, is like a wooden doll—very long, very hard, with a bust like a plant, and an arse like a rabbit."[106] Another, *Le Guide Rose*, listed deluxe houses and those worth noting in the provinces and abroad.[107] England's *Hints to Men About Town* and *The Man of Pleasure's Pocket Book* gave information on where to find "wit, pleasure, and wine."[108] In the United States similar guidebooks were available. One published in 1859 listed the better-class houses in Boston, New York, Philadelphia, Baltimore, Washington D.C. and Chicago.[109] At a later date Chicago, Denver and Louisville, Kentucky had their own sporting guides.[110] But perhaps the most famous of the lot in North America was the New Orleans *Blue Book* which lasted through more than a dozen editions.[111] It was conveniently fashioned to be carried in the inside pocket of a dress jacket. In various editions the *Blue Book* gave the names and addresses of some 400 madams and prostitutes, giving particular attention to the more expensive parlor houses, Jewish women, those of French extraction and octoroons. Detailed guides and cleverly rendered maps to the sexual pleasures of North America and Western Europe are still available in abundance.[112]

Virility and Violence

The brothel and the bedroom have been ideal environments for displays of virility.[113] During the Middle Ages in Europe and hundreds of years later in the United States manliness could be proven twice in the same night: tattoo artists worked out of brothels. One nineteenth-century method for establishing sexual prestige was the practice of a Stockholm club of military officers that required all prospective members to prove they had syphilis.[114] A method used by madams and prostitutes to get a male to make the trip to the bedroom is to make a play to his virility, perhaps by making him the butt of a joke.[115] Some of Nevada's brothel prostitutes band together to solve the problem of indecisive males by grabbing and physically carrying one of them to the bedroom. As the others do not want to be left out of post-sex discussions, jesting rituals of conquest, they soon follow. This is reminiscent of behavior in war zones where soldiers who attempt to remain faithful to their wives are mocked for not joining their companions for the trip to the brothel.[116]

One method open to males wishing to demonstrate their virility to friends is what the famous madam, Pauline Tabor, has referred to as a "pillow party."[117] Accompanied by betting companions the virile male attempts to show off his staying power. Perhaps more frequent has been the "gangbang," serial use of the same woman. Martha Stein has described the atmosphere one finds among well-educated men who frequent call girls.

> It was very like that of a fraternity party. The men sat around in their underwear, drinking and telling jokes, while waiting their turn. They would knock on the bedroom door, yell obscenities goodnaturedly, or even run in to see how their friends were doing. Sometimes they indulged in boyish practical jokes, dropping bags of water out the window, slapping each other with towels, and so forth.[118]

She also noted that when men are with others they may tip the prostitute to stay longer if they climaxed too quickly. Embarrassment must be avoided. Stein concluded that "fraternizers," 14 percent of her sample of 1,242 males, acted as if they were going to a football game or a movie,[119] "except that the intimate and semi-clandestine nature of this particular form of entertainment served in a special way to celebrate and reinforce their sense of maleness. . . ."[120]

The prostitute is very convenient. She not only works at the wrong place but she embodies the wrong values and grew up in the wrong past. She is known as a vendor of flesh and psychic payoffs. A prostitute sells power, degradation, humiliation.[121] Many capitalize on their status as debased property. They react to demands in the crudest of marketplace terms by selling access to an orifice, and nothing more. Even the argot of the street proclaims the essential facts. Those who offer only regular intercourse are "flatbackers"; those also available for oral and anal intercourse are "three-way broads." At the lower end of segments of the prostitution hierarchy, on the street and in brothels both, women will not bother to undress. It is too much trouble and the women do not believe they are being paid for the inconvenience. They will, however, expose flesh for a price. In San Jose, California in 1979 the going rate for each exposed breast was $5.[122]

All street women have a rich vocabulary for the variety of men with whom they interact. The argot may seem to function as a kind of sub-cultural glue that distinguishes insiders from outsiders, or as a shorthand device for relating past experiences and those that ought to be avoided. Important as these functions may be, the primary reason for categorizing clients derives from the threat of physical danger.[123] Among streetwalkers in the Pacific Northwest those feared the most are "beat freaks" and "dumpers." Beat freaks enjoy harming prostitutes, sometimes being hurt themselves. Dumpers just like to knock them down.[124] In Vancouver men are classified as "good tricks" and "bad tricks." Good tricks reach orgasm quickly, pay well, cause no problems and may return. They are often young or students and ask for nothing more than simple intercourse. Bad tricks, by contrast, are "nuts," "flips," "weirdos," "perverts," "freaks," "sadists" and East Indians (because the street women claim they consistently behave like bad tricks.)[125]

Prostitutes can be candid about their job, the daily realities that create their images of an ugly male world.

> I had a few bad experiences. I was beaten, I was threatened with knives, I was scared and repulsed. I had to pretend to be aroused by old men whose bellies hung down over their shriveled genitals. I had to lick men who smelled, who had decaying teeth. I had to simulate erotic passion with men who held me too tightly, who hurt my nipples, my breasts, my lips, my cunt. I was fucked up the ass till I couldn't walk and bled for three days. I had every venereal disease except syphilis and crabs. And I know I had it easy. I was not hustling out on the streets. I saw other women hooked on money, hooked on heroin, trapped by shame, by anger, by need, by pimps or boyfriends. It was hard to get myself out, even when I knew I couldn't handle it anymore. There are scars.[126]

Fantasy Fulfillment and Flagellation

Notwithstanding the argument for the significance of diversity it is often not easy to separate this need from one involving fantasy fulfillment. Surely, many men who have never had fellatio or intercourse with a woman of another race may go to prostitutes both to try to fulfill a fantasy long entertained and to try something different. Though it seems eminently reasonable to argue that fantasies are part of a diversity theme, the conundrum of "how much of this and how much of that" is mentioned not to offer a solution, one really attainable only by carefully examining male minds, but rather to draw attention to the fact that what has previously been labeled as components or examples of diversity may contain strong or dominant elements of fantasy, and vice versa.

Prostitutes tell the client what he wants to hear: that he is a great lover, that he is well-endowed, that he was just responsible for a tremendous orgasm, and that she will be anxious to see him again. Many men want to hear all of this, and a good many believe most of it. "Ooh, you're built like a football player"—according to the prostitute-author of the line, she has "made more money with that line than fifty other prostitutes with one hundred pound boob jobs."[127] A black prostitute has another saying she uses frequently: "Boy, you've got a big dick." Her rationale is at once exaggerated and yet, paradoxically, descriptive of a near-truth. "I'm black and they think that's more of a come on 'cause they think that all black dudes got dicks this long (indicating a couple of feet in length)."[128] The motivation behind the flattery is, of course, the prostitute's desire to see the clients, with pocketbook, return.

The average customer, indeed, the average man, believes that his partner ought to look pleased when having an orgasm. Picking up on "common wisdom," prostitutes often fake an orgasm by looking happy when they are supposed to since this makes the client feel he is getting top value. Ironically, the male has matters turned upside down. As Kinsey has noted, "an individual who is really responding is as incapable of looking happy as the individual who is being tortured."[129]

Verbal claims and assurances at once deceive and yet have a positive function. While the falsehood that she tells a client makes a prostitute feel she is getting back at both an individual and society, kind, exaggerated or reassuring words are precisely what the average male came for. Most prostitutes learn how to create an illusion, though learning how is not as easy as appreciating its importance, as one reflective prostitute has maintained:

> When I went into the business I had to learn to act. That was the most difficult thing for me to handle. The game is "illusion." They want to know that you dig their cock, that you came three times, that they're the best lay you ever had, that you can't keep your hands off men and the reason you're a prostitute is not because you need the money but because you really dig sex. In short, you're a nymphomaniac and they are Supercock. You must pretend to enjoy your work. The strain of pretending can be overwhelming.[130]

Faking may be repulsive, but prostitutes eventually learn to do it, and to accept it because it means money and survival in the game.[131] Yet, despite the generality, prostitutes often treat a client with deference until they get his money, then "they just don't give a shit."[132]

Many men fantasize a return to youth, to innocence, to purity, and they want to possess what they believe to be their's alone. Through the ages these kinds of desires have been translated into demands for child prostitutes, ideally "virgins." Child brothels occurred in England as early as Queen

Anne's reign. Treated as chattel and, in poor families, as useless mouths to feed, children were sold into prostitution by the age of eleven.[133] By the early 1800s London had brothels that specialized in girls under 14, some allegedly having as many as 30 or 40 boarders.[134] In the same century Liverpool was estimated to have 500 prostitutes under the age of thirteen.[135] Since the very young were in heavy demand and not overly plentiful it was primarily upper-class males who could afford to buy their services and to pay the occasional blackmail payments demanded by predators.[136]

The phenomenon of child prostitution, equally common on the Continent, played a major role in nineteenth-century campaigns against "white slavery."[137] But in the long perspective such efforts were largely for naught. Young girls are still very much in demand in European cities.[138] In the area of the *Champs-Élysées* they are known as "lollipops," while those in *Les Halles* are *les fleurs*. One report has them resembling "the teenyboppers on American TV dance parties . . . a Humbert Humbert's delight."[139]

In North America the demand for very young girls has paralleled that across the Atlantic. The "fresh stock" or "cherries" or "quails" brought extremely high prices in what amounted to a New Orleans slave market in "virgins."[140] Their cost could be quickly recovered in their rental to 20 or 30 different men who believed they were paying for the primordial act of defloration. While it might be presumed that most men knew they were not purchasing undiluted innocence this has not attenuated their interest in the illusion—or its close equivalent, youth. Decades ago in New York City youthful, and expensive, prostitutes were known as "baby pros."[141] Now those who ply the streets of the same city are called "chili dog hookers" because of their eating habits while soliciting.[142]

If F.B.I. arrest figures are a reliable indicator of actual trends the number of young prostitutes has been increasing. From 1960 to 1975 teenage prostitution arrests in the United States rose 375 percent.[143] Young prostitutes may also be on the increase in some Canadian cities.[144] Actual numbers may be more substantial than arrest figures suggest because, as street social workers and vice squads have found, girls consistently lie about their ages and often use false identification cards.[145]

Some men pay prostitutes for the pleasure of inflicting pain, but many more are masochistic. They pay for fantasy enactment and experimentation,[146] "homosexual, masochistic, transvestite, and troilistic practices that in other contexts they could only imagine."[147] Fantasy fulfillment in "kinky" or sadomasochistic sex was appreciated long ago by Freud and particularly the nineteenth century pioneer, Krafft-Ebing, in his famous *Psychopathia Sexualis*.[148]

Half a century ago flagellation was said to be common in America; advertisements for it appeared in Chicago's "massage shops."[149] Before World War II, when Paris' brothels were open and thriving, houses specialized in various kinds of *spectacles interessants*; flagellation and other "perversions'' were common, sometimes attracting high-paying audiences.[150] When the Parisian brothels were closed in 1946 these activities were still offered, but then from women working in cafes, private clubs and the streets. Simone de Beauvoir knew some of these women; they complained to her of the large number of clients with ''abnormal tastes.''[151] Sadomasochism remains popular in Europe and the United States.[152] One of the more celebrated ''houses of pain'' of recent times was uncovered in New Jersey in 1965. Monique von Cleef, the proprietor, purportedly had a card file containing the names of 15,000 clients who lived in the United States and a number of foreign countries.[153]

But nowhere does sadomasochism and particularly flagellomania seem to be so important as in England, the long-reigning throne of *le vice anglais*. The ''English vice'' derives from its widespread and time-honored occurrence in Great Britain, and its relative absence in such countries as France, Italy and Spain.[154] In Great Britain ''brothels devoted to the rod flourished,''[155] and flagellation was widespread in nineteenth century pornography.[156] Many have argued that the source of flagellomania is caning or corporal punishment in the home and the school, particularly the English public school (what, in the United States, would be known as a private school). Its effects have been so widespread that an extensive historical study concluded that:

> The fact that the rulers of Victorian Britain and her immense Empire came almost entirely from the public schools means that, among them, there must always have been a good, and probably a high, proportion of sado-masochists. It seems to me that it would be impossible to deny that this was the case. Every corner of the Empire must have had its flagellant administrators, and the Empire saw to it that these men should be allowed to continue behaving like so many public school prefects.[157]

Today advertisements for flagellation or sadomasochism in London are commonplace. They appear under headings of the following sort: ''Full theatrical wardrobe for hire—wigs, shoes, boots, chains, etc.''; ''Recaning of basket chairs''; ''Student—teacher, English-Hebrew . . .''; ''Stocks and bonds for rent''; ''Strict governess—corrective training''; ''Miss du Sade'' and ''Miss du Cane.''[158] Until recently high boots were distinctive markers of streetwalkers who specialized in sadomasochism.[159] Foot gear has been one of the more common forms of fetishism, symbolizing adulthood and sexuality, bringing to mind the classic masochistic theme of being stepped on by a female with long sharp heels.

The use of prostitutes for fantasy fulfillment may be particularly common among the higher socioeconomic classes, and especially among politicians and power brokers. Martha Stein found that of 1,242 clients of call girls, 156 wanted to be treated as slaves, and that 131 enjoyed bondage and discipline.[160] She claimed that:

The part they assigned the call girl corresponded to an idealized image of woman which exerted great power over their erotic imagination, and the correspondence was a source of excitement and pleasure. The men's individual fantasies of the ideal partner can be seen as variations of female types idealized by our culture as a whole: The Sexual Superwoman; the Beloved; the Girlfriend; the Dominating Mistress; the Child-Woman; the Earth-Mother.[161]

Another study of call girls, one that took seven years, revealed that a good many of the politicians and businessmen that frequented prostitutes wanted services that some sex researchers have described as "pathologically deviant."[162] In this study only 8-10 percent of the politicians asked for straight intercourse.[163] Many preferred some form of sadomasochism or other types of service—discipline, humiliation, and transvestite posing (Table 4-4).

Table 4-4
Sexual Preferences of Politicians and Power Brokers

	Very Frequent	Frequent	Uncommon
Straight intercourse			X
Fellatio	X		
Cunnilingus			X
Masturbation			X
Exhibitionism	X		
Voyeurism	X		
Cross-dressing	X		
Coprolalia		X	
Fetishism	X		
Golden showers		X	
Brown showers			X
Necrophilia			X
Pedophilia			X
Threesomes	X		
Semi-gay games		X	
Flagellation, donor			X
Flagellation, recipient	X		
Humiliation (verbal)	X		
Humiliation (physical)	X		
Bondage	X		
Power games	X		

Adapted from Janus et al. 1977:67.

John Gagnon has stated that there is a basic difference among clients—based on class—in what they expect from prostitutes.

The centrality of the cash exchange is high for the lower-class customer, the sexual activities preferred are limited, and the content of the sexual talk is

small. On the other hand, in contacts with middle-class males th
and not referred to again (although there may be psychic gain for
result of payment), the sexual interest may be wide, and there is
pectation of talk that transcends the immediate sexual character or the relationship.[164]

"Kinky" sex is increasingly portrayed openly in cartoons. This is
demonstrated in a study of 405 *Esquire* and *Playboy* cartoons over the past
forty years. The authors of the study concluded that:

> The liberalization of sexual attitudes has allowed the darker passions and sex-
> ual desires to come into the open. "Kinky sex," . . . while not acceptable in
> behavior, has become a part of the repertoire of fantasy. The emergence of the
> "kinky" prostitute cartoons allows the male reader to simultaneously identify
> with their darker fantasies while ridiculing them, thus bringing them under
> control.[165]

Whether or not the prostitute is commanded to engage in deviant
behavior she understands that her success depends on the ability to create il-
lusions, give assurances and fulfill the fantasies that occupy men's minds.[166]

Prostitutes as Social Workers

Despite the widespread claim by prostitutes that they continuously trick
their clients, and in a significant sense they do, clients insist they get their
money's worth, not just sexually but psychologically. Even hardened streetwalkers who daily verbalize their deceptive ruses sometimes note that they
perform a therapeutic role.[167] One Amsterdam streetwalker described her
feelings as follows:

> I hear people sayin', "Look, there's another one of them prostitutes."
> Me—mindin' my own business out of the rain, under an awning on Rem-
> brandt Square. But I think to myself: stupid bitches, a lot they know! They got
> no idea what our kind takes care of. They been married for years, and still they
> don't know nothin'. Prostitute, my ass. I'm a regular social worker, that's
> what. What we girls got to put up with! They ought to be grateful, the stupid
> bitches. Us doin' the dirty work for them so they can keep it out of their own
> house.[168]

Call girls with a steady clientele make it their business to be sensitive to
the customer's needs, needs which extend beyond the purely sexual domain.
Not surprisingly, therefore, a greater proportion of call girls are aware of
the social work role they play. And it would appear that their clients are also
more aware of the psychological component to their visits than is true of
other males. In her intensive four year study Martha Stein concluded that:

> The clients turned to the call girls not only for the satisfaction of sexual desires
> but also for the satisfaction of the emotional needs so often fulfilled by sexual
> relationships—needs for reassurance, intimacy, relaxation, adventure, self-

esteem. The call girls, by providing the clients with satisfactions important to their sense of well-being, functioned effectively as paraprofessional therapists.[169]

This case has also been made for brothel prostitutes. A study in Sweden suggested that the state should run brothels supervised by doctors and social workers for the benefit of the aged and those with personal problems and mental illnesses.[170]

It might be argued that all prostitutes are social workers broadly defined. They cater to and feed men's egos and fantasies. They reassure them about the size of their penises, about their abilities to bring a woman to orgasm and about how favorably they compare with other men as lovers. Too, many men do not want the responsibilities of a heterosexual relationship that involves marriage, financial responsibility and raising children. For these individuals, relationships with prostitutes may be the best of possible alternatives. Some men simply need help; they require someone to listen to their problems without criticizing. Their problems may be sexual, domestic or of a business nature. In these various capacities, prostitutes may be "a kind of poor man's psychotherapist."[171]

Without denying any of these propositions or functional roles, calling a prostitute a social worker or a paraprofessional therapist borders on making a fundamental error, confusing means and ends. The aim of prostitutes, call girls not excluded, is to make money, for themselves or their pimps; secondarily, perhaps unconsciously, many are also attempting to satisfy deep-seated personal needs. Even these secondary needs, however, seldom include a desire to assist men in solving their problems. To the extent that prostitutes act the role of a social worker, then, they do so in spite of themselves; their principal self-defined objective is to get the client's money, spend as little time as possible with him, and—if he is not too obnoxious or kinky—hope that he will return. Or, to put it differently, those who are not good listeners, who do not engage in a certain amount of verbal and emotional reinforcement, and who openly criticize their customers simply will not maximize return business and thereby personal payoffs.

Chapter 5 | The Legal Logic of Discrimination

A History of Legal and Illegal Discrimination

With the major exception of laws relating to pimps and procurers, prostitution laws in North America and Europe have long focused on the female. Even where both sexes have been equally culpable before the law the male has consistently received preferential treatment. In his extensive survey of European prostitution at the turn of this century, Abraham Flexner noted that "for the most part, the attitude [with regard to the application of laws] is indulgent toward the man, severe towards the woman."[1] Italy was not untypical of the times. There prostitutes were defined as "those women . . . who notoriously exercised the practice of prostitution."[2]

Prior to 1900 virtually all prostitution-related penal laws in the United States were directed against females. Abductors, procurers, exploiters, pimps, brothel owners and those who held minors for purposes of prostitution were largely free to go about their businesses. Before 1919 only Indiana had a statutory definition of prostitution and, with the exception of this state, patronizing prostitutes was not an offense. However, in more than half the states prostitutes were considered vagrants or disorderly persons. If streetwalkers were not charged under these laws, they could be apprehended under specific solicitation statutes in effect in 26 states.[3]

Vagrancy laws were inherited from England where they were originally used in the Middle Ages to provide landowners with a ready supply of labor.[4] In North America their purpose was to protect society from criminals and undesirables, the latter a catchall that over time came to apply to anyone considered a public nuisance. Since the concept of a vagrant was determined and expanded upon by those with status and power, vagrancy statutes were not consistent with the idea that laws express public opinion.

Some changes in state and federal laws relating to prostitution occurred with the vice crusades of the early twentieth century, spearheaded by the Women's Christian Temperance Union, Protestant reform groups and the Republican party.[5] Their cause was fired by public and private outcries about venereal disease, the "white slave trade," sexual discrimination, "immorality" and vice in general. The Mann Act of 1910, a milestone of sorts, was enacted to curtail "white slavers" and others in the interstate transportation of compromised women. In 1919 the federal government drafted the model Standard Vice Repression Law, providing that clients as well as prostitutes were to be prosecuted. But expectations that state legislators would enact such laws, or that they would be executed if they did, were little more than wishful thinking. Prosecution patterns in New York City are illustrative.

From 1920 to 1929 the number of males and females arraigned on prostitution charges in New York City's Magistrates' Court showed discrimination against females to be multi-faceted. Under existing law men were not arrested as customers of prostitutes. To be apprehended they had to be charged with aiding and abetting, in some cases, actually procuring. By contrast, prostitutes were picked up under vagrancy ordinances: for being on the streets in known areas of vice or prostitution, for having been arrested previously or for soliciting. The number of female arraignments was higher by a factor of three to five. During the ten-year period the number of prostitutes arraigned in court increased from 1,267 in 1920 to 3,832 in 1929. Acquittal patterns also favored males, never dropping below 42 percent of arraignments. For females the figure dropped to 27 percent in one year and never rose above 37 percent (Figure 5-1). In addition, a much higher proportion of men were given suspended sentences (Figure 5-2). For women the usual pattern involved confinement to a workhouse or reformatory. In ten years over 1,700 alleged prostitutes were committed to reformatories; only 14 men were as unfortunate.[6]

Willoughby Waterman claimed that the court was but a mirror of society.

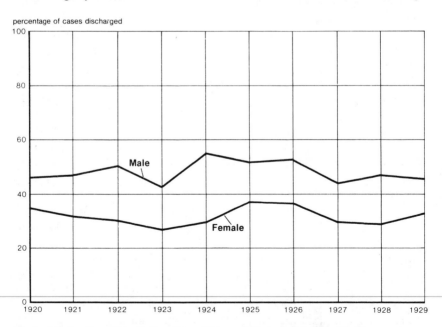

Figure 5-1 Arraigned Prostitution Cases that were Discharged in New York's Magistrates' Court
Data from Waterman 1932:72, 74.

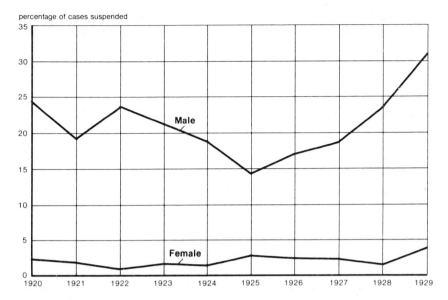

percentage of cases suspended

Figure 5-2 Arraigned Prostitution Cases that were Suspended in New York's Magistrates' Court
Data from Waterman 1932:72, 74.

(The public saw the prostitute as a disease reservoir, a sinner against family and society. As is true for the rise of massage parlor prostitution, the press played an active role in shaping public opinion. Convicted prostitutes were given newspaper space, while guilty males were virtually ignored. The unequal treatment became an easy source of bribery. During an eight and one-half year period one prosecuting Assistant District Attorney in New York's women's court received fees from prostitutes' defense attorneys for not prosecuting some 600 cases.[7]

Over time the predicament of the prostitute did not improve, and in many respects worsened. In the late 1930s more than five females were arrested for every male.[8] By 1942, 32 states had laws against soliciting, and in five of these the statutes applied only to women. Vagrancy provisions affecting only female prostitutes were in use in 23 states.[9] Seven years later a global survey by the International Abolitionist Federation showed that 38 states had laws against soliciting; only 27 countries had similar regulations.[10]

In Seattle female prostitution arrests increased from 65 percent of the total for males and females combined in 1945 to over 90 percent by 1970 (Figure 5-3). During this same period there were few changes in sex differentials for other categories of crime in Seattle.[11]

Current prostitution laws in the United States and the District of Columbia affect the prostitute in one or more of three principal ways: (1) by prohibiting the preliminary acts of solicitation and negotiation; (2) by outlaw-

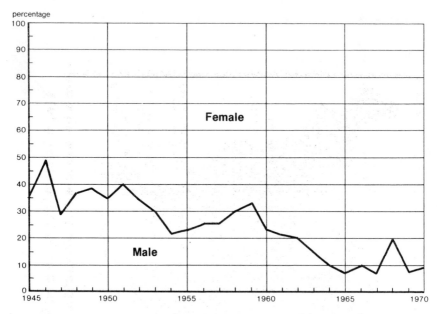

Figure 5-3 Arrests for Prostitution and Commercialized Vice in Seattle
Adapted from Schmid and Schmid 1972:202.

ing the act itself; and (3) by proscribing the prostitute's status. In 1973, 44 states had laws against soliciting, 38 prohibited commercial sex acts and 13 had statutes against being a prostitute.[12] Forty states had two or more of these statutes and five had all three (Figure 5-4). In addition to state laws prohibiting prostitution, cities of all sizes have similar kinds of regulations.

State as well as local laws do not apply equally to males and females. In seven states (Alaska, Indiana, Louisiana, North Dakota, Utah, Wisconsin and Wyoming) the statutes are expressly discriminatory against the female. Louisiana law, for example, states that "prostitution is a practice, by a female, of indiscriminate sexual intercourse for compensation." Utah's makes no distinction between prostitutes and vagrants, and states that "every woman who solicits is a vagrant." Only four states are explicitly neutral in their codes, identifying both males and females. While the vast majority of state statutes are superficially neutral, application is another matter. As of 1973 only 10 states had laws aimed at the patrons of prostitutes.[13]

In Canada the emphasis has been overwhelmingly on the streetwalker. Vancouver laws in the early twentieth century fined brothel women between $15 and $50 and jailed them for up to two months. Those who solicited on the streets could be confined for six months at hard labor.[14] Until 1972 streetwalkers were treated as vagrants in the Canadian Criminal Code. The police used a "cautioning system" in which women believed to be prostitutes were warned of their presumed status as "common prostitutes." If

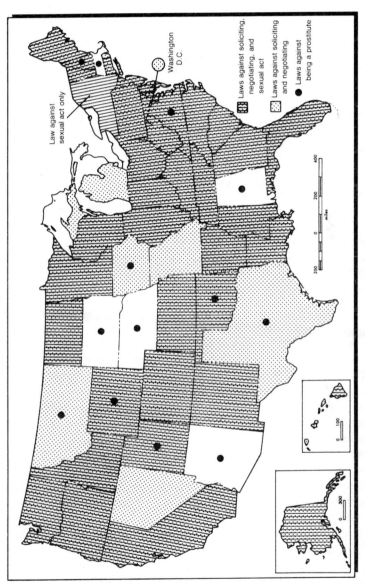

Figure 5-4 Principal Types of Laws Against Prostitution in the United States in 1973
Data from Rosenbleet and Pariente 1973:422-26.

subsequently arrested the "Vag C" warnings were used against the women in court. Under this system women were usually prosecuted for what they were considered to be rather than for what they were doing when arrested. "Once a prostitute, always a prostitute" was the rationale.[15] In addition, the Canadian law only applied to women, leaving no doubt in the French language version where reference was to the *fille publique ou coureuse de nuit.*[16]

In July 1972 Canada changed its Criminal Code so that women could be arrested on soliciting charges. The law was also amended to apply to males. The warning system was no longer used and, presumably, a woman's past arrest record was not relevant.[17] Although these changes dramatically affected male homosexual prostitutes they had little impact on the clients of female prostitutes. After 1972 pressure on the female streetwalker increased. Cops began luring women into their cars and then charging them with soliciting. The ruse worked until a Vancouver prostitute appealed her solicitation conviction on the grounds that the interior of an automobile was not a public place. The appeal was successful, and scores of convictions were overturned. Now arrests are even more difficult to make, for it must be shown that a streetwalker is actually harassing a male. This change notwithstanding, discrimination against females remains. Canadian activists have started to point out that their laws and their enforcement are, like their counterparts to the south, class specific.[18]

Arrest Ratios and Other Prejudices

The national average in the United States in the early 1970s was about seven female arrests for every male apprehension.[19] Seattle police in 1974 arrested nearly 450 females and only about 70 males on prostitution and commercialized vice charges, a ratio of roughly six to one. This is misleading for Seattle and other cities, however, because most male arrests are for pimping, running brothels or massage parlors, and especially for male homosexual prostitution. In other cities, where prostitution laws are neutral, the picture is like that in Seattle.[20] These ratios do not, of course, take into account extremes, widely disparate arrest patterns that persist in spite of changes in the law. Not until 1964 did the State of New York change the legal designation of a prostitute from a "female person" to "a member of either sex." A law against "patronizing a prostitute" did not become a part of the state's legal code for another year.[21] The effect was minimal.[22] In early 1977, 3,000 females were arrested, while the figure for males was less than one-tenth this number.

A female lawyer and civil rights activist has noted that "even in the few cases where a customer is arrested, the charge may be used to induce the man to testify against the female prostitute."[23] As late as the mid-1970s in Kansas City, Missouri, only women were being arrested.[24] The vice squad was using clients to assist in making arrests, threatening them with incarceration if they did not cooperate.

Cops sometimes "stack charges." If two policemen make an arrest, the prostitute is given two soliciting charges. Once apprehended she may be pressured into pleading guilty to a lesser charge, such as disturbing the peace. The judge goes along with the practice, cognizant that the woman has stepped onto a treadmill. Initially she may be given a 30-day suspended sentence. On a second arrest her probation is revoked and she receives the choice of 30 days in jail or pleading guilty to a prostitution charge which may carry a 90-day suspended sentence. After a subsequent arrest the woman spends three months in jail, or trades in her sentence for becoming an informant on more serious crimes. If she demands a jury trial the clogged courts get stuck with an expensive low-priority case. And the district attorney's office becomes a victim of its own methods.

(Many cities in the United States have denied prostitutes bail until they underwent venereal disease examinations, and some have quarantined them and required penicillin injections.[25] As late as 1975 in Portland, Oregon women who allegedly had "wide sexual contact" had to submit to a vaginal examination under threat of a 12-month quarantine.[26] Not only do these practices abridge basic rights, but when the women are given injections these sometimes result in yeast infections, resistance to venereal disease strains and death from drug reactions. In 1976 in Oakland, California the courts ordered—for the first time—that customers must also be quarantined and spend five days in jail awaiting examination results.[27] The quarantine practice was immediately discontinued—for both parties.)

Arrest and prosecution patterns in other parts of the Western world resemble those in the United States. Seven years of data for Montreal show a strong bias against the female (Figure 5-5). In Toronto, where both parties can be apprehended, the male is usually fined $25, while the prostitute first offender is fined $100.[28] On the second offense her charge jumps to $200. In Australia, where solicitation, brothel keeping and pimping—but not prosti-

Figure 5-5 Prostitution Arrests in Montreal
Data from Annual Montreal Police Reports 1969-1976.

tution itself—are illegal, the client is not prosecuted. Although males can be charged under laws such as those pertaining to "lewd" behavior or aiding and abetting a crime, they "never are so charged, and their names are withheld."[29]

Street Sweeps

The "street sweep" has been a favorite method of many vice squads for temporarily clearing the streets and swelling arrest figures. Using the vague provisions of vagrancy, disorderly conduct and loitering ordinances, "pussy posses," as the vice squad is known to prostitutes in some cities, make periodic sweeps of known soliciting areas, arresting virtually everyone on a charge of "willful and malicious obstruction of the sidewalks." In Detroit women were rounded up on the basis of past record and reputation. Sometimes mere location resulted in an arrest. Taken to the police station en masse, all those corralled were booked as D.P.I.s—Disorderly Persons Investigation. The purpose was not prosecution—it would not have worked—but harassment. The city wanted the streets cleared.[30]

For many years in San Francisco anyone found improperly postured or dressed in the prominent sections of the city's Tenderloin was booked on a 647c—a statute and street code for a street sweep prostitution charge.[31] Until the courts forced the police department to stop using this method in 1976, street sweeps frequently accounted for more than a hundred arrests a month, a very significant percentage of the yearly total (Figure 5-6). Street sweeps were being used in New York City as late as 1978.

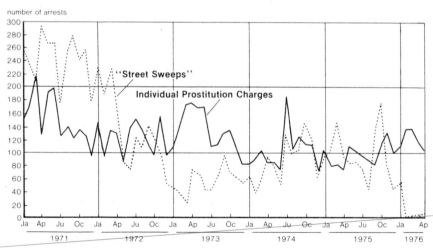

Figure 5-6 "Street Sweeps" and Individual Prostitution Charges in San Francisco
Data from San Francisco Police Records.

The street sweep has been effective in providing publicity for the vice squad, boosting the arrest figures for year-end annual reports and temporarily clearing the streets of a "visual and immoral blight." In a sense the sweep has had the same effect that white paint has on slum property. With the assistance of bail bondsmen and lawyers, pimps had little trouble getting their women released, and within 48 hours these women were soliciting along the same streets on which they had been arrested two nights before.[32] Neither judges nor district attorneys took the street sweep seriously, knowing that a non-specific charge did not make the basis of a court case. Yet, it proved effective as a form of harassment, in which the police were a "judicial punitive body, since by holding and then releasing the accused after several hours of investigation, they are actively meting out brief prison terms without benefit of a trial."[33]

Class and Color

Some prostitutes face more problems than others. As Jennifer James and Jean Withers note in *The Politics of Prostitution*, "women who work in houses of prostitution or in massage parlors are rarely arrested."[34] The pattern is an old one. In nineteenth-century Virginia City most laws regulating prostitution applied to women working in cribs and on the streets. They did not affect other prostitutes: "housekeepers," those living in and working out of hotels and those catering exclusively to rich clientele.[35] The authors of a classic study entitled *Black Metropolis* found that the police more frequently arrested streetwalkers than those working in brothels, and that among women who plied their trade outdoors in poor neighborhoods, arrests were much more likely for blacks than for whites.[36] In Chicago, the black metropolis of concern, racism was attenuated—as it was elsewhere—by social class and the ability to pay graft. A 1916 report on crime conditions in Chicago concluded that while the majority of cases brought to the morals court involved black women, black prostitutes who commanded high prices were left alone by the police.[37]

It still matters whether a prostitute hustles in a high-class or low-class streetscape. Times Square is not the lowest or cheapest locale in New York City, but the district is a good distance from the top of the street hierarchy. And its status shows in prostitution arrests (Figure 5-7).

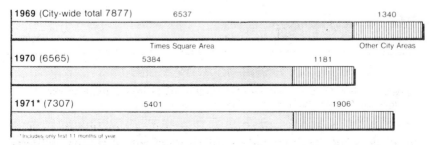

Figure 5-7 Prostitution Arrests in New York City
Adapted from Jeffers and Levitan 1973:188.

There are suggestions that the perceived class of the client also matters. A Times Square streetwalker told a researcher some years ago that:

> I can tell you one thing. I think the police won't even say anything if the guy looks like he has money. If a guy makes two hundred bucks a week . . . and has nicer clothes, the cops are afraid to bother him. It's only when the guy makes like sixty bucks a week that the cops give you trouble. . . .[38]

The discriminatory enforcement of prostitution laws is compounded for black women. Marilyn Haft has noted that:

> The women most penalized by the law are black and poor—racism is as prevalent in the business of prostitution as everywhere else in our society. Many bar owners, hotel keepers, and landlords do not allow black prostitutes to use their premises; thus black women are forced onto the streets and into blatant solicitation where the risk of arrest is highest. As might be expected, the largest proportion of arrests of black prostitutes takes place in the inner city where living standards are low, the level of desperation high, and police prejudice endemic."[39]

Surveys have long shown that the percentage of blacks and other minorities in prostitution is higher than whites in proportion to relative representation in the total population.[40] During the three-year period 1968 to 1970 just under 400 women, eighteen years of age or over, were arrested for prostitution in Seattle. Black women accounted for 54 percent of the arrests, whites for 43 percent. In terms of relative population numbers a black woman was 22 times as likely to be arrested for prostitution. Another perspective is provided by comparison of prostitution arrest patterns with those of other crimes. The Seattle arrest rate of black women for prostitution was higher than that of any other crime committed by black females, a third higher than for the second most important category of larceny. Black women were charged with prostitution four times as often as white women were arrested for drunkenness, the most significant arrest category for whites.[41]

Although blacks are not nearly so common in Canada as in the United States, other minorities take their place in the arrest statistics. Ninety percent of Edmonton's prostitution arrests in 1974 were of Indian or Metis women.[42]

These findings are not too surprising given the persistent racism in society and that found on police forces. Many of the citizen complaints registered in New York City's West Side precinct concern the "color of the people on the streets."[43] Studies in Washington D.C., Boston and Chicago have demonstrated the degree of prejudice among cops. Among white officers working in predominantly black areas, 45 percent were rated as "highly prejudiced" and 34 percent were rated as "prejudiced." In mixed and in predominantly white areas the percentages for these categories varied between 32 and 36 percent.[44]

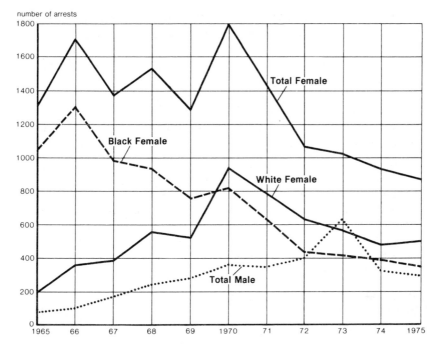

Figure 5-8 Prostitution (principally streetwalking) Arrests by Sex and Race in San Francisco
Data from San Francisco Police Records.

Data from San Francisco in the 1960s suggest the degree of racism and changes related thereto (Figure 5-8). As late as 1968 at least two black women were arrested for each white streetwalker. Significantly, in every year since 1970 white arrests have outnumbered those for blacks. Furthermore, the absolute number of black streetwalkers arrested has been more or less steadily declining, while there has been a slight increase in the number of white women apprehended. Although a closer analysis of these trends is needed, it appears that the black prostitute is now less discriminated against. The slack is being taken up by whites, probably because the San Francisco vice squad would be charged with not doing its job if the total yearly arrest figures dropped.

If the San Francisco data suggest significant change, other patterns do not.[45] The FBI Uniform Crime Reports for 1977 show that black women still account for more than half of all female prostitution arrests.[46] In Chicago nearly all of those arrested are lower-class black women, 90 percent of whom must be released the following morning for lack of evidence.[47]

Contemporary arrest patterns reflect not just racism and its cumulative impact but the continuing presence of a subculture of poverty, and the fact that there are no more rungs on an ethnic and racial succession ladder. In mid-nineteenth-century America, prostitutes were primarily Irish and German; later, especially during the early decades of the twentieth century, they came from the immigrant ghettos: Italian, Polish, Jewish. Whites and blacks alike turned to prostitution for lack of better economic opportunities. But as the new immigrants became the old and new generations found themselves higher up the socioeconomic ladder, ethnic and racial representation in the prostitute population changed. The significant fact today is that the black prostitute differs markedly from her European trade sister of fifty or one hundred years ago. The black prostitute has no place to go. There is no poor ethnic or racial minority to allow her to move off the exploitation ladder.

The Abridgment of Basic Rights

The present treatment of prostitutes in the United States is unconstitutional or subject to legal challenge on at least five grounds: (1) the right of free speech, (2) the right to privacy, (3) equal protection before the law, (4) cruel and unusual punishment, and (5) vagueness of laws.

The right of free speech is protected by the First Amendment. The Constitution provides that what one says must be "patently offensive" to be beyond the realm of protection. Only in those cases in which speech involves "fighting words," or is likely to incite lawless action, or is "obscene" is the Amendment not applicable.[48] But streetwalkers do not attempt to incite fights, and they very rarely employ four-letter words or others deemed socially offensive, "Hey, honey, how about a date?" "Would you like some fun?" or "Are you interested in a party?" are the commonplace innuendos of soliciting streetwalkers. When discussions turn to services prostitutes still do not use swear words. Obscenities are more likely to be uttered by males. Furthermore, there is virtually no evidence that men are offended by solicitations, particularly since prostitutes direct most of their efforts to males who obviously know where they are. Even in Nevada's legal brothels cursing is uncommon and the rule that no services or prices can be discussed outside the bedroom is nearly universal in the state. In those instances where offensive language is used by prostitutes, whether streetwalkers or others, more often than not it is prompted by the contemptuous behavior of males, or is requested as part of the service rendered.

In addition to the simple confrontation between a constitutional right and the facts of how prostitutes actually talk, and to whom and where, "it is axiomatic in our Anglo-American jurisprudence that the proper subject of criminal punishment is behavior, not speech."[49] Were prostitutes treated as the Constitution provides they should be, 44 states would be deprived of their principal means of making arrests. In a review of legal injustices against prostitutes Marilyn Haft concluded that "solicitation should be decriminalized for the very same reasons that laws against prostitution should be decriminalized."[50] Both are unconstitutional.

Like everyone else, the prostitute is entitled to privacy. The nineteenth-century English philosopher John Stuart Mill remarked that:

The only part of the conduct of any one, for which he is amenable to society, is that which concerns others. In the part which merely concerns himself, his independence is, of right, absolute. Over himself, over his own body and mind, the individual is sovereign.[51]

The right to privacy is protected in one form or another by the First, Fourth, Fifth, Ninth and Fourteenth Amendments.

Negotiation between a prostitute and a prospective client on the street is, as two lawyers have noted, "overwhelmingly a private, consensual affair,"[52] and, they might have added, usually between adults legally defined. The same can be said for the sexual act itself. Yet policemen intrude into the private domain all the time: on the streets and in hotels and hallways as they listen outside bedroom doors or break in to make arrests. In Michigan, Missouri and Rhode Island prostitutes are penalized for soliciting for a commercial sex act that is not illegal. Nor do these states have laws against being a prostitute. Denial of the private acts of negotiation and sex between consenting adults—issues over which there are almost never complaining parties—is an infringement of the right to control the use of one's own body, a right protected by the Fourth Amendment.

Along with the right to privacy, prostitution laws are most vulnerable under the equal protection clause of the Fourteenth Amendment. Despite changes it is all too clear that sexual discrimination in arrests and prosecutions exists. Streetwalkers, and particularly black women, are the most frequent victims of prejudice.

Evidence for positive change is hardly impressive. An Alameda County (California) Superior Court judge dismissed 252 prostitution cases in the fall of 1975 on the grounds that discriminatory enforcement violated the Fourteenth Amendment.[53] Alaska's prostitution laws have been struck down for the same reason.[54] In 1975 Seattle enacted an ordinance aimed at the client. In Oakland, California 663 females were arrested compared to 21 males in 1974. During the next year male arrests climbed dramatically—to 461—while those for females dropped slightly to 651. During a ten-month period in 1975-76 police in Washington D.C. arrested nearly 2,200 people for soliciting; over 60 percent were males. But despite these indicators national arrest figures for 1977, incomplete and suspect as they are, showed that 71 percent of all people arrested for prostitution were female and that the category remained one of the most important female crime categories. In the ten-year period, 1968 through 1977, client arrests increased 127 percent while the increase for females was 66 percent. But the female arrest base was three times that for males.[55]

During the late 1970s a number of cities began to publish the names of clients, an innovation that seems to have had a dramatic effect in reducing street activity. However, the life of the method may be very short. When the mayor of New York City urged that the names of those patronizing prostitutes be broadcast over city-owned radio and television stations, they were, but only once.[56]

Often women are harassed or arrested under vagrancy laws because they "look like prostitutes," have previous arrest records, are presumed more likely to commit other crimes, or simply happen to be in the wrong place at the wrong time. Those taken into custody on one or more of these pretenses, individually or as part of a street sweep, have been denied due process of law and also subjected to cruel and unusual punishment as prohibited by the Eighth Amendment. Though the street sweep has been abandoned in a number of cities, women are still arrested on the basis of their reputation, notwithstanding a Supreme Court decision that forbids the practice. Five states (Montana, New Hampshire, Oklahoma, Texas and Utah) and Great Britain and Canada have compounded the issue by referring to "common prostitutes" or "common streetwalkers" in their legal codes.[57] In Great Britain the 1959 Street Offenses Act was passed with the purpose of clearing the streets of the "common prostitute."[58] The word "common" has been discriminatory in implying "greater lewdness" and a record of previous convictions. Neither British nor Canadian statutes in the recent past have been clear about what constituted a "common prostitute," nor for that matter, as Monique Layton points out, have Canadian judges.[59]

Prostitution laws in the United States are vulnerable on the vagueness doctrine. What is meant by such statute terms as "immoral," "lewd" and "dissolute" has not been sufficiently clarified by the courts.[60] Despite these and other seemingly obvious problems with the prostitution laws and their enforcement, challenges to them have not proved particularly successful. Some believe that the repeal of prostitution laws in state legislatures is not imminent.[61]

Justifications and Contradictions

Prosecutors use a number of arguments to justify selective enforcement of laws. Principal among these are that women are more likely to solicit than men, prostitutes are more visible, more likely to continue as offenders and are the ones who profit from the transaction. Evidence, when available, does not uniformly support these contentions. For example, the San Francisco Vice Squad estimates that there are eight to ten times as many male customers as female prostitutes on the streets.[62] That streetwalkers may seem to be more visible is due not only to the continual presence of some prostitutes on the streetscape and their familiarity to the vice squad but also to what one is prepared to see. People are not likely to see soliciting males in known prostitution areas unless they are prepared to accept that males may be in the area to solicit prostitutes. Until recently all street decoys have been male. When their female counterparts have been used the results have been impressive. In Los Angeles on one weekend two female decoys arrested 91 men.[63] Although a prostitute has more commercial transactions than a given male, this does not necessarily mean that individual males visit prostitutes once or infrequently. Finally, the "logic" that only sellers profit from commercial sex transactions is a strange sort of myopia.

Discrimination against the female prostitute has been remarkable for its contradictions. On the basis of the words, "Do you want a date?" or "Would you like a party?" arrests have been made and jail sentences handed down. This kind of evidence remains admissible.[64] Yet, in bars across the country males hustle all kinds of women with an advance of the sort, "Hey, baby, let's you and me fuck." Hardly anyone ever complains. Nor is there much notice of the ruling of the Supreme Court in *Cohen v. California* that a man cannot be prevented from wearing a jacket in public emblazoned with the slogan, "Fuck the Draft." According to the court those annoyed can avert their eyes or walk away. Paradoxically, this is more difficult than avoiding a street solicitation, for streetwalkers, as a rule, are street-wise. They focus their advances on solicitous males, those who in one way or another indicate an interest in commercial sex.

Other logics prevail. In one 1974 court case a judge argued that the discriminatory arrest of females is justified "because the record does not support the fact that male prostitution is a problem of such significance that the legislature should proscribe the practice as a crime."[65] By a curious kind of confused reasoning the judge solved two problems at once: male prostitutes—presumably homosexual—were exempted from law because of their unsubstantiated insignificance, and males soliciting female prostitutes should not be subject to prostitution laws because they are either insignificant numerically or significant numbers of them are not engaging in acts of prostitution!

Sometimes the reasoning that protects males is an odd play on the great American motif of efficiency. During a recent 18-month period, 189 of 210 prostitution arrests in Minneapolis were of women. When the Minnesota Supreme Court was confronted with the issue of a sex bias in the arrest patterns it reasoned that "in light of current resources, a concentration on the sellers of sexual services, rather than on the buyers, is more *efficient* and thus is more likely to achieve the end sought by the local ordinance."[66] In the same year—1976—a California Court of Appeals came to exactly the opposite opinion on the matter of efficiency.[67] The recent dramatic increase in the use of female decoys, and the decline of prostitution in neighborhoods where they have been used, are evidence that efficiency lies in threatening males. When Atlanta published the names of those "prominent businessmen" soliciting prostitutes there was a dramatic—if short-lived—decrease in the number of men cruising the streets.[68]

One of the ironies of the present situation is that among so-called consensual crimes (such as drug usage, homosexuality, gambling and pornography), prostitution is the only one in which buyers are more easily deterred than sellers. The logic for not pursuing clients is founded in the intersection of social values and economic interests.

> The argument for not prosecuting the buyers is that the imposition of the social sanctions for such behavior on those who may be married and respectable is out of proportion to the gravity of their offenses. Prosecution of the buyers is almost always strongly opposed by the commercial, hotel, and convention interests on the ground that it would be bad for business.[69]

In 1957, the Archbishop of Canterbury argued that the clients of prostitutes ought to be prosecuted. His proposal was not taken seriously by British law makers on the grounds that the male did not parade as openly and habitually as the female.[70] The famous Wolfenden Report recognized that "kerb-crawling"—men soliciting women from automobiles—was a serious problem. Indeed, one source claimed that in Liverpool it was "creating pressure by local inhabitants for licensed brothels."[71] The committee that issued the Wolfenden Report argued that no action should be taken against males because the offense did not fit easily into any existing crime category, because a new law would have to be framed to deal with this kind of solicitation, because the "difficulties of proof would be considerable," and because of "the possibility of a very damaging charge being leveled at an innocent motorist."[72] An English High Court in 1966 ruled that while "kerb-crawling" by women was illegal, men were not subject to the same law.

The Imperious Hand of the State

Chapter 6

The State as Pimp

Since 1965 the number of Japanese visiting South Korea has increased dramatically, totaling in the neighborhood of 400,000 by the mid-1970s. The majority of these visitors have been men, lured by travel agency advertisements proclaiming the availability of *kisaeng* women, the Korean equivalent of Japanese geishas. By the end of the 1970s the idea had caught on elsewhere. All-male package tours were attracting well over a million Japanese men a year, perhaps 80 percent traveling to Seoul, Taipei, Manila and Bangkok to buy sex at hotels, clubs and brothels.[1] Some men were sent by their companies as rewards for sales and managerial efforts. Others, spanning the occupational gamut from small farmers to doctors and dentists, put up $300 to $400 for a four-day "sex package tour." Spurred on by the low cost and rumors that foreign prostitutes were willing to fulfill just about any fantasy imaginable, coupled with the claim that "you can't find a decent geisha in Japan," many traveled abroad two or three times a year for *kisaeng* services.[2]

By the mid-1970s more than 8,000 Korean prostitutes were available for *kisaeng* parties, enough to have significant impact on Korea's foreign trade. According to a witness at the 1976 International Tribunal on Crimes Against Women, "prospective *kisaeng* must endure lectures by male university professors on the crucial role of tourism in the South Korean economy before they get their prostitution licenses."[3] More telling is the attitude of the South Korean Minister of Education who has stated that "the sincerity of girls who have contributed with their cunts to their fatherland's economic development is indeed praiseworthy."[4] The presidents of South Korea and the Philippines and the Thai royal family have encouraged the business for the same economic reasons.[5]

Though the concept of a sex package tour may be a recent innovation in Asia, the use of women as prostitutes to further national ends is not new. In the early part of the twentieth century, the Japanese regularly shipped young girls and women to Southeast Asia to work in brothels.[6] The prostitutes were used as spies and as a source of revenue for the state. The women were forced to turn over a percentage of their earnings to the Consul.

The *kisaeng* are simply one of the more recent and blatant examples of the state as pimp. Athens had a tax on its high-class prostitutes, the *hetairae*, and its laws established brothels called *dicteria*. Bought with public money and filled with slaves, these formed a state monopoly sufficient in revenue production to build a temple to Venus. The *dicteriades* who worked in the houses got nothing for their travail. Worse, they could not enter temples or mix in religious ceremonies, they had to wear special costumes as a badge of their infamy when on the streets and their children were bastards who could not inherit property.[7]

The Romans levied tolls for the use of their roads to defray costs of protective garrisons and other services rendered. The scale of fees in 90 A.D., connecting the caravan terminal of Coptus on the Nile with Red Sea ports, shows clearly how prostitutes were regarded. To use the road a captain in the Red Sea trade was charged 8 drachmas, lookout officers and guards 10, sailors 5 and artisans 8. Courtesans had to pay 108 drachmas. The high tax was not an attempt to discourage their activity, but simply a state tax upon the occupation.[8]

An annual tax was also imposed on prostitutes, periodically adjusted to reflect their changing numbers.[9] Some emperors used the money collected for public service improvements, others distributed revenues received according to their particular ethical scruples or political needs. Constantine the Great (274-337), the first Christian emperor, referred to the brothel tax as the *chrysargyrum* (gold and silver) because so much of these precious metals came into his coffers. A later ruler, Theodoric II (c. 460), broke with tradition by not taxing brothels and their keepers. Instead, he assessed the prostitutes themselves, allegedly at ruthless rates.

Other examples abound, especially from the medieval period.[10] In Toulouse, France royal charter declared that profits from prostitution were to be shared equally between the city and its university. Seville's sixteenth-century bordellos were owned by city officials and ecclesiastical orders. The city mandated that prostitutes not wear hats, gloves, mantles or slippers. Those who leased and ran the brothels had to be approved by the local government.[11] Here as elsewhere in medieval Europe a municipality, a prince or a university could run a house unhindered but a local entrepreneur who might introduce an element of competition was repressed.[12] More significant though was the occasional extension of power from one social domain to others. During the first part of the sixteenth century Seville's government used its expanding control over prostitution to justify a more general enlargement of its powers.[13]

The Catholic Church, a government of sorts, was not immune to lusting after prostitutes' profits.[14] After the Crusades brothel traffic was so heavy and the financial returns so high that Pope Julius II founded a brothel in Rome, an innovation followed by priests and mother superiors elsewhere. Pope Sixtus IV was allegedly the first of his kind to issue licenses to prostitutes and tax their earnings. His successor, Pope Leo X, purportedly made four times as much through the sale of permits as he did by selling indulgences to repentant Germans. Even the Church across the English Channel parasitized the female body. In the Middle Ages it was happy to take ten percent of a prostitute's earnings and fill its money box with bordello property rents, notwithstanding official views that condemned prostitution.[15] Five hundred years later, during the 1920s, a standing joke among Soho streetwalkers was that their only contact with the Church of England occurred when one of its employees came around to collect rents on the many brothel properties owned in central London.[16]

The Anglican Church still owns property used by prostitutes. A prelate is said to have remarked that: "the wages of sin may be high, but being the sinner's landlord is far less dangerous and much more profitable."[17]

Exploitation need not be envisaged solely in monetary terms. In the name of strategic data gathering numerous nations have trained prostitutes and established brothels.[18] From 1940 until the end of World War II a famous Berlin bordello known as the "Salon Kitty" was used to spy on both pro-German foreign diplomats as well as on its own officers.[19] Originally opened as a high-class brothel in 1932 and patronized until 1939 by Berlin's upper crust, the *Pension Schmidt*, as it was then known, was taken over by the German Security Service and remodeled to conceal over 120 bugging devices. The house had elegant decor and served expensive alcohol and choice food to clients. It also had an unusual complement of attractive prostitutes. The renown of the Salon Kitty was such that it won the admiration of the British Secret Service. The bordello played a significant role in permitting the Nazis to be the most well informed government in the world "about the mood prevailing among its own senior representatives. . . ."[20]

After World War II the British employed prostitutes in Germany and Austria to steal secrets from Russian soldiers. A quarter of a century later they were using them as spies in the bordellos of Belfast to compromise separatists and turn them into informers.[21] The KGB and the CIA have been equally opportunistic, utilizing cleverly concealed microphones and sophisticated camera equipment to obtain incriminating evidence on foreign diplomats. The KGB makes use of prostitutes known as "swallows."[22] Highly trained in espionage, as urbane call girls or women looking for affairs, the state pays them to maneuver out-of-country dignitaries into assisting the Russians. Bedrooms are equipped with highly advanced camera equipment built into walls or bedroom furnishings. Brightness-intensifying devices increase the available light by as much as 150,000 times, permitting very good photographs in virtual darkness. To overcome problems of a continuously running camera, special transmitters that trigger photographic equipment are placed in such ingenious spots as the swallow's nipples. They cannot be discovered even with intimate sexual contact.

Of considerably greater significance, both in numbers of women involved and impact on foreign populations, is prostitution that arises during wars. Temporary gratification for mateless servicemen is often seen as reason enough to exploit the women of another nation. The Russians closed the brothels of Warsaw, Poland in early 1914; they were opened a year later by military authorities.[23] During World War II the Japanese forced women into brothels for the benefit of their soldiers; Germans did the same with young Jewish girls on the Eastern Front.[24] In the early 1950s as many as 2,000 prostitutes and 150 brothels prospered in Omisawa near the remote American air base on northern Honshu.

In Vietnam there were "Disneylands," "Sin Cities" and "boom-boom parlors"—red-light districts built by order of division commanders and the tacit approval of the Army Chief of Staff.[25] These brothel shanty towns operated in spite of the very high rate of venereal disease among servicemen, notably higher than in previous wars. The problem was so great that one commander did not allow his men to frequent the regular houses. Instead, he sequestered half a dozen prostitutes on the base and had them receive penicillin shots daily. He felt it preferable to stab the women and play with their immunity than punish his men for their pleasures.

On-base prostitution has many precedents. During the early 1920s the men at Fort Benning, Georgia had little problem entering brothels in nearby Columbus where prostitution was supposedly illegal. Even under this circumstance, however, men did not have to leave the base. "Block 23," which housed black servants, was known as the "red-light district of Camp Benning."[26] These and other practices seemed to reflect a nineteenth-century Italian attitude that prostitutes are like an army, a body "organized for service to the state."[27]

Cops and Robbers

In nineteenth-century Kansas cow towns such as Abilene, Wichita and Dodge City the purpose of anti-prostitution laws was to support the city government and the police force since revenues from other sources were inadequate. Prostitutes were arrested monthly and routinely paid a fine. Fines ran as high as $100 per woman and $200 for a brothel in Abilene. By the early 1870s the income from amercements in Wichita was so large that general business taxes, common to other frontier towns of the time, were unnecessary. There were other reasons for keeping prostitution thriving despite protests. Several of Dodge City's "soiled doves" lived with prominent city officials, including two policemen, the mayor from 1877 to 1880, the vice president of the local bank and a partner in a major saloon.[28]

Extortion by keepers of the moral order has been one near universal aspect of state regulation of illegal prostitution. A Senate investigation of New York City's police department in 1895 found that prostitution was carefully and systematically "licensed" by the police. Morris Plowcowe noted in *Sex and the Law* that:

> The system had reached such a perfection in detail that the inmates of the several houses were numbered and classified and ratable charges placed upon

each proprietor in proportion to the number of inmates, or in cases of houses of assignation, the number of rooms occupied and the prices charged, reduced to a monthly rate which was collected within a few days of the first of each month during the year.[29]

Three-quarters of a century ago Baltimore had its "Ladies' Day." Madams were periodically brought to court and fined as much as $75 for running a brothel. Minneapolis, Kansas City and Ft. Smith, Arkansas had similar systems. Although Ft. Smith officially banned prostitution, madams showed up in court every Monday morning to hand over $15 for running a house and $5 for each woman employed.[30] The bordellos of Utica, New York were near city hall in the 1950s. They survived because madams gave tickets to cops for expensive parties, donated to the election of public officials and paid $20 to vice squad members and $10 to patrolmen monthly.[31]

Corruption and geography have sometimes been intertwined, as evidenced in Minneapolis in the early years of the twentieth century. Each month the city levied a tax against prostitutes, which reportedly brought in $35,000 a year into the public bank account. Unhappy with where the money was going, the mayor and one of his associates urged prostitutes to open houses and places of business outside segregated areas so that payoffs could go directly into their pockets.[32]

That exactions have not been limited to a few select brothels or areas of a city is suggested by the Atherton investigation of prostitution in San Francisco in the 1930s. In 1937, 150 houses were known to be operating in the city, taking in nearly 4.5 million dollars. It was claimed that practically every bordello was protected by graft; figures seemed to support this. An estimated one million dollars of the city's yearly police receipts were from blackmail, about $400,000 of this from prostitution. Payments to cops might begin with "opening fees" of $500 to $750, monthly charges of $200 to $250 to be split between captains and officers and smaller, separate payments to patrolmen. In addition, there might be special assessments and periodic fines for owners who could not come up with enough "juice." Extortion made it easy for houses to stay open. In the Central Police District more than a dozen brothels operated openly. All were within a three block radius of the Hall of Justice.[33]

The predicament of madams and prostitutes in Canada has been similar. In the early years of the twentieth century Montreal police periodically raided the city's 250 to 300 brothels, not for the purpose of suppressing vice—as they were supposed to—but to collect booty. The houses often sold liquor without a license to augment profits, knowing that policemen, judges and others would resort to legal technicalities to keep them open.[34]

In Edmonton and elsewhere in the Canadian prairie provinces of the early twentieth century, the Mounties did not bother prostitutes and madams as long as bordellos were operated with "reasonable decorum." Still, once or twice a year all the women had to appear before the Mounted Police Inspector who extracted a fee of $10 to $15 from madams and $5 to $10 from each prostitute. If a charge of bootlegging or thievery was brought against a house the fees might double. Sometimes licensing gave madams an advantage. In Winnipeg, where Sabbarites ruled with such a tough hand that only churches were allowed to provide community services on Sunday, the Mounties made an exception for the brothels. But here as elsewhere community cries occasionally forced the Mounties to arrest prostitutes to show they were serious about controlling vice. When this happened madams and prostitutes reacted by entering pleas of "not guilty" in the courts.[35]

European cities and those in their former colonies are subject to the same generalization that emerges from looking at North American examples. Nineteenth-century Algeria under French control had a large population of Arabic and black prostitutes. Each woman paid a monthly tribute to the chief of police for the right to work. At one point in the 1830s the privilege of collecting the tax was sold to the highest bidder at public auction.[36] On the Continent one observer who visited a number of cities in 1913 and 1914 concluded that: "whenever the control of prostitution by regulation has been attempted it has been accompanied, if not by open corruption, at least by grave suspicion that such corruption exists."[37]

For a cop the assignment to a vice district has long been highly prized. During the Tammany Hall days cops paid for their jobs and promotions, and a police captain's position might go for as much as $15,000 in a profitable district.[38] In fact, so desirable has been duty in areas with prostitutes that the vice squad gave American English a new term: the Tenderloin. After a cop was placed in charge of an area burdened with brothels or streetwalkers he could say: "I've been eating chuck steak all my life . . . now I can afford tenderloin."[39]

In so far as possible madams preferred to deal with a chief or someone of rank, knowing all too well that one predator invited others to partake of the cake. In New Orleans during the 1940s and 1950s and in Seattle and New York City during the 1960s, the spoils from prostitution were split between the captain of a district and his "bagman." The bagman typically was a patrolman or sergeant whose sole duty was to negotiate with people controlling illegal activities. He was so indispensable that when the captain was transferred to another district, so was he.[40]

Those running brothels have often been trapped by cops at various levels, each making separate deals. A New York City or Chicago madam in the early twentieth century might not only be paying a "lookout" or a saloon keeper who was known to "protect" the entire red-light district, but she also might be making monthly payments to an inspector and a captain and nightly exactions to a patrolman.[41]

Others have followed the model of cop as robber. Bail bondsmen have had an interest in getting the bond raised. When successful this meant more money for the bondsmen and more kicked back to cops.[42] Defense lawyers have given money to policemen to omit significant parts of their testimony in court. Occasionally, they have even bribed prosecutors. The lawyers operated on the premise that there were always enough poor prostitutes who could not afford their services and would be sent to jail.[43] During the 1930s, in New York City, a ring of policemen, bondsmen, stool pigeons and Assistant District Attorneys framed innocent women, including nurses in doctors' offices and landladies, on prostitution charges for the purpose of extortion. As long as the victims payed what was demanded, charges were dropped. Otherwise, the accused might find themselves convicted of prostitution or similar charges.[44]

Extortion often involves a good deal more than the payment of money. Madams in Galveston, Texas several decades ago were required to get operating "permits" from the city police. For a modicum of protection madams turned over 25 percent of house receipts, gave the cops as much liquor as they could consume and also permitted them free access to the house women.[45] The police have often had free use of prostitutes' bodies. Robert Williams in his examination of the vice squad in America claims it was not so long ago in East St. Louis that cops entered bars frequented by prostitutes to demand—and get—free sex.[46] Not surprisingly, among their own kind prostitutes have referred to the morals squad as "the biggest pimp of all."[47]

All this kind of activity, of course, requires a certain amount of discretion and window dressing. Brothels need to be raided and streetwalkers arrested to keep citizen discontent at an acceptable level. During the 1930s San Francisco's cops accomplished this by raiding the more prosperous and visible houses.[48] New Orleans' police used a rotating system in the 1940s and 1950s when they raided a brothel. Upon entering a house the sergeant's standard line was: "Well, which of you is going to jail tonight?"[49] Laughter followed, there would be a decision as to whose turn it was, the cop might push the arrested prostitute around a little as he left to give onlookers the right impression and then the woman was taken to jail for a night or two.

Streetwalkers have not been immune to extortion.[50] Those working the streets in New York City in the early twentieth century paid for the privilege of soliciting on a particular turf, and if a woman tried to hustle beyond the beat of a cop who was blackmailing her she was arrested.[51] In some cities graft has been so common that policemen have inadvertently stopped innocent women and demanded money.[52] Like those working in bordellos, streetwalkers have had to accommodate with their bodies to avoid hassles and arrests.[53]

When English soliciting laws were enforced with new vigor after 1959 streetwalkers were supposed to be "cautioned" before an arrest was made. But policemen were not required to show proof of cautioning and women could be "warned" without their knowledge. Some cops told streetwalkers they could forget about warnings if they made appropriate cash payments.[54]

The English Collective of Prostitutes, an organization attempting to eliminate injustices, claims that the amounts paid in graft and for soliciting amount to subsidization of the British police force.[55]

In the summer of 1975 French "amazons" (those who work from cars), "candles" (in front of hotels), "hostesses" (in bars) and the Parisian "bucolic" ones (in the *Bois de Boulogne*) joined forces in large cities and rebelled against their predicament. Monique Layton summarized what happened and how they felt.

> In the city of Lyon, where the strike started, 12,000 fines were given in 1974; during the first four months of 1975, 7,000 fines had already been handed out. Some women averaged three fines a day, as well as many jail terms of 3 to 8 days. Most of them received at least one fine a week. In Paris, 35,000 fines were given in 1974 to 9,000 prostitutes. Some women came to the attention of the police 10 times a month. They accused the State of being the biggest pimp of all and of making billions of francs from prostitution. They charged that so much of their earnings went into the payment of fines that they would in fact pay far less if their income were adequately taxed; they would moreover enjoy the benefits available to taxpayers.[56]

Even call girls who infrequently experience the hassles and arrests common to other prostitutes are occasional subjects for blackmail. Harold Greenwald claims that "some of the girls secret sums of money in their apartments which may run as high as two thousand dollars, or leave sums of money in the hands of friends who can be reached at any hour in case of difficulties with the police."[57] The call girl's first instinct, no doubt founded in experience, is to bribe her way out of trouble.

Hiding Immorality

Whether or not the state has attempted to openly profit from prostitution, visibility of both its inanimate and human manifestations has been a major concern. The history of laws, formal and informal, that have attempted to reduce visibility is a long, detailed and geographically diverse one. Codified regulations and unwritten rules have zoned brothels and streetwalkers, emphasizing historical precedent, location in geopolitical sinks—the least desirable areas or among minorities, and proximity to specific public and private institutions. Some efforts to reduce visibility have stressed site characteristics: how the brothel should appear. Frequently the spatial and temporal patterns of prostitutes have been at issue. In most cases all of these concerns have been present in legal codes and in the minds of policemen.

Some form of zoning has usually accompanied a more general agenda of state intervention in prostitution, and also implied the geopolitical sink principle. In the Middle Ages Leicester and Cambridge tried to ban prostitution altogether, while other English cities attempted to restrict it to particular areas.[58] Bristol's prostitutes were categorized with lepers and, as in

London, were not permitted within the city walls. Brothels that operated outside designated areas had windows and doors removed, and occasionally an entire house was dismantled. As early as the thirteenth century Parisian prostitutes were likewise told to work beyond the city walls. Police in many German cities forced prostitutes to live and work on a few streets, often a single block in the smaller towns. Women found elsewhere were arrested, and sometimes imprisoned.[59]

Regulation as practiced throughout most of Europe during the nineteenth century involved a system in which prostitutes registered with the police, had regular medical examinations and lived and worked in designated areas. The broad aim of governments was control of venereal disease, confinement of immoral behavior and maintenance of public order. In Germany it was believed that "prostitution was the gigantic trade that held the underworld together and nurtured all other forms of violence and criminality."[60] The containment of prostitutes was thought to facilitate control over the women as well as over the army of predators and parasites that fed off them. Confinement could be seen as "some sort of attempt at prophylaxis, a sort of *cordon sanitaire.*"[61]

During the post-Civil War years American cities gave serious attention to registering prostitutes, requiring them to take venereal disease examinations and confining them to particular sections of cities.[62] Though legislation attempting to codify such matters was universally unsuccessful, largely because people felt it amounted to government sanctioning of immoral behavior, the police managed to unofficially effect the same ends—and not without support. Segregation of prostitutes was supported by many factions and for many reasons, some defying logic and common sense. Concentration was believed to facilitate control and regulation, decrease urban crime through police supervision of a "recognized crime center," increase management of the liquor trade associated with prostitution and decrease graft and exploitation of the prostitute. In addition, it was thought that a segregated district prevented crimes against morally upright women, safeguarded "normal" women from sexual perversions and the "unrestrained sexual appetites of men" and protected young boys and men from contact and temptation. People living away from red-light districts could also claim that segregation protected the community from the "offensive and detrimental proximity of prostitution."[63]

Schools, churches and various government buildings have frequently been the subject of attention in laws regulating the location of prostitution. Early nineteenth-century Paris had over 200 tolerated brothels, and ordinances there stipulated that houses were not to be within 100 yards of a church or 50 yards of a school, a palace or other public building.[64] At one time Arizona had a law stating that the owner of a bordello situated within 4,000 feet of the University of Arizona was subject to a five-year prison term, a penalty more severe than was legislated for other locations.

Missouri had similar laws and escalating penalties for houses too close to public libraries, theaters, courthouses, churches and public schools.[65]

Frequently brothels have been forbidden along major thoroughfares and in a number of instances attempts have been made to force activity into narrow streets, alleys and culs de sac. During the early 1950s in Naples prostitutes were directed into the smaller houses and off the main streets to keep them out of view of tourists.[66] In Perth, Australia high fences with barbed wire surround brothels to prevent the public from being exposed to "immoral happenings"; prostitutes are known locally as "women in cages."[67] Some governments have required that windows be painted or heavily curtained to obstruct the view of passersby or, more generally, that houses be painted in subdued colors to avoid drawing attention to them.[68] Nineteenth-century New Orleans had a law that prostitutes could not operate on the ground floor.[69]

The history of restrictions on the behavior of prostitutes outside bordellos shows that women's activities have been controlled just as much as the location and physical appearance of houses. Hamburg and Berlin, during the nineteenth century, proscribed attendance at theaters, the botanical gardens, the zoo, the town hall and other places of entertainment; prostitutes were banned from traveling on main thoroughfares as well.[70] In this century Parisian streetwalkers could not solicit along principal thoroughfares, or near railway stations, churches and schools. Nor could they wear "offensive clothing," speak to children or to men accompanied by women. Off the street, they were forbidden to live with pimps and lovers. But in Paris as elsewhere many prostitutes paid little heed to such regulations. Most worked outside the system, as "clandestines." Many Parisian street women became tired of the arrests, harassments and personal debasement and preferred to become *filles à maison* (women who work in regulated brothels).[71]

Police in a number of American cities required prostitutes and madams to register and often demanded considerable information on their backgrounds.[72] In some cities women from out of town were not acceptable employees. Here and there brothel lights could not be bright, music and alcohol were not permitted on premises, soliciting from doorways and windows was banned and "scant and fancy costumes" were prohibited on the streets.

A very common tactic was to regulate daily and weekly public activities of prostitutes and madams. Turn-of-the-century brothel prostitutes in Winnipeg needed police permission and an official escort to do their shopping.[73] At about the same time the Lethbridge City Council forbade madams and prostitutes to appear on the streets, except on Tuesdays and Fridays between two and five P.M. The city's Moral Reform League had persuaded city officials this regulation was necessary to prevent morality and immorality from "rubbing elbows."[74]

Prostitutes in the early 1900s in Richmond, Virginia were not bothered as long as they left the street by 5 P.M. on weekdays, 3 P.M. on Saturdays and did not work on Sundays and holidays.[75] In frontier Kalgoorlie, Australia where bordellos were known as "knockers" and madams enjoyed the blessing of the police force, prostitutes were not allowed into the city's commercial areas between 5 P.M. and 7 A.M. If they violated the rule they were charged with soliciting.[76] Nineteenth-century Paris had its own twist: its prostitutes could not actively hustle until the street lanterns were lit, or before 7 P.M. (whichever came later) and had to be finished with business by midnight.[77]

Notwithstanding past problems over segregation, a number of European cities still consider it highly desirable. In West Germany there are two basic approaches: a single-zone and multiple zone. The single-zone policy is illustrated by Hamburg's St. Pauli district, an adult entertainment district that measures about half a square kilometer. Munich has perhaps one of the better examples of a multiple-zone policy. There, streetwalkers are allowed to solicit in any of nine designated areas, most of which cover one or two blocks.[78] In two of the nine areas the women may ply the streets at any time, in the others only between 8 P.M. and 6 A.M. Prostitutes who do all their soliciting and negotiating off the streets can work at any time and anywhere in the city, with the exception of the cemetery and the city center (a two block area), where all prostitution is disallowed. Apart from unofficial zoning policies in most cities, small towns and rural areas in Nevada are the only places in North America that legally zone prostitution.

Unjust taxation, blackmail and corruption and restrictions on personal freedom result in good part from illegality or the regulatory intervention of the state. Illegality creates a climate that generates excess profits and in so doing presents a paradox to those who purport to represent the state: they support the repression of prostitution because that is the social mandate, and yet they do not wholly support it because there is money to be made in keeping prostitution viable. Legality does precious little to eliminate the abridgment of fundamental human rights or the iniquitous hand of the state and other predators.

Chapter 7

Oppression
in
Nevada

Currently Nevada is the only place in North America where prostitution receives open government endorsement.[1] State law permits small counties to determine for themselves whether they want prostitution. Several have used the option, with the result that nearly three dozen brothels throughout the state are legal, de facto if not in the technical sense that they may be subject to common-law abatement proceedings.

Nevada's house prostitution is insignificant when measured in terms of income, generating perhaps no more than five to seven million dollars annually. Nor does it amount to much when compared to the call girl trade in Las Vegas, Reno and the Lake Tahoe area, where as many as 3,000 to 4,000 full- and part-time prostitutes bring in many times the brothel revenue figure.[2] There is also no real comparison in terms of numbers of predators and parasites. Besides madams and some pimps who exploit the brothel women, few others have their hands in the women's money bags. By contrast, Nevada's call girls are surrounded and preyed upon by "cabbies, bartenders, bellhops, newsboys, proprietors of various establishments (liquor stores, motels, etc.), gamblers, special deputies (the private police forces of the casinos) . . . and professional pimps."[3] But what is significant is not so much these comparisons, interesting as they may be, but rather the fact that some see in Nevada's legal brothels an example with broad implications: the case for or against legalization of prostitution in North America. Though an extrapolation of the Nevada example is immediately suspect when it is discovered that the houses exist only in small towns and rural areas, the case is valuable for other kinds of insights, particularly for those without a sense of history. Because of an intricate web of local regulations, compounded by house requirements instituted by owners, the "working girls," as many prefer to be called, are robbed of their dignity and their rights, matters they often find easy to overlook because of handsome financial returns.

Locations Legal and Sanctioned

In 1980 there were approximately 35 legal brothels in the state, a picture that has not appreciably changed for many years (Figure 7-1). With the exception of the "Mustang Bridge Ranch" near Reno with its 40 or so prostitutes, most of the houses do not have more than six or seven women, and some only two or three. The total population does not exceed 250.[4]

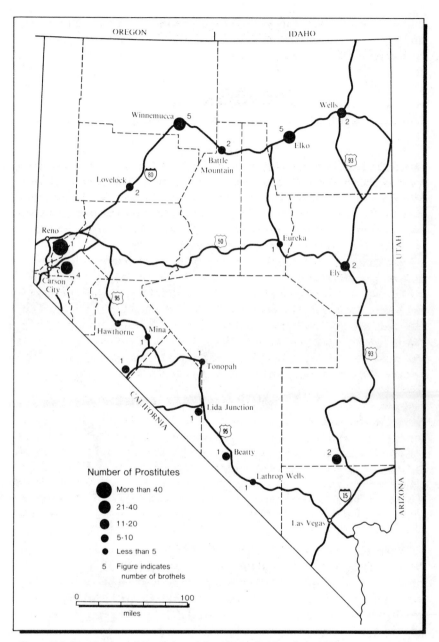

Figure 7-1 Distribution of Brothels and Prostitutes in Nevada in 1973.
Based on fieldwork by author.

Two-thirds of the brothels are in towns of 500 or more, the largest place being Elko with a population under 10,000. Others are located outside population centers (Figure 7-2). Houses are town-oriented in the northern and west-central part of the state, while rural brothels are found to the west and south. Those outside settlements are generally newer and more tied to trucking, air travel and transience—more a mirror of the hurried tempos of the industrial age than of cowboys, miners and provincial locals. Most of the isolated houses carry on business in mobile homes. Only three of more than 20 town brothels have similar facilities. A few places, the isolated ones, have landing strips to attract customers from metropolitan areas.

Figure 7-2 The ''Cottontail Ranch'' near Lida Junction
Note: The brothel has an airstrip for customers. Reproduced by permission from the *Annals* of the Association of American Geographers, 64 (1974) R. Symanski.

Where there are two or more brothels in a town, clustering is the norm. In Winnemucca, Elko, Wells and Ely the houses are practically adjacent to one another. Most occupy relatively inconspicuous sites that allow customers to enter and exit without much notice. Town brothels are invariably near the railroad tracks in declining residential areas. This feature suggests how long the red-light districts have existed.

Cribs, parlor houses and prostitutes that went by many names were as much a part of the early west as were miners, cowboys, town preachers and small merchants.[5] From Denver to San Francisco, and north to south in between, boom towns had few women, and those arriving first were usually prostitutes. On the frontier prostitution was inevitable, and the demand for women by rich and poor alike was as great as that for gold. Moral rectitude had to wait until enough women arrived to bring gentility to a male population and to change the supply and demand function, until the frenzied atmosphere of discovery, despair and fortune-making slowed, and until churches were firmly established. Prostitution was repressed in North America in the twentieth century and this forced prostitutes to find new niches. In a few places and for a few years in Nevada prostitution was illegal and the law was strictly enforced, but in general it was tolerated because, as residents will say today, "it has been here as long as anyone can remember and seems all right."

The federal government occasionally entered the picture. Storey County approved a red-light district for Virginia City in 1878. This district existed continuously until it was closed during World War II upon insistence by the Federal Security Agency which wanted to protect military personnel in the area.[6] Virginia City no longer has a red-light district, but Storey County now has the state's largest and most famous brothel—the "Mustang Bridge Ranch."

World War II closings were not taken kindly by many Nevada townspeople. Those in Beatty objected to the government's demands declaring that "after all, there isn't much to do at Beatty, we haven't television, we don't have a radio station."[7] Such sentiments die hard. In late 1979 the town's sole brothel, "Fran's Ranch," burned to the ground. Community leaders held a dance to raise money for a rebuilding effort. An organizer of the benefit stated that "Fran's quite well thought of by the majority of the people here; Fran has always been extremely gracious when it comes down to the support of local organizations, or anyone. . . ." Aware that not everyone was enthusiastic, he also noted that "not everyone likes baseball."[8]

The war took its toll. In 1943 the Wells city council enacted an emergency ordinance because:

> It had been made to appear to this Board that the absence of such an ordinance results in the spread of venereal disease, to the detriment of members of the armed forces of the United States sojourning in said city or in the neighborhood . . . and this ordinance is for the protection of their health and safety.[9]

The ordinance remained in effect until three months after the end of World War II.

In spite of opposition, most brothels in the state were closed during the war. But prostitution did not disappear; it was simply driven into cheap hotels, rooming houses or to the outskirts of towns.[10] Because of prostitution and the presence of legalized gambling and easy liquor, Elko and Ely outdrew Salt Lake City as overnight destinations for soldiers stationed at the Wendover Air Base on the Nevada-Utah border. As soon as the war ended several communities legalized or permitted prostitution within certain areas of town.

The federal government has continued its involvement in the state's bordello trade. One incident in the early 1970s involved the location of a house along a proposed section of the interstate highway. The government was concerned about having to reimburse the owner for demolition of a business that it could not condone. In another case the Bureau of Land Management ordered a brothel on federal land to relocate.[11] It did. Still another house, the "Cottontail Ranch," was also told to move. The madam had been leasing five acres of desert at $100 a year, with the option to eventually purchase the land. The property used by the Cottontail had been obtained under the Small Tract Act of 1938 which makes property available for residential and commercial use. Although the 1938 federal law did not specifically exclude brothels, the Bureau of Land Management contended that this kind of usage was illegal. The federal government lost its case.

State Laws, Local Laws and Employer Rules

The role of the federal government has been insignificant compared to the part played by state and local governments. The Nevada statutes state that a county cannot grant a license for brothels or for any business employing prostitutes if it had a population of 200,000 or more at the last national census.[12] At present only Clark County (which includes Las Vegas) with a 1970 population of nearly 275,000 is excluded by this law. Washoe County, which encompasses Reno and Sparks, had many fewer than 200,000 inhabitants at the time of the last census. But, like other cities and counties near the resort areas along the California border, Reno has specifically prohibited brothels.[13]

Gambling interests have played a major role in keeping legal houses out of Las Vegas, Reno and the Lake Tahoe area. They have been equally interested in suppressing streetwalking activity. Call girls and "independents" (those who work on their own without a pimp) are another matter. Knowing that some of the gambling clientele expect access to prostitutes, a number of casinos and hotels permit women to work the premises as long as they "do not reflect poorly on the establishment." Among the principal rules they must follow are to avoid blatant soliciting and not to steal from clients.

Other interest groups have had impact on state legislation. Brothels cannot operate within 400 yards of a school or religious center.[14] According to Marion Goldman this regulation, also reflected in most local laws, had its origin in Virginia City when, during the 1870s, anti-prostitution crusades closed a small red-light district neighboring a school.[15]

Nevada has granted county commissioners the power to license, tax, regulate and prohibit brothels. Four counties, Storey, Lincoln, Lyon and Esmeralda, license brothels by ordinance (Figure 7-3). Licensing is done to avoid being defined as a common-law nuisance and thereby subject to abatement. In 1948, in *Cunningham vs. Washoe County,* the Nevada

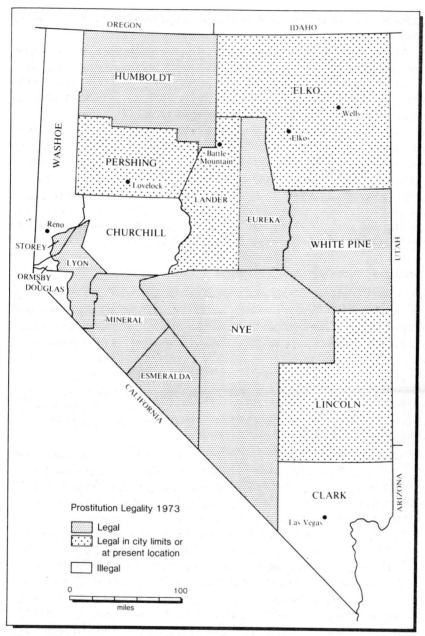

Figure 7-3 The Legal Status of Prostitution in Nevada in 1973
Data from state statutes, county and city ordinances.
See notes to chapter for specific references.

Supreme Court held that an unlicensed brothel in Reno was a common-law nuisance and that this aspect of the law could not be changed by statute.[16] Other counties license their houses as bars and boarding houses, but regulate them using prostitution ordinances. Five counties currently prohibit bordellos.

Exciusion has been rationalized by various criteria. Carson City outlaws prostitution by defaming the prostitute, describing her as someone with an "evil reputation" who engages in "prohibited conduct."[17] The City of Fallon and Douglas County have kept out brothels on the grounds that they are nuisances that offend the public sense of decency.[18]

Several counties allow the activity in towns or unincorporated areas but do not permit it elsewhere. One even restricts the location of houses to specific plots of land. The difficulty of controlling scattered brothels is the reason given by policemen for restricting them to settlements. This sentiment is not state-wide. In Esmeralda County, for example, houses must be at least five miles outside town.[19]

City and county governments have attempted to anticipate public concern. Not only do they give themselves the right to make laws as the need arises, but they enforce detailed regulations. Prostitutes must be twenty-one (eighteen in a few counties), have a work permit, be fingerprinted, photographed and examined by a physician before commencing work. In a few places the women must register their automobiles and are required to notify the police when quitting. Almost everywhere prostitutes are required to obtain weekly venereal disease examinations at their own expense.

The ordinances of Lyon and Esmeralda counties provide a striking contrast in the extent of their detail. Esmeralda County requires brothels to have location permits. They must be in uninhabited areas at least five miles from a city, town, mobile home park, or place where people normally dwell. No gaming or narcotics are permitted on the premises, and prostitutes must have weekly and monthly medical examinations. By contrast, the 1972 Lyon County ordinance, some 18 pages, is perhaps the most comprehensive in the state.[20] To insure that brothels do not constitute a public nuisance elaborate sections require data on the financial condition of the owner, addresses of prostitutes for the previous ten years, and complete information on previous convictions of the owner. A woman with a felony charge in her past cannot be employed. The sheriff can limit the hours-per-day or days-per-week that a brothel is open, the number of prostitutes that a house can have and the size of the building. He is to receive weekly reports on the health of the women, and they must have regular examinations. The bordellos may employ males only for the maintenance and repair of the premises, and no male is permitted to live on the property. The houses must be at least three miles from incorporated towns, and more than 300 yards from any public street, road, highway, private residence or business establishment. They can be closer to the latter if they receive written consent of the owner. Houses are prohibited from advertising and can only have signs no larger than three by five feet that must read "Guest Ranch—Men Only." Signs on public roads can give only the name of the brothel, approximate distance from the road and a single arrow indicating the direction. Finally, the houses must be enclosed by a fence at least six feet high with an entrance that can be opened only from the inside.

Prostitutes are required to observe a number of local regulations.[21] A few relate directly to their work. Others, less widespread, emphasize personal relationships and mobility patterns. The women are permitted outside the houses, with few exceptions, only between the hours of 10 A.M. and 5 or 6 P.M. In Wells, the hours are from 1 P.M. to 4 P.M. Winnemucca allows prostitutes in town after 4 P.M. and until 7 P.M., if the brothel is closed and the police department is notified of intentions and areas to be visited. Lander County prohibits them from leaving the houses on Sunday. Activity within the permitted hours is confined to visiting such places as doctors' and dentists' offices, beauty parlors, shopping areas and, perhaps, a movie theater. The women are explicitly excluded from bars, gaming houses and residential areas and they cannot rent rooms in town. One sheriff of Wells used to make uncommon exception by permitting prostitutes to go to local hotels with customers. Ely allows them to eat in restaurants with bars during shopping hours. Until recently one provision stated that the restaurant had to have a side entrance which the women were required to use.

Prostitutes in a number of counties are not allowed to talk to anyone on the streets, even to exchange salutations. Part of the fear is that males will be put in indelicate situations. Exaggerated concern for associations between prostitutes and males exists in Winnemucca. There, the women are not allowed to have male "friends" within the town; the term "friends" includes pimps, boyfriends, husbands and others defined by the police department.

To all of these rules there are exceptions and variations. On a prostitute's birthday, or on holidays such as Thanksgiving, the madam may obtain permission to escort her employees in a group to a bar in town. Wells permits no more than three to accompany the madam at one time. One house in Winnemucca with six or seven prostitutes has avoided problems in the past by requiring each woman to shop and attend to medical needs on a different day of the week. In rural areas, where most of these issues do not arise, prostitutes often go for their medical checkups in a group, accompanied by the madam.

Local rules and regulations also place restrictions on family proximity, employment changes and "outdates" (when madams permit prostitutes to be "bought" for out-of-house business for a day or more). A prostitute cannot be employed in Winnemucca or Battle Mountain if a member of her family lives in the county. The rule on outdates varies. Some places require a customer to meet the prostitute at the town limits and transact business elsewhere. Others stipulate that prostitute and client must leave the county. When someone quits or is fired from a house, she usually has to leave the county for a period ranging from fifteen days to three months before she can be taken in by another house in that county. Violation of these or other rules results in revocation of the work permit and perhaps banishment from the county.

To maintain a sense of decorum some police enforce in-town dress codes. During the early 1970s Battle Mountain had a rule which specified that "no girl shall be allowed uptown in bikinis, bathing suits, etc.," the very costumes found in the brothels during business hours. Prostitutes complained that the problem came in the interpretation of "etc." They could not wear short skirts and, on occasion, were told to wear pants. Winnemucca had a similar dress code, and the Chief of Police refused to issue work permits to those "improperly" dressed.

Employers compound the oppression. In general, madams require that prostitutes work for three weeks straight after which they have a week off to do as they please. This rule only hints at the atmosphere of a Nevada brothel, its regimens and rhythms.

> Like life in a submarine that submerged three weeks at a stretch, time at the Mustang Bridge Ranch had a different rhythm. The women worked in 14-hour shifts, most of them from four in the afternoon until six in the morning. Only a few worked the daytime hours, when business was slow. They worked seven days a week, three weeks in a row. They stayed at Mustang 24 hours a day. Those were the rules. Actually, there was no immediate reason to leave the sealed cyclone-fenced area. Every service was provided—hairdresser, masseuse, laundress, maids. Traveling salesmen vended racks of clothing in the back room. A snack kitchen was stocked with a dietician's nightmare: Mother's cookies, cakes, potato chips, marshmallows, candy, donuts, a wide range of ice cream.[22]

Many women are restricted in the number of telephone calls they can make per week. In one brothel prostitutes are permitted only two incoming and two outgoing calls per week, and none can be received between 4 and 9 P.M. House rules do not stop here. Many prostitutes can have no more than sugar water, tea or other non-alcoholic beverages when working. In the state's largest house women are not permitted to read, eat or knit in the parlor at any time, they are forbidden to talk about their personal lives to anyone, cannot go into another's room unless they are working a "double" on a customer, must turn in all tips to the house and are required to tip the maid a dollar a day. The prostitutes are given one concession. Except on weekends and holidays, they can leave the brothel for forty-five minutes a day to frequent a nearby bar—if they have put in a ten-hour shift.[23]

One clear effect of governmental and house regulations on the prostitutes is to make them prisoners, "inmates" as the legislators say in some of their ordinances, of the houses and towns in which they work. Occasionally the women will describe their predicament in just these terms. Yet, most emphasize the voluntary nature of their employment, and more than that, the money they are making. At the end of the 1970s an attractive, young woman could clear $800 to $1,000 a week, after the madam took a 40 to 50 percent cut of gross receipts. Whether the women pay taxes on their income is an open question. What they will talk about freely is what they can buy with their money and what they hope to invest in when they get out of the life. They also talk about the fact that nowhere else in American society can they make so much. Some simply say they like what they are doing and that they want to work with people, lots of different ones. In summary, while Nevada's brothel prostitutes are deprived of fundamental human rights and must pay predatory rates to madams and owners for the privilege of working in their houses, it would not be easy to convince most that there are better alternatives in society, or within prostitution.

Managing Visibility

The visible impact of prostitution in Nevada is insignificant, not only because of the small number of houses, inconspicuous locations and the many restrictions placed on the prostitutes' freedom, but also because the brothels cannot—by law—use prominent signs. They cannot advertise in public theaters, on public streets or along highways. A few county ordinances prohibit advertising of any sort. Brothel owners do not complain. They understand that their very existence and continuing community toleration is a function of image, so they try hard to make it as good as possible. They donate freely and generously to Little League, Boy Scouts, schools, blood banks and other fund raising activities. Yet, madams have found ways to increase their visibility with as little fanfare as possible. Attention-getting calling cards, free wall posters and exterior brothel decor are among devices used to draw in customers and gain a competitive advantage (Figures 7-4, 7-5 and 7-6). Beverly Harrell of the "Cottontail Ranch," a mobile home brothel near Lida Junction between Reno and Las Vegas (Figures 7-1 and 7-2), goes further than other madams. Proclaiming her modest house a "world famous club," she advertises through across-the-bar and mail-order sales of T-shirts, medallions, lighters and autographed copies of a book she wrote.[24]

Although the red-light districts are patrolled frequently and some county ordinances include a "consent to search" if reason is given, there are relatively few problems with the brothels. Some policemen claim there are many fewer disorder complaints related to prostitution than to bars and gaming houses. In the past madams have not admitted servicemen[25] or "hippies" for fear of trouble. And they want no part of drugs. Nor do the police. When a prostitute was caught selling small quantities of marijuana in one of Ely's houses in 1973 it was closed for a month and the woman banished from the county. Police attempt to anticipate problems by fingerprinting and registering prostitutes and, in some cases, checking their backgrounds with the F.B.I. The women must carry work cards, and brothel records must match the prostitutes present when the police make unannounced inspection calls.

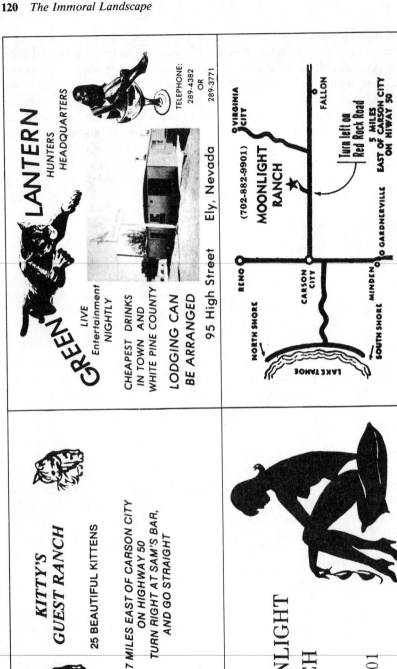

Figure 7-4 Brothel Calling Cards

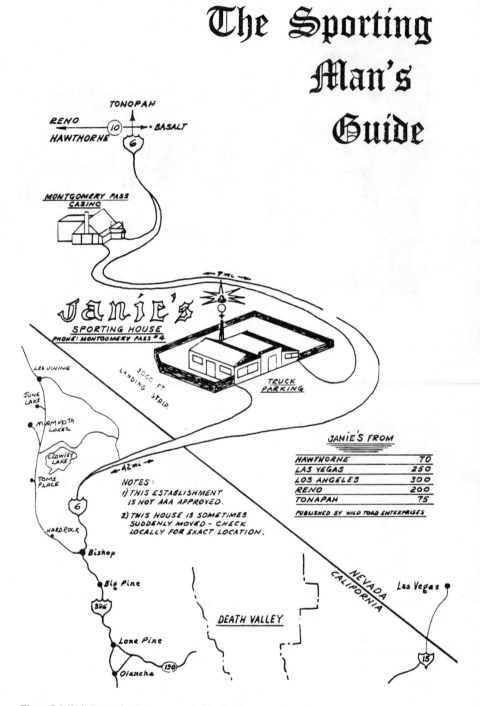

Figure 7-5 Wall Poster for Customers and Friends, Courtesy of the House

Figure 7-6 Brothel Advertising, Winnemucca

Local Attitudes Toward Legal Prostitution

Given the rather low visibility of sanctioned prostitution in Nevada it is not too surprising that many in the state favor its presence. The positive attitude is evident in casual conversations, in the words of law enforcement officers, in the voting attitudes of the populace and in the news media. A nationally publicized dispute in the 1950s involved the *Territorial Enterprise,* the newspaper on which Mark Twain served his apprenticeship, the Nevada State Highway Department and a brothel in Searchlight, near Las Vegas. The highway department complained that heavy traffic to the house had ruined the road surface and that, in addition, it was uncomfortably close to the town's one-room school house and thereby in violation of state law. The *Territorial Enterprise* advocated the "Searchlight Plan": it argued that the school rather than the brothel should be moved.[26]

A 1972 newspaper poll in Yerrington, where prostitution is illegal, found that over 90 percent of those interviewed wanted it legalized. Until the latter part of 1974 Churchill County prohibited prostitution and brothels. Then, in November of that year the county's voters decided by a comfortable margin to approve the activity.[27] A 1967 election campaign for the sheriff's office in Battle Mountain provides a striking example. The incumbent sheriff owned the town's two brothels. His challenger, who later won, privately polled members of the community regarding their views on prostitution, with the idea that he would run on a platform opposing it. To his surprise, less than ten percent wanted to get rid of the houses. Reportedly, one minister in nearby Winnemucca lost his job when he spoke out against the town's prostitution.[28]

A frequently encountered pro-prostitution argument in Nevada is the belief that spatial restriction of the activity is desirable. Since it is assumed that the activity will exist whether or not wanted, it is preferable to confine it and keep it off the streets and out of the casinos. There are no street-walkers in areas where prostitution is legal, and casino call girls are few in number. From this perspective brothels are not so much good in and of themselves but are better than perceived alternatives.

Another common attitude among townspeople is that controlled prostitution is responsible for diminishing the incidence of rape and other violent crimes. One police officer cited the fact that during a six-year period in Battle Mountain there were no proven cases of rape, while in nearby Austin, one-fourth the size, three cases occurred during the same time period. Although the relationship between rape and prostitution is unclear,[29] reasoning and decision-making are based on beliefs, not demonstrated correlations.

Parents occasionally state that open prostitution keeps their sons from early marriages, that the professional women are a good educational experience, that the houses keep their daughters "out of trouble," and that they need not worry about venereal disease. Townspeople are aware that frequent medical examinations are required and that disease problems do not usually originate in the brothels. On this their reasoning is sound.[30]

Finally, long-time familiarity with the institution has made it acceptable. When prostitution gained a foothold in the nineteenth century it persisted despite opposition. One popular view depicted the male as an animal full of sexual desires. Prostitution was seen as an acceptable outlet, better in the Victorian mind than masturbation. Too, it was felt that crib and brothel women were a stabilizing influence on the mine workers, the crux of the economy. Middle-class Nevadans of the time who opposed the idea that prostitutes were functional had neither the prestige nor the numbers to press their wishes.[31] These historical forces set a pattern not easily erased. For those living in Nevada today the brothels have been around for as long as they can remember; they are seen to be as much a part of the townscape as the drugstore, the post office and the railroad station. One suspects that many people are prepared to defend the continuance of legalized prostitution on historical grounds alone.

Despite rather widespread support for open brothel prostitution, opposition does exist.[32] The mildest form is a simple desire not to increase the number of houses. As many as half of Nevada's counties want no more than they now have. Fundamentalist church groups and new ministers who have not previously encountered legalized prostitution usually express their dissatisfaction. Legislators and district attorneys occasionally attempt to close the houses. Such occurred in Lyon County in 1971, but to no avail. The eventual solution was legalization of the county's four houses and one of the most comprehensive regulatory ordinances in the state. More recently, in eastern Nevada a district attorney launched a campaign to close the bordellos in Lincoln County after charges of arson and murder, presumably involving brothel boarders, came to public attention.[33] But dissatisfaction and vocal outcries that the houses be closed in this or that county are a minority position, and such cries are not likely to be heard by local governments that impose heavy taxes on the houses. Nearly ten years ago Lyon County was taxing each of its brothels $12,000 if they had more than six prostitutes.[34] In Storey County the "Mustang Bridge Ranch" was paying a license fee of between $20,000 and $25,000 a year, approximately 10 percent of the county's entire budget.[35]

| Chapter 8 | # Race, Class and Space |

Cityscapes have long been suffused with evidence that the poor and racial minorities pay heaviest for social morality. The particular group discriminated against—meaning prostitutes or those who live in close proximity to them—has been a matter of social, historical and geographical circumstances: those last to arrive from abroad, those least able to assimilate or better their economic situations, those with the most striking racial differences from the majority, those—like the aged—that society hardly values. In so far as prostitutes are concerned their business locations have been created and promoted by the machinery of the state, by laws and their differential enforcement that have brought the immoral and the undesirable together to form a single landscape.

Among the Poor

The costs of hypocrisy are unequally borne. The poor pay most for maintaining the illegal status of prostitution in the United States. No less sanctimonious than anyone else, they nevertheless have to live in the same areas with prostitutes, their predators and parasites, for the general benefit of the middle and upper classes who come in from respectable neighborhoods to partake of pleasure. Over half a century ago Abraham Flexner, one of the most notable students of European prostitution, found that the women of the demimonde were forced into low-rent areas where people have little control over events.[1] Of scores of American red-light districts surveyed in the early decades of the twentieth century, the largest percentage was in immigrant districts and slums—in a word among the poor and those perceived as outcast and socially disorganized (Figure 8-1).

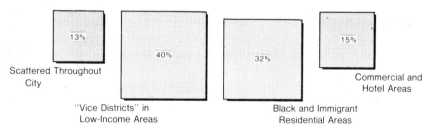

Figure 8-1 Location of 168 Brothels in a number of American Cities in 1917
Data from Woolston 1921:133.

When the famous British Wolfenden Report of the 1950s considered the question of what to do for those who must live in neighborhoods where prostitutes solicit and transact business, sympathy and forebearance were its principal recommendations.[2] Students of crime could not help but notice

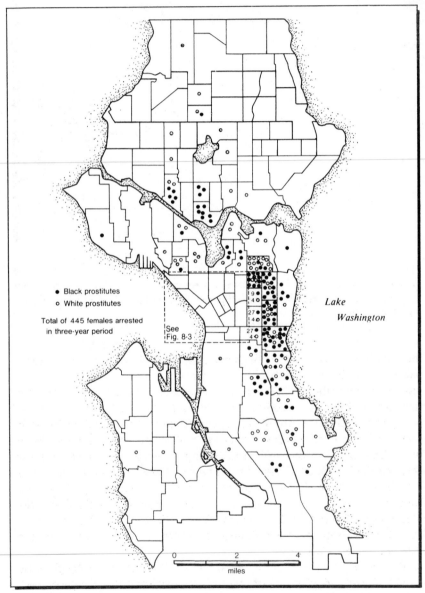

Figure 8-2 Home Addresses of Women Charged with Prostitution in Seattle from 1968 through 1970
Adapted from Schmid and Schmid 1972:243.

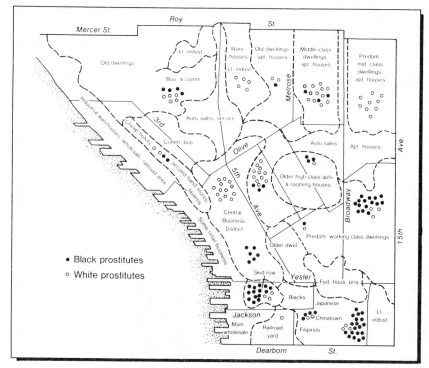

• Black prostitutes
○ White prostitutes

Figure 8-3 Home Addresses of Women Charged with Prostitution in Seattle's Central Business District and Environs
Adapted from Schmid and Schmid 1972:175, 243.

that a pathbreaking report with many commendable features was clearly biased against the lower class.[3]

If prostitutes initially do not live and work among the poor, the minorities and the down-and-outers, eventually their geography becomes synonymous with these groups. Processes put in motion by other forces in society are reinforced by prostitutes and their clients. Social and economic blight beget more of the same: prostitutes proliferate and shoppers disappear, businesses decline, more buildings are abandoned, property values drop further and so do tax revenues. Prostitutes engage in some crimes, primarily larceny, but mostly their image, their assumed criminality, invites other criminals to their side: con men, drug addicts who need money for a fix, and rapists who prey on prostitutes and other women who live in or pass through areas of solicitation.

The social geography of most contemporary cities depicts strong patterns of spatial interdigitation: poor minorities, aged down-and-outers, high crime rates and the presence of prostitutes. Seattle's police records for the years 1968-1970 show that the residences of 445 women arrested for prostitution were highly clustered in and around the central business district, in

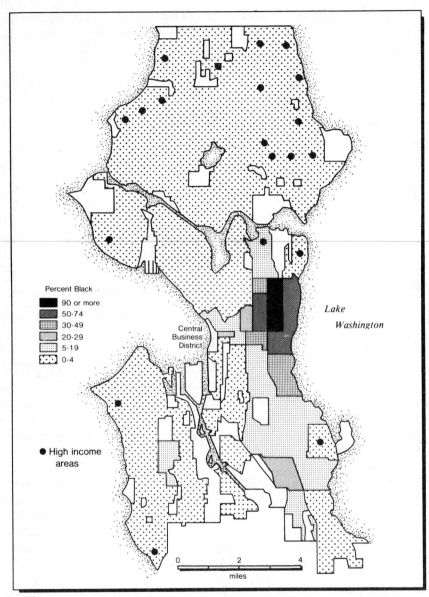

Figure 8-4 Distribution of Blacks and High Income Families in Seattle, circa 1970
Adapted from Schmid and Schmid 1972:119.

Percent Black
- 90 or more
- 50-74
- 30-49
- 20-29
- 5-19
- 0-4

● High income
areas

Central
Business
District

Lake
Washington

districts that had the highest proportions of the city's blacks, where
burglary, robbery, assault and sex offenses were commonplace, and at some
distance from middle and upper-class whites, suburban types who made use
of the women (Figures 8-2, 8-3, 8-4 and Table 8-1). Equally notable in the

Seattle data is the bias against black prostitutes; their white counterparts were more likely to live, if not work, in more respectable sections of the city.

Table 8-1

Spatial Intercorrelations of Prostitution Arrestees with other Arrestees in Seattle from 1968 through 1970

Larceny	.96	Possession of Concealed Weapon	.86
Nonaggravated Assault	.78	Forgery and Counterfeiting	.70
Burglary	.84	Sex Offenses Excluding Rape and Prostitution	.73
Robbery	.95	Male Drunkenness	.95

Adapted from Schmid and Schmid 1972:251.

Using Chinatowns to Advantage

Nineteenth and twentieth-century Chinatowns were notorious for prostitution. In the words of one historian, these ghettos functioned as "safety valves of the control system."[4] Working against the Chinese and other racial minorities was the geopolitical sink principle; public opinion and political action combine to confine obnoxious or immoral institutions to areas that have the least political clout, ideally the ghettos of racial minorities.

Chinese women were continual targets of personal debasement in the West that developed as a result of the Gold Rush. Virginia City in 1870 had a population of just over 7,000 people, including 138 prostitutes.[5] Of these enumerated women, 71 were Chinese and 4 were black. The Chinese prostitutes lived in a segregated Chinatown—the "celestial quarters"—and generally did not associate with their white counterparts. Even though 24 of the 63 white prostitutes owned property in Virginia City, none of the Chinese women did. Allegedly, those who sold their services along the town's infamous D Street were stratified and segregated. The higher-class white women occupied white-washed cottages at the head of the street, while those of darker coloration occupied cribs and inferior locations. The latter commanded lower prices and received, as did Chinese prostitutes, disapproval from the lighter-skinned women.[6]

Patterns were similar elsewhere at the time. Denver's parlor houses and better cribs were on Holladay Street (present-day Market Street), the main stem of "The Line." Although French, Italian, Irish and other nationalities worked on Holladay Street, the Chinese occupied parallel "Hop Alley." Their crib quarters were intermixed with opium dens, gambling houses and stores that specialized in articles from the Orient. Those along Hop Alley received lower prices than women on Holladay Street, though they fared better than those who worked a sidestreet called "Blue Row." There, the price for intercourse might not exceed a dime.[7] Denver's Chinese were brought in from San Francisco and it is to this city that one must turn for a fuller understanding of how a Chinatown and its prostitutes were victims of the geopolitical sink principle.

Prostitutes of Latin American descent were the first to feel the wrath of racism in San Francisco. They began arriving there in 1848, brought in as indentured labor by their ghettoized countrymen to work in their cheap cantinas and fandango parlors at the foot of Telegraph Hill. Their ghetto, in the area of Kearny and Pacific Streets, became known as "Little Chile." After 1865 it was a major nucleus of the notorious Barbary Coast.

From the beginning the prostitutes from Latin America were forced to work on a turnover principle, all-comers at cheap prices: this probably seemed reasonable enough given what they made in their home country. But they also received abuse from the general populace because of their origins. They were from Mexico, Panama and Chile. In the image of the times Latins were contemptible, dirty and morally base. A bad popular image was darkened by the press and in journals where Latin American prostitutes were seen as women of the "lowest and most degraded character." They were vilified as shameless, disgustingly lewd, *greaseritas*.[8] By day the prostitutes were sometimes robbed and subjected to criminal attacks by men who would buy their services at night. Ghettoization contributed to their predicament. They had little opportunity to learn English or to acquire the social manners necessary to work in the more respectable parlor houses scattered throughout the city. In sum, their treatment paralleled that of the Chinese who were brought in for the same purpose and worked nearby in their own ghetto.

Mere slaves to those who brought them over from the Orient, young Chinese girls were bought for a pittance in their homeland, sometimes shipped to the mainland in padded crates billed as freight, and sold as prospective prostitutes for 10 to 100 times the initial outlay, depending on age, appearance and coastal or inland destination. Supply and demand dictated prices which fluctuated between $500 and $2,000 per girl. For the most part, the young girls had been kidnapped or sold into prostitution by fathers and guardians who needed the money. Once in San Francisco the human cargo was little more than profitable merchandise to be resold or rented for use in the cribs of the Barbary Coast.[9]

Fifteen years after the Gold Rush began, the San Francisco Board of Supervisors required that large screens be placed at the entrance to the alleyways in Chinatown. The purpose was to conceal the enslaved prostitutes from passersby.[10] In 1866 the California State Legislature enacted a law expressly for the purpose of suppressing Chinese prostitution in certain areas of the city.[11] Not until 1874 was the law amended to include all prostitutes. The powers bestowed by the state were soon reflected in arrest patterns. In 1867, 14 Chinese owners of brothels were arrested. Two years later 20 Orientals were apprehended for importing prostitutes. And in one year city-wide arrests of prostitutes increased from 1 to 136. Though the records are unclear it is believed that all of the women were Chinese.[12] Whatever the racist component, it may be that, as Jacqueline Barnhart maintains, one reason for enforcing the laws against the Chinese was that they had the least financial impact on the private sector. Profits from prostitution went to Chinese males. Further, since the Oriental women were at the bottom of the social hierarchy and charged the lowest prices, they did not generate as much income as other prostitutes in the city.[13]

The treatment of Chinese prostitutes, more generally Chinese people, measured waxing and waning anti-Chinese sentiments, xenophobia and beliefs that Oriental females were "criminal and demoralizing."[14] Reactions were generally most pronounced after 1865 when increasing numbers of Chinese were brought in to build the Union Pacific across the Sierras. By the 1880s the Workingman's Party claimed to "utterly repudiate the idea of being moved by race or class prejudice," and yet declared the Chinese to be "unscrupulous, lying and treacherous," and responsible for nine-tenths of the city's syphilis.[15]

That all prostitutes were not perceived or treated similarly is dramatically indicated by the image of the French prostitute. Even her harshest critics only described her as "notorious." More often than not she was seen as one "who gave ease, taste, and sprightly elegance to the manners of the town." Indeed, she was held in such esteem that San Francisco's women who knew little of the demimonde looked to her for the latest fashions.[16]

That image and the reality of the market place were the same for French prostitutes is suggested by their place in San Francisco's "cowyard," or Municipal Brothel, a multi-storied building with large numbers of cribs rented by prostitutes. Prices in the Municipal Brothel more or less increased as one ascended. The bargain basement was occupied by Mexican women who got 25 cents. White American prostitutes on the first and second floors received 50 and 75 cents, while French women were on the third floor and received a dollar for their services. The going rate for blacks on the top deck was a half-dollar.[17]

In 1880 a significant proportion of San Francisco's brothels and cribs was confined to an area three blocks wide and nine to fourteen blocks long (Figure 8-5). The heaviest concentrations of activity were in Chinatown and several blocks to the south. One historian states that by 1885 Chinatown had some 70 bordellos, all owned by the Chinese.[18] In 1890 the City Board

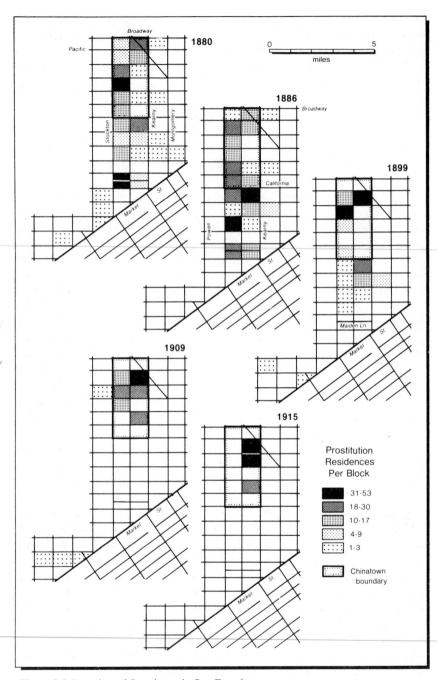

Figure 8-5 Location of Prostitutes in San Francisco
Adapted from Shumsky and Springer 1979.

of Supervisors prohibited brothels within an area bounded by Powell, Kearny, Broadway and California Streets, but the law was not rigidly enforced. In the ensuing years selective enforcement began on certain streets.

After 1875 the central business district was blocked in its southward expansion, halted at Market Street, the local "Rubicon." In reaction businesses, particularly fashionable retail establishments, invaded the southern end of the red-light district. By the turn of the century entire blocks once lined with houses of ill-repute had been cleared for respectable entrepreneurs. Within a decade one of the city's more infamous streets, Maiden Lane, had become the core of the women's apparel shopping district.[19]

The contraction of the red-light district might suggest that the prostitute population decreased or that women moved to other areas of the city. But there is no evidence for this proposition. Instead, density simply increased.[20]

With the exception of an emergent prostitution locale to the southwest—the present-day Tenderloin—prostitutes were finding it increasingly difficult to work outside Chinatown. A loose kind of de facto segregation, underway for nearly three decades, was formally institutionalized in 1909-10 by the city's police commissioners. Prostitutes were not permitted to solicit nor live outside an area nearly identical to the boundaries of Chinatown. Municipal mandates, public health requirements, and police enforcement practices expressed what had been true for more than half a century, namely that the Barbary Coast area was just about the only section of town not subject to prostitution laws.[21] Because this was home and place of work to Latin and Chinese prostitutes the public could feel secure in the belief that racial minorities were inferior, base and responsible for prostitution and associated problems.

To be sure, there is more to the explanation of the location of San Francisco's red-light district than simple racism or expansion of the central business district. Chinese men made commercial sexual use of the young girls they imported from their homeland. The sex ratio of Chinese immigrants ranged from 20 males to 1 female in 1880 to nearly 9 to 1 in 1920.[22] Chinatown also had many rooming houses, hotels and boarding accommodations that were ideal locations for prostitution. The Oriental prostitutes were no less attractive to the sizeable white population, for anonymity was insured and the price for sex was half that charged outside the district. Many of the Chinese women were reputedly willing to cater to sexual demands not easily available elsewhere. Moreover, heresay that the Oriental woman possessed vaginas with a peculiar slant created a "lookee" trade among whites, boys and old men alike.[23] In Chinatown men were relatively free from arrest and apparently many of the women were willing to take white clients who had as much interest in drinking and brawling as they did in fornication. So many ill-mannered men were seeking the services of prostitutes in the 1890s that women on the streets were reported to travel in the company of armed guards.[24]

The momentous closing of the Barbary Coast in 1917 by no means reflected deep concern for either prostitutes or the Chinese minority. San Francisco had strong factions that disagreed over a difficult problem. One group believed that the "social evil" could not be eliminated, that it provided an outlet for the sexual desires of young men, and that segregating prostitution was the best way to control venereal disease. Countering the zoning solution was the position that segregation was really a form of licensing that encouraged prostitution and the spread of venereal disease. Consorting with prostitutes was not only seen as unhealthy to young males but also immoral and unnecessary. The district had to be eliminated.

The city's businessmen, seeking their own best interests, were the major determinant of change. While initially they supported segregation as a way to protect their businesses, they reversed their decision in the name of still greater economic prosperity: imagined profits from hosting the Panama-Pacific Exposition.[25] Ministers and other opponents argued they would undermine the Exposition if San Francisco's prostitution continued to be tolerated and the red-light district were not eliminated. These concerns, the crusading of William Randolph Hearst, who used his *San Francisco Examiner* to demand the Barbary Coast be closed, and a national atmosphere of progressivism brought about the death of the Barbary Coast in 1917.[26]

The dispersal of more than 1,000 prostitutes from their locus in Chinatown radically changed the geography of the city's immoral landscape (Figure 8-6). While some women continued to offer services within the Barbary Coast or its fringes, many spread to other parts of the city, especially to the "downtown Tenderloin": Geary, Powell, Leavenworth and Market Streets.[27] One report claims that prior to 1917 the brothels averaged 15 women per house. After dispersal the number of houses tripled and reduced their visibility by employing, on average, four prostitutes. Other women, hundreds of them, worked out of flats and apartments.[28] In spite of these changes, over the years Chinatown and adjacent areas continued to be geopolitical sinks.

More on the Geography of Racism and Geopolitical Sinks

In the nineteenth century there were no surveys of how Americans felt about black prostitutes. A hint as to what the prevailing attitude may have been can be gleaned from a description of the times, the words of a detective who knew the black brothels of Water and Greene Streets in New York City in the 1870s.

> Driven to those of their own color for companionship, their isolation from all others except as servants, their native indolence, their emotional natures, all

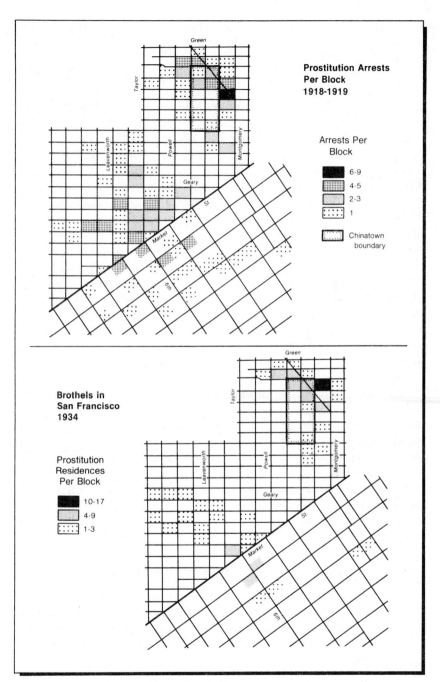

Figure 8-6 Prostitution Arrests in 1918-1919 and Location of Brothels in 1934
Adapted from Shumsky and Springer 1979.

tend to make the colored woman a free and easy one in her habits. It is an indisputable fact that these get down lower in the business than any other of their white sisters. Destitute, as a rule, of personal charms, they set themselves up with an eye to the barbarous, and when they have reached the lowest grade, are filthy and beastly beyond belief.[29]

Other chroniclers of the late nineteenth and early twentieth century voiced similar sentiments, believing that "moral laxity in colored homes was the norm"[30] and that the "Negro was addicted to sexual pleasures."[31]

When red-light districts were commonplace in the United States several cities, among them St. Louis and Savannah, had two districts, one for the clients of black prostitutes and another for whites.[32] Some American military towns along the Mexican border had three loosely defined districts, one for blacks, one for whites and another for Mexicans.[33] The red-light districts were often located among the poor and the nonwhite, as in El Paso where the city's single district was in the Mexican quarter along the Rio Grande.[34] An occasional further distinction was that some of the border brothels on the American side only accepted officers, a pattern that would be repeated numerous times in Europe during both world wars.[35] On the other side of the Mexican-American border there have long been—and still are—separate sectors for American and Mexican customers.[36] While both are staffed with Mexican women, those in the American district are younger, more attractive, better paid and confident of their higher social status.

If racial minorities have been segregated and prosecuted because of their color, they have also sometimes been conveniently ignored. In a way reminiscent of post-civil rights policies of benign neglect black prostitution in some areas has been perceived as too costly to control, or simply not worth the bother. In a careful and probing study of cities of the American prairie Daniel Elazer summarized this attitude by quoting one police chief who said that "the niggers can cut and fuck each other as much as they want, as long as they keep it quiet."[37]

Within red-light districts bordellos frequently have been segregated. In the south black prostitutes were available for white males, but the reverse situation was probably absent. Madams did not always approve of intermixing. A madam's organization in New Orleans in 1894, the Society of Venus and Bacchus, suggested that "any man who frequents nigger dives be boycotted." Another complaint was lodged against a brothel with Japanese women because it was believed that the "Japs were niggers dressed up."[38] In the 1920s Galveston, Texas had an ordinance against miscegenation. Generally ignored, the law was enforced inside the prostitution district and, as a result, neither black nor white house keepers could accept clientele of the other race. In 1929 the law was invoked against six white prostitutes who ran a bordello catering to blacks in the black section of town. When discovered by the police the women were given the choice of a heavy fine or a speedy exit from town; they unanimously chose the latter.[39] Chicago's Levee had two Japanese and two Chinese houses and at least one staffed only with black women—Black May's; all were said to have admitted only white males.[40] Information provided by Herbert Ashbury suggests that within the Levee there was some geographical segregation between the higher-class brothels and those that employed nonwhites or women of inferior quality (Figure 8-7).[41] If these very brief examples hint that black prostitutes were subject to discrimination, a closer examination of prostitution in New Orleans at the turn of this century shows more precisely how they were treated.

Color prejudice in New Orleans began in the slave market with the sale of "fancy girls," the offspring of white masters and black slaves.[42] Quadroons and octoroons (one-quarter and one-eighth black) brought in five to six times as much profit as blacks. "The choicest stock of quadroon and octoroon girls was sometimes displayed in separate quarters by their traders, already decked out in finery as befitted their future as 'fancy girls'."[43] Whatever the alleged color, many were to work in Storyville, New Orleans' infamous red-light district.

"The District," as Storyville was known to locals, was geographically graded, location being based on quality, price of service and race (Figure 8-8). The principal entry point into the District was along Basin Street near the railroad station. Once off the train, eager passengers headed first for the major parlor houses and saloons on Basin Street between Iberville and Conti Streets. This two-block core area contained the highest density and greatest number of parlor houses, the highest prices, the most elaborately furnished interiors, the best "house professors" (piano players), and the most attractive prostitutes offering the greatest range of social and sexual services. Octoroon women were a special favorite in the better houses and their names and addresses received prominence in the sporting guides.[44]

Along Franklin Street and on those streets perpendicular to Basin Street parlor houses and saloons were less numerous, though the number of cribs occupied by whites was greater. The density of cribs was highest in areas close to the railroad station and lowest along St. Louis street to the east, reflecting accessibility to the saloons. Slumlords levied exorbitant rents for crib use, sometimes renting them on a shift basis to maximize profits. When the district was at its height property owners were also charging whatever the traffic would bear for the use of alley space. Crib prices among whites were close to the $1.00 end of a seventy-five cent continuum. The tariff in the parlor houses nearby varied from $2.00 to $3.00, and was $5.00 and up in the most elegant places.[45]

To the north of Liberty Street was a zone which contained the heaviest concentration of blacks in the district, or rather the highest density of black women of interest to white males. The names and addresses of these women were listed in most editions of the *Blue Book* guides to the district (Figures

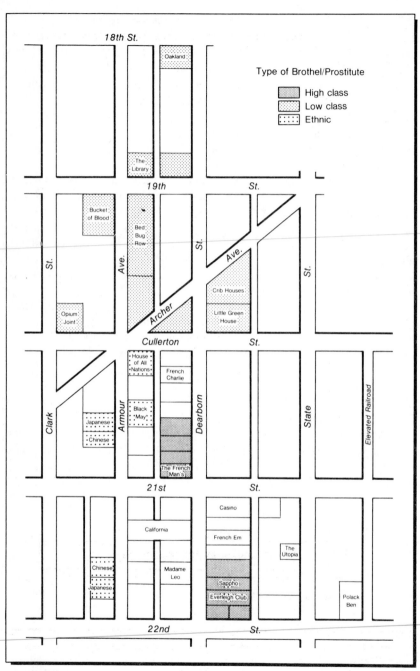

Figure 8-7 Portion of the South Side Levee in 1910
Adapted from Ashbury 1940.

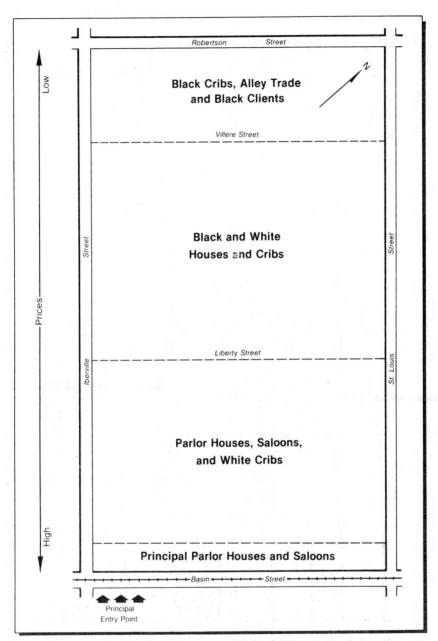

Figure 8-8 Principal Locations of Parlor Houses, Cribs and Prostitutes in Storyville, New Orleans
Based on a reading of Rose 1974, and various Blue Books.

8-9 and 8-10). That the demand for black prostitutes in Storyville was considerable is suggested by the apparent increase in their numbers over time
(compare Figures 8-9 and 8-10). Too, although the district was in decline by
the second decade of the twentieth century, the city council in 1917—the

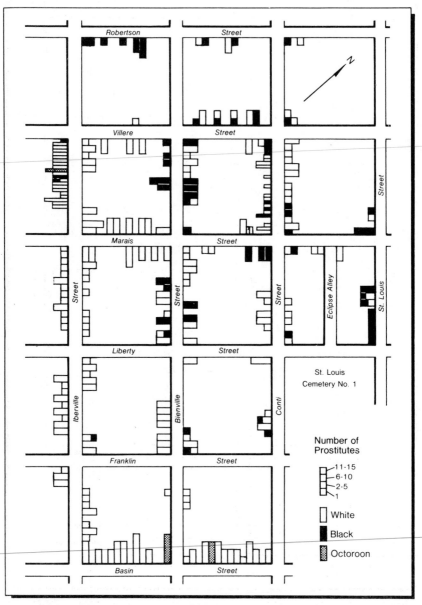

Figure 8-9 Location of Prostitutes in Storyville in 1905, according to the *Blue Book*
Data from Anonymous 1905.

year the district was closed—adopted an ordinance establishing a special red-light district for blacks.

From a geographical point of view black prostitutes occupied the worst locations: those furthest from the major entry point and principal saloons.

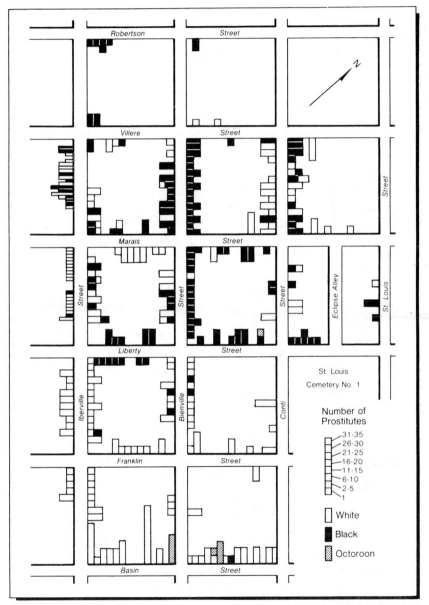

Figure 8-10 Location of Prostitutes in Storyville in 1910-1911, according to the *Blue Book*

Data from Anonymous 1910-1911.

In accord with a principle of accessibility and general desirability, prices in Storyville decreased northward and reached their lowest levels on Villere and Robertson Streets. A ghetto within a black ghetto where sex sold for a pittance in the open air or under the worst imaginable crib conditions, this area was frequented almost entirely by black males.

Segregation within Storyville expressed not only Southern racial attitude but also reflected laws that specifically legitimized separation of the races. As Al Rose noted in his fascinating study of Storyville:

> The District . . . was *legally* segregated in the sense that white and black prostitutes could not live or work in the same house and blacks were not permitted to patronize *any* of the mansions, even those staffed by black women, or to consort with white women in even the lowest of cribs. Such segregation had already become the "accepted" pattern for the city as well as for the whole South.[46]

The New Orleans law to which Rose refers was a city ordinance dated 1857. Among other things, it carried a provision that half of the $25 fine for disobeying the law was to be paid to the informer.[47] Following the half-century-old law the principal parlor houses did not allow both blacks and whites to work together. But the madams had no problem with intermediate cases: quadroons, octoroons and others were clearly not white. Nell Kimball, who ran a high-class house in the district until its closing said she was the owner of a "white whorehouse." Yet she claimed to employ women she referred to as "metisse," and "negrillonne," and others whose country of origin was Brazil. Her philosophy was to employ anyone of mixed blood as long as they looked "Spanish" and made her a profit. If prostitutes could not pass the "Spanish test," Nell Kimball would, as she said, "turn them over to a madame that ran a nigger house."[48] Another solution for a madam with both black and white women was to have the former ply their services in a nearby alley.

While the major racial contrast in Storyville was that between blacks and whites, the picture of segregation was more complex. In 1908 one observer of the district noted that in addition to special areas for blacks,

> here was a street of Jewish brothels, there two or more streets would be given up to the Italians or Slavs (generally called Polaks or Bohemians); and lastly there were the establishments of English-speaking women—Anglo-Saxon Americans, Canadians, English, and Irish. . . .[49]

Jews were singled out in the sporting guides along with blacks, octoroons and the perenially favored French. For example, the seventh edition of the *Blue Book* (1906) listed 454 women: 318 of whom were white, 58 black, 46 octoroon, 18 purportedly French and 14 Jewish.[50] In later years cries of anti-Semitism eliminated mention of Jews in the *Blue Book*; no such sentiments were expressed on behalf of blacks.

Although Storyville and districts like it are now a blurry part of American history, racism in brothels has changed less than one might have expected. Black prostitutes are commonplace in Nevada's legal brothels and they mix freely with their white coworkers. But in a few houses these women are available mainly or exclusively for white clients.[51] One brothel in the early 1970s would accept Mexican-Americans working on labor crews, but not blacks.[52] In the 1970s the "Mustang Bridge Ranch," the state's largest house, permitted black clients to enter for a drink but they had access only to prostitutes who volunteered to service them—in a special side room. Until recently only a few women would do so.[53]

Other Times and Other Places

In a broader context, evidence abounds of racism at other times and places outside the United States. In Avignon during the Middle Ages Jews were not permitted to enter brothels. London houses at the time were only slightly less restrictive; Jews were forbidden to enter Christian brothels. When the Canadian prairies were a settlement frontier and prostitution thrived, Saskatoon had separate houses for black, white and Japanese prostitutes.[54]

Victorian descriptions of black streetwalkers were often notable for their racist overtones. A "coloured" prostitute of the streets was "base . . . a shameless hag, with thick lips, sable black skin, leering countenance and obscene disgusting tongue, resembling a lewd spirit of darkness from the nether world."[55] No such view was held of "first-class" streetwalkers, white women who walked up and down Regent Street and the Haymarket, "sometimes with a gallant they . . . picked up, calling at the wine vaults or restaurants to get a glass of gin, or sitting down in the brilliant coffee-rooms, adorned with large mirrors, to a cup of good bohea or coffee."[56] A hundred years later white prostitutes in London live with West Indian or black pimps (known there as ponces), yet many will not speak to blacks in pubs nor accept them as clients.[57]

Contemporary low-class streetwalkers, often blacks or other minorities, are forced into a city's poorer, high crime areas, away from places that are busy, highly visible and the haunts of people with money and influence. In Paris high-class streetwalkers solicit near the *Étoile* at the head of the *Champs Elysées*. The city's lower-class women must work among down-and-outers, foreign workers who live cheaply and save what they can. Their districts are well-known: *St. Denis, Pigalle*, the *Barbes-Rouchechouart* area. Similar patterns are found in other European cities. Roman street women are most expensive along the *Via Veneto*. The cheapest ones solicit in back alleys, and their numbers increase away from the center of the city.[58] Along West Berlin's liveliest street, the *Kurfurstendamm*, high-class prostitutes are welcome in the exclusive cafes. Perceived class, quality and price of the women all decline as one moves away from the Kaiser Wilhelm Church, one of the street's landmarks.[59]

Discrimination based on class, without much apparent relationship to race, has also been notable. Before the Bolshevik Revolution, at a time when Moscow allegedly had 20,000 prostitutes and St. Petersburg double this number, only lower-class prostitutes, those mostly from the domestic and working classes, were forced to have regular venereal disease examinations.[60] Prostitutes in the state-regulated brothels of nineteenth-century Italy had to be registered with the police and were required to submit to regular and often degrading health examinations. Those who serviced the upper classes, rich businessmen, state officials and churchmen, were immune both from registration and examinations. This differential treatment in Italy came about not only because of bribery but also out of respect for the upper classes. Those at the bottom—the victims—openly resented the discrimination, recognizing that their predicament depended not on a concept of impartial justice but on class.[61]

Race and Class in Aruba

Some parts of the world, most notably Latin America, provide examples in which the distinction between racism and discrimination for other reasons is not so clear. Nowhere in the history of the world has there been greater expectation than in Latin America that racial discrimination would disappear. Mélange would be the key and, as is already true, mulatto and mestizo would be but two crude rubrics for a complex range of skin colors. But despite considerable mixing, and contrary to the hopes of many, racism has not yet disappeared. It is only more subtle than one is likely to encounter in North America or Western Europe. Expectations and subtleties aside, prostitution in Latin America interweaves with and reflects larger patterns and processes working elsewhere in society. The Antillean, Dutch-controlled island of Aruba in the southern Caribbean provides an interesting contemporary case study.[62]

In the mid-1930s the construction of a large oil refinery and dock expansion at St. Nicholas required a rather sizeable and dependable semi-skilled labor force. Convinced that these demands could not be met by Aruban men, large numbers of West Indians and Guayanese were brought in. To the "traditionally passive and subservient" Aruban male the nominally "single" foreigners, often darker and with different mannerisms, seemed a threat to their wives and daughters. The men appealed to the government for assistance. The government's solution, reached in consultation with refinery managers, was to import prostitutes from around the Caribbean. Initially arriving from many of the islands, after 1960 they came solely from the Dominican Republic and Colombia because of restrictive laws on the migration of single women in much of the Caribbean. Although large numbers of the foreigners returned home or were laid off after the completion of the refinery and the dock, the demand for prostitutes remained relatively constant. The reason was a change in the clientele: Aruban men now often frequented the foreign prostitutes.

The Dominican and Colombian prostitutes differed in a number of ways. The Dominican woman arrived singly in St. Nicholas but soon thereafter married an older, often destitute Aruban. She acquired a burden, someone to take her money, but the marriage maneuver also provided Antillean citizenship. By contrast, the Colombian prostitute arrived in Aruba on a three-month work permit and immediately set out to save as much as possible from her earnings. She had visions of returning to Colombia, to buy a small shop or an automobile, or simply to live better than she had before.

At present, other contrasts are evident. One is that Dominican prostitutes tend to avail themselves of government facilities for venereal disease examinations, exposing their visits to public view. The Colombian women discreetly make use of private doctors. The Dominicans work in shacks in the shanty town, the Colombians in crib-saloons that line the town's main street. The Colombian women are careful not to accept clients they fear may be diseased or, if suspicious, require clients to wear condoms. Their counterparts are apparently less cautious. Still another dimension is police treatment. If a Colombian prostitute reports a crime against her, her offender is likely to be jailed. By comparison, the complaining Dominican woman is ignored (Table 8-2).

Table 8-2
Comparison of Aruban Attitudes Toward Colombian and Dominican Prostitutes

Colombian Prostitutes	Dominican Prostitutes
Pretty	Plain
Soft-spoken	Noisy
Clean	Diseased
Single	Married
Gentle	Aggressive
Well-mannered	Crude
Compliant	Recalcitrant
See service as temporary means to rewarding end	Recognize servitude to be dead-end occupation

Drawn from Kalm 1975.

Florence Kalm has noted that a critical difference between prostitutes from the Caribbean and mainland South America is skin color. The Colombian, if not from the coast, is typically light-skinned, a mestizo; the Dominican is dark-skinned, a mulatto or a black. The Arubans, with Indian and white parentage, more closely resemble Colombians. In color Dominican prostitutes are similar to the West Indian and Guayanese imported laborers. In the Aruban mind the Dominican women and the foreign laborers coincide in other ways: they are both "noisy," "aggressive," and "recalcitrant." Yet, despite these similarities in word and treatment, apparently Arubans never voice their comparisons of Dominican and Colombian prostitutes in terms of color.

To note ascriptive parallels no more proves that racism exists than lack of reference to skin color denotes its absence. Thus, in a sense the broad question of racism in Aruban prostitution remains open and one is left more with questions than anything else. Are the voiced comparisons between dark-skinned, imported laborers and Dominican prostitutes really matters of coincidence? Are the Dominican prostitutes just what the Aruban men say they are, neither more nor less? Or could it be that the Dominican prostitutes arrive in Aruba with quite different personalities, but become crude, aggressive and otherwise unappealing because of the way they are treated? That is, perhaps the Arubans mistrust them because of their own preconceptions, with the result that with time and maltreatment the Dominican women acquire the characteristics attributed to them.

The Third Tier in American Theaters

Nonwhite skin has usually implied low social class. But age, physical attractiveness, background and opportunity are other determinants of social status on the prostitution ladder. Treatment based primarily on class is nicely illustrated in the nineteenth-century American theater where male demand for prostitutes and the laws of theater economics dictated that prostitutes be permitted, nay encouraged, to take their place near and among the cognoscenti. Though details of the American theater are of concern here, prostitutes were no less active in the theaters and music halls of nineteenth-century England and Scotland.[63]

In the fifty-year period from 1830 to 1880, lower-class prostitutes who entered the theater were required to occupy the third tier, the upper row above the dress and family circles.[64] Already widespread in the 1840s in cities such as New York, Boston, Chicago, St. Louis, Cincinnati and New Orleans, this "dark secret of the stage" was ignored in polite discussions by most of the age, despite the fact that the "assignment of prostitutes to one part of the theater had profound impact on theater design, theatrical economics, and on the extent to which theater was accepted and supported in the nineteenth century."[65]

Based fundamentally on economics, the general as well as the detailed patterns of discrimination had social, spatial and temporal components. Those confined to the third tier invariably came from the lower rungs of prostitution. They came to solicit men, to then return to the brothel for business. But for some, as in New York's Bowery Theater, place of solicitation and business consummation were the same. "They swarmed the galleries, using them not only for purposes of pickup, but also as places where their relations with unfinicky customers could be consummated."[66] In San Francisco where it is not known with certainty how third tiers were used, theaters were still famous for their "green rooms" (reception rooms) and private stalls that could be completely curtained off. That these areas may have been used for prostitution is attested to by their popularity and the fact that many stage girls and chorus actresses were part-time prostitutes.[67] Whatever happened in the third tier or the green rooms and private stalls, higher-class prostitutes could locate their clients through newspaper advertisements and agree to meet in the theater. They were able to circulate freely among respectable patrons of the theater.

Small-scale geography indicated that the low-class brothel boarders who frequented the theater were treated much like blacks in the South. The third tier contained its own bar, thereby precluding a mixing of types, if not intents. Theaters were built with a special side entrance for prostitutes and patrons of the third tier, though some customers might enter the segregated area from the other tiers later in the evening. Those who sat in the dress and family circles entered through the building front and used a central stairway. For a temporal twist of enterpreneurial ingenuity, the third tier was opened early, as much as two hours in advance of normal arrival time. Owners wanted prostitutes in the house, but they wanted them off the streets before the respectable classes arrived.

The planning and the extra building costs expended to provide for the theater-working prostitutes were economically motivated. To insure theater success, some managers gave free tickets to the women. A full house of prostitutes usually meant a full complement of men in search of pleasure. If, as occasionally happened, public pressure forced closing of the third tier, managers would later "redouble their solicitation of prostitutes."[68]

In spite of costly methods designed to please patrons and press, theater managers were eventually forced to dispense with the third tier. Occasionally they were unable to contain the activity as it spilled over into the rest of the theater. They were confronted by an influential clerical stand against the theater in general, and the problem that proximity of brothels to American stage houses was degrading to passing ladies. Too, they could not get broad-based support from theatergoers for their case. Managers found themselves in a dilemma. If the third tier remained open they would continue to be condemned in the press and to lose "respectable" patrons. Or so they were told. On the other hand, if the third tier were closed they faced financial ruin. Victorian America forced a choice. By the 1880s legitimate theaters in America no longer had a third tier. Many were also bankrupt.

Chapter 9 | Pimps and Predators

Pariah or Role Reversal?

Status as a criminal, blatant social injustices, extortion by keepers of the moral order, sexism, racism and ostracism from society all force prostitutes to seek solace where they can find it. Most—particularly street-walkers—have found pimps to be their axial pillar in their search for stability and orientation in a hostile world. In a classic study of prostitution in London three decades ago it was noted that of all the significant relationships among those involved with prostitution, "that of prostitute and ponce [rough equivalent of the North American pimp] is the really significant one, giving cohesion to an outlawed community."[1] To the extent that pimps exploit prostitutes the blame lies as much with society as with the individual. Society is at fault not only because moral and legal sanctions encourage women to seek help among social outcasts, but also because widespread oppression and discrimination against certain minorities have created environments which produce pimps. To be sure, pimping is like most institutions: once it becomes sufficiently widespread it thrives on its own inertia. Blacks become pimps not just because of exploitation or the opportunity to get back at whites, but also because they are familiar with the concepts of pimping in the black ghetto. Pimps there are heroes of a sort, role models to be emulated. Similar pressures operate on prostitutes: they want pimps because they need them, but they need them because there is peer pressure to have them.[2]

Pimps have been very much the rule rather than the exception. At the turn of this century Abraham Flexner estimated that 50 to 90 percent of prostitutes in European cities had them: the "bully" in London, the *souteneur* or *Alphonse* in France, the *Zuhälter* in Germany. Only 10 to 20 percent of the women in Paris and London did not have them.[3] Flexner was somewhat perplexed by the phenomenon, claiming that pimps treated their women brutally, took their money and provided no protection, least of all against the police. He believed that a "vestige of affection" was the main reason that prostitutes paid heavily to have them.[4]

The percentage of prostitutes having pimps in more recent years is as high as ever. Among New York City, San Francisco and Oakland streetwalkers, the figures may be 90 percent or more.[5] One estimate has 70 to 80 "bigtime'' pimps, all but one or two of whom are black, operating in New York City.[6] This does not include "coffee and cake" pimps or others who only have a single woman, make little money, or lack class among other pimps: "simple pimps," "chili pimps," "popcorn pimps," "cigarette pimps."[7] More than 100 black pimps may work in Vancouver.[8] Similar or larger figures are found elsewhere in cities of the industrialized West.[9]

In environments less oppressive than American streetscapes, fewer prostitutes have pimps.[10] Gabriel Vogliotti reckons that no more than 25 percent of women in Nevada's legal brothels have them.[11] Wayland Young believed that it was quite rare for London's prostitutes to have ponces.

> If she does, it is because she feels she needs someone to kick her out on the street at nightfall, to make sure she has the rent ready on rent day, to keep her off the bottle, to tell her what clothes she looks nice in and, perhaps most important of all, to help her see if she can't build up some sort of a sex life of her own.[12]

How accurate this observation was or whether it applied only to the period prior to 1959 when repression of streetwalking activity began is not clear.

Tempting as it may be to infer that illegality and repression alone are responsible for pimps, the institution of legal prostitution in West Germany illustrates that the issue is more complex. Barbara Yondorf ascertained that the number of prostitutes having pimps in West German cities ranged from 80 to 95 percent.[13] The reasons given by German authorities for this pattern vary. They include a need for protection from pimps and others, someone to represent them in quarrels with other prostitutes, and a person to turn to for personal help. In addition, "in a small but rather significant number of cases . . . so-called pimps are lovers, friends, or even husbands who 'manage the affairs' of their girlfriends or wives."[14] A major contrast with North America is that West German pimps rarely have a "stable" of women laboring for them.

There are further exceptions to easy generalizations that repression or illegality invites pimps onto the scene. According to one source most of Toronto's prostitutes are without pimps; the same may be true in Montreal.[15] But perhaps more significant than these exceptions are recent judgments that within the last decade in the United States some prostitutes, particularly young ones, have been working on their own in cities that traditionally have had very high percentages of pimps.[16]

Racial and ethnic composition of the pimp population has changed dramatically in the last century. In the 1880s the French "mac" was common.[17] By the early decades of this century many pimps came from the same white immigrant groups as many prostitutes, reflecting both their association with the women in ghettos and their own efforts to find their way in a seemingly hostile society. Ben Reitman knew some 300 pimps in Chicago and elsewhere during the 1920s and 1930s and contended that just over a third were black. Sixty were Italian, 47 Jewish, 26 Greek and 14 Polish. Another 44 he classified as "mixed." About one-third of the total were foreign-born.[18] No one since has had demographic data on such a large population. But all evidence indicates that with the possible exception of Las Vegas, better than 90 percent of pimps in the United States are black.[19] The picture is about the same in Great Britain.[20]

Pimping is a way of getting revenge on a white society that has dominated and figuratively castrated the black male. The pimp seeks retribution through reversing the "game." His white prostitutes are "tricks," exactly like the women's patrons who are the source of his income. In the *Black Mafia* Francis Ianni describes a scene in Harlem that reveals how pimps see the hierarchy of domination and its reversal.

> At the end of 125th Street rises the steel latticework of the Triborough Bridge. The El Dorado swooshes into the curved entrance ramp and pulls up at the toll booth. The attendant is engaged in conversation with his sergeant, who is picking up money. The attendant remarks loudly to the sergeant, "Do I charge this boy for a car, or is there a special rate for nigger whorehouses on wheels?" Since display is the essence of the player's life, Reggie is used to the hostility and harassment that his flaunting provokes in other men. He remains silent, unconcerned, pays his toll and pulls out. Once on the bridge, he simply says, "That nasty-mouthed motherfucker's paycheck be in my pocket Sunday morning."[21]

The roots of this attitude lie in the ghetto and in racism. "According to the players, black men make the best pimps because they have been tricked so long that when they 'flip over' and reverse the game, they can really get behind it with a vengeance."[22]

Since almost all big-city pimps are black many of the women who slave in their "stables" are black. But they prefer white prostitutes, not just because of the more direct link to their oppressors, but also for pragmatic considerations. White women go unnoticed more by cops, more frequently get a customer with "big money," are less likely to be challenged when entering hotels and encounter fewer problems in renting apartments. White prostitutes make a stronger commitment to pimps than do blacks. In covertly crossing the racial boundary they isolate themselves from other whites, in mind if not in fact. Pimps also benefit by receiving more respect than they might from a black woman, because the white woman is less familiar with the vulnerable points of black males in general, is unlikely to know their families or friends and has learned from the larger society to be careful about racial slurs.[23]

Pimps on both coasts often take upwards of 90 percent of the money that prostitutes earn.[24] And their demands are lordly. Gail Sheehy found that those in New York City were requiring prostitutes to bring in a minimum of $200 a night in the early 1970s.[25] A reporter several years later discovered that young girls recruited from Minneapolis were given a quota and not let back into their apartments at night until it was met.[26] They were required to toil six nights a week and might be beaten for not bringing in enough money.

Vancouver has French Canadian and Italian pimps in addition to blacks from the United States and the West Indies. While the blacks seem to resemble those across the border, white pimps—believed to have other sources of income—are usually more generous. Their prostitutes are only required to work five rather than six nights a week, and pimps may only take 50 percent of their income.[27]

The argot of the pimp world shows that the prostitute has long been regarded contemptuously by pimps: as property, as a lower form of life.[28] To those who take her money she has been perceived as a "dog," a "bitch," a "cow," a "shitkicker," and a "chick," "good only for pecking around in the dirt and for lays."[29] Even women deemed particularly valuable because of their ability to bring in money have been given animal appellations: "fox" or "mink" for a pretty, young woman and "stallion" for a tall, attractive prostitute who is a big earner.[30] But perhaps the term "stable," the collective for those who work for a pimp, in some ways is most revealing, for it presents "the image that women are like a herd of domesticated animals," a picture "clear and unmistakable."[31]

Pimps have little difficulty justifying what prostitutes receive for their money. One self-confessed drug addict, dope peddler and crap hustler, who acquired his first prostitute at 16, described the rationale:

> It's an important thing how a man carries himself in this element, in this environment. His conduct, the way he dresses, the way he carries himself, the way he conducts himself around people, around his own people. It's an important thing. He gains a certain amount of prestige. His woman wants to see him in a nice automobile, she wants to see him dressed nice. She wants to see him go into a place and pull out a roll of money and look good, because that makes *her* look good. It's her man, she represents him, that's *her*.[32]

Exploitation is as much psychological as economic. Many pimps are now "sweet macs,"[33] those who prefer to operate on the minds of prostitutes rather than on their bodies as has been true of violent "gorilla pimps."[34] Nearly a half century ago Reitman said that of the many pimps he knew the majority beat their women. "I have seen hundreds of whores with black eyes, cut lips, broken heads, bruised bodies that were acquired from their loving men."[35] Pimps still brutalize prostitutes, though apparently less frequently than in Reitman's days.[36]

Based on informal conversations and extended observations of 47 pimps and 21 prostitutes in a West coast nightclub, Lois Lee found that the contemporary "pimp game" is very much one of psychological control.[37] Using the "skull game"—unwritten manipulative strategies—susceptible women are "copped" and "turned out"—removed from the world of "straights." The psychological game of separating a woman from her past involves "flashing," "pratting," "charisma" and "cop fucking." Lee explains what they mean:

> "Flashing" is an eye catching style that involves the display of expensive clothes, car, jewelry, bankroll, etc. (all of which the pimp perceives as his "tools"), to induce the whore's attention. Once a woman's attention is drawn to the pimp, he then begins his "pratting" to pretend rejection in order to strengthen desire, ignoring her until she approaches him. He continues to "prat" her and moves into what he calls "charisma." Pimps achieve "charisma" by remaining a mystery, a puzzle and by not divulging any significant information. Once the pimp solicits a commitment that she will be "his woman," he then stages a scene for the "cop fuck." The commitment she offers the pimp may be in the form of money or a verbal commitment. . . . The "cop fuck" is the pimp's attempt to impress his newly copped woman with his sexual prowess.

One method of increasing the prostitute's social distance between "square society" and "the life" is to convince her that "straight" women are lazy, victimized, stupid, whereas prostitutes are smart and "hep." Another tactic, one that Lee ascertained to be quite common, was to move the newly "copped" prostitute away from a familiar environment, thereby increasing her dependence on him and cutting off outside support.

Control is also exerted by degrading the woman and forcing her to see that men come first in all things. A pimp will show off in the presence of others and may require a prostitute to give him "head" (fellatio) in a crowd. She is also taught to adore his body and bathe and preen him, all means of reminding the woman that her worth is less than his.

About the worst form of humiliation for a pimp is to be "georgied," to give himself sexually to a woman without being paid. It is important for pimps to see prostitutes just as clients are perceived—as "tricks." Iceberg Slim, author of the "Pimp Bible," made the case: "a pimp is really a whore who has reversed the game on whores. Be as sweet as the scratch, no sweeter, and always stick a whore for a bundle before you sex her. A whore ain't nothing but a trick to a pimp."[38]

Prostitutes are manipulated to see that the pimp's needs always take precedence, and that only by prostituting can they help him out of "pressing financial problems." Once the woman is working she is continually reminded of his definitions of adequate performance, and that if she does not bring in enough money they will not—together—be able to acquire a legitimate business somewhere in the indefinite future.

The "players" (as pimps often see themselves) investigated by Christina and Richard Milner in San Francisco in the early 1970s bear many resemblances to those studied by Lee. The Milners noted that "The Book" by which pimps play "the game" could be reduced to five commandments. The first two and most important are:

1. Man is Lord God. He shall have dominion over women and control them; also, he shall stand with his fellow men against any bitch who puts herself before man.
2. Thou shalt have no other gods before money, for money buys affection, respect, and acceptance.[39]

As they conclude, " 'The Book' provides a blueprint for a male-dominated society and a rationale for wrestling all control over males from women."[40]

Whether control is physical or psychological, the risks to pimps are few. Because laws against pimping exist almost everywhere and invariably involve stiff prison sentences, pimps rarely solicit for their women. On the street and in bars and other hustling spots, they do not publicly recognize those who fill their pockets.[41] In England where there is a distinction between pimps, who actively solicit customers, and ponces who live with prostitutes and do not hustle trade, pimps are rare and ponces common.[42]

With few exceptions, prostitutes do not report maltreatment from pimps to the police, nor will they testify against them even when pressured. Violence and emotional domination notwithstanding, ties between pimps and those who work for them are difficult to break. The cop is the enemy and pimps are not above threatening prostitutes with death if they consider turning them in. Their methods of intimidation are usually successful. In the entire state of California only 25 defendants were convicted of pimping or pandering in 1969, and only four of these were sent to prison.[43]

In spite of widespread recognition of economic and psychological exploitation, prostitutes and others have come to the defense of the pimp.[44] Jennifer James, who carried out a number of significant studies on streetwalkers in Seattle during the 1970s, believes that the pimp-prostitute relationship is little more than an exaggeration of male-female unions in the larger society.[45] In her discussions with prostitutes she found that women accepted the role reversal, and saw a number of advantages in having pimps. The primary reasons include his role as business manager, the protection, respect and status he provides and the feeling that someone cares. James discovered that the business aspect is most significant; prostitutes and pimps alike cite money as the principal reason for what they are doing. Nearly as important as economics is the protection and respect that pimps provide. Women without them are "outlaws," and second-class, abnormal denizens of the street. "Outlaws" are subject to abuse, whereas the "pimp's name is significant as a 'keep away' sign in the same way that a wedding ring traditionally has been."[46] Furthermore, the prostitute's status is directly related to that of her pimp. Indeed, a woman is defined by the man for whom she works, and will pay to work under him and gain the prestige that comes from doing so.

Status has another dimension that may work against the prostitute. Many pimps rate their "stable" women on the basis of how much cash they bring in. In Chicago a prostitute picked up by the cops will sometimes ask that her "stable" sister also be arrested so that the latter will not gain an advantage while she is in jail.[47]

A secondary set of advantages is emotional. The pimp is someone to love, someone whom the prostitute can feel good about helping and her main source of security. Despite the fact that her days and her work environment are populated with people, loneliness, alienation and insecurity are constant problems. In the subculture of prostitution the pimp is the best source of solutions.

Ironically, the main disadvantage that prostitutes perceive is having to give up their money. They are in business, but as minority shareholders without a vote on how the income is to be used. They also dislike the beatings they occasionally receive. Another negative factor cited is the loss of individuality and independence. They are constantly told when to work, how much money to bring in, how to behave, how to respect their pimp.

Although James recognizes that pimps use psychological coercion and that a prostitute "rarely settles down . . . and lives out the dream of the promised secure life together as husband and wife,"[48] she nevertheless concludes that "the satisfaction level appears to be at least as good as that of couples in the larger society."[49]

What is one to make of the picture presented by James, and the long and rather unequivocal history of how prostitutes are, in fact, treated by pimps? Although Jennifer James has done some of the most careful research in decades on prostitutes, her data for what she says about pimps are thin and just not up to par with her other findings. Furthermore, her liberal approach to prostitution in general seems to have blinded her to the reality of pimp behavior, of the very facts of the sexual inequality that she recognizes. Equally, James seems inattentive to the fact that prostitutes have been taught by pimps to see the rationale of what they are doing: prostitutes do not innovate their conceptions of right and wrong. It is, of course, possible that her findings in Seattle are rather unique, and even remotely possible that matters have changed much more substantially than anyone realizes. Neither evidence from New York City and elsewhere nor the studies of Lois Lee and the Milners on the west coast picture the pimp-prostitute nexus in benign terms.[50]

Perhaps judgments about the pimp-prostitute relationship should be set in the context of what might be in another social milieu, one different both for those who become pimps and those who are their victims. As Lois Lee has concluded, "For the prostitute, the pimp represents what she defines as a 'normal' relationship [and] he may be the only alternative in a society in which she receives only guilt and lack of acceptance."[51] Were social attitudes different, were the criminal justice system different, and were prostitutes given opportunities to see alternatives to what they now accept as normal, pimps would not be necessary or, at the very least, the relationship would be defined differently.

Cabdrivers as Pimps

Besides the state and those with the label of pimp, numerous others pimp prostitutes. Entrepreneurs who work in the garment industry, in broadcasting and a variety of service industries make prostitutes available to their clients in exchange for business.[52] Bartenders, bellhops and hotel detectives frequently demand 30 to 40 percent of prostitutes' fees just for directing customers to them or allowing a woman to sit on a bar stool or hustle in the bars and corridors of hotels.[53] Another predator with a rich history who charges extortionate rates is the cabdriver.

"Where's the action?" "Where are the girls?" "Where are things happening?" Such transparent innuendos are heard scores of times each week by cabdrivers all over the world. Although questions like these do not always imply that the inquiring male passenger is asking where to find prostitutes, often this is precisely the nature of the query. In New York City as many as one in ten males nightly might ask if no women are in the cab.[54] Cabdrivers' knowledge of cities, their widespread reputation as people who know where the "action" is, their low-class image and the very nature of prostitution laws, all contribute to the belief that they have information about the location and quality of prostitutes.

As elsewhere in the subculture of prostitution the role of those central to the activity is reflected in argot. "Cab," "cab joint" and "cab moll" are but a few of the terms once used in England and America to suggest connections among a transport mode, a job and a manner of conducting an illicit activity.[55] During the 1930s in the United States "cab joint" referred to a brothel, while "cab" had a similar connotation a century earlier in England. The widespread use of the term "cab" resulted from the brothel keeper's practice of securing a large share of clients through cabdrivers. Currency may also have derived from the occasional incidence of sex acts inside the cab. "Cab moll" denoted either a prostitute who frequently serviced customers in cabs or trains, or a madam who used cabdrivers to get business.

Cabdrivers have made the best of illegality, extracting as much from prostitutes, madams and patrons as the market would bear. Buffalo, New York was apparently typical of many North American cities in the 1930s. Drivers there got most of their income from taking men "down the line" (to the red-light district), where they received commissions on each customer. Some worked exclusively with one or two brothels, preferably the high-class ones, and might bring as many as ten clients a night.[56] Ben Reitman, a student of prostitution and house doctor for one of the largest houses in Chicago's South Side, claimed that the establishment specialized in "line loads" (taxicab customers). On a given evening he saw more than a dozen cabdrivers sitting in the parlor, waiting for their "line loads" and their $2 kickback on a $5 fee.[57]

Driver profits from prostitution have been considerable. In the third decade of this century a cabdriver might get one of the three dollars a customer paid the prostitute. Not surprisingly, when business was good at a house taxi drivers and their "chauffeur dates" often received a cool welcome from the madam.[58] Decades later those driving men to Galveston, Texas' brothels were still getting 25 percent for all business left at the front door.[59] Present-day Parisian and Amsterdam taxi drivers pocket about the same percentage.[60] Those who pimp for the American zone in Mexican border town red-light districts receive up to 40 percent of the fee paid the prostitute, and may also get a percentage of the drinks purchased.[61]

Occasionally, cabdrivers have some definite opinions about their importance and how much they ought to be paid for pimping. In the early 1950s at Formyle, Nevada (four miles from Las Vegas), some 50 or so drivers signed a petition against a large bordello. Unhappy with working conditions, one of their kind addressed his fellow pimps with the following words:

> We members of Teamsters Local 631 would like to call a special meeting and have a vote on subjects mentioned about Formyle. It seems that at different times we have had some union members working there. We recommend that all men have a paid up union card. It seems that we are helping to build a business there which isn't appreciated. We ask that the house use one price for every 15 minutes or whatever is suitable, whether he comes in a cab or not. If he does come in a cab the driver gets $1 out of every $6 spent. If a driver sells the customer in the beginning and he ever goes out in a private car the driver is ruined forever in getting a so-called "kelly". . . . Several drivers have had people that would make regular customers but after one or two trips they wind up with no "kelly."[62]

The biggest paycheck of all for cabdrivers comes when they are also the prostitute's pimp. A self-confessed pimp to homosexuals, Kenneth Marlowe, who also worked for a while behind the desk in a female brothel, noted that at one time a driver working in New Orleans carefully directed his fares to a particular woman. The ignorant customer did not know that the prostitute just happened to be his wife. According to Marlowe, husband and wife together collected 80 percent of the total bill.[63]

Several states and cities have laws directed specifically at cabdrivers—laws involving fines, jail sentences and suspension of licenses.[64] Nevertheless, some city governments have appreciated the futility of trying to circumscribe taxi drivers. Galveston used to employ the age-old approach to reducing visible immorality to an acceptable level by forbidding soliciting from taxis along the city's main streets. Presumably, working the sidestreets was permissible.[65]

Stiff penalties have kept many cabdrivers away from prostitution. For example, those in St. Louis were reluctant to take men to prostitutes in the late 1960s.[66] At that time the city was enforcing a law that carried a $500 fine, a

2-to-20 year prison sentence and loss of license. Policemen sometimes posed as "liners" (clients) to enforce the law. Dispatchers and managers of cab companies normally involved in the activity stayed away. Yet despite the risks the reputation of some cab companies indicated that their drivers could be persuaded, for a fee, to provide information on the whereabouts of prostitutes. Whatever they got in the way of a tip from a "liner" was handsomely buttressed by a 50 percent commission from the woman. Some preferred to confine their business to "use taxes," the amount charged a customer for having sex in the taxi. The male usually paid after receiving a hint that his indiscretion could be reported to the police. In addition to these forms of business, St. Louis cabdrivers had personal service contracts with the prostitutes they knew, at a 50 percent discount.

Montreal's "hustler cabbies" of the 1950s did not want any misunderstanding in view of their precarious existence with the city's cops. They made it abundantly clear to "flyers" that they wanted money for their "girl tips," notwithstanding that they also received a kickback from prostitutes.[67] To avoid serious problems with the Montreal police, women associated with cabdrivers employed a telephone and rendezvous system. If a male proved he was genuinely interested in available services the driver made a telephone call to a prostitute or her friend, gave his license plate number and agreed to park on a designated street. The prostitute drove by, looked over the prospective customer, comparing him with her mental book of vice squad members, joined those who passed her test and then was driven to a hotel. Enterprising taxi drivers might obtain as many as three or four clients a night using this method. In addition to this source of income the city's "hustler cabbies" also cheated ignorant sailors and out-of-towners. When foreigners indicated they were new to the city and wanted a prostitute the cabdriver drove gullible "flyers" to the most distant club.

Exploitation in the Housing Market

People of marginal social status have always been at a disadvantage in utilizing elements of the landscape. Often they cannot get access to housing and when they do they pay more than others for comparable accommodation. To a striking degree property used for illegal or immoral purposes is like that made available to most low-income or immigrant people. The excess rental profits made from these groups usually accrue not only to those with economic and social power but also to the very people who legislate against minorities and the morally outcast. Predators in the housing market have an obvious interest in keeping prostitution illegal. The clearer the distinction between moral and immoral, legal and illegal behavior, the higher the rent that can be extracted.[68]

The British Wolfenden Report on prostitution and homosexuality referred to slumlords of prostitution property as "flat farmers," because they charged their tenants such exorbitant rents. The weekly rate might be as high as 20 times the amount legally permitted. To avoid detection British "flat farmers" kept a false set of books showing only the maximum amount allowable by law.[69]

Greed breeds strategems to fit the occasion. To get more money some flat farmers also demanded non-returnable key deposits and payment in advance. Shortly after a prostitute took up residence in a flat, her landlord told her to leave. As an incentive she was informed that the rent was about to be raised by 50 percent or more. If the woman protested the landlord simply told her that he knew she was a prostitute, that it was for this reason she must leave, and that the court would uphold him on the matter.[70]

Contemporary London prostitutes find themselves enmeshed in an exploitation game of which high rents form only a part. They pay 50 pounds or more for a bed and sparsely furnished room; in addition, they hand over a percentage of their gross income, and they also implicitly promise to sexually service the landlord for the asking. In one week a prostitute might gross upwards of 400 pounds servicing 50 or more customers, only to find that her net after expenses leaves her with about an eighth of this amount.[71]

Gail Sheehy has drawn attention to the profits to be made in "trick pads" in New York City's "Hell's Bedroom," the prostitution streetscape centered on Times Square. One of the busiest fleabag hotels was making upwards of $150,000 a year from streetwalkers and their clients in the early 1970s.[72] The hotel—if it can be called such—had as many as 75 prostitutes working out of it, "each one using a bed eight or ten times [a day]. Each time the John donates $20 to her and $10 to the hotel."[73] Did the owner have ties at city hall? Apparently not. He managed to collect over 80 prostitution misdemeanor arrests and some 30 convictions in one 18-month period. Yet he remained in business, apparently with no greater concerns than how to acquire leases on other hotels to be used for the same purpose, or how to keep black prostitutes out of his bedrooms. He believed they mugged and robbed clients in his "clean" hotel.

Property owners at all times and places fit the general patterns described for London and New York City.[74] It was generally agreed that in San Francisco during the first decades of this century those who held real estate used for prostitution made the greatest fortunes. In a single year owners could recover the cost of their investment and much more. A collection of cribs in the Empire House paid over $125,000 a year on an investment of $8,000.[75] Another "bull-pen" in Reno, a horseshoe-shaped building that contained scores of continuously occupied cribs, made more than half a million dollars a year in rental fees, on an initial building cost of $20,000.[76]

In the prairie provinces of Canada at the turn of the century most frontier towns had segregated districts. As the towns grew the districts were moved in response to money, residential tastes and real estate dealer demands. One example of profits to be made through foreknowledge of relocation occurred in Winnipeg in 1909 when madams and boarders were forced to resettle at Point Douglas near the Red River. James Gray contends that one real estate agent who preceded the new owners into the area bought up most of the houses for prices ranging from $2,500 to $5,000. Shortly thereafter he resold them to madams for about $8,000 apiece. Once others became apprised of the imminent move, housing prices and rentals shot up dramatically. In the new district madams were charged seven times what an ordinary tenant paid for the same occupancy.[77]

At the end of the nineteenth century rooms used for prostitution in Toronto commanded much higher than normal rents. Farther east, in a French milieu, the pattern was similar. In Montreal during the early 1920s houses for poor families cost $65 to $75 a month to lease; if used as a brothel the figure rose to $400 or $500.[78]

In one respect madams differ from landlords only in their claim that they provide a number of valuable services in addition to a place for prostitutes to board and service clients, and that they are simply passing on the costs of housing and graft. Substantial as these assertions may be, their fees, almost universally 50 percent of what the customer pays, can only be described as predatory.[79]

Some madams or owners cannot claim to be offering much more than a collection of bedrooms. In Nevada's largest brothel, the "assembly-line" "Mustang Bridge Ranch" near Reno, the owner takes the position that he is a landlord and not an employer. The distinction is maintained to avoid being charged with pimping. Prostitutes in his house are supposed to set their own prices and take care of all financial matters. In fact, they do not do so. At the end of each day women who have made at least $50—which most have—are charged 50 percent of their gross income for room and board.[80]

When prostitutes have the opportunity to work in indoor settings without madams they have found it to their liking. In the Eros Centers of West Germany, multi-storied brothels with separate rooms for each woman, owners were charging prostitutes $25 to $45 a day for room rental in the early 1970s. Despite such rates many were happy with the arrangement. Whereas previously some were paying as much as 80 percent to madams, they are now keeping a comparable figure for themselves.[81]

Some prostitutes are neither willing to pay predatory rents nor lose business because their customers will not bear the room expense in addition to the woman's fee. They transact business in parks, taxi cabs, hallways, anywhere that seems convenient. "Come for a taxi-ride, dearie," was heard in London almost as frequently as "Come to my flat, luv" in the early 1950s.[82] Another reason for not using hotels or a room is that servicing someone in a car, sometimes in a park, is less demanding since an awkward position often means incomplete penetration.[83]

At times scarcity rather than price has been the issue. In Berlin during the Second World War streetwalkers found it virtually impossible to get a hotel room for even a couple of hours without first obtaining a permit from the police. Prostitute and client often had to pose as husband and wife. But even this did not always help.[84] Marie-Therese, a French prostitute who worked as a streetwalker in Berlin, vividly described how difficult it was for German women: "They get themselves fucked standing against any old wall all the time. When you go out in the morning you trip over a dozen or two used rubbers."[85]

Post-revolutionary Russia, where Marxist theory predicted that prostitution would disappear, also had housing problems that directly affected prostitutes. Many were forced to carry on their trade

> in the boulevards, in railway carriages or trucks, in dark corners of the stations, and in the entrances to better-class houses which they call *paradniki* in their jargon . . . even in taxis, literally, therefore, on the streets, which are the sole shelter because they have no abode.[86]

In recent years Parisian streetwalkers have jingled keys as they stood in doorways and alleys. The noise was less a solicitation than a way of telling males that the noise maker had an apartment. Rooms have become scarce since the police have closed small hotels that cater to prostitutes, and landlords have begun to put up expensive apartment buildings. Those without keys to rattle, particularly low-class women in *Pigalle* and *St. Denis*, have taken their clients to parks and into alleys.

Low-class or minority streetwalkers have the most difficult time renting places to do business. In the 1970s black prostitutes working in London were so discriminated against in housing, and so frustrated, that they turned to stealing from their clients. After receiving money "out front" they sent their customers off to buy contraceptives, and then disappeared.

Brothels and streetwalker "trick pads" are commonly owned by real estate dealers, bankers and other "respectable" members of the community. Properties in the Barbary Coast and Chicago's Levee used for prostitution were owned by "very prominent citizens"—businessmen and city officials. While prostitutes were harassed and arrested and madams paid graft, no effort was made to prosecute the property owners or their agents.[87] Real estate dealers in Galveston's large red-light district in the late 1920s controlled the bulk of the property. For obvious reasons, owners did not wish to be included in the city's business directory. But among those listed were three directly connected with the real estate business and four who were respectable entrepreneurs.[88] Others included a barber, a fireman, a police officer and a guard who worked for the United States customs service. A number of San Francisco's bordellos were owned by banks, real estate groups and title insurance companies in the late 1930s.[89]

Many states have made laws prohibiting the renting of rooms to prostitutes. But since the propertied class and the legislative process tend to be intimately intertwined, profiteering landlords managed to find protection in legislative riders. They can be convicted only if it can be proven that they possess knowledge of how their holdings are put to use. With such large returns on capital it is only logical that landlords wish to maintain the status quo. At the turn of the century a Wisconsin vice commission found that not only were state banks loaning money for the construction or purchase of brothels but when attempts were made to close them they were opposed.[90]

Portland, Oregon in 1913 enacted a so-called "tin plate" ordinance that required anyone owning a business used by prostitutes to prominently display a sign indicating the name and address of the owner. One rationale behind the ordinance was the belief that it would make landlords and entrepreneurs more hesitant about permitting prostitutes on premises. The law had little effect and attempts to institute it elsewhere failed. "Tin plate" legislation was killed in New York City by real estate interests who argued that it went "to too great an extreme in an attempt to control private business."[91]

Respectable citizens with financial interests in property used for prostitution try hard to avoid identification with their tainted investments. Some landlords in New York City at the turn of the century protected themselves at the expense of their wives. For example, a wife handling daily operations was expected by her husband to take full blame in the event of prosecution.[92] Other owners, not wanting to lose their profits, drew up sublease agreements so that the property could continue in use should there be a successful prosecution. Still another approach was for an owner or his agent to lease empty apartments to a janitor who then sublet them to others. Many gladly joined in, knowing that high rents would easily fill pockets all the way down the line.

The involvement of those with money and power in the prostitution housing market continues. Again it is Gail Sheehy who has highlighted the issue.[93] While few of stature in New York City wanted to talk to her about the "trick pad" business in Times Square she nevertheless discovered that owners included several Park Avenue banks, members of the city's most prestigious law firms, some of the largest tax-paying property owners in Manhattan, and others: "immaculate East Side WASPs, a prominent Great Neck heart surgeon, bona fide members of The Association for Better New York and the mayor's own Times Square Development Council."[94]

Chapter 10 | Survival in the Streetscape

To be successful, to survive in the illegal and immoral landscape the street-walker learns, elaborates upon and refines a range of stratagems. She must know the language and symbols of the streetscape, when to solicit and when to be patient, when to form coalitions, when to lay claims to territory, who she can trust or must distrust. The nature and mix of stratagems vary considerably from one milieu to another: some are similar in both legal and illegal environments, others differ among individuals and places. Whatever, with each newspaper article on street "whoring," and with each small change in court decisions or repressive measures, street perceptions change, streetwalkers adapt, reinvent, and find ways to make it in the streetscape.

Markers in the Immoral Landscape

To customers, cops, the state and those who complain or informally comment on the immoral landscape of the prostitute, appearance is a common coin for identifying habitués and geographical boundaries. Building on fact and fiction, prostitutes have used clothing and makeup to advantage in soliciting, even to the point of signaling and dictating fashion.[1]

Roman courtesans were distinguished from their lower-class counterparts by jewelry. By Roman law streetwalkers were not allowed the privilege of bejeweled trimmings. Nor, for that matter, were they permitted to dress in ways that blurred the distinction between prostitutes and "honest women." The landscape markings of Roman times were sharper than they are today. Though not always observed, Roman law proscribed in great detail that the prostitute could not wear the chaste *stola* that hides the body, or the *vitta* with which Roman ladies bound their hair. Shoes and purple robes were likewise forbidden, while dyed red or yellow hair and flowery dresses were required. Like kinds of rules and regulations were common throughout the Middle Ages. The Council of Milan in the sixteenth century forbade ornaments of gold or silver on prostitutes, and Toulouse required white scarfs and ribbons or cords on one arm as distinguishing emblems.[2] As late as 1885 Denver's town council required its "soiled doves" to wear yellow ribbons.

The twentieth-century American prostitute has had her own set of emblems. At the turn of the century she wore abbreviated dresses, had bobbed hair and stood out with rouged face and lips. Bleached hair was a means of recognition in the 1930s. In the 1940s streaking of hair in the front was something of a badge. And until the late 1950s colored stockings were markers that distinguished respectable women from prostitutes.[3]

Prostitution and the use of cosmetics have been associated, in particular, with the popular idea that face-painting leads to or indicates promiscuity. Makeup and trickery also go together. The Latin term *fucus* originally meant red dye, rouge or false color. It also means pretense, disguise and deceit.[4] Lips emphasized with lipstick, a practice that may have originated with prostitutes in the Middle East to suggest the vulva or specialization in oral stimulation, have been common among prostitutes.[5] They constitute a lie of sorts. In the West a prostitute's lips are usually off-limits and not included in the price of services. Kissing is reserved for boyfriends, husbands and pimps.

The use of exaggerated colors is also common, and is sometimes functional, sometimes not.

> It is strange how grey the night is. Colour and life cease to have any relationship. Most of the girls [in London's Piccadilly] wear bright clothes and heavy make-up, but purposelessly, for the vivid primal reds and blues, yellows, purples, and greens they choose are reduced to a dull and ineffective monotone, lifeless as a shadow. The only true colours are those of the brightly illuminated cars in the showroom windows, shiny and jewel-hard, streaked with chrome, pampered with leopard or fine, soft leather. I wear a saffron topaz ring, but as I look at it now it is glasslike, no more yellow than a splinter from a broken milk bottle.[6]

Women of the street frequently underdress in winter.[7] "We . . . must either muffle to the eyebrows, which is not particularly attractive, or hope that our frosty faces and hands will not detract from the appeal of our underclad, but at least visible, figures."[8] Rather than dress up too much, many a prostitute would prefer to alter her microgeography. In Italy, "campfire girls" and "fireflies" stand around bonfires in winter, waiting for men to approach.

In Latin America streetwalkers more obviously stand out from the local population than is true in North America or Western Europe. Garish eye and facial makeup, painted nails, tight dresses and blouses, dresses shorter than normal and sweaters lighter than usual for winter temperatures indicate the commerce of a neighborhood. The sharpest contrast is that between the young prostitute and the respected *patrona*; older streetwalkers blur distinctions between the public and the profane. When young prostitutes in interior Mexican cities became obsessed with pants before they were common dress, those near retirement stayed with the *uso general* of dresses.[9]

Appearances are a rough index of price, a suggestion of what kind of business may be transacted and of how much time the prostitute will spend with her customer. In London in the 1930s a streetwalker noted that:

> They deliberately deck themselves out in clothes that hall-mark them for what they are. Their three-inch-heel shoes, their shiny stockings, their ankle bracelets, their tiers of fox furs round the shoulders, come close to being a uniform. They need their article to be labelled if they are to have the courage to ask its price.[10]

Ten years later in London the emphasis was somewhat different and the relative asking price not so high but the attention to the right clothing was still evident.

> At night I always wear four-tiered, platform-soled shoes (that's why I'm wearing flatties now to rest my feet) and nylons. Some like fine silk stockings but I prefer nylons.[11]

Inappropriate dress evokes surprises from street denizens, perhaps deprecatory inquiries. "You're wearing flat 'eels. Are you Lesbian?"[12]

The costumes of the street have important deceptive functions: prostitutes want to appear younger than their actual age, blond when they are brunettes, French when English. English prostitutes, and others too, have made special efforts to appear French to capitalize on a common Western belief that French women are sexier, less inhibited and more attractive.[13] Wig and costume changes are meant to deceive policemen and cheated clients who may return to the streets seeking revenge.[14] For similar reasons street names—Star, Annie, Lil—have short lives.

Soliciting and Negotiating

The usual street encounter between prostitute and client is charged, an atmosphere of suspicion, indecision, comparison and evaluation. A streetwalker who worked New York's West Side between 47th and 49th Streets for nearly five years describes the situation.

> I will stand on the street, you know, and there's other girls around, and we'll be watching a dude come by. And he will walk back and forth, back and forth. Just running those eyes over you, see. Making up his mind. Trying to make up his mind who he likes, see. Now, we will be sizing him up at the same time. Is he police? Is he cheap? Is he a sporting guy? And do we know him? Around 47th Street you see a lot of dudes from out of town, but you also see a lot of them that come back time after time. Maybe they pick a different girl every time, but they keep coming back, and some of 'em you get to recognize.[15]

A decision is made to pursue the prey. A finger crooks toward the potential customer, the body postures to attract attention, and then the prostitute says, "How about some company?" or "Hello, lonesome, are you a stranger in the city?" Not all women solicit verbally, or need to do so. Mutually recognized motives may coagulate quickly and lead directly to a discussion of terms.

In repressive environments, where the competition is not that great, women wait for males to approach. Many fear and some are obsessed with the thought that all men are potential vice squad members. Jennifer James describes a typical customer-prostitute interaction.

> The man approached two women at 11:50 p.m. on a corner within one of the city's areas of prostitution (recognized as such by the police and the courts as well as by prostitutes and their customers). He initiated the conversation by asking the women where he could find prostitutes in the city, adding that he was in the Navy. One of the women asked to see his I.D., and he showed them something identifying himself as a Navy man. He then asked the women what the local rates for prostitutes were. Instead of naming a price, the women asked him how much money he had to spend. The man said he had $50, and the women suggested that he take them to a house, saying that they would take what was left of the $50 after he had paid for the room. The man asked what he would get for his money; the women replied by asking what he wanted. He requested . . . "half-and-half" (fellatio and intercourse), to which the women agreed. With the bargaining completed, the women instructed their customer to walk ahead of them to his car, so they wouldn't be seen together if any police happened by.[16]

In cities like Hamilton, Dayton and Cincinnati, Ohio teenage prostitutes sometimes as young as thirteen and fourteen operate by working the noon hour in front of restaurants and department stores. They call to an exiting male, "Nooner, baby?" A man accepts and a taxi waiting nearby takes them to a hotel. Drivers and girls have arrangements whereby the former receive personalized services a couple of times a week. The cabdriver provides transportation and imagined, or perhaps real, protection. Some customers believe the taxi driver is a pimp.[17]

Occasionally streetwalkers solicit by strolling past a customer, smiling suggestively and continuing on without looking back. Then they may pause at a store window to follow the movements of the intended prey, at the same time looking for a convenient place to stop and hustle should he follow.[18] In Rome, along the *Via Veneto*, a man may find himself walking behind a pimp and three or four prostitutes. One woman will drop back to join the male and begin negotiations. If she is unsuccessful she will let another woman attempt to get the customer interested.[19] One class of high-class Parisian streetwalkers of the 1940s was known as *tapins* ("tappers"), so-called because of the way they tapped their heels on the pavement. Were it not for this distinctive feature little might have associated them with prostitution.

Where repression is strong prostitutes walk a lot, especially those who are young and quickly draw suspicious glances from the vice squad. Walking cuts down on the possibility of arrests,[20] as it is an effective method of reducing visibility. The logical extension of foot mobility is use of a car.

The utility of motorized transport has never been lost sight of by prostitutes, either as a means of doing business or avoiding arrest. Some of the earliest automobiles used by prostitutes were known as "rolling road-houses," road-houses being bars and dance halls on the outskirts of cities where prostitutes congregated.[21] Women who solicit from cars in Great Britain, Australia and South Africa are called "kerb-crawlers."[22] At one point in the early 1960s automobiles with left-hand drives were in heavy demand from rental agencies because they made curb soliciting easier.[23] Brussel's prostitutes sit in modern sports cars with the light on and read or knit while waiting for a solicitous male.

"Car tricks" are common enough to be part of the vocabulary of the street.[24] During the 1960s French prostitutes would pick up men at a traffic light, drive to a quiet street, perform fellatio and then return quickly to their beat.[25] Some cars were allegedly outfitted with convertible back seats that served as beds.

The award for ingenuity may well belong to Australia's "commercial truck prostitutes" of the early 1960s.[26] Allegedly, underworld bosses purchased fleets of trucks, put respectable business tags on them, outfitted them with beds and enticing bedroom accouterments and even installed warning systems. A male was then employed to drive a truck to designated rendezvous points to which streetwise taxi drivers brought clients.

In a number of English-speaking countries men frequently solicit from cars.[27] They make offers as they slowly drive by a strolling prostitute, they park and wait for the women to pass, they switch their headlights on and off if the women are some distance away, and they use their horns if their glances and their words are ignored. New York City's customer-initiated "block parties" involve the male picking up a streetwalker, circling around the block a number of times while she performs fellatio and then paying her for time spent or blocks circled. While the use of customers' automobiles eliminates the motel cost and often lessens the time between one job and another, not all women like car tricks. They lose the protection afforded by a known environment of a neighborhood or frequently used "trick pad," and if driven some distance they lose rather than gain street time.

Even in the most repressive of environments some women do not consider moving from a favored spot. They hustle from doorways, near hotel entrances, at select locations where male traffic is heavy, visibility is low or escape is easy. Some hotel prostitutes station themselves near the women's washroom so they can quickly disappear when police approach.[28] A favorite spot for Times Square streetwalkers in 1971 was a construction site on Eighth Avenue. A rough tunnel of some thirty or forty feet extended over the sidewalk, permitting six or seven women to solicit out of the line of vision of undercover cops.[29]

When a male shows interest the prostitute may seek to determine where he is staying. If he claims to be in a hotel she may insist on seeing the room key and demand to see personal identification. She may pointedly inquire about occupational status, asking, "Are you a cop?"[30]

In New Orleans, the prostitute may take her potential client on a "Bourbon Street parade."[31] After meeting an out-of-town customer in a bar or club she begins by establishing details about his hometown, the hotel where he claims to be staying, his reasons for being in New Orleans. If suspicious she might excuse herself for a trip to the ladies' room to call the hotel to verify his story. Alternatively, she may suggest they go for a walk past prearranged check points. The first stop might be a friendly cabdriver; if the male is a known vice squad cop he will let her know. Another check point may be a hot dog vendor. Like the cabdriver, he remembers—for a price—who is friend and who is foe. If the prostitute still has doubts she may ask for a drink in a nearby bar. When a bartender gives the signal to "cool it," perhaps putting an ice cube in her drink, the woman politely excuses herself to make a "forgotten" call—never to return.

Prostitutes in the French Quarter participate in effective information networks, just as they do elsewhere.[32] More than a quarter-century ago South African streetwalkers kept notebooks on the Immorality Squad; they contained names and details on appearance and models and colors of police cars. The women made arrangements among themselves to exchange and update information.[33] In all these cases, predators and parasites who cooperated got trade, a percentage of the service fee, and sometimes personal service kickbacks.

Besides pooling knowledge on undercover cops, streetwalkers often cooperate in other ways. They work in groups of two or more: for protection from muggers, perceived "legitimacy" in numbers, force in protecting soliciting territories, pricing and other dealings with clients.[34] When a customer chooses a woman she will suggest that her friend accompany them; they can have a "party" or "double trick" as the women may describe it, the pleasure of two women at the same time.[35] But, as a New York City streetwalker has explained, there is more to it than a simple *ménage a trois*.

> A guy won't spend fifty apiece. He might spend thirty or forty. But for ten or twenty dollars more, he gets another girl. The guy can still only go one time. One girl frenches and the other fucks. We're both cutting our money, but the guy is excited and comes quicker. You can also steal from him. If there's a fight, two girls can win. If your stomach hurts, or you've got your period, it's better to work with another girl. So you french and I fuck. Next week, I may have my period and I do the frenching. That's just if we're working together on a trick.[36]

For some women the ideal situation arises when the client is prominent, from another city, or at a convention representing an important religious or business group. The good citizen away on business and out for a "fling with the boys" is a prime candidate for robbery. Gail Sheehy has described a scene in New York City's Belmont Plaza Hotel. Once the threesome was inside a room one prostitute would tell the customer to take a shower, adding, "sweetie, then we'll do you like you never been done before."

> While he was panting his fantasies under the hot spigot, the pair would split. His clothes went down the air shaft and his wallet went with them because, as anyone knows, an Iowa Shriner is too moral a man to make a scene in the altogether. The wallet would be fat with cash and a wad of credit cards.[37]

Streetwalkers may cooperate among themselves by agreeing not to provide services below a minimum price. Those who undercut their street colleagues encourage wrath, perhaps reprisal.[38] Occasionally the women band together when their market or profits are threatened in other ways. In Fresno, one of northern California's major prostitution areas because of its location on a major trucking route, truckers agreed that no prostitute would be paid more than ten dollars. In reaction the women picketed the truck stops, arguing that "price fixing" was "in restraint of fair trade."[39]

Streetwalkers are often fine-tuned to the rhythmic activities of the vice squad. After the English "meatwagon"[40] or the New York City "pussy brigade"—as the vice squad is referred to by other cops[41]—make their usual nightly rounds, solicitations often increase noticeably. Some of the most intense hustling occurs during the thirty-minute change of guard in late afternoon.[42] Policemen do not like to make an arrest near the end of their shift; arrests mean time-consuming paperwork without overtime pay. In Jalapa, Mexico streetwalkers normally hit the streets between four and five P.M. and work until 11 P.M. before returning home or going to a brothel for extra late-night trade. Some, however, do not enter the avenues until early evening after the frequent rounds made by patrols between five and seven P.M.[43]

A few women show little concern for cautionary strategies. They verbally accost potential clients, sometimes so indiscriminately as to include couples.[44] Verbal barrages may be sprinkled with prices that decrease as the prospective client gets further from the soliciting prostitute. Often the most blatant and aggressive examples occur in port cities, where women pinch and grab at passing men. Gail Sheehy has recorded the case of a few New York City streetwalkers who stabbed and burned with acid men who ignored them.[45] Their behavior may in part be conditioned. Some men enjoy negotiating with prostitutes and then insulting them.

Caution is necessary because an arrest means lost "trick money," a "nut" or quota that cannot be met, and an unhappy pimp. For a good hustler an arrest costs $200 or more for each night not on the streets. Caution is necessary in an English city because a warning citation means the time is that much closer when it will be imperative to move elsewhere to avoid a fine or jail. Getting picked by New York City's "pussy posse" or

Chicago's "whore wagons" or Vancouver's "pigs" and "bulls" has other meanings: chauvenistic indignities at the precinct station, tenure in a dank tank where sweat, sweet perfumes and stale urine mix, and unjust venereal disease examinations. Treatment is often richly sprinkled with law-enforcement cynicism: "It's just picking up the cunt, bringing it in, and letting it go loose again."[46]

Mixing Environments and Stratagems

Besides the solitary pavement, prostitutes hustle in bars, cafes, "grindie" theaters, around shipping docks and trucking stops. They get business through the telephone, referrals from colleagues and CB radios. Some women use but a few of the stratagems and environments available to them; many mix and diversify their options. Choice of work place and method of soliciting are based on perceived short-term advantage: money to be made, inclement weather, the likelihood of arrest. Streetwalkers in London during the late 1940s mixed public soliciting with privately arranged meetings. This was "the professional pattern for nearly all prostitutes, from the highest to the lowest."[47] Their aim was to establish a regular clientele through street work and return only to the streetscape as they lost their regulars or needed more business.

In San Francisco's North Beach prostitutes take seats near a bar entrance, sometimes sitting at the same table every night. They choose locations that facilitate their ability to spot vice squad and customers, and their locational predictability helps return business.[48] Too, their pimps can sit in the same bar and watch their behavior, calculate the money their stable women are making and brag to one another about what great men they are in exploiting women. All this can be done while pimps are spatially separated from prostitutes, allowing them to avoid arrest when their women are apprehended (Figure 10-1).

Experience with the police begets a multitude of indoor adaptations. Some prostitutes wait in cafes for a telephone call from their pimps who provide them with appointments.[49] An erstwhile New York City stratagem was for a prostitute to roost with a crossword puzzle. When approached by a male she asked him how much he was willing to pay. He bid by defacing the puzzle; she marred it until the bid price was acceptable.[50] More than 30 years ago a South African variant for part-time prostitutes involved a customer leaving money and a slip of paper with his name and address at a cafe table. The tea or lunchtime waitress noted the particulars and then met him when she got off work.[51]

One club in Vancouver, British Columbia has a reputation that extends throughout Canada.[52] Two types of prostitutes work there, those with black pimps and those with white ones. Women without pimps who attempt to work in the club are forced out by other prostitutes or their pimps, or they are recruited. Tables in the club are reserved for prostitutes on two floor

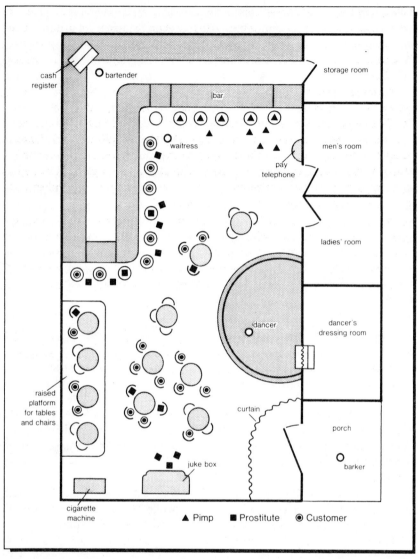

Figure 10-1 A Bar in San Francisco
Adapted from Milner and Milner 1973:21.

levels. The women must pay a cover charge to enter, a tip to the doorman and a fee for the table—extra if the table is a good one. If they return to the club after scoring with a customer prostitutes have to pay another door charge, and double for a table. The maître d' also demands kickbacks for clients referred or for use of a back room for oral sex. In return for business and fees the club reciprocates by announcing over the public address system when cops are coming—using a code name, and pages prostitutes for telephone calls when they begin hustling undercover cops. That the club was a good place for soliciting and that it profited from the presence of prostitutes is attested by its annual door revenues of $185,000 a year in the mid-1970s.[53]

Burlesque houses, when they existed, were favorite solicitation sites for pimps and streetwalkers.[54] They have been replaced by adult book stores, XXXX-rated theaters or pornographic movie houses justly designated as "grindies." Skid-rowers, the necessitous and the friendless of all classes in search of second-hand sex thrills come to these wretched, urine-permeated establishments to spend naked afternoons and hopeless nights. Ticket prices are outrageous and the misguided patron sees no more than dulled color strips of people in nude camps, "sex movies" with no plots, little or no dialogue and perhaps not even the sex they came to see. Sometimes low-class streetwalkers, particularly those inexperienced in the ways of the street, invade the grindies hunting for customers or tarrying outside until they exit. Their successes are checkered because the debauched denizens of the immoral landscape cannot bear the going tariff; a hand must proxy. But there are always takers, and some take anything.

> Guys come out hot and bothered and ready for anything, and I tell them to try me because old stuff knows more than young stuff does, and before they say yes or no . . . I take them past the trick store for a laugh to break the ice and I say, "What do you want to do, go into a hall some place and save three bucks or get a real bed in a hotel?"[55]

Using the landscape to advantage is not a recent ploy. Roman prostitutes often gathered near the Circus Maximus to solicit men as they returned from the games. Whether fact or fiction, it was believed that the spectators had been sexually aroused "by the gladiatorial shows, the mutilations by and of wild animals."[56]

Streetwalkers in port cities have often solicited on ships. In England in the early nineteenth century sailors often had to stay on board, but women were allowed to join them in numbers proportional to the men's good behavior.[57] London after World War II was a different matter. Prostitutes hustling along the docks might engage the assistance of a seaman or laborer to get them on board a newly arrived ship where they could solicit in the corridors or at cabin doors. Some were reckless enough to spend an entire night aboard, knowing that they faced the prospect of being at sea by morning.[58]

A hustling niche of relatively recent vintage is the truck stop. "Pavement princesses," as the women are known, buy CB radios and make waves with suggestive identification codes such as "Cat Lady," "Eager Beaver" and "Blue Bird." For the eager truckers a meeting place is quickly and conveniently arranged. On the national CB bands "Hookersville," a truck stop on Highway 99 just south of Fresno, California, has a group of five motels that are used by the pavement princesses. Some, of course, just climb into the truck beds; it saves time for the women and money for the customers. Elsewhere, truckers are tenderly entreated to frequent "health clubs"—male sporting havens only open to those who carry their Interstate Commerce Commission cards.[59]

Accommodating Behavior

Illegality forces streetwalkers to enter into cooperative agreements with policemen. They want to avoid street hassles, an arrest and court prosecution.

> [There is] a lot of give and take between the women and the cops; they've known each other for a long time and they're known to watch out for each other. There's not even the semblance of hostility between them. In fact, there may be something quite the opposite, a total passivity on the part of the woman in relation to the police, but there is a whole lot of . . . "accommodating" behavior too. The scene in court is astonishing: the woman is absolutely flirting throughout the whole proceedings. She's doing it when she comes in; she does it when she's going out with the cops and the clerks. It doesn't break down for a minute. That interchange is very weird to watch . . . but you know the woman's security and advantage lies in maintaining this relationship.[60]

Australian prostitutes, like others almost everywhere, have a way of seeing things pragmatically. When charged with prostitution some plead guilty and pay the fine. They fear retaliation from cops.[61]

Accommodations may be no more complex than what used to be a London "courtesy." When policemen approached streetwalkers many ambled to other areas to solicit.[62] More generally, courtesies may be the exception. Prostitutes speak crudely of what matters on the streets.

> Never talk back to the flatfoots. That's the golden rule the social workers never tell you. If you answer back the mother-fucking bastards instead of giving you a couple of days will slap you in the can for a month—and top it off with a false report.[63]

A streetwalker stays out of trouble by befriending policemen on her stroll and by giving them what they want—information about illegal activities more serious than soliciting.[64] She pays them off with money and her body. She provides information on drugs, gambling operations and arsonists. Advantage accrues from being employed as a stick (shill) in gambling houses and from working around bars and clubs where gossip flows like cut-rate drinks. The streetscape, of course, is not peculiar for accommodating behavior. When red-light districts were commonplace in the United States prostitutes often acted as stool pigeons for police.[65]

Streetwalkers do not want their positions endangered; many have little compunction about revealing the identity of out-of-towners. Some prostitutes form friendships with vice officers, discussing personal problems—financial, marital—and personal likes and dislikes—football scores and happenings in the economy. They support and reinforce rationalizations concerning the least supportable aspects of a policeman's job, "of hiding in men's toilets, pretending to be johns, or spying on people carrying on their private affairs."[66] Occasionally acting out the role of a supporting wife-on-the-job may not be enough to keep a woman out of jail if she steals from a client or blatantly solicits when the heat is on, but it may make the difference between a polite warning from a "friend" and a ride to the local precinct.

Occasionally police and prostitutes develop deep ties. In the streetwalking locales of post-war London some cops helped women on their beats by giving them money to assist them through an illness when they could not work. It was not just that constables received information on local criminals, rather, at this time prostitutes were seen as a natural part of the streetscape.[67]

New York City is probably the more common case. There, prostitutes get breaks, but they still wind up in the station house with considerable regularity. The plainsclothes officers in New York know the regulars, they give them names expressive of both derision and affection, and they even tell them to throw away their drugs or weapons before they are hauled away.[68] But such concessions ultimately count for little. The cops are still "pigs," "bulls" and "assholes" who abuse their power.[69] The women "accommodate" them as long as they can, as long as they see advantage, and then they move to a new neighborhood or another city—anywhere they believe there to be fewer hassles.

Strolls and Territories

Prostitution streetscapes are composed of strolls, loosely defined areas where the women solicit. Strolls vary in size by time of day, day of the week and season. Generally prostitutes move about more during the day than at night, more during winter than summer. In the first case they do so to reduce detection, in the second to keep warm. Friday and Saturday are invariably busy, especially near major convention centers and downtown hotels. Stroll sizes and amount of circulation vary. Older women may use smaller areas than their younger competitors.[70]

On the stroll the prostitute moves around to entice or enjoin customers, reduce boredom, keep warm and reduce visibility. Part of most streetscapes resemble common greens, areas to which all have unimpeded access. Here women assemble in groups of two to four, laughing, talking and joking among themselves. With the arrival of a possible client they break into singles or pairs, only to regroup once he is out of scoring distance. One description of London street behavior underscores how gatherings may be time-specific occurrences:

> The girls start the evening well spaced out along the recognised trade-routes—the half-lit streets behind Piccadilly or Leicester Square, around the maze of Shepherd's Market, and in the purlieus of Paddington. It is only later on, when they have taken a customer or two, and are becoming careless, or when they have had no luck at all and are becoming sulky, that they congregate in twos and threes for a triumphant or embittered gossip.[71]

Bus stops and intersections with traffic lights are preferred soliciting sites. Choosing a location near a bus stop allows for the excuse that one is just waiting for a bus.[72] More important, a male halted in his forward progress is an easier hustle than an ambulatory one. The time from red to green light is sufficient to induce hesitation and permit a hit. Traffic flow complements light changes. In Sacramento, California's major prostitution area "the easternmost corners have the advantage of being on busier streets with greater north-south evening traffic flow than is found on the little-used streets of the western edge of the stroll." In Sacramento and other cities prostitutes like to hustle on one-way streets to reduce the need to shout a solicitation, thereby lowering the risk of arrest.[73]

Telephone booths figure into stroll definitions. The loud ring of a phone at an open booth enables a pimp to contact his women and respond to market place demands. A pimp can thus move his women as convention and port schedules dictate. As well as moving to other local soliciting sites the women can, when cheap air flights are available, do business between not-too-distant major cities (such as San Francisco and Los Angeles).[74]

Many women frequent the same stroll day after day, and some establish territorial claims. Regularity of work place means regular customers and regular sources of income, less pressure in meeting nightly quotas set by pimps, fewer problems from new faces who turn out to be "weirdos," "freaks," "nuts," and now and then killers. Regularity or predictability and homogeneity go together. Like selects for like: similar types of prostitutes and clients come to define particular streetscapes. In the 1930s Parisian men who desired obese women went to the Rue Quincampoix. The tripe-sellers and butchers termed the objects of their desire *nanas* (something nice to eat) and *morues* (codfish).[75] Men familiar with New York City capitalize on their knowledge that those who solicit in "Hell's Bedroom"—the Times Square area—are often young girls who offer bargain basement "quickies." On the East Side the street women are better dressed, older and more expensive than their Times Square counterparts.

The generalization that prostitution districts tend to have similar kinds of women does not imply that the criteria that determine work place are always straightforward. Vancouver had a number of streetwalking areas in 1977 which, in broad terms, could be distinguished on the basis of price and status among prostitutes (Figure 10-2). At the top of the hierarchy was an area intersected by Georgia and Hornby Streets, where the cost of a "trick" was $50 to $100. Only prostitutes who solicited in some of the clubs felt superior to these women. Along Davie Street prices began at $40 and went as high as $80. At the bottom of the hierarchy were the Granville and Hastings streetscapes, the latter overlapping the city's Skid Row. While average prices in these areas were $30 a "trick," roughly the price of one cap of heroin, Granville streetwalkers tended to look down on those who worked in or near Skid Row.[76] In spite of these generalizations a fieldworker who knew the areas and many of the women maintained that "age does not seem to be a discriminating element in the choice of the area, and neither do natural looks. Grooming, self confidence and drug addiction are the factors which will determine the women's preference for a certain zone."[77] Furthermore, even though there was not much mobility among the various streetscapes, except when cops hassled the women, prostitutes who hustled for black pimps worked almost everywhere.

Working the same stroll infuses much needed predictability into an illegal, sometimes dangerous environment. Knowledge of place means that prostitutes become familiar with the quirks, prejudices and demands of

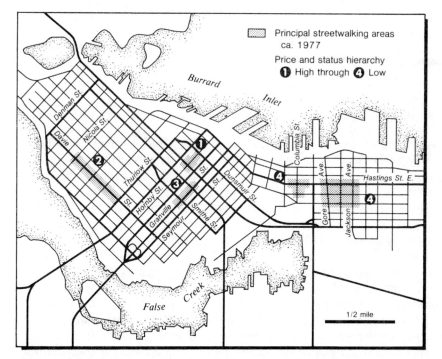

Figure 10-2 Principal Streetwalking Areas in Vancouver, British Columbia
Adapted from Lowman 1980; and data in Layton 1975:100-104.

hotel owners, bellhops and elevator boys, good, bad and indifferent types of potential customers who come to the area and—most important of all—the policemen who patrol. Knowing the physical and social lay of the local land makes it easier to decide when to solicit and when to hesitate, when to expect the vice squad and when and where to run when arrest is imminent. "The tie that binds whore to turf is more than sentimental. It takes a long while to learn a territory, its faces and places, its cops and plainsclothes. On strange turf a slip up is almost inevitable. . . ."[78] In new places a prostitute simply does not know the signposts of the streetscape, the excuses that cops will accept.

Place consistency, if not territoriality, advantages the pimp. He can quickly check to see if his "bitch" is working rather than acting like a "jive-ass" or a "flaky ho" (one who is unstable and does not work hard at her job). He is in a better position to adjudicate territorial claims or cause trouble for competitors. Place stability is also economical; knowing where one's women are gives a pimp more time to "flash" among other "players."

Though prostitutes themselves emphasize familiarity and predictability as reasons for returning to the same stretch of pavement or making claims to territory, each also has a way of drawing attention to idiosyncratic advantage. A London streetwalker two decades ago put it this way:

> I always stand here, where Half Moon Street and Piccadilly meet, and every brick of this shop front, every fault in its paintwork, every crack in the pavement is familiar to me. There is a certain safety and advantage in this familiarity, too: I know the quickest route to take if I spot the police, the best angle of light from the street-lamp for my face and figure, the most comfortable section of wall to lean on when the minutes drag. Besides, they expect to find me somewhere near this corner if they come back for more, and a good many of them do.[79]

A prostitute may refer to "her corner" and a pimp occasionally designates a given street or a section of a block as "his territory." In the extreme case, a pimp's name will label a place.[80] If he has a number of women in his stable they may all use the same corner or have nearby overlapping strolls. Geographical contiguity facilitates his watchdog function and forms a power base against other prostitutes who wish to hustle the same locale, and toward men who become verbally or physically abusive. In some cities pimps belong to loose confederations that respect other's territories.[81]

Territorial claims are based on how long a prostitute has worked a stroll, how much verbal and physical power she can exert alone or by calling on cooperative street sisters, and the degree to which her pimp will intervene on her behalf. Some women are very possessive of their turfs and will shout down or physically battle those who attempt to intrude.[82] In Paris a prostitute will call the police when another woman invades her domain.[83] Fights are most likely to arise when traffic is heavy.[84] Decades ago Coney Island was known for its low prices, caused by competition and the high incidence of "freebies." It had a crowd of opposites—many young girls in their teens and also many who were as much as fifty or sixty years old. One distinctive feature of Coney Island that created a good deal of competition was that it had a very definite seasonal peak of activity—the "golden" months of June, July and August. Most of the prostitutes did not frequent hotels, but found that areas under the boardwalk sufficed for transacting business. Some used the same places on a day-to-day basis, and when others impinged on their territories conflicts were often resolved with fist or knife fights.[85]

The dangers of strolling someone else's turf are particularly acute for newcomers or "outlaws," those who refuse to work for a pimp.[86] In Boston's infamous "Combat Zone" an unwritten code declares that all prostitutes must have pimps. Pimps or their women beat those who try to beat the system. Their rationale is simple. One Combat Zone prostitute allegedly gave more than $80,000 to her pimp in eleven months. Another pimp had 13 prostitutes working for him, each good for at least $800 per week.[87]

Two decades ago women had to pay for the right to work the streets of Piccadilly and Leicester Square. There, as elsewhere, monetary investments increased the likelihood that a prostitute would fight rather than flee when her space was violated.

> Every prostitute that you may see upon such notorious sites is certainly paying at least £20 per week, and often much more, for the right to be there. She is not likely to stand by and watch a strange girl infringe upon her costly pitch. If she is herself not inclined to take off her shoe and deal with the intruder, helped gladly by any other girl of her trade and acquaintance in the vicinity, she has only to send for her Johnson, who will muss up the newcomer with all the ferocity and lack of hesitation that one can expect from a type whose only pride is in his ability to intimidate a woman. He will shred her face unforgettably.[88]

At one time in the United States one prostitute would pay another "for the right to seek customers on particular days . . . or buy . . . the right to work a locale from a woman who had previously been established there, in a manner similar to that in which a physician buys a practice."[89]

Enforceable claims to turf vary temporarily. A territory for Shirley who works the shift of dregs—2 to 6 A.M.—is differently defined for Mo who solicits the same turf from 9 P.M. until she meets her pimp quota. Territoriality has meaning in another temporal context. Weekend and summertime prostitutes cause the density of streetwalkers to increase, thereby augmenting competition for customers and the best spots from which to solicit. Weekend prostitutes often hold down another job; they hustle the busy nights to make up what their jobs do not pay them. Some just do it as fancy commands.

Territories vary in size and permeability, and they mirror technology. "Streetwalkers on wheels" or "kerb-crawlers" also lay personal claims to city real estate. But by the very nature of their mobility their territories are inclined to be larger, more amorphous, and more often overlapping with those of competitors than is true of the machine-less walkers.[90]

Territoriality sometimes has racial overtones.

> [In New York City] down on Third Avenue and Twelfth Street . . . the north-west corner in front of the tacky dinette and dingy bar is populated day and night with drunks wandered off-course from the Bowery, junkies on the nod and street hookers also on heroin. Their pimps are often indistinguishable from the rest of the rag-tag army that loiters there. The scruffy hotels where hookers take their clients for $6.00 a room are found on the side streets. These hotels and the pavements in front of them are often the scenes of muggings, knifings and murders. Third and Twelfth is reserved almost exclusively for black hookers, or for those white hookers with black boyfriends or pimps. A white prostitute attempting to break into the business there is warned only once to move to another block. A subsequent visit has been known to land a contender in Bellevue Hospital.[91]

In the same city in 1971 a researcher working in the Times Square area found that black prostitutes solicited the west side of Eighth Avenue from 44th to 49th Street. White women hustled the east side of the street and both sidewalks above 49th Street.[92]

Territoriality occasionally has international dimensions. Some years ago when Dutch and French prostitutes found their own governments hostile to soliciting many fled to Brussels. Because of their foreign appeal and their attractiveness (some were from the South Pacific and former French and Dutch possessions) the women were able to charge higher prices than locals. They also took over part of the high-class market—NATO and multinational personnel. Resentment of what was seen as territorial infringement was expressed in the murder of pimps who accompanied their "migrant workers."[93]

Established social ties, the investment in time and effort to secure one's right to choice turf, and the predictability that comes from knowing a streetscape, its denizens and its transients, all attach prostitutes to a place. But unlike many others such attachments for prostitutes must be temporary, changeable and irregular. Because men want diversity in sexual offerings and because pockets of demand rise in accord with occasional or unusual events, there is obvious advantage for a prostitute to occasionally change her streetscape address. The vicissitudes of repression and place-to-place differences in community attitudes toward prostitution are equally strong imperatives that override the gains of working a single open-air address.

Chapter 11

Mobility as Strategy

In the Name of Country and Profit

Historically, prostitutes have been strikingly mobile. They marched with the Roman legions and in one year of the Crusades more than 13,000 camp followers were counted. When the Duke of Alva's army invaded the Netherlands 1,200 prostitutes accompanied the invasion. In 1476 nearly 2,000 prostitutes followed the army of Charles the Bold.[1] Three hundred years later several hundred followed the British from Halifax to Boston.[2] Both armies in the American Civil War were accompanied by large numbers of prostitutes, many of whom disguised themselves as men to avoid detection by officers.[3]

Liverpool, in the middle of the nineteenth century, lacked sufficient prostitutes to meet the demands of a disembarking navy. As a result, when large ships arrived, brothel owners wrote to correspondents in London asking that women be sent. Although undoubtedly exaggerated, it was claimed that by reason of the numbers traveling between London and Liverpool "the traffic [occupied] a respectable position in the ensemble of the trade of Great Britain."[4] But Liverpool was not unique for its periodic influx of prostitutes, nor was the navy the only reason for intra-island trade in Victorian Britain. The prostitute population of Edinburgh decreased rather drastically in the summer and again during the university vacation in the fall. Some women traveled with the wealthy customers on excursions, others moved to villages to be near their clients. In Edinburgh the prostitute population increased during horse races, especially those at Musselburgh. The women came from all of the country's major cities for these famous summer races. Not surprisingly, when there were gatherings at racecourses elsewhere prostitutes were present.[5]

Brothels were common on both Eastern and Western fronts during the First World War. Prostitutes "were housed in abandoned castles, in little village houses which had been more or less spared by the war, in wooden barracks which had been erected for this purpose, or in empty wagons."[6] Places of business were only as permanent as the battle lines, and because these changed with surprising regularity in some areas, motorized bordellos were used. Those with blue lights were for officers, those with red ones for everyone else.[7]

During wars the United States military has been so concerned about venereal disease and the moral effects of prostitution on troops and local communities that it has taken its case to Congress. During World War II, Congress and the Secretary of War designated that brothels could not be within five miles of military installations, and in both major wars red-light districts near virtually all bases were closed. But such restrictions did not prevent supply meeting demand. Prostitutes and eager customers met in cafes, dance halls, hotels, rooming houses and on the street.[8] On the outskirts of towns cabin camps, the early forerunners of motels, were so popular with prostitutes that the media referred to them as "hot-pillow joints." The women traveled to bases and nearby towns in cars, buses, trains and trailers, occasionally picking up servicemen in their own automobiles and taking them to rented facilities in trailer parks.[9] The popularity of cars and trailers was institutionalized in the soldier jargon, "chippie wagons."[10]

Those who serviced the military frequently arrived at the base the night before payday. They came into cities like Louisville from as far away as Memphis, Atlanta and Detroit. After two or three days of intense activity the tired women packed their bags and returned home. A common observation in Killeen, Texas, near Fort Hood, used to be that everyone could tell when it was payday at the base because prostitutes from Dallas and Austin were the principal human cargo at the local Greyhound bus station. As the economic status of the G.I. changed, so did the periodic influx of out-of-towners. Soldiers now frequently drive to Dallas, Austin, San Antonio and the well-known *zonas rojas* along the Mexican border, several hours distant.[11]

When the military attempted to suppress prostitution, prostitutes simply moved to nearby towns, or periodically relocated within walking distance of their former place of business. Attempts to suppress San Bernardino's D Street motel prostitutes, who serviced the men at March Field, were countered by moves to motels down the street.[12] In the late 1950s the military tried to control venereal disease by making Mexican brothels off-limits after several cases were reported in the same house. Prostitutes reacted by arranging to rent rooms privately. Because they continually changed addresses it became increasingly difficult to control them.[13]

Circuits and Circulation

Prostitutes often display considerable pattern in their movements. A detailed examination of sexual behavior in Somerset County in early seventeenth-century England noted that one class of prostitute was the so-called "vagrant whore." Sometimes accompanied by a male or another prostitute she went from parish to parish earning what she could at inns, markets, fairs and crossroads. Some labored a regular circuit to service diocesan clergy, their friends and relatives.[14]

During the nineteenth century a "parlor house circuit" extended from South Dakota to California and south to New Mexico. A Colorado round included Georgetown, Aspen, Denver and Cripple Creek. The gold rush fever of Deadwood, South Dakota brought a large number of miners, gamblers, saloonkeepers and prostitutes to the town. One year alone saw as many as 2,000 men and women join the rush for gold, so many that "the Denver Tenderloin showed signs of becoming depopulated."[15] More money, small male populations, declining demand for one's face or body, word of better working conditions elsewhere, police crackdowns and the search for madams easier to work for were all reasons that stimulated mobility. Travel was visible and frequent enough to give rise to the term "cat wagon," the means by which many prostitutes moved from one camp or town to another.[16]

On the Canadian frontier prostitutes worked on the Winnipeg to Pacific Coast passenger trains, a pattern that has a contemporary parallel among Russian women who solicit on the Lenningrad to Moscow line.[17] For some of the early Canadian women the details of their routes were defined by the travel patterns of their male poolshark companions. Destinations also depended on expected receptivity. For a while, Edmonton, Alberta was attracting prostitutes from as far away as Montreal. It was a particularly good place to go when the Mounties were handing out "floaters"—invitations to leave town. Whatever the specific destination of peripatetic prostitutes, their arrival was often heralded at the railway station.

> The railway news agents could always tell when there was a new girl in town by the number of local blades who sidled up to them on the station platforms to buy contraceptives. Many newsies on the branch lines made more money selling such supplies than they did from their fruit and magazines.[18]

Few places now qualify as legitimate frontiers, but one which does is Alaska. The influx of men without wives who accumulate very large paychecks draws prostitutes from all over the lower forty-eight. One measure of how many women were going north to hustle trade is that between mid-1974 and mid-1975 prostitution arrests in Fairbanks increased more than 4,000 percent.[19]

Recently, European prostitutes have allegedly followed circuits defined by criminal syndicates and pimps.[20] In the Netherlands during the 1960s women stayed for two or three months in Amsterdam, then moved on to such places as Rotterdam and The Hague for similar periods of time. This general pattern was periodically broken by any large gathering of people: various once-a-month marketplaces, or events such as the Roermond egg market. On these occasions prostitutes synchronized their movements, chartering buses that converged on active centers for several days. Other European prostitutes work for madams who regularly send them on assignment to Amsterdam, Paris, Rome, Frankfurt, Hamburg and Berlin. One

London madam claims to have as many as 200 women working for her on such major city circuits.[21]

More than 50 years ago in the United States a group of pimps known as "The Independent Benevolent Association" moved prostitutes among brothels and cities as opportunities dictated.[22] When the Mafia was deeply involved with narcotics, bookmaking and prostitution in the 1930s, women were rotated among houses from San Diego to Seattle. Pimps kept the prostitutes moving "so the customers wouldn't get bored nor the cops wise."[23] Investigators on the Kefauver Committee uncovered a vice ring operating out of New York City which regularly moved women among such cities as Wilkes-Barre, Pittsburgh, Youngstown, Cleveland, Forth Worth, Gary, Chicago, Buffalo, Elmira and New York.[24] Another circuit focused on New Iberia, Louisiana and covered some eight states, while still another centered on Phoenix City, Alabama, once known as the "Sodom of the South." Prostitutes sometimes moved from city to city at predictable intervals—in one instance on a regular three-week schedule. These geographical courses were loosely organized confederations, not tightly controlled operations run by syndicates.[25] The head of Oakland, California's vice squad maintains that organized circuits still exist. On the West Coast pimps "sell girls back and forth, or trade them like ballplayers."[26]

"Country tours," as they are called by prostitutes in Australia, are tuned to seasonal weather conditions.[27] Like avian species that migrate between seasons, the women go south in the summer when the weather is warm and the foraging good, and then progressively move northward as winter approaches. A goodly number of Storyville's white brothel boarders were seasonal migrants from the north. Accompanied by gamblers, lovers and pimps they headed south in the fall and returned home in the spring. Profit was one motive for their itinerant behavior, climate another.[28] In present-day Europe some prostitutes work in Italy, Spain and Greece in the winter and then return to their northern turfs in summer.[29]

Places that define circuits tend to be relatively large. Among contemporary West Coast streetwalkers a familiar route begins "in San Diego, moves through Los Angeles, San Francisco, Portland, Seattle, and Vancouver, B.C., to Alaska. If the coast proves unsatisfactory, the next stop is Hawaii or inland to Salt Lake City."[30] A "road ho" or "circuit ho" usually travels with a pimp and at least one other prostitute. The group may work as many as ten cities, gearing precise movements to weather and large conventions.[31]

In Jalapa, Mexico prostitutes first travel to nearby places they know, then to lesser-known cities at a greater distance, and finally out of state (Figure 11-1). Out-of-state places share certain features: they are relatively close to home or large, such as Acapulco, Iguala, Puebla, Teziutlan, Tuxtepec and Villahermosa. Choice of a house in which to work depends on gossip received from colleagues, personal acquaintance with brothel owners, the

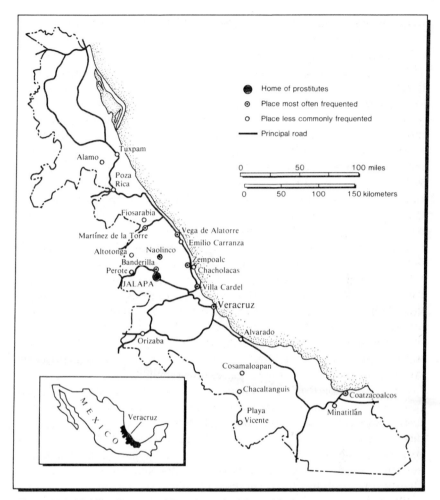

Figure 11-1 Mobility Patterns of Prostitutes in Jalapa, Mexico
Adapted from Barrera Caraza 1974.

possibility of working seven days a week, and whether or not the owner will allow children to live with their mothers on the premises.[32]

Besides climate, city size and proximity, local or regional conditions sometimes serve as determinants of circulation patterns. "Camp hos" of the Pacific Northwest make the rounds of logging and construction sites. A pimp and two or three women may negotiate business terms with a foreman.[33] Their British Columbian counterparts, "camp to camp hookers" as they are known among other prostitutes, move about in groups of three to five for up to five months a year.[34]

Some prostitutes do not exactly work circuits yet regularly travel long distances on business. One example is the "weekender" prostitute: a secretary, waitress or clerk who works in southern California and commutes on weekends to Las Vegas to solicit in the Strip hotels. Leaving on Thursday night and returning Sunday evening she may take along little more than a handbag.[35]

The amount of circulation, both within and between cities, is suggested by brothel turnover rates. In the United States during the early twentieth century nearly 90,000 changes of address occurred among 32,000 prostitutes during a three-year period. More than a third of the moves were interstate; the typical prostitute had practiced in more than one state, some in as many as six.[36] Figures from the nineteenth century suggest similar trends. Officially registered prostitutes of Hamburg changed their addresses, on average, twice a year, while 85 percent of Zurich's brothel boarders were staying no longer than five months, and over 60 percent less than two.[37]

A study of 72 streetwalkers by Jennifer James in Seattle showed that over 60 percent of the women moved at least 500 miles once every three months, remaining at one address for periods ranging from a weekend to three or four months. Another third moved this distance at least two or three times a year.[38] Of 77 eastern Nevada house prostitutes more than a quarter stayed ten days or fewer before quitting or moving to another brothel, while nearly 60 percent remained for less than a month in a single house. Only a few women spent as many as three or four years at one location.[39] In Latin America and Australia turnover patterns are similar.[40]

The demand for diversity has been a significant reason for the mobility of prostitutes. In nineteenth-century Belgium "there was a lot of movement of girls between brothels; it was probably sound business to vary the merchandise."[41] San Francisco's parlor-house madams of the 1870s held monthly receptions to show off their new arrivals and to proclaim their backgrounds and previous work locations: New York or New Orleans, Omaha or Denver, the Continent or Great Britain.[42] Whatever a woman's roots, they were exploited for their positive connotations. The imagined world of other places has great appeal to men entering a brothel. Thus for their benefit the madam might talk effusively of "a diminutive blonde who had served her apprenticeship in New York's famed Seven Sisters, a tall redhead from Lou Harper's Mansion in Chicago, or several buxom girls from Kate Townsend's in New Orleans, one of the most luxurious parlor houses of all during this period."[43] Many decades later managers of expensive Hollywood bordellos were as vocal as some of San Francisco's madams. When a new woman entered a house, sometimes someone who finally knew she would not make it as a screen star, the madam, proud of her new acquisition, advertised that a "fresh pink" was available.[44]

A study of mobility patterns among prostitutes in Jalapa, Mexico discovered that nearly half of 22 women interviewed said they left a brothel because of declining demand for their services, and they thought they could do better elsewhere.[45] Many of those working in the legal brothels of

Nevada move to different towns to take advantage of the premium males place on diversity. In Winnemucca, Nevada, where two houses are adjacent to one another and under the same ownership, employed women move freely between them.[46]

The madam's desire for continually changing faces not only has promoted mobility and created job insecurity,[47] but has also given rise to a parasitic class of bookers and brokers. In early nineteenth-century France, brothel owners had agents who continually supplied them with fresh young girls from the countryside.[48] A hundred years later in New York City it was the custom of bordellos to "operate after the manner of vaudeville circuits, with a change of entertainers each week." Bookers made a business of circulating prostitutes among houses, a service for which they were accustomed to taking a ten percent commission on the women's earnings.[49] New York City still has brokers who work for a percentage of revenues; they now send women around the country rather than to various city burroughs.[50]

Phrases of the present-day streetscape highlight the importance of novelty. Vancouver's streetwalkers speak of "out-of-town girls"—those who reputedly monopolize the market for a while because they are new.[51]

The matrix of reasons for mobility is a large and full one. Stealing from a client may be the sole reason for changing one's base of operations.[52] If the "game" was on an out-of-towner, moving uptown or downtown for a few days may be enough. If the client is a regular the smart "thoroughbred" will move to another city.

For white prostitutes in the United States family pressures may create an initial impetus to mobility. Once a white woman becomes a prostitute and her kin learn of it, she is an outcast; frequently they would rather she not exist. A common pattern involves her leaving home by the age of 16 or 17, never to return. In striking contrast, black prostitutes often maintain close ties with their families and therefore may work in the city where they were raised. Even if blacks do travel, they seem much more prone to return home to reaffirm kin ties. Among 40 black streetwalkers interviewed in Seattle, 30 worked in the city where they had resided a good part of their lives and where their families lived. As much as parents, brothers and sisters are homebound magnets to the black prostitute, equally magnetic are the woman's children. Paternity is not as important as it is to a white; she knows black friends and perhaps close relatives who are "trick babies" and neither she nor those around her harbor the deep prejudices that whites do. She supports her children and wants to be with them. Yet, ironically enough, these very facts sometimes account for occasional mobility, as when she comes under investigation by the child protection arm of the welfare department. Fearing that she could lose custody of her offspring, she knows that a solution to the problem requires that she leave her children with her parents and move to another city.

Some women move because they enjoy traveling, and the attraction of travel may even have brought them into prostitution. Some are mobile because they feel restless, because they cannot or do not want to hold a "straight" job, and because on the street or in the brothel they have strained relations with "stable" sisters or house companions. Other women find themselves temporarily mobile because of difficulties with their pimp. They leave town for a few days to allow their man to recover dignity he feels he lost when his "bitch" did not react in the proper fashion. "A pimp's image (reputation) is his most important asset."[53]

Mobility and geographical spread of a stable feeds a pimp's image. A "fast-stepper" moves his women about adroitly, "where business is best, where the streets are 'cool,' where he has business connections, or where he wishes to live at any one time."[54] Status, appellation and mobility are interrelated. "Red" is a local or regionally based pimp; "American Red" works cities that extend across the entire map of North America; and "International Red" may be just what his name implies, a high-status pimp with all the class of a jet-setting executive. He has lawyers and bondsmen around the globe who take care of problems as they arise. Fast-stepping International Red is the polar opposite of the "half-stepper," who has low mobility, a meager income and too much involvement with the local police. Precisely because of his low mobility and that of his women, the half-stepper's reputation is likely to be thin.[55]

Among other labels of the immoral landscape with strong mobility connotations are "thoroughbred," "lady," "old-timer," "ripoff artist" and "turn-out."[56] A thoroughbred stands at the top of the social hierarchy; she has style and knowledge of the "game" and moves around North American cities and the offshore islands with considerable ease. The lady is similar but younger. Also highly mobile within the United States, she is less likely to leave the country than the thoroughbred. The old-timer, as the name indicates, has been around for a long time. More place-based than thoroughbreds and ladies, she travels among cities mainly to teach and recruit, to check on her stable sisters and to insure for the benefit of her man that they do their job. The ripoff artist overlaps some of these categories; she steals from clients. If successful she has high status among her peers, but to be successful she must be mobile. Finally, the "T.O." (turn-out or young beginner) is directed to move from place to place by pimp or stable sister to avoid problems with her family or the law.

Even the argot employed within the pimp stable shows the ineluctable linkages among social status, success and mobility. A stable "star" is highly mobile and of considerable importance to her sisters because of the money she brings in. The "main lady," the one the pimp usually favors and depends on to watch over the other women is, largely by definition, tied to place. Only if the pimp has prostitutes working elsewhere will she, like the corresponding old-timer, travel. The contrasting counterpart to the main lady is the "fly-by-night," the unstable prostitute who moves from stable to stable. Though her mobility among pimps and streetscapes has little to do directly with police harassments, she illustrates, in name if not in fact, an often repeated pattern for coping with stress and repression.[57]

Repression and Mobility

Notwithstanding the considerable advantages to soliciting the same streetscape, intra-city movements have been commonplace. Indeed, as measured by number and frequency of moves, those occurring within and between neighborhoods are more important than circulation at regional and national scales. Illegality and periodic repression are principal causative agents.

Vigorous repression has been countered by mobility almost everywhere. When Storyville was closed in 1917 prostitutes and madams immediately moved to other, often respectable, parts of the city and continued with business as usual.[58] During Storyville's twenty year existence few houses operated outside the district nor had many streetwalkers. The New Orleans' problem was captured in music after the district was closed.[59]

> Legislature voted the District down . . .
> Damn good way to spread the hookers over town.
> Tell me how long will I have to wait?
> Can I have it now—
> Or must I hesitate?

Its jazz musicians, racism and infamous red-light district aside, New Orleans was not peculiar. At about the same time in New York City and numerous other places across the country the police were making strenuous efforts to repress streetwalking and brothel activity. Successful by some measures, prostitution generally spread elsewhere: to cabarets, nightclubs, dance halls, tenement houses and tenement "call flats" where arrangements were made by telephone, and to streets and neighborhoods that had previously known little of the "social evil." Madams who did not wish to close their doors permanently essentially had two choices: they could pay "protection" money to the police or they could run a "fly-by-night" and move around as much as necessary to avoid predators. The major problem for madams who moved periodically was that of reaching steady customers without endangering their reputation among friends and relatives. One way around the difficulty was to send announcements that the "library" (brothel) or its "books" (prostitutes) had relocated. Sometimes clients were reminded it was time to renew their "membership in the library" or that there were "new books on file in our new quarters."[60]

A change of address coupled with new methods of soliciting business have been common adaptations to repression. Upon the insistence of the occupying forces after World War II, the brothels of Japan were ordered closed by imperial decree. Soon thereafter special "restaurants" known as *tokushu inshoku ten* (*tokuin* for short) took their place. In addition, new areas of brothels, disguised as bars and restaurants, known as *aosen* (the Blue Line) districts arose adjacent to the older bordello quarters, known as *akasen* (the Red Line).

By 1953 one estimate placed the number of Japanese prostitutes at more than 300,000.[61] Besides those who worked as *tokuin* or *aosen* waitresses, 100,000 "waitresses" and "hostesses," 30,000 streetwalkers and nearly 40,000 geisha were also engaged in prostitution. Two years later the high estimate for Japan was 600,000.[62] Not until 1958, ten years after the imperial decree that brothels be closed, were the *tokuin* houses closed. The result was predictable. Disguised bordellos and rendezvous centers sprung up in the form of *kafue* (bars), *machiai* (meeting places) and *ryōriya* (Japanese-style restaurants).

When governments have repressed brothels the changes have seldom been as anticipated, and not always welcome. In 1946 clerical, social and political controversy in France led the legislature to close the country's houses. An investigation before and after the law was effected showed that during 1945-46, prior to brothel closings, Paris had approximately 1,600 house prostitutes and another 20,000 working the streets.[63] More than two-thirds of the latter were not registered with the police, did not carry medical cards and therefore were subject to arrest. When brothels were shut several changes occurred. House women moved to the streets and, for them, the pimp or *souteneur* replaced the madam. Also the geography of prostitution altered. Whereas previously few streetwalkers solicited between the *Place de la Concorde* and the *Place de l'Etoile*, after the 1946 law was enacted as many as 200 prostitutes stationed themselves in this area.

Official records of the Paris Prefect of the Police and the *Brigade Mondaine* indicated no increase in the number of streetwalkers after the postwar brothel closings. These statistics, however, are suspect. House prostitutes constituted less than ten percent of the total, these kinds of censuses are notoriously inaccurate, and the police look better if no changes occur. Something must have happened. Within a half-dozen years after the brothels were closed, Mme. Richard, the legislator who initiated the bill that forced prostitutes into the streets, admitted she had made a mistake. In retrospect she felt it was better to have houses and a lower venereal disease rate than an uncontrollable street problem.[64]

Italy's 1958 Merlin law abolished legalized brothels and the licensing of streetwalkers. Prostitutes almost immediately sought out new niches; the women began to make appearances at theaters, art shows and business conventions. Perhaps as many as 2,000 attended a single Sunday soccer match. Among other changes was the emergence of "klaxon girls" in Rome, Genoa and Milan. They solicited from, and became inextricably identified with, their cars. There were, for example, Maria of the Appia, Yvette of the Opel and Rossana of the Dauphine. The particular automobile reflected both social mobility and success. A woman began soliciting in a small Fiat 600 or something similar and, as income improved, moved up to an Alfa Romeo or Ford equipped with reclining seats and interior bar. The mobile prostitutes solicited men walking the streets, but they preferred those in cars. Motorists were more affluent and did not need to be returned to the pickup spot. Strategies varied. One favorite involved pulling alongside a car and while one woman kept abreast of the potential client the other solicited by unbuttoning her blouse. Less affluent streetwalkers developed a different approach. To protect themselves from the police they employed lookouts who worked on Lambrettas. The lookouts rode ahead of an approaching patrol car to warn others that the vice squad was following.[65]

Mobility and arrest history are related. A three-year study noted that:

> Streetwalkers, if they are known to the police, are arrested as soon as they appear on the street. Prostitutes who continue to appear on the streets after making bail are repeatedly arrested. . . . In such a climate, mobility increases rapidly as most of the informants limit their working time in a city to a week or so, and then move elsewhere.[66]

The pressures are ever-present. The vice squad clamps down along a five-block stretch of the immoral landscape because a major political convention is coming to town, or because three hotels registered five complaints in a week, or because election time has arrived once again. In the history of American cities any kind of local electoral campaign has constituted enough reason for sweeping the streets of undesirable elements. Street prostitutes are displeased whatever the rationale, but they possess neither voice nor vote. They amble downstreet or upstreet a half-dozen blocks to little explored avenues; they saunter over to turf abandoned two months earlier when citizen complaints made that area "hot"; or they work a few of the local bars where—for a price—they are permitted to hustle discreetly.

A move of some distance provides anonymity and a fresh start with the local vice squad; further advantage may accrue from inconsistency in prostitution laws and their application. In 1976 San Francisco elected a new mayor and district attorney who ran on a platform de-emphasizing non-violent crimes, including prostitution.[67] This permitted spending the city's limited resources on more serious offenses. Shortly after the new policy came into effect the cops claimed there were more prostitutes on the street than at any time during the previous ten years.

In that same year a survey was made of San Francisco's Tenderloin. Street activity in a five-block area was recorded three times a week for a period of seven months. Results showed that when San Francisco and nearby cities were quiet, 12 to 35 regular streetwalkers were present. The number swelled to between 75 and 90 when a crackdown took place in Oakland and when nearby Palo Alto closed its massage parlors under a

Red-light Abatement Act. The Tenderloin population decreased to its regular number when the vice squad reacted with heavy repressive measures.[68]

Similar pulsations occur in other Bay Area cities. Oakland police repress streetwalkers and they move to nearby Emeryville. The Emeryville vice squad reciprocates and Oakland receives what it had before—if not more.[69] The story is repeated hundreds if not thousands of times each year throughout North America.

In 1967 New York City reduced its maximum penalty for prostitution from a criminal offense to a violation and from a year in jail to fifteen days or a $250 fine. In practice, those arrested were allowed to settle three or four cases at once, paying only a fine of $150.[70] The city also ended a 30-year practice of permitting cops to both make an arrest and act as prosecutor, a dual role that made it very difficult for a woman to beat the charge against her. As a result of these changes pimps and their prostitutes came to New York City from all over the country to enjoy not only liberal prostitution laws and a city that treated girls over sixteen as adults, but also the status of working the "main switchboard."[71] It was not long before "midtown became the nation's largest flesh showroom."[72] By 1969 the police reported a 70 percent increase in arrests.[73] Before the year ended the maximum penalty for prostitution was raised to 90 days in jail or a $500 fine and the law's status changed from a violation to a misdemeanor. If prostitutes could not be reformed or jailed at least they might move to someone else's turf.

That state and local governments differ in their prostitution laws or application is not surprising. That city governments would not understand that a geographically selective law within its own political boundaries invites prostitutes to move down the block or across town to get around the law is more difficult to appreciate. Yet, there is evidence that local governments do not appreciate the geopolitical principle that a law must be applied uniformly to all places if it is to be effective.

For nearly a dozen years Sacramento, California streetwalkers worked the "4th and T" street stroll, an area encompassing about four city blocks (Figure 11-2).[74] Typically, one could find between five and twenty prostitutes on any given night, alone or in small groups numbering no more than six. Only when police activity was particularly intense were the streets clear. Under normal circumstances the cops encountered a number of difficulties in making arrests, the most serious involving judicial requirements regarding what was needed to make a conviction stand, and the legal astuteness of the streetwalkers. Prostitutes' tactics ranged from asking for driver's licenses and proof of occupation to a demand that the customers undress completely before sexual activity began.

Thinking that they had a solution, Sacramento judges in early 1977 told first-time offenders they would be put on probation rather than sent to jail if they did not frequent the 4th and T stroll locale. If caught in the area an

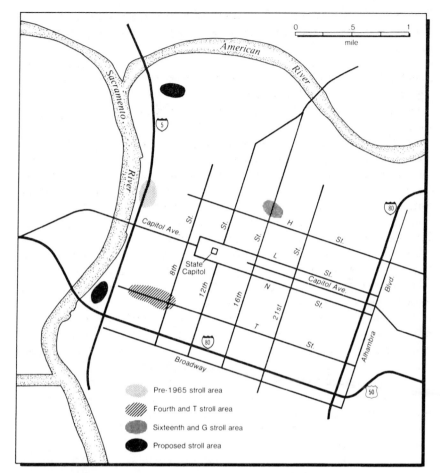

Figure 11-2 Proposed and Actual Prostitution Areas in Sacramento, California
Adapted from Kent and Dingemans 1977:65

arrest would constitute a violation of parole and thus the women could be sent to jail. The solution quickly perceived by prostitutes was to move to a new area, at 16th and G streets (Figure 11-2), which was not specified as off-limits by the court. Too, the locale had advantages: good street lighting, a brisk traffic flow and easy access to "trick pads." When this geographical change provoked strong public reaction the vice squad increased arrests around 16th and G streets. The courts increased the size of the bail bond and, in some cases, jailed the prostitutes. This second attempted solution worked no better than the first. With no place to go and with the public unwilling to create an official stroll, repression in the 16th and G street region was accompanied by a return to normal activity in the original 4th and T street area. In all, six months elapsed from old to new locale and back again to home base.

As elsewhere, some in Sacramento thought that the real solution was to create an officially sanctioned stroll elsewhere in the city, away from residential areas (Figure 11-2).

But that proposal was quickly withdrawn within 24 hours of its announcement in the local newspaper. In this town, as in most, this action was deemed politically unfeasible, and it was widely believed that this would lead to an influx of additional streetwalkers as had recently occurred in San Francisco when enforcement of prostitution laws slackened.[75]

Local perceptions in this instance were correct.

Chapter 12

Closing Brothels and Clearing the Streets

The Demise of American Red-light Districts

From the post-Civil War period until the beginning of the second decade of the twentieth century cities of all sizes tolerated red-light districts. Some grew and became vital through a passive historical process of slow accretion and lack of community concern. Others were products of moral outcry and geopolitical processes. Only a few cities—Baltimore, Washington, D.C., Chicago, Cincinnati and St.Louis—attempted to get their districts legalized or use a licensing system. St. Louis did so in 1870 but its licensing system was abolished three years later. Other cities were unsuccessful. In all but three states—Arkansas, Louisiana and New Mexico—red-light districts were against the law. Yet as many as 50 cities actively regulated them and by the dawn of the twentieth century there may have been 150 official and unofficial districts.

After the turn of the century public outcry against vice increased and crusades initiated before World War I proved unprecedented in their scope and intensity.[1] For every argument that had supported red-light districts there arose its opposite. In the changing social climate of progressivism it was claimed that segregation, and more generally prostitution, increased a city's crime rate, exposed males to immoral behavior they might otherwise not have known and—for those who visited the districts—promoted education in abnormal behavior and sexual perversions. It was alleged that segregation increased the amount of prostitution and venereal disease. The red-light district was seen as a "festering sore" that lustful men who consorted with prostitutes spread to the rest of the community. Other perceived negative aspects of prostitution included its role in stimulating alcohol consumption, graft through illegal toleration, crimes against women by encouraging sexual promiscuity and, in general, promotion of the moral degradation of the community.[2] In addition to these many arguments segregation itself was a fundamental problem in other ways. Many people were willing to have red-light districts, as long as they were in someone else's neighborhood. But even if this could be solved there was still the issue that the majority of a city's prostitutes worked outside the districts.[3]

By the second decade of the twentieth century dozens of cities and some states formed vice commissions to determine the extent of the "social evil" and the future of red-light districts. The commissions not only examined their own situation through detailed field investigations, but also looked at experiences elsewhere.[4] Studies by George Kneeland in New York City and Abraham Flexner in Europe were particularly influential.[5] The commissions took note of the fact that European countries had long histories of attempts to deal with prostitution through registration of the women on police records and mandatory medical examinations to control venereal disease. Success was mixed at best. On the subject of segregation Flexner had this to say:

> Segregation in the sense of an attempt to confine the prostitutes of a city or even the majority of them to a single locality or even to a few definite localities is not undertaken in any European city from Budapest to Glasgow. If, as is the case, they cannot be caught and inscribed, how are they to be caught and segregated? European cities, having universally failed in the attempt to inscribe prostitution, necessarily refrain from any endeavor to segregate any considerable part of it. Nay, more, no European city succeeds even so far as to confine to bordells or bordell quarters even the inscribed part of the prostitute army which has been expressly ordered to stay there.[6]

The first major vice commission investigation was conducted in Chicago in 1910. By 1911 the idea had spread to other large cities in the Midwest—Minneapolis, Kansas City and Cleveland (Figure 12-1). The follow-

Table 12-1

Number of Prostitutes and Geographical Patterns of Brothels in Various European Cities, circa 1910

City	Number of Brothels	Location Pattern	Number of Prostitutes	Estimated Total Number of Prostitutes
Bremen	25	One Street	75	?
Brussels	6	Scattered	37	Over 3,000
Budapest	13	Scattered	260-300	Several thousand
Cologne	98	Scattered	194	6,000
Dresden	81	On 32 different streets	293	?
Frankfort	10	Scattered	100	?
Geneva	17	Scattered	86	?
Hamburg	113	On 8 dispersed streets	780	?
Paris	47	Scattered	387	50,000-60,000
Rome	22	Scattered	125	Over 5,000
Stockholm	30	On 6 dispersed streets	98	?
Stuttgart	10	Scattered	22	?
Vienna	6	Scattered	50-60	30,000

Adapted from Flexner 1914:173.

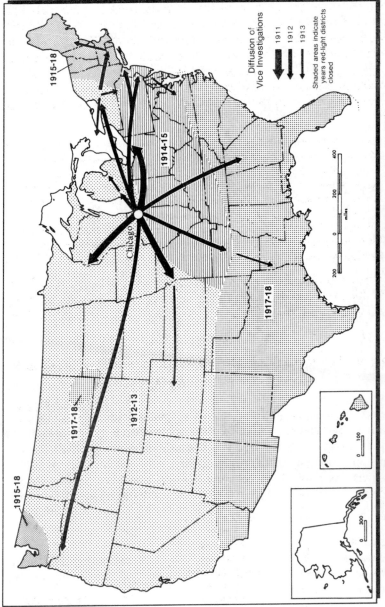

Figure 12-1 The Diffusion of Early Vice Investigations and the Closing of Red-light Districts to 1918
Based on data in Mayer 1918; Pfeiffer 1918; Everett 1919; and the Journal of Social Hygiene 1915-1920.

ing year vice commissions were established along the Eastern Seaboard, in New England and in a few major cities in the West and South. From 1910 to 1912 cities above 100,000 conducted formal studies, but by 1913 and 1914, when inquiries peaked, at least half a dozen places under 50,000 had set up investigations.

With few exceptions, wherever vice commissions were formed red-light districts were closed within one to three years of the reported findings (Figure 12-1). Their strong recommendations were buttressed by the passage of red-light abatement laws. Between 1911 and 1915, 21 states and Washington, D.C. passed them, and by 1920 they were in effect everywhere except Oklahoma, Nevada and Vermont. These laws permitted individuals to bring court action against brothels and red-light districts without having to rely on the initiative of the police or district attorneys.[7]

The one area of the country that lagged behind in initiating investigations and closing their districts was a broad belt extending across the entire southern reach of the United States. Only when Congress and the armed forces decided that prostitutes were a threat to troops in training for the Great War were red-light districts closed. By 1918 perhaps 200 cities had closed their red-light districts.[8]

By 1928 every state except Nevada had abandoned the policy of segregating prostitution. According to scores of yearly field surveys conducted by the ever-vigilant American Social Hygiene Association (ASHA), prostitution—as measured by their criteria of volume, visibility and effect on the community—had been declining nationwide since the vice investigations and closings began some fifteen years earlier. But after 1928 the ASHA found that activity was increasing, as was visibility.[9] This pattern more or less persisted until another world war found communities once again engaging in vigorous repression.

While cities almost everywhere claimed success in coping with the social evil, at least until the end of the 1920s, prostitutes and their predators and parasites began adapting immediately. As early as 1920 numerous authorities agreed that the closures and intense repression reduced the prostitute population. But they also granted that women formerly segregated had spread throughout cities and taken up business under new guises.[10] The vice commissions bore part of the responsibility. All recommended abolishing the districts, yet only 28 percent wanted to prosecute brothel proprietors, and a mere 24 percent felt that patrons should be charged with a crime. Conclusions and solutions were imprinted with the marks of shortsightedness in other ways. Only a third of the vice commissions were interested in repressing streetwalking, and less than a third showed any concern for raising the wages of working-class women.[11] Attitudes notwithstanding, many cities made strenuous efforts to suppress prostitution, but found that the women continually foiled their best endeavors.

The variegated attempts to control prostitution are probably best illustrated in the New York City experience. New York has had more privately organized groups of citizens attempting to control prostitution than any other city, but despite their best efforts, an investigator concluded in 1932 that after each new legal loophole was closed, the prostitutes found new ways to function.[12]

Few could deny that the cityscape resembled a moveable seesaw. As public and police attention focused on brothel activity prostitutes moved to the streets. With repression on the streets the women moved back to the houses, to new streetscapes and developed new ruses. Mobility was the geographical motif that tied together a variety of strategems, insured viability and created an ever-changing mosaic of immoral landscapes.

Chicago: The Complexities of Adaptation

During the post-Civil War period prostitution was a highly profitable enterprise for Chicago's underworld. At this time there may have been more than 250 brothels and 2,000 prostitutes in the city. Streetwalkers were common and plied their business with impunity.[13] An 1845 Illinois law had declared brothels illegal, but society tended to regard prostitution as inevitable and not worth repressing.

After the Chicago fire of 1871 a number of vice areas grew to prominence. Taken together they bespoke the moral code of the times, in name if not in fact, and gave a distinctive flavor to the landscape. The "Black Hole," a cluster of cribs and brothels, and "Coon Hollow" on the South Side, catered to blacks. Also on the South Side were the "Badlands," "Satan's Mile," "Hell's Half-Acre," "Dead Man's Alley" and the "Levee," so named because of the disorderly nature of levee districts in river towns almost everywhere. In later years the Levee would encompass other districts and become infamous as Chicago's principal red-light district.[14]

By the late 1880s there were at least three recognizable districts, one on the south side, one on the west side and one to the north—"Little Hell." Significant as these districts were, they were home to less than half of the city's prostitutes. By 1910 when Chicago's vice commission was under way the police department knew of some 500 brothels and 1,900 madams and prostitutes. Equal or greater numbers operated without police knowledge or interference. None of these figures included streetwalkers or part-time prostitutes.[15]

Chicago was the nation's first city to sponsor a municipal investigation of prostitution and the first to attempt to eliminate its districts. Although there was opposition from the city's cops who preferred informal regulation, their voices were barely heard by muckrackers, those concerned with social hygiene and those agitating against white slavery. Some were evangelical and uncompromising, others attempted to be rational and humanitarian. Whatever the color of their crusading banners, reformers were generally of one mind in wanting impartial and uniform justice and an end to districts that were purportedly bringing in $15 million a year in profits.[16] The formal closing of brothels may have seemed like a victory to moral reformers; it was merely a prod to prostitutes, madams and others to use their ingenuity.

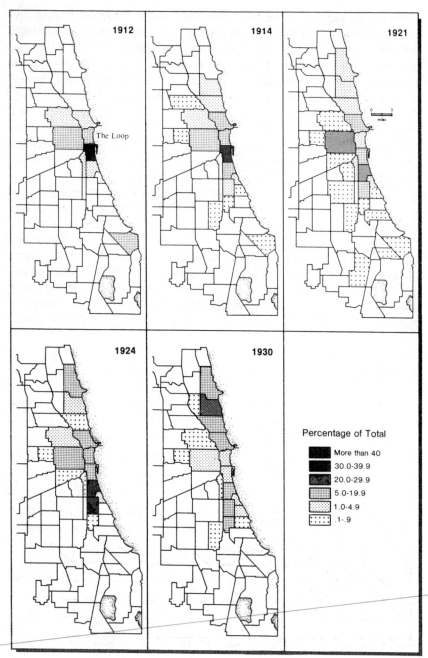

Figure 12-2 Places of Prostitution in Chicago, according to the Committee of Fifteen
Data from Reckless 1933:281-285.

When the city first attempted to close the Levee in 1912 prostitutes were told by their pimps, their madams and saloon keepers to move to residential neighborhoods.[17] In protest, they were also advised to visibly parade downtown, wearing more than usual amounts of lipstick, and to solicit on the streets. All was for naught. The police closed 135 places that harbored prostitutes, most in the South Side. Still, it took nearly two years to effectively shut down most of the Levee. Madams with high-class houses continued to operate. Some hired young boys and hoodlums to act as lookouts, others filled the pockets of cops and those in the right places. But despite payoffs and discretion where it had been lacking previously, most found that business viability entailed a concept of mobility.

The initial years of repression were particularly active, a fact evident in the changing distribution of arrests between 1912 and 1914 (Figures 12-2 and 12-3). In 1912 prostitution arrests were being made in only eight of 70 statistical tracts, and the majority came from but two tracts. Within two years police were collaring women in twice as many areas. With the major exception of more intense efforts during and after the war years the pattern of arrests in 1914 more or less forebode the future. While prostitutes were seized in just over half of the 70 tracts during the nearly two decades examined, a mere ten accounted for about 90 percent of total apprehensions.

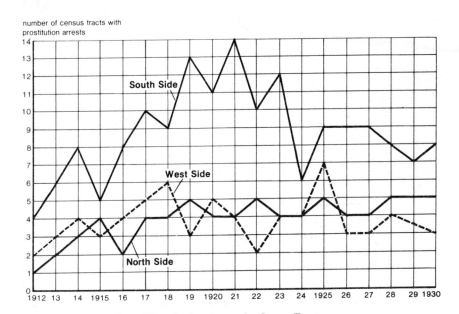

Figure 12-3 Distribution of Prostitution Arrests by Census Tract
Based on an analysis of maps produced by author from Reckless data for each year.

From the Levee and nearby areas prostitutes spread to a number of neighborhoods where previously they had worked only occasionally or not at all. The South Side experienced the highest rates of arrests and the most dramatic fluctuations, no doubt reflecting—however imperfectly—prostitution activity and movement into and out of the area as repression waxed and waned (Figure 12-3). Many women were not moving much further than near neighborhoods when chased by the police, soon returning to familiar turf when repression slackened.[18] Over time prostitution in this part of Chicago extended its reach southward, never abandoning a core area that was evident before the city took measures to get rid of its "social evil" (Figure 12-4).

The hand of the law was the major determinant of the relocation process. After repression began brothels had little place persistence. Fewer than eight percent of bordellos raided more than five times maintained the same

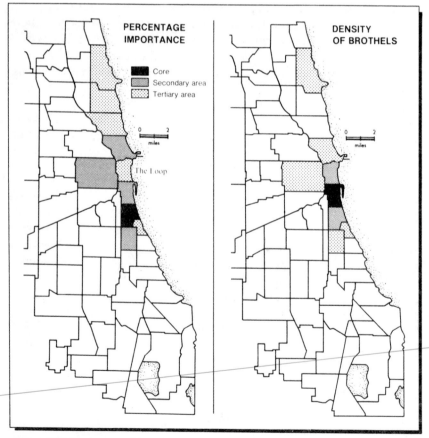

Figure 12-4 Persistence of Prostitution in Chicago, 1910 to 1929
Data from Reckless 1933:281-285.

address, and 67 percent were first offenders at the booked location. Relocations were responsive to differential repression within the city. It was not uncommon for flats, apartments and hotels to be reoccupied when the cops relaxed. Houses with the greatest address longevity were those able to secure police protection, which usually meant they were tied into organized crime. The underworld was most active in the centralized areas, especially the South Side. Others who did well were "rich cafe owners and those supported by powerful politicians."[19] Prostitutes stayed four times as long at the same address in centralized areas as did those further out, and nearly eight times as long as roadhouse operations on the outskirts of the city.

Dispersion of activity resulted in significant changes in types of business locations. By 1930 three broad zones could be distinguished. Near the Loop prostitution occurred primarily in flats and cheap hotels. In a zone more distant women serviced their clients principally in houses and large apartment buildings. In districts still more remote from the core most commercial sex transactions took place in apartments and flats.

One effect of intensified police repression was that the total amount of prostitution activity apparently decreased. One estimate put the number of full-time prostitutes in Chicago in 1910 at 5,000. They worked in some 1,000 houses, averaging about five women per brothel. By 1923 the prostitute population had been halved, as had the number of bordellos. After 1915 the streetwalker population may also have declined. However, interpretation of this claim is complicated because dress differences between streetwalkers and non-prostitutes blurred over time, because it became more acceptable for women in general to be on the streets alone, and because of increasing sophistication in solicitation methods.

Brothel visibility and business practices changed noticeably from pre-repression days. No longer did flashing lights and blaring music suggest the presence of promiscuous women, no longer did open solicitation from windows fronting on the streets occur, and men were discouraged from lingering near places where prostitutes worked. Some houses were protected by "tunnels for escape, warning buzzer systems, secret panels, trick doors," and the prospective client might find himself "sent into a dummy smoke shop, from there directed to outside passages, through alleys and yards to the back door of a house or apartment which [was] absolutely dark."[20] When business was finished, the customer was directed to leave by another exit.

Prior to repression cabdrivers often acted as guides for visitors to the red-light district. After closings began they took on the role of acting as "steerers" and "runners," especially for women who moved frequently among houses. Taxi drivers were vital to organized syndicates, but even more so to unattached prostitutes. Those working alone had to rely on connections with bartenders, hotel clerks, waiters and cabdrivers if they were to compete effectively. Although taxi drivers were well-compensated for their efforts, receiving a healthy commission on each client delivered, and were a vital adaptive agent in a new setting, by the mid-1920s their pivotal role had declined. Principal reasons included lack of discrimination in referring customers—resulting in frequent arrests, misunderstandings with prostitutes, predatory monetary demands for their services, occasional evangelical preaching and the risk of being reported to the companies for whom they worked, or being taken to court if independents. One prostitute in 1920 described her disaffection for cabdrivers.

> I was in with the cabbies. They knew my number and sent me up a lot of tricks. They get $2 out of every $5 spent, you know. If they don't trust you, they will stick around and collect then and there. But I always had them come back in the morning and get their money. I didn't want them ringing the bell any more than was necessary. But they're a dumb lot. They send up just anybody. They're just as liable to send up some spy, reformer or plain clothes man. They can't tell the difference. I'm through with them now. It's too risky.[21]

Repression presented problems for organized crime that necessitated counter strategies. One Chicago syndicate used a system of shifting prostitutes among slum properties they owned. The property might have a semi-permanent "for sale" or "for rent" sign in front, with a poor black family living in one or two rooms. A couple of times a week a boss of operations told taxi drivers and others soliciting clients which houses to use. If difficulties with the police were anticipated particular houses went unused until matters improved.

The most sustained attempt at repression in Chicago occurred between 1923 and 1927 when a closed-town policy existed. It was most strikingly manifested in the flight of prostitution to roadhouses on the outskirts of Chicago.[22] Some were located as far as 50 miles from the Loop. Although they first appeared when repression began, their popularity rose when police activity was most intense. Walter Reckless, the principal student of prostitution in Chicago at this time, claimed that roadhouses thrived because the edges of the city were sparsely settled and had a "decadent rural culture."[23] In fact, lax repressive measures and jurisdictional matters seemed to be the central reasons. Uncertainty existed among city, county and state authorities over who had the right to prosecute roadhouse operations. Further, when county police were involved they only weakly enforced the law. Nevertheless, old Levee owners who opened up the suburban fringes still found it necessary to pay graft, use a tipoff system for impending raids and occasionally change addresses.

Graft and bribery played a major role in the persistence of prostitution in Chicago. A 1931 report before the United States Senate stated that as much as $10,000 a week was paid to the city's police bureau to "lay-off" vice establishments.[24] For security brothel owners might have to pay a substantial initial fee followed by monthly payments. Often these were simply for protection against closing. In some cases payoffs gave the owner a monopoly in a certain area of the city. Fees varied according to the number of establishments maintained. "Pocket guides" or notebooks were kept by those responsible for carrying out vice raids. These listed secure places, prices and those that could be raided. One notebook that belonged to a lieutenant revealed extortion rates ranging from $40 to $150 per week per house. The notebook also showed that some brothels were "chief's places," the total take was his, whereas for others the extortion monies were split three ways.[25]

Payments were not always made in money, or rather not just in cash.[26] House owners were sometimes told where to buy their groceries, their liquor, their insurance. Neighborhood bosses and brothel owners might "guarantee" that so many votes would be delivered for a political candidate in exchange for protection. Because not everyone in the city hierarchy was receiving graft, now and again raids were carried out on a seemingly indiscriminate basis. Protected houses were usually warned in advance of impending raids. The raids occasioned a temporary closing, movement to another location or a short vacation for the operator.

Notable relationships existed between the mutating locations of prostitution and socioeconomic characteristics of the population. In contrast to frontiers, more females than males lived where activity was most concentrated. In general, these were also areas with the lowest proportions of home owners.

By 1930 the city's neighborhoods with the greatest incidence of prostitution coincided with those possessing the highest percentage of blacks. A dramatic shift had taken place since repression began. Chicago had relatively few blacks in 1912, and prostitution was a white phenomenon occurring in white neighborhoods. By 1930 considerable activity had shifted to the South Side Black Belt, where residential inhabitants were both black and poor, and where brothels were predominantly boarded by black women (Figures 12-5 and 12-6). Major reasons for this included heavy black migration into the least desirable neighborhoods, few job opportunities for these new arrivals, except as maids and porters, and greater harassment of black prostitutes. But most significant of all was application of the geopolitical sink principle. Real estate agents consistently rented flats and buildings in the Black Belt to those they knew to be engaged in prostitution. Blacks and prostitutes were already there and the agents justified their behavior by noting that the Black Belt was a "festering slum."[27] Only 26 percent of the buildings were in good repair in 1912.[28]

When pushed and harassed prostitutes and their predators took paths of least resistance: to neighborhoods of declining respectability and those with increasing concentrations of blacks. When the police pursued prostitutes they consistently pushed them away from commercial districts and white

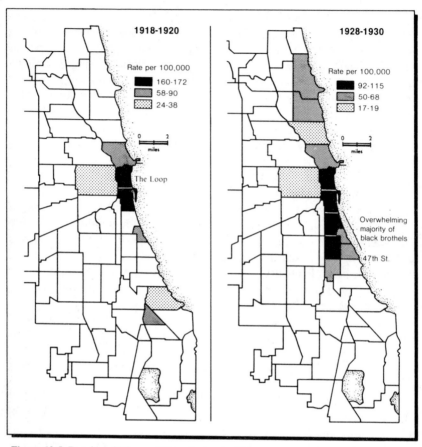

Figure 12-5 Density of Places of Prostitution in Chicago
Data from Reckless 1933:281-285.

neighborhoods and into or near the Black Belt. In twenty years of repression relatively few good residential areas were invaded by prostitution.

In his probing study of Chicago's slums and ghettos from 1880 to 1930 Thomas Philpott pinpointed some of the issues.

> No white people . . ., not even the sort who patronized whores and gaming tables, cared to live next door to bordellos and casinos, any more than they wanted to live near Negroes. Since it was not possible or at least not politic, to suppress vice, the police segregated it. Black people were helpless to prevent the authorities from locating the red-light district where they lived . . ., just as they were unable to stop whites from segregating them.[29]

The problem was compounded by the fact that prostitution in the Black Belt was mainly for whites, and it was whites who principally received profits from the trade.[30] It is not surprising that blacks did not support repression,

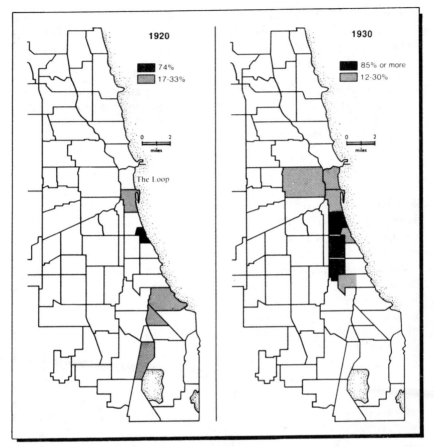

Figure 12-6 Percentage of Blacks in the Population
Data from Reckless 1933:281-285.

believing that it was only a vehicle for pushing prostitution deeper into their own neighborhoods.

Racism had other dimensions in Chicago. Very few brothels had blacks and whites working under the same roof. In 1929, 44 percent of the houses had only black women, while 55 percent were staffed solely with whites. Black and white clientele did not mix to any extent. Those few places where the races came together, "black and tan resorts," were invariably more subject to police raids.[31]

Black prostitutes constituted 70 percent of the morals court cases in 1929. By this time it was a "generally accepted fact that Negroes are more liable to arrest by police than whites," resulting in good part because "police officers share in the general public opinion that Negroes 'are more criminal than whites,' and also feel that there is little risk of trouble in arresting Negroes, while greater care must be exercised in arresting whites."[32]

In spite of blacks bearing a disproportionate share of the cost of living in immoral landscapes for the benefit of whites there were enough women working elsewhere in the city that an Illinois crime survey in 1929 could not help but conclude that:

> the crusades against vice, even when they succeeded in achieving the objectives at which they aimed, as in the abolition of the segregated vice district, do not seem to have extirpated the social evil; they have, however, driven it deeper into the community life, where it tends to find concealed forms of expression.[33]

London: A Different Problem

If Chicago provides an historical example of how brothel prostitutes and those associated with them adapt to repression, then London at a later date is a case study of what happens when the state attempts to suppress street-walking.

The act of prostitution has not been illegal in London since Cromwell's Puritan reign in the seventeenth century. During the early nineteenth century the British Parliament enacted a law to protect the public from annoyance by prostitutes.[34] According to later revisions, "every common prostitute or nightwalker loitering or being in any thoroughfare or public place for the purpose of prostitution or solicitation to the annoyance of the inhabitants or passengers is liable to a fine of forty shillings."[35] Whenever arrested for supposed nuisance a prostitute appeared before a judge, pleaded guilty, paid forty shillings and then returned to the streets. Many women saw the fine as a form of taxation or license fee and claimed that they were arrested approximately every two weeks, or on a "rota basis." Some even knew when they were about to be apprehended and might make arrangements with the police in their area to arrest them at another time if they had a pressing personal task to undertake. The system had many shortcomings but it promoted understanding and a certain amount of accommodating behavior among street women, clients and cops. It also permitted the development of relatively stable social structures and expectations.

The most important prostitution districts in London in the 1940s were Soho, Mayfair, Hyde Park, Paddington and Victoria[36] (Figure 12-7). Each could be differentiated from the others in number and age of prostitutes, where business was principally transacted and whether it was a source or receiving area for women moving up and down the social hierarchy.

The largest and most infamous area was Soho. A noted prostitution district for more than a hundred years, it was principally populated by two classes of women. One was composed of those who regularly worked the area, were well-known to the police and arrested on a regular basis and generally took several clients in an evening, each in quick succession. The second and more numerous group included those who worked infrequently,

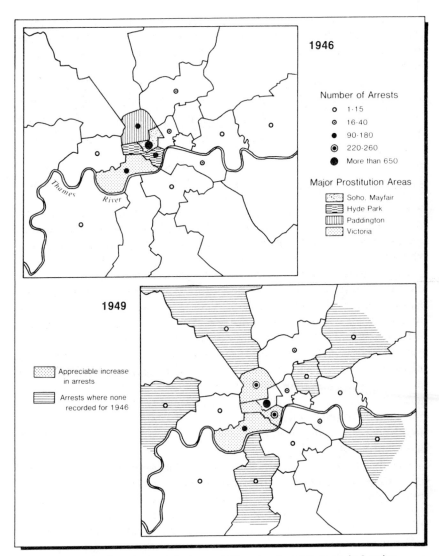

Figure 12-7 Major Prostitution Districts and Changing Arrest Patterns in London
Data from Rolph 1955:185.

were not known to the police and therefore seldom arrested, and often came in from another part of London by taxi or tube train to spend under a half-hour picking up a serviceman or a single all-night customer. Neither of these classes was among London's most attractive or expensive nor, by comparison with streetwalkers elsewhere, were they particularly considerate of their clients. Their outstanding trait was their degree of organization and professionalism. Most would transact business by taking their customers to relatively expensive rooms, while some serviced men in the lanes off Soho streets, or in taxicabs. Soho was an area prostitutes entered when they came into the life and from which they would leave for places down the social ladder.

Neighboring Soho was Mayfair, the most exclusive and discreet prostitution district in London. Mayfair was less heterogeneous than its neighbor in the types of prostitutes found there, and was characterized by women who hustled full-time. Mayfair prostitutes dressed well, were attractive, "charming and sympathetic" to their upper-class clientele and demanded high prices. Indeed, they were proud of their label: "the aristocrats of street prostitution."[37] Business was transacted in rented rooms, usually separate from their own residences. Somewhat like Soho, Mayfair was a place where prostitutes began and might spend their entire street life. Only a few moved down to Soho or upward into Mayfair from other locales. Although these two districts—London's West End—accounted for half of the city's convicted prostitutes in 1949, few ex-juvenile delinquents and criminals could be counted among the women.

A third and rather heterogeneous area was Hyde Park, a district inhabited by the very young and old, those trying prostitution for the first time and by housewives who came to work only in the afternoon. While the prices were generally lower than in other areas, they varied depending on where services were performed. Many who worked in Hyde Park did not have flats for business. Often clients were serviced in the park or in men's cars. Hand masturbation was a frequent request. Prostitutes from other districts came to work in the park after losing their flat through illness or financial difficulties. Finally, some younger women moved from Hyde Park to other streetwalking locales, though many stayed because they liked working in the park.

Paddington was similar to Hyde Park. It was populated by many young prostitutes who could not afford to keep separate rooms. Some streets bordering Paddington were frequented by older women. Prices were low in this district and services were performed in cars, dark back streets, cheap hotels or in the womens' rooms. Unlike Soho, Paddington lacked conspicuous competition among prostitutes and seemed to attract less aggressive women. For many it was an area of transition; they began there and left for other locales. Occasionally they returned but seldom stayed long enough to be known and subject to arrest.

Victoria was London's fifth major prostitution district. Primarily a reception area for older women from Soho or Hyde Park, its streetwalkers had the highest average age and rate of arrest. Despite the lower-class status of the district, the prostitutes charged the relatively high prices to which they had become accustomed elsewhere. Rooms were almost always used for servicing customers. Because the locale was a receptacle for those on the way down and those who had plied the trade in Soho, it had "an atmosphere of dogged commercialism: the women [were] hard, often socially embittered and demonstrably out to defeat their customers."[38]

A final district worth mentioning was Stepney, distinctive for its popularity with young prostitutes and runaways from places other than London. Many of the men who lived in the district were foreigners, unsettled immigrants or seamen waiting for ships to leave. They provided accommodations for wayward young girls who then turned to prostitution. Soliciting occurred in cafes and other public places, and sexual activities took place in the streets and private rooms. Many women would go with a man for the entire night at a low price, sometimes asking for no more than a bed for the evening. Those who turned to full-time prostitution often moved to another district. Some remained and set up household with a man they met in Stepney, as wife, lover or prostitute.

While other areas were used by streetwalkers in London in the 1940s—Waterloo Station and the Euston Road district being two—these generally had few prostitutes and were less well-known than the others. Too, women could be found near railway stations, shipping docks, military barracks and in and around various commons and parks. These prostitutes were a quite heterogeneous lot. Some worked continually, others did so sporadically; some only worked the streets, others went primarily to cafes and public houses.

As depicted here, prostitution districts in London were relatively well-defined and stable. But the situation changed in the late 1940s. During the war years soldiers kept prostitutes busy. Some, of course, were busier than others and their work load depended as much on where they hustled as on their personal attributes. Victoria, for example, was near the train station and this was a definite locational advantage as arriving soldiers headed for the nearby pubs and cafes. Heavy male demand, protection afforded by indoor environments and periodic blackouts meant that women did not have to labor at soliciting.

Once the war was over all this changed. Soldiers were gone, less money was circulating, prostitutes became bolder and more visible in their ways and the police responded by cracking down. The result was predictable. In some areas the number of prostitutes arrested increased—dramatically so in Hyde Park; total prostitution charges climbed noticeably in all districts; and London's immoral landscape began to look like a ripe tomato smashed on a table (Table 12-2; Figure 12-7).

Victoria vividly illustrates the changes. The total number of charges for prostitution in the district during 1945 was a mere 45. But in 1946 the figure skyrocketed to 593, climbed to 691 a year later and then hit a peak of 879 arrests in 1948. In Victoria there were other changes after the war. The percentage of streetwalkers over the age of 30 increased. A selection process had occurred: amateur and young prostitutes found it difficult to cope with police harassment and increased competition, because of fewer clients and

Table 12-2
Prostitution Arrests and Charges by District in London

District	No. of Prostitutes Arrested				No. of Prostitution Charges[1]				Average No. of Charges per Prostitute	
	1946	1949	+/-	%	1946	1949	+/-	%	1946	1949
Soho Mayfair	800	655	-145	-18	2,949	3,045	+96	+3	3.6	4.3
Hyde Park	116	259	+143	+123	275	702	+425	+155	2.4	2.5
Paddington	176	221	+45	+26	346	471	+125	+36	2.0	2.1
Victoria	145	96	-49	-34	593	807	+214	+36	4.1	8.4

[1] Includes charges for solicitation only; the only other charge of consequence is for vagrancy which only affects the figures for Hyde Park. For Hyde Park this would increase the number of charges for 1946 by approximately 6% and for 1949 by 13%. A few of the prostitutes were arrested in more than one area.

Data from Rolph 1955:185.

because of brothel women who had taken to the streets. The amateurs and the young ones responded by soliciting less frequently.

A comparison of arrest patterns for Hyde Park for 1946 and 1949 shows differences when compared with Victoria and other districts. Of London's major prostitution areas, the percentage increase in arrests was highest in Hyde Park (155%), more than four times that of Victoria (36%; Table 12-2). In Hyde Park more women were arrested a given number of times, and several were arrested half again as often as were those working the park three years earlier (Figure 12-8). A unique feature of Hyde Park, not indicated in Table 12-2 and Figure 12-8, was the six-fold increase in arrests for indecent behavior, from 15 in 1946 to 92 in 1949. Many of the prostitutes were young and new, did not have flats for business and lacked the experience of servicing men outdoors.

Soho and Mayfair showed no appreciable increase in total arrests between 1946 and 1949, but other changes did occur. Many of the younger prostitutes had moved out of these areas and those remaining were older, more persistent and less subtle in soliciting. Persistence was reflected in a significant drop in the number of prostitutes arrested (from 800 to 655) while the total number of charges remained about the same (2,949 vs 3,045), in the increased average number of charges per woman (3.6 to 4.3), and in the tendency for some prostitutes to be arrested a greater number of times (Table 12-2 and Figure 12-8). That times had gotten harder was also apparent in the decreased brothel trade in the West End and in the greater

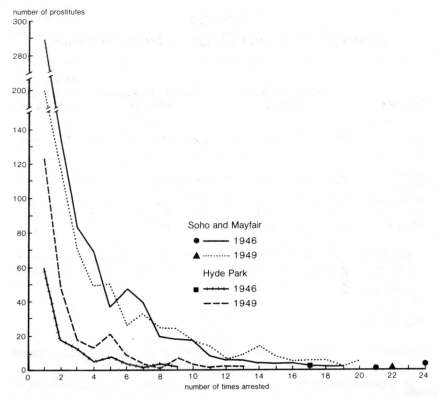

Figure 12-8 Arrest Patterns by District and Year
Data from Rolph 1955:192.

number of women without hustling flats. Decreased demand and increased rents showed up in arrests for public intercourse. In 1946 only a single prostitute in Soho and Mayfair had been charged for this type of behavior; by 1949 the number had jumped to 61.

The picture in Paddington and other districts was not unlike that described for Victoria and Hyde Park: a general increase in number of charges, more business being transacted within public view and, as in Soho and Mayfair, movement within the districts away from areas where room rents had increased. In short, while the post-war years had specific effects on each locale and on different classes of women, all areas shared to some extent the effects of decreased demand, tighter money and police reaction to prostitutes' attempts to maintain previous income levels.

If any specific group benefited in the late 1940s it was French prostitutes who came to exploit their renowned reputations. For a while some even took out dual citizenship by marrying Englishmen, on the condition that a divorce would quickly follow. Mayfair, not surprisingly, was hardest hit by this mini post-war invasion.[39]

Despite changes, some small, some significant, social hierarchies persisted in London's prostitution districts. They persisted, more or less, until the Street Offenses Act of 1959. Under the new law it was no longer necessary to demonstrate that a prostitute was a public annoyance. Simply the fact that she was loitering or soliciting on the streets constituted an offense. A second arrest was more costly than the first and by the third she could be sent to jail for three months. The new system provided that a streetwalker was to receive two cautioning notices before being arrested. Obviously prostitutes could and did solve the problem by changing their names and moving to new turf.[40] A change of name and address might be accompanied by legislative relief. The Street Offenses Act did not repeal all previous laws, nor did it eliminate local inconsistencies.[41]

The immediate effect of the Street Offenses Act was to force prostitutes to leave familiar surroundings. Arrests were one indication that the street scene had altered. During the first three months after the Act was put into effect London arrests for street solicitation were down by almost 90 percent when compared to a similar period in the previous year.[42] But business went on more or less as usual. Prostitutes began working in pubs and cafes and hustling at open doors and windows. By 1960 the courts moved against the women by extending the meaning of solicitation to include window tapping and other forms of invitation, on the grounds that these constituted solicitations "projected to" someone.[43] Other prostitutes put up fluorescent red doorbells and small signs such as "French Model" that left little doubt about their occupation. A note near the doorbell might indicate that Lulu or Mimi could be found on the second floor, easily reached because the street door was open.[44] In case such advertisements were missed, men were hired to pass out cards with addresses and prices. Women in Mayfair, and others with resources or resourcefulness, adapted by renting cars. Renting permitted a continual change of colors and makes, making it difficult for cops to recognize their adversaries. Shortly after the new law came into effect at least 50 London prostitutes were using this method.[45]

A number of women moved their base of operations to hostess clubs and "near beer" establishments where they were forced to pay a percentage of their earnings to the owner or manager. Some received a kickback on the expensive champagne they forced on males, others did not. All had to spend inordinate amounts of time listening to verbal abuses and dealing with drunks, men with foul breath and wandering aggressive hands.[46] The system promoted fraud. Men were enticed into clubs on the implied promise they would be able to have intercourse, often with attractive teenagers. The young girls made assurances, got payment in advance and then agreed to meet gullible customers at addresses that did not exist.

A common stratagem involved advertising in newspapers and shop windows. Paddington, Bayswater, Soho and other districts became popular for the use of "coded" advertisements. Service and address cards were put in shopkeepers' windows, ostensibly to tout legitimate sales. The cards read "Lovely fireside rugs made to order," "Dusky dolls for sale" and "Young kittens for sale." The first referred to intercourse on the floor, the second to a pair of black and white prostitutes, the third to simple intercourse. Other ads were more explicit or used easily recognized jargon: "Large chest for sale" and "Teenage doll giving French lessons."[47] If doubt remained in a male's mind concerning the nature of the services all he need do was make a phone call.

In Soho, Mayfair and other districts many prostitutes specialized in "extras" and "kinky" sex. Up to half of the window or newsstand advertisements fell into these categories, further evidence for the importance of "English Culture" (sadomasochistic requests). Prostitutes found they could receive two, three or sometimes several times their normal straight intercourse fee for beating men with ropes, whips or walking sticks, or for allowing customers to abuse them in one of these ways. A sadistic act cost a client as much as a pound a stroke.[48] Some prostitutes specialized in "bondage and correction." A man was firmly tied with a rope and then beaten with a cane. In general, few women were willing to receive such blows, even for a good price, and those who did were older and on their way down.

Shopkeepers, tobacconists and others cooperated with prostitutes in posting cards because it was profitable.

> They charged two pounds a week for each advertisement or card on Praed Street, and there were about 100 in the window for all the call girls there were. That meant the shopkeeper made himself 200 pounds a week tax free, and all the call girls got business. Men stood in a long line to read the advertisements and picked what they liked, for some of the girls had their picture on the card as well, almost naked.[49]

As early as 1960 the card business was so profitable to shop owners that whole windows were filled with ads, and some places had no goods inside to sell.[50]

The police were not very successful in combating card soliciting. They tried to prevent people from congregating to read them and they took their case to court, and lost. The only consolation, if it could be called one, was that nineteenth-century London prostitutes had successfully used the same method. At least there was no repetition of the practice of having men parade up and down Regent and Bond Streets with sandwich boards announcing the offerings.[51]

After 1960 the "country lane beat" variant of prostitution increased in popularity. Prostitutes worked main roads at the periphery of the city, planting themselves on the route to Oxford, near Denham, and in Buckinghamshire, and later between Lambourne End and Ongar in Essex. At first their customers were truck drivers, but later they included those of the upper-middle and upper classes. Often business was transacted in a nearby field or the client's car. A distinguishing feature of this locational adaptation was that the women only worked the country lanes until the late afternoon and then moved either to Soho or to the London docks where sailors were easy prey.[52]

Some women returned to the streets they knew so well, despite heavier fines and the possibility of a jail term after the third conviction. Since the heavy fines could not be considered a minor business expense, many women began putting up court defenses. And they were successful because few arresting officers could afford to spend up to a full day in court for a simple prostitution charge. Nevertheless, those who worked the streets came out later at night and bargained less over price in order to reduce visibility. Since many who solicited out of doors did not have flats a usual place of business was the back seat of an automobile.

Cops lost in other ways, enough to make many question whether the Street Offenses Act had been a good thing after all. Previously a policeman knew all the women on his beat and he could focus his attention on blatant solicitators. After the Act cops had much greater difficulty in keeping track of prostitutes. Under the old system policemen received payoffs from the women; now they received less or nothing at all. The "punter" or client also suffered. Prostitutes began to make promises and then not deliver; they ran with the money received "out front." Even the venereal disease rate is alleged to have increased, not too surprisingly in view of pressures to be clandestine. If there was a clear winner in the new system it was the landlord, and anyone else who could blackmail the prostitute for what she was doing.[53]

In summary, the Street Offenses Act of 1959 forced prostitution to take other forms, with both social and geographical consequences. The resulting repression broke down a relatively stable prostitution hierarchy—a set of districts with meaning to prostitutes, their patronizers and policemen—and it removed most of the ostentatious solicitation in most districts. A few women remained on the streets and risked the heavy penalties of arrest and prosecution. But most went to the country lanes, to clubs, to coded ads and to work for madams who maintained discreet call-house operations. A reading of history might have told legislators that a simple mode change was a likely reaction to repression.

Chapter 13

Massage Parlors and Other Strategems

As long as a disapproved activity is covert many people seem willing to ignore it, or at least attenuate their judgments about it. For such institutions as massage parlors, club hostesses and escort services the meaning of visibility would seem to reside as much in the social acceptability of a word or way of stating something as in the true nature of things. Disguises produce a social irony. So long as some segment of the population believes that massage parlors, escort services or similar operations are more or less what they claim to be, then such businesses will cater to innocent expectations. To be sure, they may offer prostitution services, but these may be limited or only part of the offerings. However, if society begins to seriously label these kinds of enterprises as fronts for prostitution, then they will be handled as such in legislation, owners and employees will see advantage in behaving as labeled and treated and clients in their demands will consistently ignore the falsehood contained in an institutional label. Social labeling is self-fulfilling, and very often self-defeating; it is a feedback process in which the labeled activity is transformed to more closely resemble the label and its various connotations.[1] At some point no one will be fooled into believing that, for example, massage parlors are anything more than brothels. And yet, by some twisted social logic, the fact that they are called massage parlors rather than brothels insures their continuing existence.

From "Locals" to Everything

The association between massage parlors and prostitution is not new and existed even when authorities tolerated or regulated prostitution. A chronicler of Chicago's "dark places" in the latter part of the nineteenth century claimed that numerous massage parlors were really brothels.[2] More than two decades later when thriving red-light districts dotted the North American landscape vice commissions repeatedly concluded that such places were fronts for commercial sex. New York City had an estimated 300 parlors.[3] A 1915 Toronto report charged that virtually all of the city's masseuses were prostitutes.[4] Europe has not been an exception historically, and the Amsterdam police in recent years suspected that up to 125 of the city's massage parlors were, in fact, brothels.[5]

Increases in the number of massage parlors mirror repression. This was true when America's red-light districts were closed, when Italy's brothels were shut in 1958, and when prostitutes were forced to leave London's streets in 1959.[6] According to one observer, the dramatic rise of parlor prostitution in Italy could be measured simply by examining advertisement listings for manicurists and masseuses.[7] So intense was the rivalry that many changed their names to begin with A, or a string of them, working on the assumption that those at the beginning of the list have an advantage.

While the continuing repression of streetwalking activity has been a factor in the proliferation of massage parlors in the United States in the 1970s, their numerical explosion owes much to the expectations of returning servicemen, most of whom encountered the sexual massage while on Rest and Relaxation during the Vietnam War. In Bangkok, Thailand, for example, 7,000 prostitutes reputedly worked in massage parlors at the height of the war.[8]

Though most heavily concentrated in the largest cities, massage parlors are found in places of all sizes. A 1972 tally for select cities, emphasizing the larger ones, showed the following: San Diego had 50; Pittsburgh, 28; Atlanta, 13; Denver, 12; New Orleans, 11; Columbus, Ohio, 16; Memphis, 8; and New York City, 75 to 100.[9] In testimony before the State of Washington House Subcommittee on Social Concerns in 1975 Barbara Yondorf claimed that prostitutes in massage parlors and body painting studios in King County (principally Seattle) accounted for as much as one-third of the total (Table 13-1).[10] In late 1977 the Washington D.C. Licensing Bureau listed some 50 massage parlors in the city. Of these, 22 were within walking distance of the White House and financial district, and another 11 were near foreign embassies (Figure 13-1).[11]

Table 13-1

Prostitution in King County, Washington in 1974

Type of Prostitute	Females	Males
Streetwalkers	200	150
Massage parlor & body painting studio prostitutes	3-400	?
Prostitutes working out of bars, baths, steam rooms, etc.	300	150
Topless dancers	50	—
Entertainment industry prostitutes	75	?
Call girls (boys)	100	?
Prostitutes in brothels	200	?
Total	1225-1325	300 +

Drawn from Yondorf 1975:4.

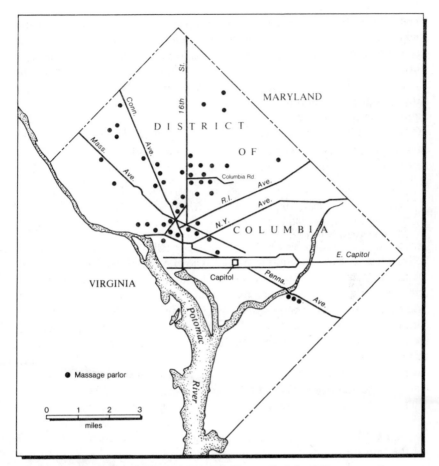

Figure 13-1 Licensed Massage Parlors in Washington D.C. in 1977
Adapted from Stopp, Jr. 1978.

As significant as the visual revitalization of the immoral landscape is the nature of the institution's transformation and that of the women who work in it. Through the interplay of social values and pressures expressed in legislation, enforcement and the media, and the self-seeking behavior of entrepreneurs, employees and clients, massage parlors mutate from businesses that specialize in hand masturbation to brothels—often low-class—that cater to nearly every demand and fantasy. This metamorphosis demonstrates how social labeling leads to a self-fulfilling prophecy.

Self-serving mechanisms are put into operation the first day a woman is employed.[12] The astute manager gives the new employee an unusually large amount of business, perhaps telling her she will only have to perform "locals" (hand masturbation). Women with no previous prostitution experience may believe they will have to go no further. But they learn otherwise, and quickly adjust. They discover that customers "tip" more for fellatio and intercourse than for a local and that their financial success depends on tips, since the owner takes up to 80 percent of the "massage" fee.[13] They also learn that unless they are willing to substitute their mouth for their hand they will lose business, and probably their jobs.[14] In this setting a woman may become a prostitute because she has few alternatives for employment. Or if she does, she has none that pays as well. Reservations about the job are blurred, eventually buried, by habit, long work hours, pressures from employers and coworkers, but most of all by visions of what the money will buy.

> For those who adjust to the routine, the rewards are very lucrative indeed. What a masseuse makes in "tips" she keeps. She pays no taxes on them and is not assessed any portion by the studio. These tips range at times to $800 for a five-day week.[15]

Newspaper exposés and licensing laws play an important role in the changing behavior of owners, employees and clients. To avoid pimping charges those who run parlors are careful to hire new women as free lance models, rather than as employees.[16] The "models" may be required by local ordinances to have regular venereal disease examinations; effectively they are treated like prostitutes. In the press and on the streets the women are called "sluts," "white trash" and "whores." Some attempt to bolster their declining image by demanding that they work with their hands only. But they are victims of labeling and they begin engaging in self-labeling and invidious comparisons. In ranking themselves with others they feel it better to be a "hand whore" than a "whore," someone who will do almost anything.[17] In a lineup for clients they begin referring to themselves as part of the "meat display."[18]

Customers learn about the medical requirements, feel the women must be safe, at least safer than someone picked up in a bar or on the street, and this adds to both trade and the demands placed on the "masseuses." Men consistently ask for fellatio and intercourse, expressing no interest in locals. The number of "grabby customers" increases dramatically, men complain to the parlor manager they did not get what they came for, some even demand their money back. If a woman does not want to go beyond locals she is informed that street prostitutes can be hired to take her place.

Clients hear that massage parlors are nothing more than "whorehouses." Street hustlers and the language of the landscape suggest they must be right. "Shangri-La," "Fantasia," "Roman Massage," "Ancient Palace of Leisure" and "Total Orgasm" are more suggestive than traditional brothel marquees. "Full body service," "Greek" (anal intercourse), "half and half" and "dominant" are among the verbal and written promises thrown at passersby by barkers, found on street markers, in handouts and in newspaper advertisements. Place names and terse pledges appear with increasing frequency in the underground press: the *Naked News* in New York

City, the *Saturday Evening Swinger* and the *Berkeley Barb* in the San Francisco Bay Area and the *Hollywood Press*. New York City's *Screw* rates the parlors, giving a rundown on exactly what kind of sex and attention one can expect for his money.

When laws are lax, entrepreneurs take advantage of the situation. West Hollywood in the early 1970s paid little heed to its parlors. The owners responded by advertising briskly and boldly in the underground press. The "Kama Sutra," the "Institute for Sexual Intercourse" and the "Sexual Catharsis Center" were three places that promised as much as any brothel in history.

Knowing their image has altered, owners realize that handsome returns can be had by catering to less common requests. They actively begin to seek the "weirdo." Advertisements for "Greek" and "dominance" increase in newspapers. Massage parlor managers who are change laggards begin to imagine the money lost to competitors, for prices and profits rise roughly in proportion to deviation from normal sexual services such as a local or simple intercourse.

Healthy returns encourage other entrepreneurs to enter the lucrative massage parlor business. Established owners open additional parlors and introduce practices appropriate to maintaining high profit levels and a competitive edge. In less than four years the number of massage parlors in Austin, Texas increased from two to twelve. One family which controlled three of them expanded into a nearby city and, in 1977, talked of beginning operations in other states.[19]

To stay abreast of rivals some owners direct their employees to spend part of their time visiting the parking lots of bars, night clubs and strip joints to leave suggestive calling cards on car windshields. The invitations often have a personal touch. As competition stiffens, operators may agree among themselves that each establishment should have its own territory for distributing calling cards.[20]

Others share in the harvest of the massage parlor business. Many of the parlors take major credit cards. Banks and financial institutions are not adverse to making money off the earnings of prostitutes, and hardly anyone thinks of raising the issue that state laws prohibit pimping.[21] Parlor owners frequently have to pay double or triple the rent a legitimate business would expend for the same premises.[22] Police ask to have their pockets enriched for closing their eyes. In some cities graft is expensive, especially if the owner is female.[23] Local governments require license fees, ranging from $500 to $5,000. These predatory rates are legitimized by public outcries of "whoring," and the belief that massage parlors presage the beginning of a red-light district.

The police frequently attempt to suppress massage parlors. During one two-year period in Chicago they made 280 raids on 63 businesses, arresting 950 women. When Chicago cops discovered they could not arrest women using prostitution statutes because there were no laws against "masturbation," they applied the Illinois Obscenity Statute. In general, periodic raids have proved to be short-term solutions at best.

Where the police crack down on places that offer virtually everything, as they did in New York City in mid-1971, owners readjust. Desperate managers solved their problem by renting stalls to streetwalkers.[24] Others reopened under a new name and relabeled the services that got them in trouble. One parlor decided to operate under the guise of a dance studio, another got rid of its "half and half" offering and instead offered nude reading encounters. Some owners returned to the older pattern of "massage and masturbation only."

With continued repression owners and employees require customers to take off their clothes before terms are discussed, and women learn to tell men where not to put their hands—all to avoid solicitation charges or entrapment. In the 1970s the New York City police department forbid its officers from undressing to get an arrest.[25] The city's massage parlor prostitutes avoided problems by requiring customers to undress before services and fees could be discussed. The city countered by hiring private detectives to purchase services and tell of their experiences in court. It worked, until the method came under heavy public criticism.

If repression is intense and continuous prostitutes ask their clients for extensive background information, and examine credit cards and other pieces of information. Some even tell men to return in two or three days after their stories have been cleared.

Strategies are invented and elaborated to meet the strength of the repressive challenge. New York City selectively enforced its general business laws by requiring those with massage parlors to meet higher standards on building, fire and safety codes. However, the only real effect, as one observer put it, was that the city begat "the cleanest, safest, and most well-lighted brothels in the country."[26]

The ingenuity required is usually not that great because governments generally prove to be ineffectual. By 1979 only 15 states had laws pertaining specifically to massage parlors, and these did little to distinguish between genuine massage therapists and prostitutes working in massage parlors.[27]

B-Girls, Escorts and the Three Act Play

Men generally expect women in massage parlors to behave as prostitutes, and their expectations are usually, but not always, met. The very fact of claiming to be something other than a brothel, combined with the illegality of prostitution, makes it relatively easy to defraud gullible males. Based on a veiled promise of sex, clients pay in advance, get less than they believed would be forthcoming and then complain they were cheated. When confronted with the ruse parlor owners and employees respond by reminding clients that prostitution is illegal. The men have little recourse, especially before the law.

There are, of course, other institutional forms besides massage parlors that have profited from the illegality of prostitution: B-girls, hostess hustlers, those who play the "Murphy game" and women who work for escort services and encounter studios. B-girls, "come-ons," and "drink hustlers" or "hostesses" have a rich history and association with prostitution.[28] Employed by bar owners their ostensible purpose is to serve drinks, be companionable, sexy and apparently sexually available. True purposes and intents are another matter. Erica Stone has described how the B-girl hustle worked in some of San Francisco's topless and bottomless bars in the early 1970s.[29] A customer is encouraged to buy a bottle of champagne for $30, a price that includes a few suggestive smiles or the woman's presence at the table for a short while. When the bill for the first bottle is paid the B-girl informs the customer that she works for tips, and that the standard rate is $10. Depending on the amount of business and how good a mark the male appears to be, she might sit with him and visually and verbally cater to his fantasies. The hustler often helps the man drink the cheap champagne to get him to order a second bottle. If he tries to be physically aggressive the woman may knock the bottle to the floor and then hustle him for another one.

The sexual ruse involves encouraging the customer to stay and drink, with the implicit promise (explicit for wary types) she will meet him later at a designated place. Most men believe that B-girls are prostitutes, that working in topless and bottomless clubs is simply a convenient and relatively safe way to peddle an illegal service. Their beliefs are often badly shaken. In one San Francisco club that Stone describes the men are told to appear after closing hours at a club called the "Pam-Pam." If a customer should return the following evening enraged that the woman did not show up as promised she simply tells him that she waited an hour or so at the "Pam-Pam East," a block or so away, and he did not come as agreed. There are few complaints and news of fraud spreads slowly to other males. Men are too concerned about giving the impression they got what they were after, and too embarrassed to tell the tale of how they were cheated by women posing as prostitutes. Predictably, the real winner is not the B-girl but the bar owner who takes all the profits on the drinks and a percentage of the tips.

In London "clip-joint girls" solicit men on the streets to join them in a dimly lit basement room, a near-beer club where the hostess requires several rounds of exhorbitantly priced drinks—cold tea—to "get in the mood."[30]

> The next step is to get the man to hand over the money. This is usually achieved by pretending that the money is required as a deposit for the key of an apartment to which they will shortly adjourn. The man is told to wait for the girl a little way down the street and of course she never comes.[31]

Since the women do not have intercourse with the men (police refer to them as "professional virgins") and have no reputations as "common prostitutes" they cannot be charged for soliciting.[32] The police are dependent on complaints from defrauded males, which they seldom receive.

The ruse of inducing a male to pay for a key to a nonexistent place has been a common one, even where prostitution has been tolerated.[33] In San Francisco's infamous Barbary Coast one dance hall dive known as the Seattle was notable for the sale of keys by its barmaids.[34] The Seattle did not permit employees to leave the premises with customers, but women were free to lead them down imaginary blind alleys. As practiced at the dance hall for more than a year, and at other places on the Barbary Coast, a barmaid convinced an anxious male she could not meet him on premises after closing hours since her jealous lover always walked her home. If he really wanted to meet her, however, she would sell him a key to her room where they could meet later. Keys sold for from one to five dollars and some women were reputed to have had as many as a dozen takers in an evening. The keys, of course, were for nonexistent doors. Supposedly, from time to time one could see "furtive figures . . . flitting through the streets searching hopelessly for doors which their keys would open."[35]

A similar method in common use since the Barbary Coast closing is what the author of the Pimp Bible, Iceberg Slim, has referred to as the "Murphy game."[36] A con man stands on a corner in a known prostitution district, solicits men with promises of a beautiful woman and a great time "just around the corner," and then sells the baited male a key to a nonexistent apartment. To the wary mark who asks why he must pay in advance, the Murphy man cites the need to protect the prostitute from the police.

A variation of the Murphy game involves "knobbers," males who disguise themselves as female prostitutes.[37] Some lure unsuspecting men into alleys to negotiate a price and then, with the aid of an accomplice, rob them. Others claim it is "the wrong time of the month." They perform fellatio in a truck, a hallway, an alley. Gail Sheehy, who learned about prostitution as a foot-wise journalist, conveyed a prostitute's indignation at those who worked near Lincoln Tunnel in New York City in the late 1960s: "damn knobbers strutting their silicone breasts past dumb Jersey truck drivers, the cops say they're better-looking than the real thing, it's an insult."[38]

Where keen competition prevails a type of quasi-prostitution sometimes appears. In Amsterdam during the mid-1960s two kinds of bars were common: one sold only wine or beer while the other dispensed all forms of alcoholic beverage. The first had lower- to middle-class clientele and competition among barmaids was intense. Upon entering the premises a customer was approached by a woman who invariably asked for expensive, low-quality champagne. If the customer spent enough money the woman took him to a rear booth or private dining room, put a napkin on his lap and masturbated him to orgasm.[39]

Many women who work as B-girls, topless dancers and strippers are prostitutes.[40] Some must prostitute to keep their jobs. Like women working in
brothels or massage parlors they are required to turn over a sizeable percentage of their earnings to club owners.[41] One college-graduate feminist
who moonlighted as a topless dancer in the New York City-New Jersey area
discovered that many women found it hard to avoid the temptation to triple
or quadruple their incomes by spending time in the "backrooms," performing fellatio or masturbation, or leaving after work with clients set up by the
manager.[42] A study in Toronto concluded that "prostitution is almost an inevitable consequence of stripping" because strippers perform at stag parties, because they are regarded as prostitutes and because they are always
being propositioned.[43] Yet, precisely because not all B-girls and strippers
engage in prostitution routinely, men frequently feel cheated out of what
they believe available merely for the asking and payment of a fee.

Among the more recent entrants into the immoral landscape are escort
services and nude encounter houses. Many of the escort service agencies
may be no more than what they claim: places where men hire young women
for an evening of companionship—dinner, dancing, talking—without
physical sex. While men believe the women are prostitutes, many of the
agencies claim that they are not fronts for prostitution and that most of
their clients are not interested in such services.[44] These claims are dubious at
best. Commonplace advertisements strongly suggest that employees are
prostitutes.[45] While the escorts or "outcall girls" may not engage in sexual
activities during the hours formally contracted for with the agency, many, if
not the overwhelming majority, are sexually available later for a large
"tip." As with B-girls and those working in massage parlors only women
who will prostitute themselves can make sizeable incomes or find palatable
the trying hours they spend with an array of demanding men while most of
the "legal"profits accrue to their employers.

More so than B-girl hustling, stripping and escort services, the nude en-
counter house derives its existence and vitality from illegality.[46] The modus
operandi, the usual one, is simple enough. Large garrish signs labeled
"House of Ecstasy," the "Oral Intercourse Center," the "House of Oral
Sex" and the "Tunnel of Love" suggest the possibilities (Figure 13-2).
Well-programmed, aggressive barkers add a human touch with words like,
"Come in, mister, there are pretty girls inside to satisfy your every need."
And what the male barker outside cannot verbalize, the female counterpart
inside does: "For your money you get the room, a girl, and you get to
climax." The ruse continues with the customer being required to sign a
form stating that he is not a cop or offended by unconventional sex acts.[47]
Anxiously, the mark chooses from among the females available, pays his
money which is immediately pushed through a slit in a safe or passed to
someone else, goes into a small cubbyhole, perhaps adorned with mirrors and

Figure 13-2 San Francisco Establishments that Feed Off the Illegality of Prostitution

posters of nude women, and then watches as the female before him strips to bra and panties, exactly as permitted by law. When the client gets verbally or physically aggressive he is politely told he can stare, take his clothes off, masturbate or practice the ancient art of "oral love," that is, talk. For a higher price he can obtain "full body contact," which means he gets to hold hands with the woman.

If the male persists in believing that encounter house employees are prostitutes he can enter another stall for an additional $50 to $100. The second cubicle may differ from the first only in that it has a red light or perhaps the presence of an additional woman. But as before nothing happens, nothing more than the often-repeated lines to remind the male of laws against prostitution.

If the irrepressible mark has deluded himself into believing that it is only a matter of money to get what he wants and he still has some left, then he may be advised that he can buy into Act III, a "Japanese tongue bath."[48] Client and woman go to a hotel, she encourages him to get into the bathtub, puts his clothes under a bed, and leaves. All that remains is for the male to gather his composure and, if the sting overrides his sense of dignity, contact the police.

Police departments receive hundreds of complaints each year on such ruses, especially from foreign tourists. No one knows how many more go unreported because marks feel too foolish to report their misadventures. In the first couple of years after a dozen or so encounter houses opened in San Francisco the vice squad claimed to have received over 400 complaints.[49] Some marks meted out their own justice, with their fists, with firearms or with arson. When complaints have been persistent cops have attempted to make arrests and build consumer fraud cases. But it is the client's word against that of the woman or house owner. Further protection is provided by ambiguous—if highly suggestive—come-ons, laws against prostitution and inept or corrupt governments. Sometimes carefully constructed evidence has been ignored or purposely mishandled by city prosecutors and appeals boards.[50]

Hypocrisy, consumer fraud, corruption and the creation of undesirable consequences through social labeling and self-fulfilling behavior do not result solely from illegality. Yet, there seems little doubt that with regard to prostitution such effects are either magnified or directly attributable to laws that are both unjust and self-defeating. Clearly, existing ways of handling prostitution in North America ought to be changed. The burden of history and common sense forces one to argue against the status quo and for more just solutions.

In Quest of Just Solutions

In North America approaches to prostitution have been and continue to be unjust, self-defeating and clearly in need of change. The development and evaluation of any policy necessitates a consideration of what, fundamentally, can and cannot be altered, an examination of competing alternatives and strategies for carrying out the proposed plan. One can proceed as an idealist and talk about unlikely worlds, engage the issues with dour pessimism (realism, some might say) or try to steer some middle path between the two. I believe in the just, I believe in the probable, and I also believe that, important as logic and common sense are, appeals must ultimately be made to self-interest, the interests of those who control the system of concern or make use of its components. Self-interest is the nature of capitalist societies; nay, it is the very nature of all living things.

The Probable and the Improbable

There is no reason to believe that monogamy, or some form of serial monogamy, will not continue to be the prevailing mode of sexual pairing among humans, as it has for thousands of years. It is a well-known anthropological finding that even among the scores of societies that permit polygamy, only a relatively small number of males (invariably the rich and the powerful) have more than one wife. Most societies are essentially monogamous. Nor is there any reason to believe, based on history and the anthropological record, that sex will ever be easily available to any significant segment of society. The vast majority of known societies have and continue to perpetuate rules and norms that proscribe indiscriminate copulation.

Because male promiscuity is biologically based and culturally reinforced in most societies, and because sex is unlikely to be freely available to all men, prostitutes will continue to meet a demand. Prostitutes are useful, not fundamentally because they protect the family or help society define the boundary between acceptable and unacceptable moral behavior—as sociologists and others have long contended—but because they provide an outlet for a biological imperative. Even if one does not accept arguments that emphasize the biological basis of prostitution, there is still no reason to expect the demise of the institution. Prostitutes simply provide too many services that are not easily available and that men are willing to pay for. For some men, prostitutes function as therapists, for others they embody the perfect outlet for sadomasochistic urges and for a great many they permit the fulfilling of fantasies.

Feminists such as Susan Brownmiller believe that prostitution should be eliminated because it contributes to the "mass psychology of rape" by putting sex into an explicit exchange format.[1] Besides ignoring the reality that almost all human interactions are exchanges of one sort or another, Brownmiller is making an unsubstantiated assertion about rape. Not only is there virtually no evidence that commercial sex promotes rape, to say nothing of the possibility that rape may not be primarily a sexual act, there is also some indication that prostitution may even lower the rape rate.[2] In any event, the connection between rape and prostitution is a subject for research, not one for irresponsible polemics. It should also be added that if a fraction of the money that is spent to control prostitution were used to prevent rape, men and women alike would be much better served.

Some on the left who argue for the elimination of prostitution have bought the myths that women do not enter prostitution on their own initiative, and that they do not like what they are doing. Some may not, but many prostitutes—perhaps the majority—do.[3] Paul Gebhard and his associates at Indiana University found that two-thirds of 127 prostitutes interviewed had no regrets about their job choice.[4] Other studies have reached similar conclusions.[5] Furthermore, prostitutes do not seem to be interested in rehabilitation. When Italy's brothels were closed in 1958, centers of "social re-education" were established. Women ignored the program, going to the streets instead.[6] In 1971 Detroit was awarded $150,000 under a Model Cities program to rehabilitate 60 prostitutes. The great majority were uninterested because they would not be able to make as much in new jobs as they could make as prostitutes.

Another social reality of some universality is that men write the rules that run social systems, and they control such systems. One might reasonably hope that social and economic inequalities between the sexes will improve. But even if females reach parity with males it does not necessarily follow that they will be unwilling to sell access to their bodies, particularly if men follow history in their willingness to pay more for sex than for most other services. Thus, even if sexism and economic oppression eventually disappear, it is simply naive to believe that prostitution will no longer exist.

The liberalization of attitudes toward acceptable sexual behavior during the last couple of decades has probably not resulted in a significant loosening of moral attitudes toward prostitution. From a cross-cultural perspective it is clear that the majority of societies condemn the institution. But while there may be no great change in how people feel about prostitutes, people can be persuaded to change the way prostitutes are treated before the law. Such has already been accomplished in a number of western European countries.

% of people in diff areas that agree that pros should be legalized

Arguments for Decriminalization

The prevailing opinion along a sizeable segment of the political spectrum in North America favors decriminalization of existing prostitution laws.[7] Decriminalization would put prostitution outside the law; it would be neither illegal nor legal. This position has received support from the National Organization of Women, the National Commission on the Causes and Prevention of Violence, the Select Committee on Crime of the House of Representatives, state chapters of the American Bar Association, prostitute's organizations, psychiatrists, intellectuals, students of prostitution and even some police forces. A few surveys suggest that the public may favor decriminalization, or would if they knew more about how it compared with the present system or legalization as an alternative. Eighty-three percent of those polled in San Francisco in 1974 preferred some form of decriminalization.[8] Another survey in Boston in the late 1970s found that 77 percent of those questioned felt that either some kind of decriminalization or legalization was better than the current system.[9]

The battery of arguments for decriminalization is formidable and difficult to ignore. Arguments counter alternatives and appeal to common sense, elementary notions of justice and the allocation of scarce resources. And, not of least significance, decriminalization appeals to the best interests of those who make use of prostitutes. Arguments for decriminalization also make effective use of the very kinds of historical and cross-national evidence that have been considered here.

Illegality involves a misunderstanding of the purpose of the criminal justice system. The aim of the criminal justice system is not to impose public standards of morality upon the private acts of consenting adults, immoral though they may be by widely held social standards, but rather to protect people and property from the harmful effects of others. Decriminalization would not only rectify this misdirected use of the justice system but it also would have the virtue of not implying that the initiation or act of prostitution is a privilege of the state.[10]

government involvement

One compelling reason among many for not legalizing prostitution, even if the reason is not among the half dozen or so that involve concepts of justice, is the long-held fear among many Americans that legalization means that the state approves the institution. More than half a century ago it was recognized that few legislators would back legalization, if only out of fear that it would ruin their political careers.[11] That fear is still germane.[12] Decriminalization poses no comparable problem, for it says only that a particular type of behavior is not subject to criminal sanctions, not that it is right or wrong. That legislators and the public seem to appreciate this distinction is indicated by recent decriminalization, by nearly half of the states, of private, non-commercial sexual activities among consenting adults.

Because of the large number of full- and part-time prostitutes in North America, and the much larger pool of men who frequent them at one time or another—69 percent according to Kinsey—prostitution laws are obviously ignored.[13] As George Halleck, one-time Superior Court Judge of the District of Columbia, has noted, efforts to enforce laws under such conditions lead to disrespect for laws in general.[14] Furthermore, since both the prostitute and her client freely enter into a transaction that serves both parties, making complainants a rarity, prostitution laws "in the end can be enforced only by resorting to the sort of police tactics which are intolerable in a free society."[15] Cops behave criminally to obtain minor criminal convictions, they are tempted by graft and often accept it, they selectively discriminate against the poor and racial minorities according to their own prejudices, they lie to themselves about the probity of their own behavior and through all this they make a mockery of the very system that they are supposed to exemplify. Thus, a perversion of a minor law has spillover effects of a more general and pernicious nature.

Questions of justice aside—issues that seem all too clear—one inescapable reason for breaking with the status quo concerns the obvious mismanagement of scarce public resources. Even without considering the nature of the offense, the extremely high rates of recidivism and the more general futility of the effort, prostitutes are simply very expensive to arrest and jail. They draw excessively on the criminal justice system, which by any set of reasonable criteria should be devoting its time and money to crimes of violence, crimes against persons and crimes that deprive people of their property. One can only conclude that social morality and hypocrisy are not just expensive but a good deal more costly than most people realize.

The case for decriminalization is compelling from other perspectives, in particular, one cast in a simple framework that compares illegal markets with those that lack criminal sanctions. The analysis is as applicable to abortions, drugs and alcohol as it is to prostitution. As George Hilton pointed out, illegal markets have several features that differentiate them from others, characteristics that are invariably undesirable.[16] Most "become the source of political pressure for perpetuation of the prohibition" and "convince large segments of the population that the illegal markets are run by nasty people who are best prohibited."[17]

Illegality impedes the flow of information about a product or service and thereby increases search costs. During Prohibition men had to spend time and money finding a speakeasy or a bellhop who knew where to find alcohol. Likewise, the owner of a speakeasy had to screen customers for fear they were agents enforcing the Volstead Act. Men in search of prostitutes must ask cabdrivers, bellhops and bartenders and are expected to pay for such information. Informants profit from their monopolistic situation.

In an illegal market the buyer has few assurances about product or service quality. During Prohibition labels on bottles were sometimes faked and buyers bought methyl alcohol, with disastrous consequences. Consumer fraud in massage parlors, encounter studios and escort services is widespread. Those who solicit the services of a streetwalker may be robbed and mugged, deceived into buying the services of a "knobber," or get less than they thought they had negotiated for. Prostitutes learn to verbally suggest that they will deliver a good deal more than they actually do. Cheated customers usually have little recourse, in no small part because they fear they will be subject to arrest if they report their mishap to the police. By contrast, men who frequent Nevada's legal brothels are rarely cheated. When they feel they have received less time or service than that bargained for, a complaint to the madam will usually rectify the misunderstanding. Other problems, such as having one's wallet stolen, are nonexistent.

Because sellers of an illegal good or service are labeled as criminals, they come to see themselves as such and associate with those who break all kinds of laws having nothing to do with prostitution. Bootleggers were seen and treated as criminals and often broke a variety of laws to be able to transport and sell their product. Many prostitutes come to see little difference between themselves and those who sell cocaine or heroin, steal automobiles or mug people in dark alleys.

Illegality creates higher earnings for the seller, a condition that the economist Alfred Marshall called "quasi-rents." Quasi-rents result from the risks of being arrested, from social opprobrium and from excessive demand. The difference between what women can earn in ordinary employment and in prostitution makes the institution very attractive. Again, Nevada provides an instructive example. There, in the late 1970s, one could purchase simple intercourse under safe and hygienic conditions for $20 to $25. The same service with a comparable woman in San Francisco at that time was at least double this amount.

Quasi-rents are subject to predation: by those who monopolize information about the service, such as bartenders and bellhops, by those who provide necessary services such as pimps and housing landlords, and by those who ease or make possible circumvention of the legal code such as cabdrivers, lawyers and cops. Where prostitution is legal, or illegal and veiled as something else, governments also take a share of quasi-rents. In Nevada they do so with heavy taxes on brothel owners, whereas in major cities local governments charge predatory rates for massage parlor licenses.

This comparison between illegal markets and others has several implications for what should happen to prostitution under decriminalization. If prostitutes were free to discreetly advertise and privately but openly discuss with prospective customers their prices and services, information would become more standardized. The result would be selection against prostitutes less than explicit about their offerings. Women who cheated their clients would be more often reported to the police, since legal restraints for consorting with the women would be absent. With freedom to advertise, information about the availability of prostitutes will increase, and men will spend less time and money finding exactly what they want. The services of those who derive income from passing out information or bringing buyers and sellers together will become less valuable, because without laws against prostitution others will enter the market to capitalize on the quasi-rents now made by bellhops, cabdrivers and bartenders. Competition from those entering the market will continue until the size of the quasi-rents is no longer attractive. If quasi-rents to predators drop, then prostitutes' net income will increase. This will open up possibilities for prostitutes: their economic position will improve because their costs will drop, they will be able to reduce prices in the hope of attracting more business, or they will be able to give better service for the same price since their profits will increase.

With decriminalization prostitutes and clients are more likely to report thievery, fraud and maltreatment to the police. Since prostitutes will not be considered criminals for their sexual behavior they will be less likely to engage in criminal activities that jeopardize their principal source of income. The perception of greater safety may increase the willingness of some men to frequent streetwalkers, men who are now reluctant to do so. The potential result, of course, is more money for the prostitute. Without a criminal label attached to prostitution, women would be free to move in and out of the activity as fancy and personal demands dictate. The present system keeps some women in prostitution when they would prefer to leave, precisely because they have arrest records, a problem that makes it difficult to get jobs in the "straight" world.

What would happen to pimps after decriminalization is problematic. If, in fact, prostitutes primarily need them as buffers between themselves and the hostile environment centered on cops and courts, then over time the need for them may largely disappear. Even under the best of circumstances, however, it would take time for the pimp population to dramatically decrease, because of habit and inertia in the system, because pimps confer status on streetwalkers, and because prostitutes on the whole are like most other people—they want someone of the opposite sex in their lives. If the pimp has been a cushion and protector for the prostitute in a larger sense, not only against cops and the courts but also against customers and others, then the percentage of women requiring pimps may remain high irrespective of changes in the status of prostitution. An instructive example is contemporary West Germany where the great majority of prostitutes have pimps, even though prostitution is legal.[18] In any event, it seems only logical that with decriminalization prostitutes will have more choice. They will not need pimps to provide bail money or arrange for lawyers, they will have an easier time of reporting maltreatment to police, and yet if they so choose they can have pimps.

Some prostitutes say they want the status quo of illegality.[19] They reason that it is precisely this characteristic of the market that keeps prices up.

They believe that either legalization or decriminalization will induce numerous women to enter the market and, as a consequence, prices will drop. At first glance the argument appears sound. But proponents make the questionable assumption that a change in legal status will automatically bring a change in social attitudes, or a willingness of most women to ignore the moral code. A paradox raised by Kingsley Davis decades ago focused on why so few women enter prostitution, given their plight and the money to be made.[20] Illegality alone is not an explanation. The social norm that keeps many women from entering prostitution, to say nothing of a simple distaste for the job, will continue to act as a barrier. Of course, additional women would likely enter the market were it decriminalized but it is unlikely there will be dramatic changes in the numbers employed. Even if women did resort to prostitution, a good many would work on a part-time or occasional basis since entry and exit would be relatively easy. If, simultaneously, full-time prostitutes had a shorter working life than at present, because of lack of barriers to other jobs, overall supply might not vary that much. Finally, with greater turnover it would be more difficult to organize the women and prey on their earnings.

On the assumption that prices might drop—as the comparison between Nevada and San Francisco suggests they might—prostitutes may still be better off following decriminalization than under the present system. With fewer predators there would be fewer demands on their quasi-rents.

Decriminalization might financially benefit males who now frequent call girls. Streetwalkers would become more attractive since they and their customers would not be subject to arrest, and information on the availability of all prostitutes would improve. Hence, prices charged by call girls should drop. Call girls would have to be more open about their business to maintain similar levels of activity, facilitating the collection of income taxes.

Fears that decriminalization invites a rash of new problems have little basis, at least when compared with the recent history of other activities that have been decriminalized. By the early 1970s Hawaii had decriminalized public drunkenness, homosexuality, abortion and all sexual acts between consenting adults except prostitution.[21] In the years that followed there was no upsurge in the rates of abortion or public drunkenness, and drunks no longer got dried out at public expense. Homosexuality was more open than previously, but the police had no reason to believe that its prevalence in the islands had increased.

Concern among law enforcement officers that organized crime and other criminals will be attracted to prostitution if it is decriminalized seems unwarranted.[22] Though Nevada's brothels are legal and therefore not strictly germane to the issue, there is, nevertheless, no evidence for the involvement of organized crime. Under decriminalization it is improbable that brothels, by far the easiest form of trade to control, would monopolize the market. If numerous women were to enter prostitution on a part-time basis, working through advertisements and perhaps occasionally on the streets, it would be difficult for criminals to organize them to advantage. These factors, plus the much greater profits to be made from narcotics and gambling, make big-time criminal involvement in decriminalized prostitution unlikely.

The Dilemma of Incompatible Interests

Decriminalization would seem to solve most of the prostitute's problems, but it would not necessarily protect the public's rights, however much one may disagree with the quality of the moral judgments of many individuals. Without legalizing prostitution there are a few ways in which the state can control it, even though the danger exists that its bureaucratic tentacles would become oppressively entangled in the lives of prostitutes.

Despite a long history of recognition that high visibility promotes public outcry, oppressive laws and repression, governments have repeatedly concentrated prostitutes in specific areas of cities. Much like criminalizing women by treating them as criminals, the state has exacerbated the problem of prostitution by encouraging, often forcing, prostitutes to congregate. All evidence shows that unofficial and official segregation attempts, presently exemplified by Boston's Adult Entertainment Zone, are failures both in fact and in public perception.[23] Yet cities continue to propose the establishment of districts comparable to Boston's.

In the 1970s the New York Chapter of the American Civil Liberties Union proposed a red-light district for New York City.[24] The city's vice squad chief contended that the only place people would permit one would be along the piers. One city in New Jersey had the idea of locating its prostitutes near an old city dump.[25] In the San Francisco Bay Area there have been suggestions in recent years to permit prostitutes to use Alcatraz Island, a plan reminiscent of one made over a half-century ago by a Minneapolis vice commission that proposed that prostitutes be confined to Nicollet Island.[26] When, in the 1970s, the Rotterdam City Council received complaints that prostitution was spreading into residential areas it approved a plan to concentrate prostitutes in a 400-bed ship alongside an old abandoned area of the harbor.[27] The women did not like the idea because the cost of their rooms would be very expensive, and equally because it would give them too much prominence. These kinds of suggestions do little to alleviate what seem to be all too obvious problems: high visibility, the impossibility of confining even a substantial proportion of prostitutes to a single district, the attraction that clusters of sexual activity have for thieves and other criminals, and the fact that such districts require considerable policing. Nor do proposals such as the city-dump solution treat prostitutes and their customers with respect. Fortunately, such recommendations rarely find public support.[28]

One obvious solution to the problems that arise from clustering prostitutes is to use multiple zoning ordinances, the purpose of which is to keep visibility below levels that prove to be offensive. This could be accomplished by three processes undertaken simultaneously. One would encourage prostitutes to discreetly solicit in newspapers, magazines and telephone directories. Another would promote the dispersal of brothels and streetwalkers throughout a city. A third measure would require that only so many brothels and streetwalkers be allowed in designated zones.

For locating brothels, cities could adopt some variant of the Detroit "Anti-Skid Row Plan" which specified that sex-related businesses be at least 1,000 feet apart.[29] This plan was adopted to preserve the quality of urban life by not blighting an area with high densities of socially undesirable services. Several years after the Detroit ordinance came into effect the desired results were apparent.[30] Additionally, it appears that the number of topless bars, adult book stores and pornographic theaters was significantly reduced.

A prostitution zoning plan could specify the density of brothels per city area, the manner of advertising, limits to brothel size and number of employees and the permissible nature of soliciting out-of-doors. Other regulations, such as those relating to parking, could also be instituted. However, beyond requirements such as these the brothel and its employees should not be regulated more than other businesses. The government would have the right to see that taxes are paid, that building and safety code requirements are met and that employers meet acceptable labor standards.

For brothel prostitutes as well as all others there should be no regulations requiring women to have venereal disease examinations or carry cards to the effect that they are disease-free, as is common in many parts of the world. To require prostitutes to undergo examinations, but not their clients—a widespread practice—is clearly discriminatory. This argument aside, it is in the best business interests of prostitutes to remain free of disease. There will probably be no greater number of irresponsible practitioners in the sale of sexual services than is true for most practices over which society lacks control. If the Nevada situation is indicative no one need worry about disease. Without exception customers are carefully examined and if any hint of disease is present they are asked to leave the house.

But there are other problems with arguments for required venereal disease examinations. Even when women are periodically inspected there can be few assurances, short of their own care in accepting clients, that prostitutes will remain disease-free. If a woman is examined once a week this does not preclude the possibility that she can still infect dozens of clients shortly after being inspected. Other problems include the sheer difficulty of policing prostitutes, the tremendous cost of trying to do so, and the fact that required examinations take one more step toward bringing prostitution under governmental, and potentially oppressive, control.

The proper role for government is the establishment of programs for the eradication of venereal disease. Facilities for diagnosis and treatment ought to be established. In the event that prostitutes should prove to be a health hazard, contrary to what current evidence suggests, the public could be warned in the same way it is now told of the dangers of cigarette smoking.

Of 279 people surveyed by Barbara Milman under the auspices of the Harvard Center for Criminal Justice, 68 percent favored legalized brothels in preference to the current system. Thirty-four percent of those polled were members of the business community and another 31 percent were classified as "residents of neighborhoods."[31] The survey also included a number of policemen from around the country. Milman did not specify exactly what was meant by a legal brothel or how much control would be exercised by the state. However, since knowledge of Nevada's oppressive rules is not widely known it can be assumed that people do not think of regulations in these terms. But whatever future polls might show, particularly when clearer distinctions are made between decriminalization and legalization, what seems certain from Milman's and other surveys is that the public would prefer prostitutes to be in houses rather than on the streets.

Similar feelings exist outside the United States. In the mid-1970s suggestions for licensed brothels arose in London, Birmingham, Liverpool and Southampton.[32] Many Italians would prefer to see the old system of brothels reinstituted. Whether such houses would have to be under strict state control to be acceptable or could be run like any other business is not presently known.

Prostitutes could form collective brothels.[33] For some, particularly those in Great Britain and France, this would solve the housing shortage problem. Minority prostitutes would be most advantaged since they are usually discriminated against in where they can solicit and service clients. In a broader sense, all prostitutes as well as their customers would benefit. The prostitute could raise her fee to include part of what the client normally pays for a room and in return give more or better service. If prostitutes choose to work for madams, laws could be established that limit their charge for services to 10 to 15 percent of the prostitute's fee, rather than the usual 40 to 50 percent.

Streetwalkers could be permitted to solicit in most areas of the city. This would not only reduce the total number of brothels present, but would also provide prostitutes the alternative of working outdoors. Customers that do not like the brothel atmosphere would also gain. As with houses spatial constraints on density could be established. For example, perhaps two streetwalkers would be permitted for every two or three blocks. Alternatively, city planners could specify an acceptable number of prostitutes for a zoned area of a half dozen or more blocks, anticipating that women might prefer to congregate. In this case, the number allowed should be kept quite low to prevent a reoccurrence of a well-known problem.

Because some areas would be more preferred than others and many streetwalkers would want to solicit in the favored zones, somebody could institute either a lottery or rotating system to give everyone equal access. Policemen would give civil fines comparable to parking tickets to those who solicited in areas when it was not their turn.[34] The fines might escalate to make it expensive for women to disobey the lottery or rotation system with any regularity. Prostitutes on both sides of the Atlantic have expressed preference for a fine system as an alternative to current practices.[35] They are confident that they can prove they are not a nuisance or law-breakers and that there will be few problems as long as complaints are filed by someone other than cops. Finally, as Margo St. James has suggested, revenues from fines could be channeled into services that benefit prostitutes. The money could be used to set up day-care centers and psychological counseling services, and to provide for educating women who seek alternative means of gainful employment.[36]

That an escalating system of civil fines might effect the desired goals is suggested by the West German experience. In 1974 prostitution was moved from the criminal to the civil code books. This change has not increased the difficulty of controlling prostitution. Police have found that by the time a prostitute receives her third or fourth civil fine for disobeying zoning ordinances the expense becomes great enough to prevent further violations.[37]

Other criteria that could be used to determine the densities of prostitutes in particular zones include general population densities at critical soliciting hours and the willingness of entrepreneurs to have prostitutes on their premises. For example the financial districts of some American cities have very little human activity at night. Owners of some bars, clubs and hotels will want prostitutes available to encourage business. Allowable densities in these areas could be higher than in other zones within the city.

Finally, some provision should be built into city zoning plans to accommodate inter-city movements of prostitutes who are responding to periodic fluctuations in demand that arise from events such as conventions. Exactly how this should be handled depends on local conditions. For this reason, if no other, specificity in zoning policies must be placed in the hands of local governments.

Tactics to Speed a Slow Process

Despite the arsenal of historical and contemporary evidence condemning legal and illegal prostitution and the many sound arguments in favor of decriminalization, there is no suggestion that many states are about to change their laws. While numerous people and organizations have worked in behalf of decriminalization, their numbers and impact are small compared to those who have fought for the right to legalize abortions or to give homosexuals their rights. Change only comes when the clamor is loud and when the personal and public costs become all too apparent.

A number of tactics have been employed by prostitutes and others to bring about change. Obviously, the greater the number of these that are utilized simultaneously, and the more widespread their use, the sooner prostitutes will receive fair treatment. Some of the tactics that have been or ought to be used, or at least considered, are worth outlining.

Efforts should be made to educate the public, and particularly those engaged in the legislative process and the administration of justice. Besides emphasizing the merits of decriminalization and the history of problems with legality and illegality, particular attention ought to be given to current discriminatory treatment of prostitutes, the abridgment of constitutional rights, the poor use of public resources that could more wisely be spent on serious crimes, and the fact that illegality creates criminals and criminal behavior in the very process of trying to effect opposing ends. Hard facts and vivid comparisons should be used to dispel public concerns and misconceptions about venereal disease and drug usage among prostitutes. Not least of all, it should be emphasized that there are more sensible ways of dealing with the visual blight of landscapes, that much of the problem arises precisely from unofficial policies of concentrating prostitutes and sex businesses in small areas of a city.

Prostitutes have formed unions in a number of countries, including the United States, England, Mexico, France and Sweden. They have done so to get better working conditions, to alter their public image and to work to change the laws that oppress them. One such organization, COYOTE (an acronym for Call Off Your Old Tired Ethics) was founded in San Francisco in 1973 by Margo St. James, a former prostitute. Its purpose is to educate the public in some of the very ways suggested, to rally support for a change in existing laws and to assist prostitutes with their daily difficulties. Although the organization spread to a number of American cities and has prompted some legislators to introduce decriminalization bills, it continues to be hampered by inadequate funding. Support for this and similar organizations is badly needed, for as the history of unions in America clearly shows, any organized effort that effectively brings together those with a common cause is likely to speed the process of change.

In recent years newspapers in a number of American cities have published the names and addresses of men arrested for soliciting prostitutes. Despite the method's apparent appeal to those who seek justice, it is doubtful that it should be encouraged. While it may have the salutary effect of clearing a particular streetscape, and may satisfy those who wish to see the customer receive the same treatment as the prostitute, it only compounds injustices and diverts attention away from more fundamental changes in the law.

Until there is positive evidence of change, prostitutes will use whatever non-violent subversive means they can. One suggestion voiced is that they should threaten to reveal the names of prominent customers, particularly government officials.[38] The tactic has a certain intuitive appeal, but is probably not very realistic. Most prostitutes that have clients with power and influence are call girls. For them streetwalkers' problems are as remote as they are to average citizens. Those who would encourage such a tactic work from at least two erroneous assumptions: that call girls care about those that they, in fact, socially disdain, and that, even if they did, they would jeopardize their own business. In this case, in this place, and at this point in history, self-interest, not class-interest will largely determine change.

For the streetwalker the best line of attack on an ancient unjust system is to continue with old ways: lie, cheat, steal, move when necessary, do whatever needs to be done to avoid hassles and arrests. And when arrested, *never* plead guilty, and do everything necessary to make the public pay in dollars and cents. That is what the public understands best.

Without abandoning hope and efforts to alter the existing system, the sideline realist, like the prostitute and the cynic, can always find solace in the thought that change will come when enough people who make legislative decisions clearly see the costs involved: the huge bill from prosecuting prostitutes for a crime without a victim, the legitimate crimes that have too few resources devoted to them, and the money that the state loses from untaxed revenues. All decisions—cultural and biological—are ultimately determined by the calculus of costs and benefits.

Appendix

Nancy Burley
and
Richard Symanski

Women Without: An Evolutionary and Cross-Cultural Perspective on Prostitution

A focus on prostitution in the urban, largely industrialized West does not adequately address certain questions of a more general nature. Where and under what kinds of conditions is prostitution usually found? More importantly—to those with interests transcending the historical—can the study of the origins of prostitution further enlarge our understanding of the evolution of the species? By addressing such questions it is possible to break away from the present, the near past and societies we think we know. By looking at the behavior of humans not so close to us, we can suspend some of the moral values that often make intelligent discussion of the institution so difficult. A cross-cultural perspective may also shed further light on fundamental conflicts between the sexes.

By drawing on the large body of data contained in the Human Relations Area Files (HRAF), a coded accumulation of ethnographic material on approximately 300 societies, the overwhelming majority of which are non-Western and non-urban, we attempt to give cross-cultural perspective to prostitution in a way not heretofore attempted. Furthermore, by using current principles and concepts in evolutionary theory we couch these findings in ways that are compatible with the major theory addressing the evolution of all sexual species.

Cautionary Signposts

The ethnographic record is the best source available for examining the cross-cultural incidence of prostitution and its possible evolutionary significance. Yet, the painstaking field studies by anthropologists contain several limitations that must be mentioned lest someone unaware make more of the evidence than is warranted. Recording the incidence and nature of prostitution in low-technology societies has probably been a low priority for all but a few ethnographers. Despite a generally open mind for bizarre and circumscribed practices, the widespread disdain for prostitutes has undoubtedly hindered the ability of many to see or inquire about them, or to receive accurate accounts from informants.

A further problem is definitional. In the literature on several societies ethnographers categorically state that prostitution is absent and then immediately follow with clear examples of its existence. The contradiction is rarely softened by a claim that the society in question does not have a concept of prostitution, or that outsiders would equivocate over the meaning of examples. Compounding this difficulty is disagreement among those who have studied the same group: one person will state that prostitution exists, another that it does not. In many cases it is not clear whether or not prostitution occurs, since no mention is made of its presence or absence.

Even where prostitution is labeled and perhaps described in detail other problems arise. Only a single instance may be cited, and numerical data on incidence are almost always absent. The great majority of studies on non-Western peoples have been done by males, a problem of perhaps considerable magnitude.

The distinction between pre- and post-contact prevalence of prostitution is seldom clearly made, though there may be an indication that it increased after contact. In many cases intruders either quickly destroyed or badly disrupted the integrity of the social system. When this occurred the latent potential for prostitution may have quickly become manifest, or low levels of incidence may have been magnified. One of the more evident examples of this problem, worth mentioning because we do not give it further attention, appears among societies of the environmentally-rich Pacific Northwest (Figure 1). There, prostitution was apparently rare before the appearance of traders and loggers.[1]

Whites wanted woodcarvings, costumes, masks, blankets and, not least, sexual services from the Indian women. These societies had a long tradition of exchanging large quantities of goods collected or made from the products of their environment, riches that were then used in ceremonial feasts (potlatches) that validated social rank among individuals and groups. White demands for goods and women and Indian demands for the products of whites set in motion rounds of ceremonial feasts that became more frequent and more important. One result was that prostitution became "an important and honorable way of earning income for status-seeking ventures."[2]

The Pacific Northwest societies are, perhaps, an example of the contact problem in dramatic relief, dramatic because strong concepts of property and exchange could easily be translated into the renting of women's bodies. But important as contact may have been for prostitution in this part of the world, the problem does not detract from the more general picture.

Our principal approach to surmounting these various difficulties has been to examine all societies (approximately 300) presently found in HRAF for the one category (548) that most often mentions prostitution. We have also looked at several others (595, 674, 684, 768, 834, 836) on sex and related matters for the 60 societies constituting the HRAF "representative

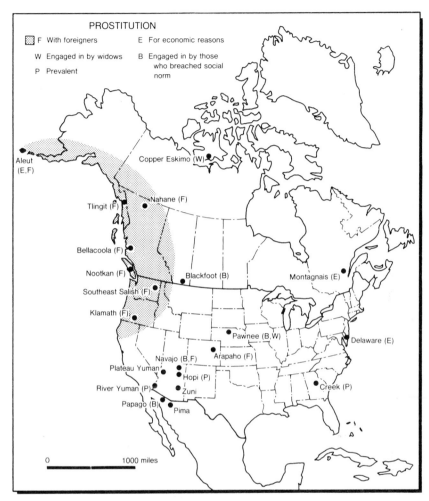

Figure 1 Prostitution Among Native Americans

sample." We have tried to focus on recurring themes and their possible meaning, but without sacrificing reference to individual examples that are such a rich part of the ethnographic record. Merely as a matter of convention we have employed the "ethnographic present," treating societies as if the practices described were extant. Obviously in many cases they are not.

An inquiry into the sociobiology of any human phenomenon begins from several premises, a few of which are reiterated here. One premise, contrary to what many social scientists dogmatically believe, holds that there is continuity between nonhuman and human life. This premise does not deny that culture is radically different than the behavioral plasticity and capacity for transmission of information in nonhuman species, but holds that our long evolutionary past is relevant to understanding aspects of contemporary human behavior.

A second and related premise is that adaptations are germane to past environments. Species are continually evolving, and what may have been adaptive in past environments may not be so at present. That behavior seems biologically out-dated or nonfunctional in a new environment may mean only that there has not been evolutionary time enough for biological and cultural imperatives to track in tandem. Because men continue to visit prostitutes even though there is little possibility of reproductive payoff does not mean that such gains were not received at some time in the past. Likewise, the fact that most women in the West now use some form of birth control that allows them to be promiscuous in no way vitiates an argument that in the long stretch of evolutionary time women had a much lower tendency toward promiscuous behavior than men.

A further starting point for analysis is that individuals do not consciously calculate reproductive costs and benefits. Rather, those individuals who pursue strategies that enhance their reproductive success are, on average, selected for. For convenience and parsimony of expression biologists often speak as if individuals strategically plan their behavior. Those unaware of this convention frequently assume that biologists think that animals have conscious understanding of the law of natural selection. This interpretation is incorrect. The correct way of interpreting these statements is that animals, including humans, often behave *as if* they were consciously attempting to enhance their biological fitness.

Based on a few unfortunate pronouncements, many people jump to the conclusion that because a sociobiological argument has been presented for a given trait, this means that specific genes exist for that trait: for jealousy, for aggression, for prostitution. This, of course, is hardly the case. All that should be argued in most cases is that polygenic inheritance, fashioned over evolutionary time, gives individuals the capacity for certain kinds of behavior in particular environments.

Another premise concerns the significance of cultural norms. Societal attitudes toward particular activities do not necessarily reflect the ''adaptiveness'' of those activities to individuals. The very nature of natural selection is such that competition among non-relatives is to be expected. Individuals of different status in society will be influenced differentially by a particular norm. Nor can we expect all individuals to assert their will equally: those who are the most dominant or successful—the rich and the powerful—are more likely to influence the norms and codes of society than others. In general, they will favor rules that benefit themselves and, in so doing, often discriminate against subordinate, less powerful members of society.[3] When individuals are sufficiently powerful, they may even encode rules that others must follow, but to which they pay little heed.

Finally, it seems that many liberals and radicals are disturbed about an apparent normative component of sociobiological reasoning. This reaction results from confusion between descriptive statements of what is or was the case and those regarding what *ought* to be the case. Consideration of the biological motives underlying human behavior can be a disturbing experience. But emotions reveal different truths than those sought in science. We, like other "sociobiologists," do not condone the multitude of ways in which humans, acting in their own best interests, treat others. We simply seek to understand and describe the evolutionary process by which the behavioral repertoire of our species has been molded.

Biological Preconditions

In evolutionary perspective, prostitution can be defined as relatively indiscriminate sexual activity for non-reproductive profit. Prostituting females offer sexual services to a number of males for the purpose of acquiring resources or access to them. Females who engage in prostitution lack the "intent" of bearing offspring fathered by most copulatory partners, and they may even attempt to avoid bearing offspring that might result from such copulations.

This definition of prostitution is founded in contemporary sexual selection theory and ultimately results from the very definitions of the sexes. Because females make large, energy-rich gametes, while those made by males are small and energy-poor, females make many fewer reproductive cells than males. In addition, females typically put more energy into rearing their offspring. For these reasons, any female is potentially able to make fewer offspring than any male. Males, therefore, have a strong biological incentive to compete for and exert control over females, who for them constitute a limiting reproductive resource.[4] Males may profitably view females as "property," a resource to be defended. Females, on the other hand, benefit little from such a perspective on males because their reproductive capacity is intrinsically limited. For this reason, polygyny is a widespread mating pattern among animals, whereas polyandry is exceedingly rare.[5]

Because females' investment in each offspring successfully reared is usually considerable, they should be highly selective of mates. If females cannot control or do not "know" the timing of ovulation, they should be selective in their choice of all copulatory partners—transitory as well as those who are relatively permanent—because without such knowledge they place themselves at risk. A female without control over conception should, in theory, only copulate with males whose "quality" she judges adequate for paternity.

Females should be sensitive to male genetic quality in so far as it affects the quality of offspring produced. Genetic quality may be measured by a variety of cues, including vigor and general appearance of health. Besides giving attention to genetic quality, females should benefit from assessing the amount of resources potential partners are likely to commit to offspring. In some species females are unable to reproduce without material support provided by males, and in many the number and health of offspring may be related to male assistance. Forms of material investment often provided by males include defense of a breeding site (such as a territory), building and maintenance of shelter (such as a nest) and the provisioning of food for mothers and young. In general, then, among species in which females cannot reproduce efficiently on their own, they should obtain some evidence of both genetic and resource-providing quality before beginning reproduction, even before becoming vulnerable to pregnancy.

Although natural selection favors females that discriminate among copulatory partners, it favors males that are less discriminating. Compared to the amount of effort needed to raise offspring, the energy males invest in single copulations is very small. Therefore males that copulate whenever suitable opportunities arise are selected for. Males will benefit from leaving a female after copulation whenever their probability of locating another female is substantial, and when there is a possibility that the "abandoned" female will raise one or more young without their assistance.[6] Lack of further investment may lower that female's reproductive success (she may raise fewer offspring than she could with his help), but the male's concern is only for his own reproduction. His best interests dictate that he engage in sexual behavior as circumstances permit. Because the costs and benefits of indiscriminate sexual behavior are considerably different for the sexes, females are generally less available as sexual partners than are males. It is this very discrepancy, an imbalance between supply and demand, that forms one precondition for the existence of prostitution. This precondition is present almost universally among sexual species.

Another necessary precondition for prostitution is that males provide some reproductive resource other than their genes. In some species male contribution to offspring consists solely of genetic material. In these cases females lack a possible motive for copulating other than to acquire genes. In many species, however, males typically provide females with non-genetic resources that aid in the reproduction of young. Furthermore, the amount of male investment, in theory, is proportionate to confidence of paternity; males are likely to contribute to the extent to which they are certain of being the real fathers of their mates' offspring.

The exchange of "sexual favors" for the economic support and protection provided by males is a feature incorporated into many mating systems. In and of itself this characteristic does not define prostitution, contrary to assertions by some liberals and feminists. The presence of an exchange concept, however, is a preadaptation necessary for prostitution to arise.

For prostitution to evolve, females must find a way around the biological imperative that they be selective of their sexual partners. One way of doing so (as women who have access to artificial contraceptives know) is to control paternity or the likelihood of becoming pregnant. Forgetting recent human inventions, females that advertise that they are reproductively available when in fact they are not are engaging in deceit. Deceit tends to be most effective when opposing selective pressures to detect it are small.[7] Since males are selected to copulate whenever the cost of doing so is relatively low, they may become evolutionarily "trapped" into being occasionally deceived regarding female intent. If attempts to avoid deception are energetically expensive or lead males to make mistakes, thereby failing to copulate with fertile females, it will be uneconomical for males to try to ascertain whether deceit is occurring. Prostitution may result.

Another circumstance that contributes to prostitution, even in the absence of deceit, occurs when females place greater value on certain "goods" than do the males who proffer them for sexual access. This is likely to happen when males control resources needed for survival or reproduction. For example, consider a localized food resource that a dominant male can successfully defend. Since he has more than enough food for himself, any food used as an exchange item is of relatively little value. But for a given female without access to food, just the reverse is the case. Under such circumstances the female may be willing to copulate for the resource required, and the male should be readily disposed to the transaction.[8]

Many species are known to possess one or more of the necessary preconditions for prostitution. Females are known to deceive males regarding the reproductive value of given copulations. They may, for example, display false estrous behavior when they are not ovulating (as in lions),[9] or even when they are already pregnant (as in langurs).[10] Males readily copulate with females under these circumstances. Pre-copulatory gifts are presented by males of numerous species, including many that do not form long-term pair bonds. There is evidence that copulatory timing or order affects the probability of paternity in some of these cases.[11] Hence females may be able to simultaneously select mates by copulating with a desirable male at the right "time" and also receive resources by doing so indiscriminately at other times. There are, of course, counter-selective pressures operating on males who give resources to females when the probability of genetic repayment is nonexistent. For this reason, prostitution should not be rampant, but—where the preconditions exist—should appear in low to moderate frequencies.

The biological argument for prostitution is supported by the fact that prostitution is found in a multitude of societies (Table 1). For only a dozen of those included in HRAF it is explicitly stated that no prostitution exists without claims to the contrary. The question of whether the other 150 or so societies in HRAF have prostitutes is moot. Whatever the case, and working

Table 1
The Cross-Cultural Incidence of Prostitution[1]

North America

Society	Source	
Aleut	Coxe	1804
	Jones	1969
Arapaho	Hilger	1952
Aztec	Sahagún	1955
Bellacoola	McIllwraith	1948
Blackfoot	Wissler	1911
Copper Eskimo	Jennes	1922
Creek	Swanton	1924-25
Delaware	Heckewelder	1819
Hopi	Titiev	1972
Klamath	Voegelin	1942
Mam	Wagley	1949
Montagnais	Burgesse	1944
	Lips	1947
Nahane	Honigmann	1949
Navajo	Leighton & Kluckhohn	1947
	Valkenburgh	1938
Nootkan	Drucker	1951
Papago	Underhill	1946
Pawnee	Dorsey & Murie	1914
Pima	Underhill	1946
Southeast Salish	Cline et al.	1938
Tarahumara	Bennett & Zingg	1935
Tarasco	Beals	1946
Tepoztlan	Lewis	1951
Tlingit	Jones	1914
	Knapp & Childe	1896
	Krause	1956
Yucatec Maya	Steggerda	1941
Yumans (Plateau)	Smithson	1959
Yumans (River)	Whited	1894
Zuni	Smith and Roberts	1954

South America and the Caribbean

Society	Source	
Araucanians	Faron	1961
	Latcham	1909
	Titiev	1951

[1] This table includes all societies in which prostitution was noted, even if only a single example was cited by the ethnographer.

Only those societies which are part of the Human Relations Area Files (HRAF) have been included in this listing. Obviously, there are many more societies contemporary with those here that also have prostitution. For example, Puerto Ricans and Haitians are included on the list, whereas Columbians and Costa Ricans are not.

For convenience, the culture area classifications are the same as those used by George Murdock.

Aymara	Bouroncle-Carréon	1964
	LaBarre	1948
Bororó	Cook	1909
Bush Negroes	Hurault	1961
Cagaba	Preuss	1926
Callinago	Breton & LaPaix	1929
Caraja	Cook	1909
	Krause	1911
Cuna	Stout	1947
Goajira	Gutierrez de Pineda	1950
Haiti	Herskovits	1937
Inca	Garcilasco de la Vega	1869-71
Jamaica	Kerr	1952
Mataco	Fock	1963
Mosquito	Conzemcius	1932
Puerto Rico	Steward et al.	1956
Timbira	Nimuendajú	1946
Trumaí	Murphy & Quain	1955
Yanoama	Vinci	1959
Yaruro	Petrullo	1939

Europe

Society	Source	
Czechoslovakia	Pelc	1925
Georgian Britain	Harrison	1881
Greece	Sanders	1962
Imperial Rome	Lewis & Reinhold	1966
Lapps	Itkonen	1945
Serbs	Lodge	1942
Stuart Britain	Malcolm	1810
Tudor Britain	Stow	1971
Yugoslavia	Erlich	1966

Middle East

Society	Source	
Amhara	Messing	1957
Bahrain	Bahrain	1937
Eritrea	Worthington	1946
Ethiopia	Worthington	1946
Hausa	Smith	1954
	Smith	1965
Iran	Massé	1938
Kanuri	Cohen	1960
Kurd	Masters	1953
Kuwait Bedoins	Dickson	1951
Saudi Arabia	Bailes	1952
Senegal	Crowder	1959
Siwans	Cline	1936
Somali	Lewis	1962
Sulubba	Glubb	1943
Turkey	Stirling	1965

Table 1 Cont'd.
The Cross-Cultural Incidence of Prostitution
Middle East

Society	Source	
Wolof	Gamble	1957
	Gorer	1935
Yemen	Heyworth-Dunne	1952

Africa

Society	Source	
Azande	Czekanowski	1924
	Wyndham	1936
Bemba	Richards	1939
Bushmen	Kaufmann	1910
	Thomas	1959
Dogon	Paulme	1940
Fang	Balandier	1955
	Tessmann	1913
Ila	Smith & Dale	1920
Kikuyu	Dundas	1915
	Leakey	1953
Lozi	Turner	1952
Masai	Hollis	1905
Mende	Little	1951
Mongo	Hulstaert	1928
Mossi	Dim Delobsom	1932
Ngoni	Barnes	1951
Rundi	Czekanowski	1917
Shilluk	Howell	1953
	Pumphrey	1941
Tonga	Colson	1971
Twi	Field	1970
Yao	Stannus	1922

Russia

Society	Source	
Chukchee	Borgoraz-Tan	1904-1909
	Sverdrup	1938
Turkestan	von Schwarz	1900

Asia

Society	Source	
Ainu	Pilsudski	1910
Burma	Christian	1942
	Ferrars & Ferrars	1901
Cambodia	Thompson	1941
China	Lamson	1934
	Yang	1954
East China	Murphy	1953
Formosa	Grad	1942
	Stanford University	1956c
Formosan Aborigines	Guerin & Bernard	1868

India	Cornell University	1956
	Karve	1953
Inner Mongolia	Washington	1956
Indochina	Broderick	1942
Kanada	Srinivas	1952
Kashmir	Modi	1913/1916
Kerala	Iyer	1912
Korea	Hulbert	1906
Lepcha	Gorer	1938
Laos	Reinach	1901
Malaya	Logan	1886
	Williams-Hunt	1952
Malays	Firth	1943
	Djamour	1959
Manchuria	Lattimore	1935
	Shirokogorov	1924
Mongolia	Ma	1949
	Maiskii	1921
North China	Chao	1948
	Stanford University	1956b
Okinawa	Glacken	1953
Sinkiang	Lattimore	1950
South China	Kulp	1925
South India	DuBois	1906
Southeast China	Stanford University	1956a
Taiwan Hokkien	Gallin	1966
Thailand	Thompson	1937
	Zimmerman & Valdhyakara	1934
Tibet	Peter	1963
Vietnamese Tonkin	Gourou	1936

Oceania

Society	**Source**	
Alor	Dubois	1944
Aranda	Basedow	1925
Bali	Covarrubias	1938
Iban	Sutlive	1972
Ifugao	Lambrecht	1932-41
Makassar	Chabot	1950
Manus	Mead	1930
Marquesas	Suggs	1963
Marshalls	Erdland	1914
	Kramer & Nevermann	1938
Murngin	Berndt & Berndt	1954
Santa Cruz	Graebner	1909
	Speiser	1916
Tiwi	Hart & Pilling	1960
Tonga	Koch	1955
Toradja	Adriani & Kruyt	1951
Trobriand Islanders	Malinowski	1929
Truk	Damm	1938
Woleai	Damm et al.	1938
	Spiro	1949
Yap	Senfft	1907

on the conservative assumption that some percentage of societies said to have prostitution may not, it is still clear that the institution has occurred in enough societies, and with sufficient frequency in scores of them, to necessitate an inquiry into the nature of cultural predispositions. What, then, is it about cultural norms and values in general and the individual motives of males, females and parents in particular that sometimes greatly magnify biological preadaptations?

Cultural Predispositions

Among humans, female biological predispositions may be enhanced by at least two commonly encountered societal expectations: the explicit (or thinly veiled) recognition that female sexual services constitute a commodity of exchange, and the denial to women of choice with regard to copulatory partners (including spouses). The first causes women to recognize and perhaps capitalize on what in some societies is their only resource—their bodies. The second condition favors reduced female selectivity, since women and girls are conditioned to deny their negative feelings toward sexual activities with men not of their own choosing.

It is a norm in many societies that men give money or gifts in exchange for sexual services, even where females are thought to enjoy sexual activity as much as males.[12] Specifics differ from one group to another, but in varying degrees such customs and more general attitudes increase women's awareness of their potential economic value as sexual objects. Fang women learn from their men that they "rank first in value as goods for trade," ahead of goats, guns and cloth.[13] Among Bush Negroes "the men who have the most success with women are always short of money,"[14] while the claim that rich Hopi men are most successful in their "love affairs"[15] strongly suggests that Hopi women are in the habit of accepting money for sexual activity. Pygmy men are more formal and work through an intermediary; they pay the parents for the privilege of having an affair with the daughter, or for the explicit purpose of defloration.[16] Upon being engaged, a Nootkan girl is told to "sleep with her husband and have intercourse with him, for that is what men buy wives for."[17] Among peoples such as the Hopi and Mongo, women acknowledge that they use such customs as a source of additional income.[18]

In some societies women have the right to choose their own spouses, but in others they do not, particularly for their first marriage. They may even be denied the right to divorce a husband they do not like. Among the Koreans, for example, a woman has little recourse if she does not like her husband. Girls are married at an early age and after marriage they are no longer considered a part of their parents' family.[19] Truk women may be legally lent (or prostituted) by their husbands against their will.[20] And women may not be allowed to refuse the sexual advances of dominant males. Among the Mataco women cannot reject the advances of a chief.[21]

The reasons that males visit prostitutes cannot be sharply distinguished from their reasons for engaging in many other forms of sexual activity. At the basic sociobiological level, males are selected to be promiscuous, at least to the extent that promiscuity is relatively inexpensive. Since prostitution and courtship exist as a continuum, the vast majority of copulatory opportunities involve costs to males in terms of time and/or material goods. In the male perspective, prostitution realistically may represent nothing other than a relatively explicit sexual transaction.

Certain characteristics of prostitution may be attractive to men and so make it possible for prostitutes to charge them more than the value of goods normally provided for sexual services during courtship. Prostitution activities are less demanding of a male's time than other, less explicit, and possibly deceitful, forms of sexual aggression. They are likely to be less disruptive to his life, since emotional content of the relationship is minimal. Sexual activity with a prostitute may also be much less dangerous than seduction of married women and marriageable girls, particularly for relatively powerless men in society. For these reasons males may respond readily to female acknowledgment or advertisement of availability for gain.

A major biological stimulus to visiting prostitutes may be that the polygyny threshold in humans is relatively steep. Because wives and offspring require considerable resources, only the richest men in most societies can afford to maintain more than one woman at a time.[22] There may, nevertheless, be numerous males possessing more than enough resources to maintain one wife, but not enough to support two. Without some outlet for investing in fractions of "reproductive units" (i.e., wives and their offspring) the reproductive success of these males is limited to that accruing from monogamy. Up to some point they may adaptively invest more energy in their legitimate offspring, but eventually they will reach the point of diminishing returns, where further investment no longer increases reproductive success of offspring and therefore is biologically wasteful. Similarly, there are likely to be males with greater capital than needed for their own support but with insufficient resources for a wife. Both these groups of males may benefit from placing extra resources into low investment, high risk opportunities that may range from seduction of unwary women through participation in prostitution.

Prostitution is a mechanism for males to make low-cost, low-return reproductive investments with surplus resources at their disposal. Other categories of women that fill similar roles include slaves, mistresses and secondary wives. Both society's norms and a man's wealth will determine which of these types of women he will invest in. The wealthiest of males can afford maximum investment in numerous wives and thus they should have relatively little use for prostitutes. However, societal rules may prevent them from practicing the degree of polygyny they can afford, forcing them to use their investment to include women other than wives. For example,

Islamic law forbids men from having more than four wives. But there is no religious or legal limit to the number of concubines a Hausa male can have, and wealthy men support many. Although the letter of religious law is followed, secular law has been written to permit the offspring of concubines to gain the status of legitimacy upon their father's death and to inherit equally with the offspring of "wives."[23] Legally, concubines are not wives, but sociobiologically they appear to be.

Just as courting and prostituting behaviors cannot be easily dichotomized, neither can the status of women with respect to marriage. The above example illustrates how powerful individuals can manipulate laws to their own advantage, thereby redefining the nature of relationships between males and females. A more frequently encountered example of the same principle involves the status of secondary wives. They may have the status of legal wives, as among the Hausa, or they may be considered something akin to "informal" wives, with the inheritance rights of their offspring varying. For example, neither secondary wives nor their offspring inherit among the Cagaba, the Dogon and the Ifugao.[24] Among the Fang and the Masai, offspring of subordinate wives receive a fraction of the inheritance of principal offspring.[25] Where the offspring do not inherit or have no guarantee of inheritance, such wives are the equivalents, biologically, of mistresses or concubines. By keeping mistresses or secondary wives males may be able to adjust their investment as circumstances permit. As their wealth increases they can increase investment in these women, but they can also withdraw resources as circumstances become unfavorable. In this way they do not jeopardize the fate of offspring of their primary spouses.

Another reason for making social distinctions among classes of women that males support is the desirability of passing on a substantial amount of wealth to a fraction of one's offspring. Power is often wealth-dependent. Rather than parceling out resources evenly and fragmenting the power of a lineage, males may benefit by having a group of principal inheritors and a separate group less well provided for. The substantial reproductive success of males in the former group is practically insured, while that of those in the latter is not.

Men in power, however, may have many means of providing for offspring who receive no inheritance. A possibly extreme tactic occurs among the Lozi, a society in which kings are harem polygynists, maintaining many wives and concubines. The degree of polygyny practiced by these men is so great that many commoners go without wives. In his majestic generosity, a king sometimes gives loyal subjects pregnant concubines, who become legal wives. Not surprisingly, the king himself is responsible for the condition of the women given away.[26]

Slaves, mistresses and wives of varying status, then, all provide males with ways to distribute resources to circumvent the polygyny threshold or to insure the transmission of power to some of their sons. But mistresses and wives require substantial investments, and slaves, although demanding less, require that males have considerable control. Even where slavery is permitted, it may still be the case that only the relatively affluent and powerful can exercise reproductive control over such women. Although providing little return, most prostitutes (excepting courtesans who might be biologically classed as mistresses) require minimal investment. The wealthiest men in affluent societies have no need to patronize ordinary prostitutes, but such women can be expected to be attractive to relatively poor men in affluent societies and to a large fraction of men in less affluent societies.

Societies vary considerably in their treatment and expectations of women, their degree of sexual permissiveness and in distribution of wealth. In order for women to voluntarily engage in prostitution, there must be both conditions that make it advantageous for them to do so and an environment that makes it possible. Where prostitutes are strongly discriminated against, women may become socially and spatially marginalized. Women may resort to deceit to counter formal or informal proscriptions. For example, Kurdish Moslem prostitutes may pretend to be Christians to avoid the threat of death.[27] Among the Bemba, it is recorded that a prostitute left her kin group and successfully established herself in a new environment by claiming to be a close relative of the chief. The chief's acquiescence was gained through bribery, and her presence in his group tolerated.[28]

Under other circumstances the occurrence of prostitution may result from male or parental initiation. In these instances, females are often forced into the situation and may or may not stand to benefit. In most cases, the primary rewards probably accrue to initiators. Below we consider female motives for turning to prostitution, and male and parental motives for initiating or encouraging it.

Female-Initiated Prostitution

In almost all societies women are economically dependent on men—their husbands, their male relatives, or both. In some cases dependence results because women cannot own substantial amounts of property, in others because they are considered to be property. Even the very fruits of female labor are often controlled by males. Coupled with a frequent lack of female control over resources is the strong expectation that all females should be married. The perceived role of women as wives and mothers is a mighty one, and society commonly makes no provision for the support of women in any other capacity. Unmarried women may be seen as "unnatural" and as economic burdens. In some societies kin refuse to support unmarried female relatives.

It follows that one stimulus to prostitution occurs when certain females are considered "unmarriageable." This status may be conferred on a woman for reasons of her own making, or as a result of circumstances beyond her control. Probably a major factor contributing to unmarriageable status is male reluctance to support offspring other than his own. Natural selection strongly disfavors individuals who contribute to the offspring of non-relatives. Men in many societies appear to have internalized natural selection's dictum, making it difficult for women with children to marry. In many cases unmarriageability results simply from male refusal to marry women with dependents, but in some instances formal rules are involved. Among the Ganda widows without children are permitted to remarry, but those with offspring are forbidden to do so.[29] Whether the result of formal or informal proscription, women with children sometimes find themselves excluded from a female's basic means of economic support. Despite the likelihood of social opprobrium it may be beneficial for widows, divorceés and unmarried women with children to turn to prostitution to support themselves and insure their offspring's survival; such behavior is reported for a number of societies.

Women may find it difficult to locate mates not only when they already have children, but also when men perceive a strong possibility that they will, in the future, produce offspring fathered by others. This possibility makes them, from a male's point of view, poor marital risks. Women who have been divorced on the grounds of adultery may be unmarriageable for this reason, as may unmarried non-virgins and other women who have acquired a "tarnished" reputation (Table 2).

Table 2
Classes of Women Who Become Prostitutes Because of Lack of, or Restricted, Opportunities for Marriage

	Widows	
Society	**Source**	
Araucanians[2]	Titiev	1951
Bororó[1]	Cook	1909
Cagaba[2]	Preuss	1926
Copper Eskimo	Jennes	1922
Formosan Aborigines	Guérin & Bernard	1868
Goajiro	Gutierrez de Pineda	1950
Hausa[1]	Smith	1954
Ifugao	Lambrecht	1932-1941
Marshalls	Kramer & Nevermann	1938
Pawnee[2]	Dorsey & Murie	1914
Rundi	Czekanowski	1917
Serbs[2]	Halpern	1958
	Lodge	1942
Sumatra	Ploss et al.	1935
Tepoztlan	Lewis	1951

Divorcées and Others Whose Marriage Has Failed

Society	Source	
Amhara[1]	Messing	1957
Bororó[1]	Cook	1909
Kanuri[1]	Cohen	1960
Kikuyu	Leakey	1953
Malays[1]	Firth	1943
Mongo	Hulstaert	1928
Mossi	Dim Delobsom	1932
Somali	Lewis	1962
Taiwan Hokkien	Wolf	1965
Tonga	Colson	1971

Non-virgins, Unmarried Girls, Adulterers and Other Women of Questionable Moral Character

Society	Source	
Araucanians	Faron	1961
Blackfoot	Wissler	1911
Burma	Ploss et al.	1935
Creek	Swanton	1924-25
Kashmiri	Modi	1913/1916
Pawnee	Dorsey & Murie	1914
Somali	Lewis	1962

Orphans

Society	Source	
Kuwait Bedoins	Dickson	1951
India	Cornell University	1956
South China	Kulp	1925

Diseased and Outcast Women

Society	Source	
Aztec	Sahagún	1955
Creek	Swanton	1924-25
Ifugao	Lambrecht	1932-41

Lack of Suitable Husbands

Society	Source	
Kikuyu	Leakey	1953
Malays	Djamour	1959
Manchuria[3]	Lattimore	1935
Okinawa[3]	Pitts et al.	1955
Rundi	Czekanowski	1917
Shilluk	Howell	1953
Taiwan Hokkien	Wolf	1965
Tibetans[3]	Peter	1963

Unmarried Women (Reason for Marital Status Unspecified)

Society	Source	
Twi	Field	1970
Caraja	Cook	1909
Chuckchee	Sverdrup	1938
Delaware	Heckewelder	1819
Fang	Tessmann	1913
Hausa	Smith	1954
Marquesas	Suggs	1963
Mende	Little	1951
Mongo	Hulstaert	1928
Tepoztlan	Lewis	1951

[1] Remarriage is possible.

[2] Women are not permitted to remarry. Where not indicated, marriageable status of the women is unknown.

[3] Unavailability of husbands said to be due to skewed sex ratio or to polyandrous mating custom.

Men may act not only to protect their own reproductive interests, but those of their relatives as well. As a result, a widow may be prohibited from remarrying to insure that her husband's resources remain committed to his offspring or to his kin. Among the Ganda, for example, where widows with children are not permitted to marry, they are nevertheless allowed to engage in amorous activities so long as they do not become pregnant. When such a woman does become pregnant, her unfortunate lover is required to pay a heavy fine to the clan of her deceased husband.[30]

An alternative means by which kin can retain a dead man's resources is through forced marriage of the widow to a brother or other kinsman of the deceased. This practice occurs in a number of societies in Africa (e.g., the Bemba and the Tiv), in South America (Bush Negroes and the Goajiro), in Asia (the Santal) and in Oceania (the Aranda).[31] But marriage to a kinsman does not necessarily insure that the widow will receive support. For example, among the Aranda, women are forced to support themselves and their children despite marriage to their former husband's brother.[32]

The widow's lot is particularly hard. In some societies where age is highly respected, her position may be secure (e.g., Bush Negroes)[33] or she may be supported by her grown sons (e.g., Kanuri).[34] In many societies, however, women are not so fortunate. They may be considered burdens to their kinsmen. Among the Copper Eskimo, men are allowed to relieve families of their problem by simply carrying widows off, a practice called "marriage by capture." A widow perhaps less fortunate might "offer herself . . . to any man who wants her for a day or week, in the hope that someone will finally keep her permanently."[35] By contrast, unmarried girls are assets and not subject to marriage by capture. Among the Cagaba, widows are considered beasts of burden and must do the hardest work.[36] The Andaman Islanders also look down upon widows and sometimes drown or otherwise murder them.[37] Less violent means for disposing of this undesirable class of women have been used by Koreans, who consider it virtuous for widows to commit suicide. Many women apparently oblige.[38]

Since widows are regarded so poorly, it is not surprising that in many societies they turn to prostitution (Table 2). Widows-as-prostitutes are only occasionally observed in some societies, but the phenomenon is a routine feature of others. The Marshall Islanders consider widows to be ordinary prostitutes, and the Pawnees drive them out of the tribe, forcing them to live as prostitutes at the outskirts of the village.[39] Poor Moslem widows with children in Serbia "work as unlicensed prostitutes, even in their own homes."[40] In Greece in the early twentieth century young widows without support sought village girls to introduce into prostitution.[41] Because women so often survive their husbands, there have probably been numerous opportunities for them to discover that prostitution is a way to support self and offspring.

Another condition that contributes to prostitution is the occurrence of dowries; the requirement that a female's family make a payment at the time of marriage or contribute substantially to her support afterwards. Where such resources are needed for marriage, poor and orphaned women and girls find themselves unmarriageable. Lack of dowry is a motivation for prostitution reported among the Taiwan Hokkien,[42] and lack of relatives leads to prostitution in several societies (Table 2).

Other women that may find it difficult to marry are the deformed and diseased (Table 2). Women falling into this class are probably excluded from matrimony because they are unproductive, both economically and biologically. If prostitution enables them to reproduce successfully we can consider their behavior biologically adaptive. In many cases, however, they are probably not superior reproductive competitors, and at most, may manage to extend their own life expectancy. That women with such problems are able to market themselves at all attests to the strength and nature of male demand for sexual activity.

Women whom men consider marriageable may nevertheless opt out of their conventional role as wives and mothers and become prostitutes when they perceive that the activity affords more opportunities than does marriage. This condition is most likely to appear when the field of potential spouses is of sufficiently low quality that males are not worth the reproductive commitment concomitant with marriage. In order for the decision to become a prostitute to be biologically advantageous, it is necessary that the long-term reproductive success of a woman as prostitute exceeds her reproductive success if she were to marry the best of the available males. Both genetic quality and long-term investment capabilities of males should be considered in the assessment process. If a female is better able to support herself and her offspring through prostitution than she could expect through marriage, or if the average genetic quality of her offspring would be as good or better through random copulation than through union with a particular male, a biological stimulus to prostitution exists.

Among the Shilluk, females consider that ownership of cattle is a prerequisite of male marriageability and will opt for prostitution when males meeting this requirement are not available.[43] Women in several other societies report that a shortage of acceptable mates led them to prostitution (Table 2).

Acceptable males may be in shortest supply in those few societies that are routinely polyandrous. In polyandrous human societies resources are quite limiting and brothers typically cooperate to support the offspring of one female.[44] While in most places females are in demand by males, where polyandry prevails males constitute a limiting reproductive, as well as economic, resource. To circumvent this difficulty, and to avoid marrying males with few resources at their disposal, females may resort to prostitution.

Lack of confidence in the quality of potential mates can be a problem in those societies in which women lack control over their marital partners. Under such circumstances we might expect some reluctance to marry. For example, in some societies women do not meet their spouse prior to betrothal or marriage. In others they may know their spouse prior to marriage but may have feelings of ambivalence or dislike towards him. Ambivalence toward marriage may be compounded by the fact that in some societies women are essentially powerless to divorce their husbands. They may also have realistic concerns about the consequences should their husbands die, divorce or abandon them. All of these factors may lead them to attempt to reject marriage to particular individuals. However, women, and particularly girls, often have little recourse when they rebel against familial decisions except to become financially independent of their families. Since most societies do not provide women with outlets for economic autonomy, women may perceive prostitution as a viable alternative (Table 3).

Table 3

Societies in Which Prostitution is Used as a Means of Avoiding Marriage in General[1], Or Marriage to a Particular Male[2]

Society	Source	
Azande[1]	Czekanowski	1924
Hausa[2]	Smith	1955
Kanuri[1]	Rosman	1962
Navajo[1]	Reichard	1950
Papago[1]	Underhill	1946
Taiwan Hokkien[2]	Wolf	1965

Of course, women find alternatives to forced or undesirable marriages in addition to prostitution. For example, Pawnee girls may attempt to influence the mate-selection process by finding a way to sleep with the boy of their choice. Upon revealing their misconduct to their parents, the latter work to effect a marital agreement between the families of the two young people. But such subterfuge may not work. A boy may simply refuse to marry a girl with whom he has had sexual relations. At that point, the girl's parents ostracize her, forcing her to become a prostitute.[45]

A further factor contributing to the relative desirability of prostitution in some societies is the quality of life of married women. Secondary wives in polygynous societies are often considered subordinate to, and may even become servants of, first or primary wives. For this very reason, first wives often encourage their husbands to become polygynous. As mentioned earlier, the legal rights of secondary wives and their offspring are quite variable. Societal norms appear biologically advantageous to first wives, who use others' labor to rear offspring; and to men, who hedge their bets by contributing fully to some offspring, while providing lesser amounts to others judged "high risk." This state of affairs should greatly reduce the benefits of marriage to women whose possibilities are limited to becoming secondary wives. At one time among the Kikuyu the ranks of prostitutes were increased by "girls who in olden days would have become second wives in a polygynous household."[46] They could not find men who wanted them as first and senior wives. This case may illustrate as well as any how female counter-strategies are selected for in societies in which the status of women is sufficiently low to permit routine exploitation of their labor for the primary benefit of others. Prostitution is just one of several possible alternatives.

Women also indicate that they turn to prostitution to avoid the hard work and drudgery of marriage. This suggests that the life of a prostitute is less onerous than that of a married woman in some non-industrialized societies. If Malay divorcées in Singapore have difficulty in remarrying and are reluctant to engage in such poorly paid and strenuous occupations as gathering firewood and laundering clothes, they may become prostitutes.[47] Among the Amhara and Bemba prostitutes can afford to hire men to do work normally befalling women.[48]

In a few societies in which prostitutes are not strongly discriminated against, women use prostitution to locate superior mates (Table 4). Amhara women consider customers short-term husbands, and although the "pair bond" typically lasts for only one night, women watch for men they consider potentially desirable husbands and encourage them to become repeat customers.[49] Alternatively, women can use prostitution to increase their own desirability as mates. In Algeria, Ulad-Nail girls use prostitution to save up a dowry.[50] Among the Mongols, attractive prostitutes have high economic and social status, and even the wealthiest of men are not adverse to locating marital partners in their ranks.[51] But whether association with prostitution helps or hinders female marriageability, prostitution can be so economically rewarding that its impact on marital status may be only a secondary consideration.

Table 4

Societies in Which Prostitution is Used as a Means Of Mate-Getting,[1] and Those in Which Prostitutes Have High Social Status or are Quite Wealthy[2]

Society	Source	
Amhara[1]	Messing	1957
China[1]	Lang	1946
Kanuri[1, 2]	Rosman	1962
Lydia[1]	Ploss et al.	1935
Malays[1]	Firth	1943
Mongolia[2]	Maiskii	1921
Ulad-Nail[1]	Ploss et al.	1935
Wolof[2]	Gorer	1935

The motives expressed by many sorts of women in numerous societies are, at their core, clearly economic: men create a demand and women find an economic advantage in meeting it. In the Fox Islands during the middle of the eighteenth century it was common for a number of Aleuts to have from two to four wives. They often exchanged them or sold them in bad times for a bladder of fat or to Russian hunters for a "trifling compensation."[52] In the harsh desert environment of the Goajira, prostitution was definitely motivated by economic considerations. "During the summers, which are the periods of scarcity and misery, their conduct finds, if no approbation, at least excuse among their relatives, who see in their way of life a means of income which assists in part to supply the most basic necessities of life."[53] In addition to the circumstances discussed above that favor participation in prostitution, the basic economic motive is recognized by ethnographers and the people themselves in a number of additional societies (Table 5).

Up to this point we have considered prostitution as a full-time occupation, or at least as a basic means of support, an alternative to marriage. In some places, however, married women participate in the activity on a part-time basis, apparently for the primary purpose of augmenting income (Table 6). Most ethnographers do not specify whether or not husbands are aware of their wives' activities; in some cases, evidence suggests probable ignorance. Circumstances that favor husband-wife cooperation versus those that favor female deceit are discussed in a subsequent section.

It is easy to see why society frowns on prostitution that results from the alternatives sought by unmarriageable women and those rejecting their

Table 5
Additional Societies in Which Women Turn to Prostitution for Economic Support

Society	Source	
Aymara	Bouroncle-Carreón	1964
Bali	Covarrubias	1938
China	Fried	1953
Goajiro	Gutierrez de Pineda	1950
Kurd	Masters	1953
Iban	Sutlive	1972
Serbs	Halpern	1958

Table 6
Societies in Which Married Women Engage in Part-Time Prostitution

Society	Source	
Aleut	Jones	1969
Bali	Covarrubias	1938
Bushmen	Kaufman	1910
Dogon	Paulme	1940
Goajiro	Gutierrez de Pineda	1950
Hausa	Smith	1955
Hopi	Titiev	1972
Kuwait Bedouins	Dickson	1951
Siwans	Cline	1936

social circumstances. The first group includes women of low status and those already considered a burden or unwanted. They are likely to become objects of discrimination and ridicule before turning to prostitution and this attitude may simply become intensified afterwards. Although negative feelings toward low-status women are to be expected, those in power may not actively seek to suppress prostitution activity of these females, especially since it decreases the women's dependence on others.

The second group of women, those who reject their social role, poses more of a threat to the male-dominated moral order. Prostitutes may have considerably more personal autonomy than other women, no doubt due in part to their economic independence. To keep more women from pursuing this alternative, it is in the best interests of those with authority to condemn prostitution and to make life as difficult as possible for those practicing it. This significantly reduces benefits to prostitution as perceived by females and may keep the number of women so employed at lower levels than might otherwise be the case. However intense pressures may be on these particular women, they are but a subcategory of more general attempts to keep prostitution at low levels by leaving little doubt about the institution's social meaning.

A rather widespread social norm holds that the space that defines the core of society's social relationships should reflect prevailing moral values. In a sense, that which is located within the village or most of its spaces is sacred, that which lies beyond in the wilderness, in transient, public and heterogeneous social spaces is profane. The dichotomy, of course, is a loose one and does not apply to just any infraction of just any cultural norm. If a violation of rules is widespread, relatively inconsequential or engaged in by those with power and privilege, the breach may hold no geographical consequences. But when the taboo is strong, when the transgression clearly defined or absolute rather than relative, then the social and geographic spaces of those who generally follow the moral code have been profanely invaded. Violators must live in their own geographic space, one that either they alone define or one in which their identity is of little or no consequence to those offended. These spaces—social geographic sinks—may be within the village, but specifically circumscribed; they may be just outside the geographical limits of where most social interactions occur; or they may simply be part of the ill-defined or offensive landscapes of other places—unused spaces, other villages, the cities of foreigners.

Prostitutes are geographically set apart from their own societies in a variety of ways. Where women have access to a town or city they frequently move there. Cities provide anonymity and sufficient demand to allow full-time pursuit of prostitution. In 31 of the societies with prostitution the women work or reside in towns and cities, often those with port or commercial activity. Women without the opportunities or desire to work in these places may be itinerant, moving among their own people or neighbors (Table 7).

Some societies segregate their prostitutes within the settlement or force them to live and work beyond the geographical limits of normal social interaction (Table 7).

Table 7
Geographic Patterns of Prostitution

Society	Mobile Prostitutes		Source	
Araucanians	Titiev		1951	
Caraja	Krause		1911	
Navajo	Reichard		1950	
Siwans	Cline		1936	

Those Who Live and Work on Outskirts of Settlement

Society	Source	
Inca	Garcilasco de la Vega	1869-71
Laos	Reinach	1901
Mongolia	Maiskii	1921
Pawnee	Dorsey & Murie	1914
Siwans	Cline	1936
Yap	Furness	1910

Those Segregated Within A Settlement

Society	Source	
Bororó	Cook	1909
China	Lamson	1934
Hausa	Smith	1955
Manus	Mead	1930
Okinawa	Cohen	1958
Santa Cruz	Graebner	1909

Prostitutes Reside in Village—Unspecified Whether or Not Segregated

Society	Source	
Caraja	Krause	1911
Hopi	Titiev	1972
Mam	Wagley	1949
Manchuria	Lattimore	1935
Mataco	Fock	1963
Sierra Tarascans	Beals	1946
Trumaí	Murphy & Quain	1955
Yanoama	Vinci	1959

The Inca force prostitutes to live alone in fields in poor huts, each woman to herself. Prostitutes are not allowed to enter towns or interact with other women.[54] Among the Bororó segregation means working in the "great hut," a large building in the center of an encampment or village reserved for bachelors and public functions. Females are only permitted to enter the great hut as prostitutes, to participate in funeral ceremonies, or when being punished by their husbands, who take them to the hut and allow the men of the village to sexually assault them.[55]

Finally, there are cases in which it is known only that prostitutes reside in the village, and they may or may not be geographically isolated (Table 7). Some of these women may be identified less by geography than by appearance. Among the Creek, prostitutes are women who commit adultery or are cast out by their husbands. Their distinctive badge is cut hair or an ear and a painted face.[56]

Prostitution Initiated by Males and Parents

In some societies women do not enter prostitution voluntarily. Instead they are forced into the occupation by their husbands or fathers (Table 8), jointly by their parents (Table 9), or by their abductors (Table 10), perhaps to be purchased by new "parents" or unrelated males.

Table 8
Societies in Which Females are Reported to be Forced into Prostitution, by Their Husband,[1] Father,[2] or Uncle.[3]

Society	Source	
Aleut[1]	Coxe	1804
Bellacoola[1]	McIllwraith	1948
Burma[2]	Ploss et al.	1935
Chuckchee[1]	Borgoraz-Tan	1904-1909
Fang[1]	Balandier	1955
Hopi[1]	Titiev	1972
Manchuria[1]	Shirokogarov	1924
Marshalls[1]	Kramer & Nevermann	1938
Montagnais[1]	Burgesse	1944
Murngin[1]	Berndt & Berndt	1954
Olo-Ngadjoe[1]	Ploss et al.	1935
Sumatra[1]	Ploss et al.	1935
Timbira[3]	Nimvendajú	1946
Tiwi[1,2]	Hart & Pilling	1960
Tlingit[1,2]	Knapp & Childe	1896
	Krause	1956
Trobriand Islanders[1*]	Malinowski	1929
Yucatec Maya[1,2]	Steggerda	1941

* Indicates that activity is engaged in by chief or headman.

Table 9
Societies in Which Girls are Reported to be Forced into Prostitution by Their Parents or Family

Society	Source	
Creek	Swanton	1924-25
China	Levy	1949
India	Karve	1953
Manchuria	Lattimore	1935
Mongolia	Ma	1949
Okinawa	Maretzki & Maretzki	1963
Santa Cruz	Davenport	1962
Taiwan Hokkien	Wolf	1965
Truk	Damm	1938
Yap	Senfft	1907

Males' motives for encouraging or enforcing prostitution are as diverse as those of females, but most retain the common thread of economics. However, one motive that is probably the exclusive domain of males has a political basis. In places in which polygyny is permitted and in which a small fraction of the male population has reproductive access to a large proportion of the female population, prostitution may be initiated or condoned by males in power in order to reduce discontent and rebellion by the less fortunate males in the society. Official support for the institution permits it to flourish and organized brothels may result (Table 11).

Political motives are evident in some African and Oceanic societies. Among the Fang and Yap, bachelors secure the cooperation of their chiefs to obtain prostitutes through purchase or capture.[57] Also among the Fang, chiefs may only keep three or four of perhaps a dozen or more wives. The others are divided among friends and adherents or hired out to acquaintances for cash payments.[58] Young males among the Manus are reported to be willing and eager to go to war for the opportunity it affords them to rape women and obtain slave-prostitutes.[59] This theme has apparently been repeated frequently throughout human history.[60] Marshallese and Trobriand headmen rent concubines and wives from their extensive harems, a practice that may have both political and economic motivations.[61] The Marshallese headman keeps close watch over his women's activities, perhaps permitting him to monitor those of subordinate males. Alternative adaptations for appeasement and control of subordinates are found among the Azande and Lozi, societies in which the powerful maintain large harems. Polygynous Azande males express concern about retaliation by bachelors and give cast-off concubines to their lessers while Lozi kings sometimes give concubines away after impregnating them.[62]

Polygyny is both the outcome of, and a reinforcer of, male reproductive competition. Hence, where prostitution is organized for the primary benefit of bachelors, theory leads us to predict that prostitutes would be recruited from outside groups, since many of the young women within society are fathered by its powerful males.[63] This expectation is supported by the limited data available; the pattern occurs in all five societies for which information is available on both points (compare Tables 9 and 10). Also, we would expect that the reproductive benefit to patronizing prostitutes in these instances would be minimal since it is not to dominant males' advantage to encourage subordinates to reproduce. Unfortunately, data on prostitute reproduction are almost nonexistent. The only evidence uncovered concerns the Santa Cruz Islands, where sons of prostitutes are killed at birth and daughters are reared to become prostitutes.[64]

The rich and powerful may also organize brothels and other forms of prostitution for their own use, particularly where extensive polygyny is not legal. In Okinawa, where pleasurable aspects of sex—to men—are identified with prostitutes, an old custom provides that after a man is married he leaves his wife at home and goes to a public brothel.[65] In Okinawan society

Table 10
Societies in Which Prostitutes are Typically Slaves, War Captives, or Women Who Have Been Purchased

Society	Source	
Blackfoot	Wissler	1911
Caraja	Krause	1909
Fang	Balandier	1955
Goajiro	Gutierrez de Pineda	1950
Imperial Rome	Lewis & Reinhold	1966
Koreans	Hulbert	1906
Manus	Mead	1930
Santa Cruz	Graebner	1909
	Speiser	1916
Saudi Arabia	Bailes	1952
Thailand	Thompson	1937
Toradja	Adriani & Kruyt	1951
Yap	Senfft	1907

Table 11
Societies in Which Prostitution is Known to be Openly Tolerated or Government-Sponsored

Society	Source	
Amhara[2]	Messing	1957
Caraja[1]	Krause	1911
China[2]	Lamson	1934
East China[2]	Murphy	1953
Fang[1]	Balandier	1955
Hausa[2]	Smith	1955
Indochina[2]	Broderick	1942
Koreans[1]	Moose	1911
Malaya[2]	Williams-Hunt	1952
Manchuria[2]	Shirokogorov	1924
Manus[1, 2]	Mead	1930
Marshalls	Erdland	1914
North China[2]	Stanford University	1956b
Okinawa[2]	Maretski & Maretski	1963
Santa Cruz[1]	Graebner	1909
Taiwan[2]	Wolf	1965
Thailand[2]	Thompson	1937
Tibet[2]	Peter	1963
Trobriand Islanders	Malinowski	1929
Wolof[2]	Gorer	1935
Yap[1, 2]	Lingenfelten	1971

[1] Those in which customers are principally young men or bachelors.
[2] Those in which brothels are reported.

women are expected to remain faithful, while a man's sexual behavior is limited only by his finances. Prostitutes are available to a rather broad segment of the male population, there being a continuum of brothel types and reasonably well-defined classes of prostitutes. These distinctions prevail in a number of Asian societies in which prostitution is openly tolerated (Table 11).

Less affluent men may have motives for prostituting women, motives more economic than political or reproductive. In general, pimping may arise as a strategy to assert control over resources under at least two conditions. In societies in which male control over resources is typically limited, pimping may provide males with a means of increasing assets. Alternatively, it may be used as a counter-strategy to reassert male control over resources in places in which females voluntarily engage in prostitution to attempt to increase their control. In general, we would expect the sale of wives' sexual services to be more common where males' confidence of paternity is generally low and/or male investment in offspring is low. Under these conditions the benefits of prostituting wives are more likely to exceed the costs than in those circumstances in which males provide substantial investment in their offspring.

In at least three societies permitting polygyny, the Fang, the Trobriand Islanders, and the Lapong district of Sumatra, men marry some wives for the primary purpose of prostituting them.[66] This is one way of exploiting the labor of subordinate women to contribute to the reproduction of primary wives. In some cases the reproductive risks of selling access to even "primary" wives may be small in comparison to the economic rewards of the activity. For example, one form of prostitution involves a husband-wife agreement to defraud unwitting men. A woman allows herself to be "seduced" by a man, whereupon her husband cries adultery. The victim is required to reimburse the husband substantially for violation of his property. Among the Ila this ruse is called "hunting for wealth," since the "aggrieved" husband is paid in valuable cattle. Supposedly the husband thinks more of his wife for prostituting herself in this manner—because she adds to his wealth. But it is only after she has earned several cows that she may be able to keep one for herself.[67] The Lozi have a different angle on this theme. They have an upper limit to the number of cases a man can bring to court to sue for adultery: beyond that limit, his wife is considered to be a common prostitute.[68]

An activity that may be only marginally classified as prostitution occurs in societies that practice wife exchange. Wife exchange occurs in some societies in which males often travel long distances without female companions. Upon reaching their destination, their host may offer his wife for the night in return for a small gift. Although it is generally thought that such offers are made freely, limited evidence suggests that rather specific reciprocity is involved. Soon after having been visited, males make trips to receive return hospitality. This system of exchange has been capitalized upon by traders and other outsiders who offer goods instead of their own women in exchange, and it appears that males readily adapt to the change of currency.[69]

There are at least three types of "parentally" enforced prostitution. Among the Formosans, the Taiwanese, the Taiwan Hokkien, and possibly in some other Asian societies, prostitutes and respectable citizens adopt "daughters" for the explicit purpose of turning them into prostitutes.[70] The economic motive of exploiting the labor of non-relatives is clearly the basis of this form of prostitution. Prostitutes sometimes also raise their own daughters to become prostitutes, or their offspring may be forced by the larger society to enter prostitution (e.g., Kuwait Bedouins; Sierra Tarascans).[71] In a few cases the result is the formation of a caste of prostitutes (e.g., the Kanada; India).[72] Finally, biological parents may knowingly sell their daughters to procurers or otherwise deliberately force them to become prostitutes (Table 8).

The prostitution of daughters may be biologically adaptive if it increases the family's fitness through accentuating the mate-getting and reproductive alternatives of offspring other than the daughter involved. This situation is likely to prevail where sons require substantially more resources to marry than do daughters, so that parents can profitably prostitute daughters to increase the resources of sons. It may also be expected to occur under circumstances in which daughters are frequently unmarriageable, as is the case in the few regularly polyandrous societies. Under these conditions, daughters may simultaneously contribute to their sibs and enhance their own reproduction through prostitution. In Taiwan, parents admit to prostituting daughters in order to obtain heirs, as well as for economic gains.[73]

In societies in which marital custom provides that males pay handsomely for the right to marry females, we would expect parents to oppose the tendency of a daughter to become a prostitute. However, where females do not provide this income, where females must provide dowries of considerable worth, or where the price of prostitutes is relatively high and parents need money, the likelihood of selling daughters into prostitution increases. People in the Santa Cruz Islands report they sell their daughters into prostitution because they get ten times more than a bride price would bring. The purchased girl is used and provided for jointly by three or four bachelors who may also hire her out for feather money, pigs or coconuts. When the men tire of her they take her to another village and auction her off, an important event among the local populace.[74] A somewhat similar pattern in which parents are well rewarded is found among the Yap.[75]

Does Kinship Matter?

To the extent that prostitution is, in some sense, biologically advantageous, there should be a relationship between those who initiate the activity and kinship structure. Each "class" of individuals (husband, father, parents, married or unmarried female) should promote or engage in prostitution in accord with who profits from doing so. By considering the characteristics of different kinship and mating systems it may be possible to make predictions regarding this relationship.

In general, females appear to have the most autonomy and the greatest access to resources in matrilineal societies, those in which descent is traced through the female line. In contrasting numerous matrilineal societies with others, Robert Textor found that matrilineal inheritance and matrilocal residence occur more often in societies typified by matrilineal descent.[76] Matrilineal inheritance does not necessarily mean that females have control over wealth or resources but rather that wealth is transferred through the female line. For example, at death a man's resources may pass to his sister's sons. Where matrilocality is the rule, males, upon marrying, leave their kin group to reside with their wife's relatives. In societies displaying patrilocality, a much more common practice, females join their husband's kin group, thus diminishing social interactions among those to whom they are most closely related. Matrilocality may contribute to female autonomy because females maintain close ties with their own kin.

In comparison with societies characterized by patrilineal descent (that traced through the male line) or double descent (that traced through both lines), matrilineal societies tend more often to be purely monogamous. They are also societies in which wives are obtained relatively easily. Bride price or bride service, if present, is usually small. In patrilineal and double descent systems, polygyny is more common, and the procurement of wives involves considerable effort or expense. Premarital sexual behavior is more often permitted, tolerated or less severely punished in matrilineal than in patrilineal or double descent societies. In addition, extra-marital sexual relationships are more often tolerated and divorce and abortion are more common among matrilineal groups.[77] While matrilineal societies are sometimes considered sexually permissive, it may be more accurate to say that such societies relax the double standard. In a good many non-matrilineal societies penalties for infringements of restrictions on sexual behavior fall more heavily on females than on males.

Of course, within societies classified as matrilineal or patrilineal, considerable variation in attitudes and practices occurs. Alice Schlegel constructed a five-category typology of domestic authority within matrilineal societies. She found that in some husbands' authority strongly predominates, whereas in others it is adult brothers who are in control. When husbands have considerable command over domestic affairs, societal characteristics tend to resemble those found in patrilineal systems. According to Schlegel, the greatest personal autonomy for females occurs where male authority is divided between, and apparently fragmented by, husbands and brothers.[78] These differences notwithstanding, overall females have more autonomy in matrilineal societies.

One might suppose that where prostitution occurs it would be initiated generally by individuals of the sex with greater control. By this reasoning, females would be more likely to initiate prostitution in matrilineal societies, and would be more frequently forced into the activity in those which are patrilineal. Such an expectation is short-sighted, for it does not consider the benefits to be acquired from prostitution.

Social and economic pressures on females to engage in prostitution appear much less marked where matrilineality occurs. Females in matrilineal societies probably have greater choice over their marital partners and greater ability to terminate undesirable relationships. Thus, they should be less stimulated to opt for prostitution in order to avoid a forced marriage. Also, given that males are not required to provide substantial sums of money or labor to obtain mates, male wealth should be a relatively unimportant mating consideration in matrilineal societies—at least in those characterized by matrilineal inheritance. Since polygyny is less common in matrilineal societies, females less often face the prospect of becoming secondary wives. Because females may also have somewhat more control over resources, they are at less of an economic disadvantage. For all of these reasons, it would appear that females are more likely to benefit from turning to prostitution in patrilineal societies, even though male control may be sufficient to prevent them from doing so.

The selective pressures operating on males are quite different. In patrilineal societies males often have to supply substantial amounts of time or resources to obtain wives, and upon their death they tend to leave their wealth to their wives' sons. Under these circumstances a man's biological fitness depends heavily on his wife's fidelity. If she engages in sexual activity with other males, her behavior may lower his fitness by causing him to contribute to another man's offspring. Although males may be able to force their wives to become prostitutes in patrilineal societies, it is usually not to their advantage to do so. An exception to this generality occurs when the status of secondary wives is low and males do not have to invest heavily in them. In this case, the economic advantages of coercing women into prostitution may offset the biological costs of resulting pregnancies, particularly if the males' behavior permits them to obtain more wives (through increased wealth) or to channel more resources to "legitimate" offspring.

In matrilineal societies, a man's confidence of paternity is often quite low. Indeed, it has been suggested that the domestic authority displayed by women's brothers in many such societies results from lack of confidence of paternity.[79] A male is certain of being related to his sister through his mother. If he cannot be certain he is the father of his wife's offspring, he profits from contributing less to them and more to his sister's offspring. Therefore, when a male's confidence of paternity is sufficiently low and his investment in his wife's offspring also low, he may benefit from forcing his wife or daughters into prostitution if he can then channel some of the profits back to his sister and her offspring. Men in matrilineal societies may have good biological reasons for prostituting their wives and their wives' daughters. However, their ability to do so may be limited by their domestic authority.

By this line of reasoning, females should be more inclined to initiate prostitution in strongly male-dominated societies, while males should tend to force women into prostitution in weakly male-dominated societies. In both cases there may be contravening social pressures that limit the ability of would-be initiators to behave as predicted.

To examine this hypothesis, societies were classified by kinship pattern (matrilineal, patrilineal or double descent), mating system (monogamous, occasionally polygynous, frequently polygynous) and the sex initiating prostitution. Included under female-initiated prostitution are societies in which the literature reports the following motives as leading females to enter prostitution: economic need, avoidance of marriage, lack of available marriage partners and mate-getting ability (Table 12).

There are problems with this attempt at classification that deserve mention. First, it rather arbitrarily dichotomizes the possibilities for initiation of prostitution. In actuality, females may become prostitutes voluntarily (as voluntarily as humans engage in any activity) or they may receive varying degrees of pressure from spouse or kin. The categorization reflects language used by ethnographers, who may not in all cases have intended to imply that women either voluntarily or forcibly submitted to prostitution.

Since there is variation within kinship systems in degree of female autonomy, it is not reasonable to expect that in all cases females have greater autonomy in matrilineal societies. To explore the extent of variability we categorized degree of social restrictiveness on female behavior using a modified version of the classification developed by Kenneth Eckhardt.[80] In this classification one point was assigned to societies for each of the following patterns displayed: matrilineal descent, matrilocal or avunculocal residence, and lack of property exchange or token exchange at marriage. Societies could score from zero (restrictive of females) to three (permissive toward females). In all cases for which data were available, matrilineal societies scored 2 or 3 on this index, whereas patrilineal or double descent systems scored 0 or 1 (Table 12).

The classification does not control for amount of prostitution, nor for disagreement among sources regarding the nature of kinship and mating systems. And there is, of course, Galton's problem regarding whether or not the societies can be considered independent units.

Despite these difficulties, available data tend to support the idea that females use prostitution to circumvent social restrictions, and males are more likely to force wives and "daughters" into prostitution when their investment in offspring and confidence of paternity is low. Of 22 societies classified as patrilineal or double descent systems, females were recorded as initiating prostitution in 18 (82 percent) and males in 5 (23 percent) (Table 12). Of the 12 societies classified as matrilineal, females initiate prostitution

Table 12
Lineality Patterns, Mating Systems and Sex-Specific Initiation of Prostitution

Prostitution Initiated by Husbands and/or Fathers	Prostitution Initiated by Women and Girls

Societies with Patrilineal or Double Descent
(Total = 180)

Burma[4]—M	Araucanians[1]—P
Chuckchee[1, 5]—P	Aymara[1]—M
Fang[1]—P	Azande[1]—P
Murngin—P	China
Yucatec Maya—M	Chuckchee[1, 5]—P
	Dogon—L
	Iban[1]—M
	Kikuyu[1]—P
	Mongo[1]—P
	Mossi—P
	Okinawa[1]—M
	Rundi—P
	Serbs[1]—M
	Shilluk[1]—P
	Siwans—L
	Somali[1]—P
	Trumaí—P
	Wolof[1]—P

Societies with Matrilineal Descent
(Total = 65)

Hopi—M	Twi[3]—L
Marshalls[2]—M	Bororó[2]—P
Timbira[2]—M	Creek—L
Tiwi—P	Goajiro[2]—P
Tlingit—L	Marshalls[2]—M
Trobrianders[2]—L	Navajo—L-P
	Pawnee—P

Sources for classification of lineality patterns: Eckhardt 1971; Schlegel 1972; Textor 1967. Sources for classification of mating system: Murdock 1965; Textor 1967. Sources for number of societies: Schlegel 1972; Textor 1967. Symbols: M = monogamy; L = limited or occasional polygyny; P = polygyny common. [1]indicates societies scoring 0 or 1 on index modified from Eckhardt (1971), suggesting strong male dominance in society. [2]indicates societies scoring 2 or 3 on index modified from Eckhardt (1971), suggesting male dominance weak or absent. [3]indicates society classified differently by Textor and Schlegel; Schlegel's classification used here. [4]indicates that society probably should be classified as parent-initiated, rather than father-initiated (see text). [5]indicates society classified according to Eckhardt 1971. Note that two societies (Chuckchee and Marshalls) have both male- and female-initiated prostitution.

in 7 (58 percent) and males in 6 (50 percent). Although matrilineal societies tend more often to be monogamous, 86 percent of those in which females initiate prostitution practice some degree of polygyny (Table 12). This suggests that under the most favorable conditions—matrilineal, monogamous societies—females, as a rule, do not find prostitution advantageous.

A final consideration is the distinction between father- and parent-initiated prostitution. In societies in which prostitution is initiated by the husband, the consequences may not be advantageous to the mother or the daughter. By contrast, in parent-initiated prostitution the economic and, possibly, the biological interests of the mother and father are aligned.

Forms of behavior that restrict the opportunities of particular offspring but enhance the overall reproductive success of the family are sometimes termed "parental manipulation."[81] Geographically, the pattern of returning resources to the family through prostitution is a predominantly Asian custom. Prostitution has long been quite common in Asian societies. Perhaps not coincidentally, some of these same societies are typified as requiring absolute obedience from offspring. The ability of mothers and fathers to force daughters into prostitution may result from the fact that it is in their joint benefit to do so. Males may be less often able to force the daughters of their wives into prostitution when their authority is weak or when wives' interests are not aligned with their own.

In summary, the cross-cultural causes of prostitution are diverse. Women and girls appear more likely to initiate prostitution activities when their economic and biological options are strongly restricted by social norms that protect male investment and advantage. Males appear more likely to force women into prostitution when their biological interests are not well-protected by society. Parents may successfully force daughters into prostitution when the interests of mother and father are aligned, and especially when society does not extend individual rights to dependent children. The overall incidence of prostitution is affected by many factors, some biological, others cultural, but it does not appear that norms regarding sexual behavior have a determining effect on frequency. Based on the data examined here, prostitution may be slightly more frequent in matrilineal societies, which tend to de-emphasize the double standard, than in patrilineal and double descent societies, which enforce it (18 versus 12 percent). However, this difference does not address the important question of relative frequency of prostitution within societies.

The many faces of prostitution reaffirm the social and biological dictum that those with advantage seek to perpetuate that advantage, whereas the disadvantaged seek to counter or circumvent the conditions that make them socially subordinate and reproductively inferior. Women are often without because of the rules that men make, but some women counter—wisely perhaps—by capitalizing on their one asset that men must value to be evolutionarily competitive.

Source Notes for the Main Text

Chapter 1

1. Morris and Hawkins 1969:15.
2. "New York Court . . ." 1978.
3. "Sexual Solicitation . . ." 1979.
4. Jennings 1976:1250.
5. Rossi et al. 1974.
6. Milman 1980.
7. Gallup 1976:803.
8. Geis 1972:192.
9. Geis 1972:128.
10. Pilpel 1970:61.
11. Sheppard 1979.
12. Haft 1974:23.
13. Stinchcombe 1963; Lowman 1980.
14. Atkinson and Boles 1977.
15. Kaplan 1977.
16. Mercier 1979.
17. Marx 1977:37-40.
18. Lemert 1968:93; MacNamara and Sagarin 1977:106.
19. Jones 1978:9.
20. Gebhard 1966b.
21. Yondorf 1979:420-21.
22. Sandford 1975:218.
23. Choisy 1960:88-89.
24. Gunther 1957; Stafford 1967.
25. Winick and Kinsie 1972:14; Sheehy 1974:12.
26. San Francisco Vice Meeting 1976.
27. Moses et al. 1976.
28. Yondorf 1979:426.
29. Dirasse 1978.
30. Sheehy 1974:12.
31. Noll 1974.
32. Texier and Vézina 1978:283-90.
33. Winter 1976:33-34, 230.
34. Geis 1972:192.
35. *Discreet Gentleman's Guide . . .* 1975:4.
36. Yondorf 1979:425.
37. Christian 1960:60-61.
38. Philadelphia, Vice Commission of Philadelphia 1913:15.
39. Philadelphia, Vice Commission of Philadelphia 1913:15.
40. Chicago, Vice Commission of Chicago 1911:32.
41. Woolston 1921:118.
42. Ashbury 1933:232.
43. Ashbury 1933:313.
44. Rose 1974:30.
45. Rose 1974:96.
46. Rose 1974:31.
47. Rose 1974:29-30.
48. Exner et al. 1977:482.
49. Exner et al. 1977:483.
50. Exner et al. 1977:483.
51. Pomeroy 1965; Gebhard 1969.
52. Young 1967:115-16; Greenwald 1970:25-26.
53. Velardi 1976:260.
54. Heyl 1979:121-22.
55. Heyl 1979:121-22.
56. Layton 1978:170.
57. Young 1967:124.
58. James and Withers 1975:xv.
59. San Francisco Committee on Crime 1971:19-20.
60. Neckes 1976.
61. San Francisco Committee on Crime 1971:20.
62. San Francisco Vice Meeting 1976.
63. San Francisco Committee on Crime 1971:1.
64. Haft 1975:25-26.
65. Moses et al. 1976.
66. Morrill 1977.
67. San Francisco Committee on Crime 1971.
68. Geis 1972:199.
69. Schmid and Schmid 1972:256.
70. McKay 1974.
71. Rolph 1955:26-33.
72. Gemme 1971.
73. San Francisco Committee on Crime 1971:4, 25.
74. San Francisco Committee on Crime 1971:24.
75. Becker 1968:170.
76. Ehrlich 1973.

Chapter 2

1. Sanger 1937:456.
2. Kneeland 1913:198.
3. Syracuse, Committee of Eighteen 1913:103; Newark, New Jersey, Citizen's Committee 1914:156; Layton 1975:20-21.
4. Sanger 1937:456.
5. Kneeland 1913.
6. Lemert 1968:71.
7. Sheehy 1974; Raab 1977; Palmquist and Stone 1978.
8. Palmquist and Stone 1978.
9. Morgan 1975.
10. Addams 1912:59, 145; Borrelli and Starck 1957:62; Lemert 1968:71.
11. Tancer 1973:215; Teresa de Gallo and Algate 1976:4.
12. Roebuck and McNamara 1973:237.
13. Layton 1975:20-21.
14. Egyptian Government 1935:12-13; Bellamy 1973:60-61; Burford 1976; Winter 1976:246; Bullough and Bullough 1978:71.

15. Bullough 1964:189; Bridenbaugh 1968:120-22; 316-18; Pivar 1973:20.
16. Bullough 1976:515.
17. Richardson 1970:4.
18. Pivar 1973:27.
19. Richardson 1970:27. Also see Wagner 1971:261.
20. Richardson 1970:27; Wagner 1971:261.
21. Parent-Duchatelet 1836, Vols. I and II; 1857; Evans 1976:106.
22. Colquhoun quoted in Henriques 1968:51.
23. Geijer quoted in Henriques 1968:52.
24. Trudgill 1976:107.
25. Vintras 1867:29-41.
26. Knox 1857:232.
27. Quoted in Trudgill 1976:107.
28. Turner 1959.
29. Pearson 1972:77.
30. Bullough and Bullough 1978:117-29.
31. Walton Vol. I, 1899:247.

32. Bullough 1964:144; Cobb 1970:235; Baker 1975:27.
33. Baker 1975:27.
34. Data are from Parent-Duchatelet 1836, Vols. I and II; and 1857.
35. Després 1883:6-7.
36. Hufton 1974:311.
37. Baker 1975:27.
38. Parent-Duchatelet 1836, Vols. I and II; and 1857.
39. Walton 1899, Vol. I; Bullough and Bullough 1978:158-60.
40. Bullough and Bullough 1978:158.
41. Parent-Duchatelet 1857:306-307.
42. Bullough 1964:111.
43. Flexner 1914b:24-25.
44. Sandford 1975:217; "Francia . . ." 1978.
45. Evans 1976:108.
46. Henriques 1968:78-80.
47. Schultz 1977:8-9.
48. Layton 1975:217-18.
49. Wisconsin Legislative Committee 1914.

50. Elazer 1970:226.
51. Elazer 1970:226-28. The discussion of prostitution in Illinois draws on Elazer 1970.
52. Layton 1975:7.
53. Texier and Vèzina 1978.
54. The map is based on personal familiarity with general patterns in the state, and also arrest and population data.
55. "Fresno Has Distinction" 1975.
56. The material on Boston draws on Milman 1980.
57. Evans 1976:109.
58. Bullough and Bullough 1978:123.
59. On the image of pimps see Milner and Milner 1973.
60. Goodman and Cohen 1977.
61. Lane 1975, Part II:3.
62. Gorner 1977; Fields 1976.
63. Mankoff 1974:429.
64. Karp 1971:54.
65. Sheehy 1974:16-17.

Chapter 3

1. Great Britain, *Report of the Committee on Homosexual Offenses and Prostitution . . .* 1963:142.
2. Great Britain, *Report of the Committee on Homosexual Offenses and Prostitution . . .* 1963.
3. Great Britain, *Report of the Committee on Homosexual Offenses and Prostitution . . .* 1963.
4. Gosling and Warner 1960:9.
5. Gosling and Warner 1960:21-23.
6. Gallup 1976:427.
7. Storch 1977.
8. Storch 1977:62.
9. Gibson 1979:292.
10. Steiner 1977:91
11. League of Nations 1924:55.

12. Moses et al. 1976.
13. San Francisco Committee on Crime 1971:41.
14. National Public Opinion Research Institute 1952.
15. MacNamara and Sagarin 1978:8-9.
16. Winick and Kinsie 1972:33-34.
17. Winick and Kinsie 1972:33.
18. Bullough 1964:260.
19. Bullough 1976.
20. Burford 1976:74, 91.
21. Drago, Vol. II, 1972:4.
22. Forbis 1973:199.
23. Barrera Caraza 1974:36.
24. Roberts 1953:159.
25. Federal Bureau of Investigation 1978.
26. Milman 1980.
27. Rosenbleet and Pariente 1973:422-27.

28. Quoted in Boles and Tatro 1978:72.
29. Toynbee 1978.
30. Riegel 1968:438-39; Caugherty 1974; James 1976b; Jennings 1976.
31. San Francisco Committee on Crime 1971:30.
32. San Francisco Vice Meeting 1976.
33. d'Orban 1973.
34. Yondorf 1979:423.
35. Layton 1975:53-60.
36. Winick 1973:160.
37. Sheehy 1974:35-36.
38. Ianni 1975:10.
39. James 1975c.
40. Millett 1973:117-18.
41. Goldstein 1978.
42. Layton 1978:166-67.
43. Chambers et al. 1970.
44. The following paragraphs draw on James 1975c.
45. James 1972b.

46. Milman 1980.
47. Woolston 1921:54-55.
48. Flexner 1914a; Woolston 1921.
49. Flexner 1914a:367.
50. Christian 1960:94.
51. Geis 1972:192-93; Sandford 1975:153; United Nations 1959:8.
52. Wilcox 1962; Idsoe and Guthe 1967.
53. Martinez and Centeno 1974:22-23.
54. James 1973b.
55. Gemme 1971:33.
56. "No Bail for Prostitutes . . ." 1975; Lane 1975, Part II
57. Moses et al. 1976:15-19.
58. Yondorf 1979:427.
59. Edwards 1972.
60. James and Burstin 1971.
61. Scherzer 1971:25-26.
62. Rolph 1955:93.
63. North Carolina 1972:46-47; Davis 1973:12; "Hookers and Their Johns . . ." 1979.
64. President's Commission on Law Enforcement . . . 1967:189.
65. Association . . . 1968:11-16; Commission de Police . . . 1977:104-119.
66. Winter 1976:88-90.
67. Sandford 1975:217.
68. Yondorf 1979:423.

69. Ianni 1975.
70. Kobler 1972:114-15.
71. Bullough 1964:252.
72. Powell 1939.
73. Milman 1980. References to Boston in this section are drawn from Milman.
74. Kneeland 1913; Woolston 1921. Also see any of the various crime commission reports issued between 1910 and 1920: Newark, New Jersey 1914; Lexington, Kentucky 1915; Minneapolis, Minnesota 1974.
75. Hilton 1971:133.
76. Rolph 1955:90.
77. Yondorf 1979:425.
78. James 1972a:114.
79. Amir 1971:117-19.
80. Brassaï 1976.
81. Rolph 1955:90.
82. Sheehy 1974:86.
83. Milman 1980. A study in Seattle also found that prostitutes from minority groups were somewhat more likely to engage in larceny: Hilton 1971:109.
84. Rolph 1955:89.
85. James 1971.
86. Freed 1949:99.
87. Gebhard 1969.
88. James 1972b:174-75.
89. Milner and Milner 1973:82.
90. Layton 1978:88.

91. James 1972b.
92. Doherty 1976.
93. Carmichael 1975:146.
94. Binderman et al. 1975:215.
95. Longstreet 1965:95; Davis 1974:102.
96. Davis 1974:102.
97. Wilson 1974:141.
98. Bondenson 1968:75.
99. Fabian 1954:52-53; Bryan 1967:154.
100. Winter 1976:153.
101. Bloch 1934:69-70.
102. Bryan 1967:154.
103. Wilson 1974:119.
104. Gebhard 1966a:2.
105. Lorenzen 1974.
106. Babington 1969:227.
107. Quennel 1950:42.
108. Ashbury 1933:256. The following draws on Miller 1962:61-63.
109. Ashbury 1940:124-27; Ellington 1972:203.
110. Kneeland 1913:77.
111. Freed 1949:99; Morrison 1967:111-12; Hilton 1971:113.
112. Vogliotti 1975:20.
113. Kinsey et al. 1953:613-14.
114. Kinsey et al. 1953:613-14.
115. Freed 1949:55.
116. Tower 1856:335; Henriques 1968:257-58.
117. Hilton 1971:112.
118. Hilton 1971:112.
119. San Francisco Committee on Crime 1971:28.

Chapter 4

1. Henriques 1968:99; Goldman 1972; 1977; Scott and Tilly 1975:57-58; Burford 1976:140-41.
2. Hufton 1974:313-14.
3. Pearson 1972:33.
4. Goldman 1970:12.
5. Addams 1912:59.
6. Bell 1909; Roe 1909; Janney 1911; Fifth International Congress 1913; Flexner 1914a; Rosen 1976; Rosen and

Davidson 1977.
7. Newark, New Jersey, Citizen's Committee 1914:164.
8. Woolston 1921:61-71.
9. Bullough 1965:53.
10. United Nations 1959:22-23.
11. Burford 1976:145.
12. Sanger 1937:475.
13. Waterman 1932.
14. Drake and Cayton 1962:596-97.
15. Drake and Cayton

1962:598.
16. Hirshfeld 1937:159.
17. Freed 1949:164, 182-88, 191-94, 369.
18. Teresa de Gallo and Alzate 1976:5.
19. Roebuck and McNamara 1973:238.
20. "Child Prostitution . . ." 1974.
21. United States Bureau of the Census 1979.
22. James 1975a.
23. Kuttner 1971.

24. Gebhard 1969.
25. Gebhard 1969:29.
26. New York City, Committee of Fourteen 1915.
27. Stuckey 1977:224.
28. James 1976a; James and Meyerding 1977a.
29. Anonymous 1974.
30. Some students of social deviance have made a distinction between primary and secondary social deviance. See Lemert 1951; Lemert 1972:62-63; Rosenblum 1975.
31. Young 1967.
32. Davis 1971.
33. Winick 1962.
34. Sanger 1937:206; League of Nations 1943:25-32; Murtagh and Harris 1957:180-86; Khalaf 1965:65; Pearsall 1969:288-89; Liswood 1970; Mathis 1970; Polatin 1970; Schimel 1970; Millett 1973:54.
35. Janus et al. 1977:68.
36. Stein 1974:312.
37. Stein 1974:312.
38. Terman 1938.
39. Melody 1969:104; Heyl 1979:92.
40. Coleman 1973:6.
41. Winick and Kinsie 1972:184.
42. Edwards and Masters 1963:222, 324.
43. Edwards and Masters 1963:324.
44. Rose 1974:77.
45. Rose 1974:77.
46. Mankoff 1974:603.
47. Layton 1975:108-109.
48. *Discreet Gentleman's Guide . . .* 1975:54.
49. Mankoff 1974:51, 438.
50. Roebuck and McNamara 1973:239; Teresa de Gallo and Alzate 1976:5.
51. Millett 1973:127; James and Meyerding 1977b.
52. Ashbury 1933:174.
53. Ashbury 1933:174.

54. Kobler 1972:36.
55. Murtagh and Harris 1957:12-13.
56. Winick and Kinsie 1972:42, 247.
57. Freed 1949:102; Rose 1974.
58. Terman 1938.
59. Davis 1929; Burgess and Wallin 1953.
60. Adam 1973:521; Mankoff 1974:257-59.
61. Mankoff 1974:257.
62. Benjamin and Ellis 1954: 101; Scott 1954:17, 20-21; Cross 1965:95; Geiger 1968:22.
63. Lewinsohn 1971:29.
64. Dawkins 1976; Clinard 1963:39; Sahlins 1976; Symons 1979.
65. Bateman 1948; Grunt and Young 1952; Wilson et al. 1963; Trivers 1972; Burley 1977.
66. Hite 1976:321-26.
67. Sahlins 1976.
68. Engels 1942; Gunther 1957:331; Kellen 1972:147; Mankoff 1974:445; Brokhin 1975.
69. Davis 1937; Davis 1961; Benjamin and Masters 1964; Khalaf 1965; Henriques 1968; Karp 1971; Winick and Kinsie 1972; Leonard 1979; Leonard and Walliman 1980.
70. Rotenberg 1974:63.
71. Egner 1958:57; Rosenbleet and Pariente 1973:374; Gibson 1979:24.
72. Erikson 1962; Polsky 1969:184-87.
73. Bullough and Bullough 1978:271.
74. Adler 1975:57.
75. Smith and Bullough 1975.
76. Stein 1974:222-24.
77. Barnett 1976.
78. Ashbury 1940:134.
79. Partridge 1961.
80. James 1972b; Milner

and Milner 1973:36.
81. Bullough 1964:288, 290.
82. Winick and Kinsie 1972:44.
83. Bullough 1964:288.
84. Forbis 1973:199.
85. Gentry 1964:218.
86. Hirshfeld 1935:71; Bullough and Bullough 1978:289; Butterfield 1980:44.
87. Hirshfeld 1937:148.
88. Wilson 1974.
89. Milner and Milner 1973:264-65.
90. Esselstyn 1968:130.
91. Glover 1945; James and Meyerding 1977b.
92. Parent-Duchatelet 1857; Kneeland 1913; Flexner 1914; Sanger 1937.
93. James and Meyerding 1977b.
94. Kinsey et al. 1948:600.
95. James and Meyerding 1977b.
96. Sheppard 1979.
97. "Hookers and Their Johns . . ." 1979.
98. Simmons 1952.
99. Steiner 1977:90.
100. Stein 1974.
101. Janus et al. 1977.
102. Jeffers and Levitan 1973:21-34.
103. Kneeland 1913; Roberts 1953:66; Blanch 1955; Winick and Kinsie 1972; Stein 1974.
104. Guyot 1883; *Women That Pass the Night* 1906.
105. Bloch 1934:89-90.
106. *Pretty Women of Paris* 1883.
107. Cross 1965:47-48.
108. Pearsall 1969:257-59.
109. *Directory . . .* 1859.
110. *The Sporting and Club House Directory . . .* 1889; Anonymous 1892; *G.A.R. Sporting Guide* 1895.
111. Semper Idem 1936.
112. Hurwood 1973; Erickson 1974; Green

1974; Mankoff 1974;
*Discreet Gentleman's
Guide . . .* 1975;
Jackson 1976.
113. Schwartz 1973.
114. Flexner 1914a:45.
115. Johnson 1973.
116. Hirshfeld 1937:160.
117. Tabor 1973:154-56.
118. Stein 1974:140.
119. Stein 1974:153.
120. Stein 1974:137.
121. Millett 1973:57-58, 93;
Schwartz 1973; Sheehy
1974:11.
122. Bauer 1979.
123. James 1972a:114.
124. James 1972a:114.
125. Layton 1978:90,
173-76.
126. "How to Remember
. . ." 1978.
127. Atkinson and Boles
1977:10.
128. Atkinson and Boles
1977:10.
129. Kinsey et al. 1953:606.
130. Anonymous 1974:5.
131. Millett 1973:59.
132. Rolph 1955:88.
133. Burford 1976:175.

134. Drzazga 1960:96.
135. Pearsall 1969:291.
136. Sanders 1970:431.
137. Butler 1896; Bell 1909;
Terrot 1960; Waldberg
1969.
138. Yondorf 1979:429.
139. Mankoff 1974:49-50,
57.
140. Ashbury 1938: 391-92;
Longstreet 1965:198.
141. Harris 1960:94-104;
Shoemaker 1977.
142. Palmquist and Stone
1978.
143. Federal Bureau of
Investigation
1965-1978.
144. Mercier 1979.
145. San Francisco
Committee on Crime
1971:34.
146. James and Meyerding
1977b.
147. Stein 1974:312.
148. Krafft-Ebing 1965.
149. Gibson 1978:45.
150. Shaw 1950:132.
151. Beauvoir 1974:627.
152. Greenwald and
Greenwald 1973;

Mankoff 1974:500,
538; *Discreet
Gentleman's Guide
. . .* 1975:54.
153. Cleef 1975:220-21.
154. Gibson 1978:x.
155. Gibson 1978:233.
156. Ryan 1839; Gibson
1978:163-64, 233-64.
157. Gibson 1978:313.
158. Davis 1966:213; Young
1967:136; Mankoff
1974:601.
159. Gebhard 1976:159-60.
160. Stein 1974:243-544.
161. Stein 1974:313-14.
162. Gagnon and Simon
1967.
163. Janus et al. 1977.
164. Gagnon 1968.
165. Bradley et al. 1979:18.
166. Erwin and Miller 1960;
Tabor 1973.
167. Rolph 1955:91-92;
Winick and Kinsie
1972:168.
168. Mol 1964:34.
169. Stein 1974:1-2.
170. Henriques 1968:340;
Ullerstam 1966.
171. Ellis 1965:11.

Chapter 5

1. Flexner 1914a:104.
2. Gibson 1979:40.
3. Hooker 1921:114-16.
4. Rheinstein 1954;
Chambliss 1973.
5. Lubove 1962; Feldman
1967; Riegel 1968;
Wagner 1971.
6. Waterman 1932:71-77.
7. Waterman 1932:76.
8. Federal Bureau of
Investigation 1939.
9. Gould 1942:540-41.
10. International
Abolitionist Federation
1949.
11. Schmid and Schmid
1972:199-203.
12. Rosenbleet and Pariente
1973.
13. Rosenbleet and Pariente
1973:422-27.
14. Layton 1979:109-10.
15. Canada, Report of the

Royal Commission
1970:370.
16. Canada, Report of the
Royal Commission
1970:369; Canada,
Report on Sexual
Offences 1978:33-34.
17. Layton 1979:111.
18. "Women Blast Hooker
Law" 1979.
19. Haft 1974:14.
20. Haft 1975:29; Kizer
1975:1; Moses et al.
1976; Tampa
Prostitution Committee
1976.
21. James 1975b:16-17.
22. Haft 1974.
23. Haft 1975:28.
24. Wade 1975:421.
25. "No Bail for Prostitutes
Without VD . . ." 1975.
26. *Portland Scribe* 1975.
27. Jennings 1976:1252.

28. Stuckey 1977:231.
29. Wilson 1971:66.
30. La Fave 1965:450-61.
31. Based on fieldwork in
1976, discussions with
San Francisco vice
squad and streetwalkers
and examination of
arrest records.
32. San Francisco
Committee on Crime
1971:23, 40-42.
33. Sagarin and
MacNamara 1972:367.
34. James and Withers
1975:xvi.
35. Goldman 1972:38.
36. Drake and Cayton
1962:595-96.
37. Illinois Crime Survey
1929:854.
38. Karp 1971:178.
39. Haft 1975:24.
40. Drummond 1953:222.

41. Schmid and Schmid 1972:215, 242.
42. Layton 1975:8.
43. St. James 1976.
44. Black and Reiss 1967:492.
45. Kizer 1975; Tampa Prostitution Committee 1976.
46. Federal Bureau of Investigation 1978.
47. Flannery 1976.
48. Haft 1975:35-36.
49. Wade 1975:425.
50. Haft 1975:369.
51. Quoted in Kaplan 1977:662.
52. Rosenbleet and Pariente 1973:420.
53. "Victoire vs Ferdon" 1975.

54. Wade 1975:419.
55. Federal Bureau of Investigation 1978.
56. Sheppard 1979.
57. Rosenbleet and Pariente 1973:422-27.
58. Thomas 1972:16-17.
59. Great Britain, *Report of the Committee on Homosexual Offenses and Prostitution* 1963:136; Layton 1979:111.
60. Rosenbleet and Pariente 1973:376.
61. Rosenbleet and Pariente 1973:421.
62. San Francisco Vice Meeting 1976.
63. Marx 1977:37-40.
64. "D.C. Prostitution

. . ." 1978.
65. Quoted in Boles and Tatro 1978:83.
66. "Discrimination Defense . . ." 1976:15; underlining mine.
67. "Discrimination Defense . . ." 1976:15.
68. Boles and Tatro 1978:81.
69. Kaplan 1977:598.
70. Walker 1965: Geis 1972:185.
71. Thomas 1972:17.
72. Great Britain, *Report of the Committee on Homosexual Offenses and Prostitution* 1963:147-48.

Chapter 6

1. Witness 1, Japan 1976; Witness 2, Korea 1976; Stokes 1979.
2. Witness 2, Korea 1976:177.
3. Witness 2, Korea 1976:178.
4. Witness 2, Korea 1976:178.
5. Stokes 1979.
6. Broderick 1942:98-99.
7. Sanger 1963:181-82.
8. Lewis and Reinhold 1966:147
9. Burford 1976:18-19.
10. Sanger 1937; Lewinsohn 1971; Burford 1976.
11. Bullough and Bullough 1978:142, 144.
12. Henriques 1965:50; Simons 1975:67.
13. Perry 1978:195, 209.
14. Sanger 1937:161; Lewinsohn 1971:135, 157; Burford 1976:102.
15. Taylor 1953:22.
16. Cullen 1975:4.
17. Scarlet 1974, Part II:38.
18. Hirshfeld 1937:245.
19. Norden 1974.
20. Norden 1974:241.
21. Lewis 1977; Morrill 1977.
22. Lewis 1977:14, 16, 165.
23. League of Nations 1932:53-57.

24. Brownmiller 1976:61-62.
25. Brownmiller 1976:96-98.
26. Report of the United States Interdepartmental Social Hygiene Board 1922:45.
27. Gibson 1979:119.
28. Leonard 1979; Leonard and Walliman 1980:156-73.
29. Plowcowe 1951:256.
30. Drago 1972, Vol. II:52.
31. Williams 1973:96.
32. Wagner 1971:154-55.
33. Brown 1937; Gentry 1964:265-66.
34. Montreal Committee of Sixteen 1918:14-17.
35. Gray 1973:123, 34, 51.
36. Drzazga 1960.
37. Fosdick 1969:375.
38. Drzazga 1960:145-46.
39. Kinsie 1953:242.
40. Williams 1973:24-25.
41. Kneeland 1913:150; Williams 1973:25.
42. Barnes and Tralins 1961:100.
43. Powell 1939:117-18.
44. Plowcowe 1951:252-53.
45. Jackson 1974:191-92.
46. Williams 1973.
47. Hartmann 1946:11.
48. Draper 1940.
49. Williams 1973:184.
50. Barrera Caraza 1974:88.

51. Miner 1916:135.
52. Drzazga 1960:147.
53. Layton 1975:196.
54. Sandford 1975:154.
55. "PLAN . . ." 1977.
56. Layton 1975:213.
57. Greenwald 1970:45.
58. Bullough 1964:113.
59. Bullough and Bullough 1978:117-19.
60. Evans 1976:119.
61. Burford 1976:52.
62. Riegel 1968:448-49.
63. American Social Hygiene Association 1921:43.
64. Sanger 1937:141-42.
65. Drummond 1953:212.
66. Pomeroy 1972:421.
67. Winter 1976:50.
68. Sanger 1937:142; Khalaf 1965:147; Gray 1973:197.
69. Rose 1974:8.
70. Evans 1976:118.
71. Flexner 1914a:405; de Leeuw 1934:160.
72. Woolston 1921:102-107.
73. Gray 1973:66.
74. Gray 1973:197.
75. Miner 1916:132.
76. Winter 1976:55.
77. Flexner 1914a:405.
78. Yondorf 1979:421.

Chapter 7

1. This chapter draws heavily on fieldwork conducted from 1973 to 1979. It is an update and a slightly different perspective of Symanski 1974.
2. Reasons and Delugach 1977.
3. Reid and Demaris 1964:92-93.
4. Figures are based on fieldwork. But also see Sweeney 1948:435; Symanski 1974; Vogliotti 1975:162.
5. For accounts of prostitution in the nineteenth century see Ashbury 1933; Drago, Vols. I and II, 1972; Barnhart 1976; Goldman 1977.
6. Bucchianeri 1973.
7. White 1970:177.
8. "Brothel Remains a Hot Spot" 1979.
9. *Wells Emergency Ordinance No. 24.*
10. American Social Hygiene Association 1945:500; Patterson, Ulph and Goodwin 1969:565; Elliott 1973:313.
11. *Reno Evening Gazette,* August 30, 1971 and October 9, 1971; *Las Vegas Review-Journal* 1973.

12. *Nevada Revised Statutes 1971:* Ch. 244.345.
13. Sweeney 1948:435; *Carson City Municipal Code,* 1973; *Douglas County Ordinances; Washoe County Ordinance No. 137.*
14. *Nevada Revised Statutes 1971:* Chs. 201.380, 201.390
15. Goldman 1972:36.
16. Bucchianeri 1973.
17. *Carson City Municipal Code,* 1973.
18. *Fallon City Ordinance;* Thran 1973.
19. *Elko County Ordinance 1971-G; Lander County Ordinance LC 6-72; Winnemucca Municipal Code,* 1973; *Ely City Ordinance; Esmeralda County Ordinance No. 124; Lincoln County Ordinance No. 1971-6; Pershing County Ordinance No. 53.*
20. *Esmeralda County Ordinance No. 124; Lyon County Ordinance No. 77.*
21. The following is based on mimeographed rules given to madams and prostitutes by sheriffs and police, and also personal discussions with these people.
22. Green 1973:50.

23. Green 1973:47.
24. Harrell 1975.
25. Winick and Kinsie 1972:197.
26. Beebe 1962.
27. Ebbels 1975.
28. Winick and Kinsie 1972:197.
29. Kinsey et al. 1948:698; Kinsey 1950; Barber 1969.
30. A long-time state sanitation engineer who had close knowledge of the state's brothels knew of no epidemic that ever originated in them; White 1970. Only one reactive blood test for syphilis came from a regulated house between 1970 and 1972; Edwards 1972. All prostitutes are required to carefully examine all clients, without exception, before any form of sexual activity. If there is any suggestion of disease they are refused service.
31. Goldman 1972.
32. *Nevada State-Journal* 1973.
33. Lindsey 1977.
34. *Lyon County Ordinance No. 77.*
35. *Reno Evening Gazette* 1972.

Chapter 8

1. Flexner 1914a:176.
2. Great Britain, *Report of the Committee on Homosexual Offenses and Prostitution* 1963.
3. Geis 1972.
4. Barth 1964:109.
5. Blackburn and Richards 1979.
6. Goldman 1972:34-35.
7. Miller 1962:51-54.
8. Barnhart 1976:86-118.
9. Ashbury 1933:168-73; Barnhart 1976:121, 196.

10. Gentry 1964:150.
11. Heizer and Almquist 1971:163; Barnhart 1976:128.
12. Barnhart 1976:130.
13. Barnhart 1976:186.
14. Heizer and Almquist 1971:164.
15. Barnhart 1976:126.
16. Barnhart 1976:134.
17. Ashbury 1933:269.
18. Light 1974:369-70.
19. Bowden 1967:275-315.
20. Shumsky and Springer

1979.
21. Shumsky and Springer 1979.
22. United States, Bureau of the Census 1960.
23. Light 1974:370-72.
24. Light 1974:377.
25. Johnson 1915.
26. Lubove 1962; Feldman 1967; Burnham 1973.
27. Johnson 1915.
28. Brown 1937.
29. Warren, Jr. 1970:110-11.

30. Johnston 1910:456.
31. Harris 1898:5.
32. Woolston 1921:104.
33. Exner 1917:209.
34. Johnson 1917:492.
35. Exner 1917:208; Hirshfeld 1937:143-46; Winick and Kinsie 1972:226-27.
36. Based on fieldwork from 1973 to 1977.
37. Elazer 1970:230.
38. Rose 1974:27-28.
39. Price 1930:31, 53-54.
40. Ashbury 1940:265.
41. Ashbury 1940.
42. Bancroft 1959.
43. Day 1972:46.
44. Anonymous 1905; 1910-11; Semper Idem 1936; Rose 1974.
45. Ashbury 1938:436; Rose 1974.
46. Rose 1974:67.
47. Semper Idem 1936:19.
48. Longstreet 1965:82.
49. Johnston 1910:459.
50. Semper Idem 1936:58.
51. Vorenberg and Vorenberg 1977:29.
52. Castle 1974:47.
53. "Back at the Ranch" 1970; Vogliotti 1975:172-73; Vorenberg and Vorenberg 1977:29.
54. Flexner 1914a:104; Taylor 1953:218; Sanger 1937:101; Burford 1976:70; Gray 1973.
55. Quennel 1950:43.
56. Quennel 1950:40.
57. Rolph 1955:127.
58. *Discreet Gentleman's Guide* . . . 1975:49-50.
59. Mankoff 1974:341-43.
60. Halle 1933:253.
61. Gibson 1979:69, 269.
62. This example is taken from Kalm 1975.
63. Henriques 1968:58-60, 130-31.
64. This example draws heavily on Johnson 1975.
65. Johnson 1975:575.
66. Murtagh and Harris 1957:203-205.
67. Barnhart 1976:183.
68. Johnson 1975:581.

Chapter 9

1. Rolph 1955:136.
2. Milner and Milner 1973:107-57.
3. Flexner 1914a:32-33.
4. Flexner 1914a:32.
5. Sheehy 1974; Lane 1975, Part IV.
6. Ianni 1975:12.
7. Winick and Kinsie 1972; Milner and Milner 1973:30.
8. Layton 1975:172.
9. Freed 1949:88; Vorenberg and Vorenberg 1977:35; Yondorf 1979:427.
10. Teresa de Gallo and Alzate 1976:2.
11. Vogliotti 1975:159.
12. Young 1967:126.
13. Yondorf 1979:427-28.
14. Yondorf 1979:427.
15. Stuckey 1977:231; Texier and Vézina 1978.
16. Margo St. James, in personal conversation; Lane 1975, Part IV; Farrell 1977.
17. Woolston 1921:48.
18. Reitman, 1936:166.
19. Margo St. James, in personal conversation; Sheehy 1974:97; Ianni 1975; Lee 1975; Women's Jail Study Group 1976.
20. Young 1967:127.
21. Ianni 1975:11.
22. Milner and Milner 1973:163.
23. Martinez and Centeno 1974:96, 114; Layton 1975:170-71.
24. Sheehy 1974:14; Lane 1975, Part IV; Palmquist and Stone 1978.
25. Sheehy 1974:14.
26. Raab 1977.
27. Layton 1975:154-57.
28. Milner and Milner 1973:265.
29. Harris and Freeman 1967:47.
30. Harris and Freeman 1967; Jackson 1974.
31. Milner and Milner 1973:278.
32. Jackson 1974:190.
33. Ianni 1975:7.
34. Beck 1969; Milner and Milner 1973.
35. Reitman 1936:47.
36. James 1973a; Palmquist and Stone 1978; Mercier 1979.
37. The following draws on Lee 1975.
38. Beck 1969:15.
39. Milner and Milner 1973:38.
40. Milner and Milner 1973:48.
41. Milner and Milner 1973:17-19; Ianni 1975:13.
42. Sion 1977:58.
43. San Francisco Committee on Crime 1971:36.
44. Silver 1974, Part I:4.
45. The following draws on James 1973a.
46. James 1973a:153.
47. Flannery 1976.
48. James 1973a:158.
49. James 1973a:159.
50. Winick and Kinsie 1972:101-10; Schimel 1973; Sheehy 1974; Yondorf 1979:427.
51. Lee 1975.
52. Jeffers and Levitan 1973.
53. Winick and Kinsie 1972:115.
54. Sagarin 1974:216-17.
55. Partridge 1961.
56. Winick and Kinsie 1972:113-14.
57. Reitman 1936:129-30.
58. Price 1930:26.
59. Jackson 1974:193.
60. *Discreet Gentleman's Guide* . . . 1975:95; Cordelier 1978:38.
61. Roebuck and McNamara 1973:236.

62. Reid and Demaris 1964:103.
63. Marlowe 1964:113-14.
64. George 1962:728.
65. Price 1930:27.
66. Henslin 1971:197-207.
67. Vaz 1955:183-85.
68. Forman 1971:103-24.
69. Great Britain, *Report of the Committee on Homosexual Offenses and Prostitution* 1963:172-73.
70. Rolph 1955:65.
71. Scarlet 1974, Part II:10.
72. Sheehy 1974:79.
73. Sheehy 1974:79.
74. Flexner 1914a:326;

Wisconsin Legislative Committee 1914:80-82; Woolston 1921:92; Sanger 1937; Barrera Caraza 1974:78; Winter 1976:86.
75. Barnhart 1976:193-94.
76. Winick and Kinsie 1972:146.
77. Gray 1973:50, 65.
78. Clark 1898:147: Haywood 1923:14.
79. Adler 1959; Barnes and Tralins 1961; Stanford 1966; Tabor 1973.
80. Vogliotti 1975:164.
81. Kaye 1974:12.
82. Scott 1954:128.

83. Rolph 1955:59.
84. Cointre 1966:81.
85. Cointre 1966:81.
86. Halle 1933:61-62.
87. Gentry 1964:248; Barnhart 1976:187, 193-94; Ashbury 1940:290; Chicago, Vice Commission of Chicago 1911:87.
88. Price 1930:8-9.
89. Draper 1940:4.
90. Wisconsin Legislative Committee 1914:82.
91. Waterman 1932:30.
92. Kneeland 1913:94.
93. Sheehy 1972; 1974:19.
94. Sheehy 1972:71.

Chapter 10

1. Barnhart 1976.
2. Sanger 1937:75, 91-96.
3. Winick and Kinsie 1972:34.
4. Drew-Bear 1975:31-32.
5. Benjamin and Masters 1964:58.
6. Anonymous 1960:12.
7. Barrera Caraza 1974:65.
8. Anonymous 1960:84.
9. Barrera Caraza 1974:64-66.
10. Cousins 1938:276.
11. Rolph 1955:77.
12. Cousins 1938:276.
13. Cross 1965:61-63.
14. Karp 1971:186-87.
15. Wells 1970:60.
16. James and Meyerding 1977b.
17. Evans 1975:43.
18. Winick and Kinsie 1972:147.
19. *Discreet Gentleman's Guide* . . . 1975:50-51.
20. Karp 1971:177; James 1973a:148.
21. Woolston 1921:153.
22. Winter 1976:42.
23. Swingler 1969:81-83; Sion 1977:55.
24. Layton 1978.
25. Henriques 1968:268.
26. Winter 1976:64-65.
27. Freed 1949:132; Rolph 1955:57-59; Winter 1976:42.
28. Prus and

Vassilakopoulos 1979.
29. Karp 1971:175-76.
30. Layton 1979:113.
31. "Do Police Look Other Way . . .?" 1974; "It's the Old Storyville Game" 1974.
32. Karp 1971:181.
33. Freed 1949:23.
34. Morrison 1967:88ff; Karp 1971:181; Winick and Kinsie 1972:149; Winter 1976:62-64.
35. Layton 1978.
36. Hall 1973:27.
37. Sheehy 1974:222.
38. Winter 1976:10.
39. "Fresno Has Distinction" 1975.
40. Morrison 1967:88.
41. Millett 1973:156-57.
42. Sheehy 1974:98.
43. Barrera Caraza 1974.
44. Sheehy 1974:22.
45. Sheehy 1974:23.
46. Millett 1973:156-57.
47. Rolph 1955:55.
48. Milner and Milner 1973:17-20.
49. Sion 1977:120.
50. Winick and Kinsie 1972:154.
51. Freed 1949:134.
52. Layton 1975:105-106.
53. Lowman 1980.
54. Drzazga 1960:7.
55. Murtagh and Harris 1957:7.

56. Partridge 1960:45.
57. Henriques 1968:61.
58. Rolph 1955:53-54.
59. Carroll 1977.
60. Millett 1973:157.
61. Wilson 1971:86-87.
62. Anonymous 1960:21.
63. Cointre 1966:144.
64. Rolph 1955:18; Atkinson and Boles 1977; Winter 1976:212.
65. Woolston 1921:109.
66. Atkinson and Boles 1977.
67. Rolph 1955:104.
68. Sheehy 1974:88.
69. Layton 1978:90, 173-76.
70. Barrera Caraza 1974:6.
71. Fabian 1954:53.
72. Flannery 1976.
73. Kent and Dingemans 1977:65.
74. Lane 1975, Part IV:12.
75. Brassaï 1976.
76. Layton 1975:100-104; Lowman 1980.
77. Layton 1975:100.
78. Sheehy 1974:89.
79. Anonymous 1960:3-4.
80. Hall 1973:15, 17.
81. Ianni 1975:13.
82. Winter 1976:60.
83. Cordelier 1978:191.
84. Gosling and Warner 1960:120; Sion 1977:16.
85. Murtagh and Harris 1957:8-10.
86. James 1972b:175.

87. Cullen 1976.
88. Fabian 1954:55.
89. Winick and Kinsie 1972:148.
90. Winter 1976:60.
91. Coleman 1973:15.
92. Karp 1971:63.
93. "Sex Gang Warfare" 1976.

Chapter 11

1. Henriques 1968:55.
2. Brindenbaugh 1968:317.
3. Davis 1974:103.
4. Knox 1857:214-15.
5. Knox 1857:233; Henriques 1968:100-101.
6. Hirshfeld 1937:143.
7. Basserman 1968:234.
8. Pfeiffer 1918; Hearing Before the Committee on Military Affairs . . . 1941.
9. National Advisory Police Committee 1943:42.
10. Kinsie 1941:333.
11. Kelly 1974.
12. Winick and Kinsie 1972.
13. Christian 1960:68.
14. Quaife 1979:146-50.
15. Drago 1972, Vol. II: 2-3.
16. Bullough 1973:204.
17. Gray 1973:28, 132-33; Bullough and Bullough 1978:329.
18. Gray 1973:28.
19. Kizer 1975; Snapp 1975.
20. Gebhard 1966a:2.
21. Borrell and Cashinella 1975:122.
22. Woolston 1921:83, 86.
23. Reid and Demaris 1964:19.
24. Drummond 1953:222-23.
25. Thornton 1956:775.
26. Lane 1975, Part IV.
27. Winter 1976:51.
28. Henriques 1968:257.
29. Jeffers and Levitan 1973:145.
30. James 1975a:354; Smothers 1976.
31. James 1972a:106.
32. Barrera Caraza 1974:241-48.
33. James 1972a:106.
34. Layton 1978:169.
35. Reid and Demaris 1964:95.
36. Woolston 1921:50.
37. Evans 1976:112; Flexner 1914a:184.
38. James 1975a:351-52.
39. Symanski 1974:371.
40. Barrera Caraza 1974; Winter 1976:57; Primov and Kieffer 1977:247. 1977:247.
41. Pearson 1972:51.
42. Gentry 1964:148.
43. Gentry 1964:148.
44. Winick and Kinsie 1972:177.
45. Barrera Caraza 1974:236-41.
46. Symanski 1974.
47. Barnhart 1976:108.
48. Sanger 1937:143.
49. Powell 1939:41.
50. Jeffers and Levitan 1973:39.
51. Layton 1978:171.
52. The following draws on James 1975a.
53. James 1975a:357.
54. James 1975a:358.
55. James 1975a:358.
56. James 1975a:358.
57. James 1975a.
58. Longstreet 1965:255-56.
59. Rose 1974:166.
60. Kneeland 1913:28.
61. Iga 1968.
62. Matsumoto 1960.
63. Shaw 1950.
64. "Paris Reconsiders . . ." 1952; Halphen 1960; Benjamin 1973:873.
65. *Time* 1960.
66. James 1975a:353.
67. Burns 1976.
68. Galloping Horse 1977:4.
69. Oman and Ensminger 1974.
70. Geis 1972:198-99; Sheehy 1974:14-15.
71. Ianni 1975:12.
72. Sheehy 1974:15.
73. Geis 1972:198-99.
74. The example is drawn from Kent and Dingemans 1977:73.
75. Kent and Dingemans 1977:73.

Chapter 12

1. Lubove 1962; Wunsch 1976.
2. American Social Hygiene Association 1921:43.
3. Mayer 1918:197-98; Broughton 1942:12.
4. Chicago 1911; Grand Rapids 1911; Hartford, Connecticut 1913; Philadelphia 1913; Syracuse 1913; Honolulu 1914; Little Rock 1913; Newwark 1914; Lancaster, Pennsylvania 1914-15; Minneapolis 1974; Wisconsin Legislative Committee 1914.
5. Kneeland 1913; Flexner 1914a.
6. Flexner 1914a:175-76.
7. Anderson 1974:220.
8. Mayer 1918:197.
9. Johnson 1935.
10. Woolston 1921:125.
11. Mayer 1918.
12. Bullough 1964:198.
13. The following paragraphs draw on Ashbury 1940:98-123.
14. Ashbury 1940:246; Wendt and Kogan 1943; Miner 1931:286.
15. Ashbury 1940:292.
16. Haller 1970; Haller 1971-72; Anderson 1974.
17. Ashbury 1940:301, 303-309.
18. The rest of this section draws on Reckless 1933.

19. Illinois Crime Survey 1929:855.
20. Reckless 1933:96.
21. Reckless 1933:147.
22. Russell 1931.
23. Reckless 1961:51.
24. Drummond 1953:206.
25. Illinois Crime Survey 1929:855-59.
26. Washburn 1934:68-69.
27. Spear 1967:24.
28. Spear 1967:24.
29. Philpott 1978:158.
30. Philpott 1978:158; Spear 1967:25.
31. Spear 1967:44.
32. Reckless 1933:26, 28.
33. Illinois Crime Survey

34. Great Britain, *Report of the Working Party . . .* 1976.
35. Great Britain, *Report of the Committee on Homosexual Offenses and Prostitution* 1963:136.
36. The description of these districts draws on Rolph 1955.
37. Rolph 1955:48.
38. Rolph 1955:49.
39. Scarlet 1974, Part III:70.
40. Scarlet 1972:21.
41. Sion 1977:73.

1929:863.

42. Greenland 1961:210.
43. Jones 1960:704; Greenland 1961:213.
44. Sion 1977:64-65.
45. Gosling and Warner 1960:11-12.
46. Scarlet 1974, Part III:70.
47. Davis 1966:213.
48. Young 1967:138.
49. Morrison 1967:182-83.
50. Jones 1960:705.
51. Flexner 1914a:306; Pearsall 1969:265.
52. Davis 1966.
53. Thomas 1972:18; Scarlet 1974, Part III.

Chapter 13

1. Skolnick 1975; Velarde 1976; Farrington, Osborn and West 1978.
2. James 1891:118-26.
3. Kneeland 1913:45.
4. Woolston 1921:144; Rotenberg 1974:34-35.
5. Cross 1965:45; *Discreet Gentleman's Guide . . .* 1975:96.
6. Kneeland 1913:10; Mayer 1919:344; *Discreet Gentleman's Guide . . .* 1975:54, 73; Sandford 1975:71-72.
7. Mankoff 1974:497-98.
8. Bryant and Palmer 1975:227.
9. Bryant and Palmer 1975:228.
10. Yondorf 1975:4.
11. Stopp, Jr. 1978.
12. Velarde 1976:252-59.
13. Chandler 1974; Garvin and Anthony 1977, Part I.
14. Rasmussen and Kuhn

1976:276; Sion 1977:116.
15. Wallach 1973:42.
16. Van Gelder 1973:98.
17. Bryant and Palmer 1975:241.
18. Bryant and Palmer 1977:136.
19. Garvin and Anthony 1977, Part I.
20. Garvin and Anthony 1977, Parts II and IV.
21. Gorner 1977.
22. Bryant and Palmer 1977:133.
23. "National Tattle" 1977:5.
24. Sheehy 1974:95.
25. Strom 1977:16.
26. Quoted in Strom 1977:20.
27. Wald 1979.
28. Flexner 1914a; Winick and Kinsie 1972; Rose 1974:69.
29. Stone 1973.
30. Davis 1966:209-20.

31. Greenland 1961:215.
32. Greenland 1961:215.
33. Williams 1973:70.
34. Ashbury 1933:282-83.
35. Ashbury 1933:282-83.
36. Beck 1969; Winick and Kinsie 1972:112; Sheehy 1974:16.
37. Freed 1949:133.
38. Sheehy 1974:91.
39. Gebhard 1966a.
40. Skipper and McCaghy 1971.
41. Boles and Garbin 1977:117-18.
42. Fulbright 1973.
43. Salutin 1973:144.
44. Shaw 1977:196.
45. Spence 1980.
46. Hong et al. 1975; Silverman 1977.
47. Hong et al. 1975:467.
48. Silverman 1977.
49. Silverman 1977.
50. Silverman 1977.

Chapter 14

1. Brownmiller 1975:392.
2. Barber 1969.
3. "Prostitutes Ignore . . ." 1971.
4. Gebhard 1969.
5. Jackman, O'Toole and Geis 1967; Exner et al. 1977.

6. Geis 1972:192.
7. Albin 1977; Arnett 1975; Brunhart, Congdon and Tepley 1976; Bullough and Bullough 1978; de Crow 1974; George 1974; Gitchoff et al. 1973;

Halleck 1974; Holmes 1972; "Hooker Law . . ." 1978; James 1976b; Mead 1971; Megino 1976; Millet 1973; Orlando Task Force 1977; "Power to Prostitute . . ." 1977;

Runkel 1976; Schultz
1977; Silver 1974, Part I
and II; "Women Blast
. . ." 1979; Women
Endorsing
Decriminalization 1977.

8. Jennings 1976.
9. Milman 1980.
10. Millett 1973;
Brownmiller 1975.
11. Minneapolis 1974:33-34.
12. Schultz 1977.
13. Kinsey et al. 1948:597.
14. Halleck 1974.
15. Halleck 1974:60.
16. Parts of the argument
that follow are based on
Hilton 1975.
17. Hilton 1975.
18. Yondorf 1979.

19. "A Prostitute Speaks"
1967; Coleman 1973:3;
Koper 1976:6; Winter
1976:16.
20. Davis 1937.
21. "Legalize
Prostitution?:" 1974.
22. Megino 1977.
23. Lindsey 1976; "Trouble
Along 'Combat Zone' "
1976; Milman 1980.
24. Vorenberg and
Vorenberg 1977:34.
25. Strom 1977.
26. Lane 1975, Part III;
"Send Them to
Alcatraz" 1975;
Minneapolis 1974.
27. "Hookers Battle Plan
. . ." 1978.

28. Ayres 1975; " 'Red-
Light' District . . ."
1975; "Trouble Along
'Combat Zone' " 1976.
29. Morrill 1977; Ward
1977.
30. Ward 1977.
31. Milman 1980.
32. Sandford 1975:159.
33. "An Ideal" 1977.
34. "Barristers Urge . . ."
1974; James 1976b.
35. Lipton 1977; "PLAN
. . ." 1977.
36. Margo St. James, in
personal conversation.
37. Yondorf 1979:432.
38. Margo St. James, in
personal conversation.

Source Notes for the Appendix

1. McIllwraith 1948; Krause 1956.
2. Bancroft-Hunt 1979:18.
3. For example, Kurland 1979.
4. Trivers 1972; Wilson 1975.
5. Orians 1969.
6. Dawkins and Carlisle 1976.
7. Dawkins and Krebs 1978.
8. Symons 1979.
9. Bertram 1976.
10. Hrdy 1977.
11. Parker 1970.
12. For example, the Trobrianders: Malinowski 1929.
13. Bennett 1899:70.
14. Hurault 1961:158.
15. Titiev 1972:164.
16. Turnbull 1965.
17. Drucker 1951:304.
18. Titiev 1972; Hulstaert 1928.
19. Griffis 1882; Moose 1911.
20. Kramer 1932.
21. Pelleschi 1896.
22. Murdock 1965; Irons 1979.
23. Smith 1965.
24. Preuss 1926; Park 1946; Paelme 1940; Lambrecht 1932-41.
25. Tessmann 1913; Trézenem 1936; Merker 1910.
26. Gluckman 1959.
27. Masters 1953.
28. Richards 1939.
29. Roscoe 1911.
30. Roscoe 1911.
31. Slaski 1951; East 1939; Herskovits and Herskovits 1934; Gutierrez de Pineda 1950; Mukherjea 1962; Schulze 1891.
32. Chewings 1936.
33. Kahn 1931.
34. Cohen 1960.
35. Jennes 1922:159.
36. Brettes 1903.
37. Sen 1962.
38. Griffis 1882.
39. Kramer and Nevermann 1938; Dorsey and Murie 1914.
40. Lodge 1942:85.
41. Sanders 1962.
42. Wolf 1965.
43. Howell 1953.
44. For example, Goldstein 1976.
45. Dorsey and Murie 1914.
46. Leakey 1953.
47. Djamour 1959.
48. Messing 1957; Richards 1939.
49. Messing 1957.
50. Ploss et al. 1935.
51. Maiskii 1921.
52. Coxe 1804; Sarychev 1806.
53. Gutierrez de Pineda 1950:252.
54. Garcilasco de la Vega 1869-71.
55. Cook 1909.
56. Swanton 1924-25.
57. Balandier 1955; Lingenfelten 1971.
58. Tessmann 1913.
59. Mead 1930; Mead 1937.
60. Brownmiller 1976.
61. Erdland 1914; Malinowski 1929.
62. Evans-Pritchard 1929; Lagae 1926; Gluckman 1959.
63. For example, Irons 1979.
64. Graebner 1909.
65. Pitts et al. 1955; Glacken 1953.
66. Tessmann 1913; Malinowski 1929; Ploss et al. 1935.
67. Smith and Dale 1920.
68. Gluckman 1972.
69. Borgoraz-Tan 1904-1909.
70. Stanford University 1956c; Wolf 1965.
71. Dickson 1951; Beals 1946.
72. Srinivas 1952; Cornell University 1956.
73. Wolf 1965.
74. Graebner 1909; Davenport 1962.
75. Senfft 1907.
76. Textor 1967.
77. Eckhardt 1971; Schlegel 1972; Textor 1967.
78. Schlegel 1972.
79. Alexander 1974; Hartung 1976; Kurland 1979.
80. Eckhardt 1971.
81. Alexander 1974.

Bibliography
for the Main Text

Adam, Corinna, "A Special House in Hamburg," *New Statesman*, April 13, 1973, pp. 521-22.

Addams, Jane, *A New Conscience and An Ancient Evil* (New York: Mac-Millan, 1912).

Adler, Freda, *Sisters in Crime: The Rise of the New Female Criminal* (New York: McGraw-Hill, 1975).

Adler, Polly, *A House is Not a Home* (New York: Popular Library, 1959).

Albin, Leslie, "Florida NOW Wants Changes in Prostitution Law," *Sentinel Star* (Orlando, Florida), October 2, 1977.

American Social Hygiene Association, *Social Hygiene Legislation Manual, 1921* (New York: American Social Hygiene Association, 1921).

American Social Hygiene Association, "The War Against Prostitution Must Go On," *Journal of Social Hygiene*, 31 (1945), pp. 500-507.

Amir, Menachem, *Patterns in Forcible Rape* (Chicago: University of Chicago Press, 1971).

Anderson, Eric, "Prostitution and Social Justice: Chicago 1910-1915," *Social Service Review*, 48 (June 1974), pp. 203-28.

"An Ideal," *Coyote Howls*, 4 (Autumn 1977), p. 16.

Anonymous, *The Denver Red Book: A Reliable Directory of the Pleasure Resorts of Denver* (Denver: 1892).

Anonymous, *Blue Book*, (New Orleans: 1905).

Anonymous, *Blue Book* (New Orleans: 1910-11).

Anonymous, *Streetwalker* (New York: Viking Press, 1960).

Anonymous, "Prostitution: 'Freedom in an Oppressive World'," *The Boston Phoenix*, February 26, 1974.

Arnett, Dixon, Assemblyman. Twentieth District, California Legislature, letter to Margo St. James, July 18, 1975.

Ashbury, Herbert, *The Barbary Coast: An Informal History of the San Francisco Underworld* (Garden City, New York: Garden City, 1933).

Ashbury, Herbert, *The French Quarter: An Informal History of the New Orleans Underworld* (Garden City, New York: Garden City, 1938).

Ashbury, Herbert, *Gem of the Prairie: An Informal History of the Chicago Underworld* (New York: Alfred A. Knopf, 1940).

Association des Chefs de Police et Pompiers de la Province de Québec, *Le Crime Organisé: Aspect Nord Américain* (Montreal: 1968).

Atkinson, Maxine, and Jacqueline Boles, "Prostitution as an Ecology of Confidence Games: The Scripted Behavior of Prostitutes and Vice Officers," in Clifton D. Bryant, ed., *Sexual Deviancy in Social Context* (New York: New Viewpoints, 1977), pp. 219-31.

Ayres, Gene, "Planners Say No to Porno Controls," *The Oakland Tribune*, October 23, 1975.

Babington, Anthony, *A House in Bow Street: Crime and the Magistracy London 1740-1881* (London: Macdonald, 1969).

"Back at the Ranch," *Newsweek*, March 9, 1970, pp. 78-80.

Baker, Alan R. H., "France from Waterloo to World War II, No. I: A Nation of Peasants," *Geographical Magazine*, 48 (October 1975), pp. 24-30.

Bancroft, Frederic, *Slave Trading in the Old South* (New York: Ungar, 1959).

Barber, R. N., "Prostitution and the Increasing Number of Convictions for Rape in Queensland," *Australian and New Zealand Journal of Criminology*, 2 (1969), pp. 169-74.

Barnes, Ruth (Madam Sherry), with S. Robert Tralins, *Pleasure Was My Business* (New York: Lyle Stuart, 1961).

Barnett, Harold C., "The Political Economy of Rape and Prostitution," *The Review of Radical Political Economics*, 8 (Spring 1976), pp. 59-68.

Barnhart, Jacqueline Baker, "Prostitution in San Francisco from the Gold Rush to 1900," unpublished Ph.D., University of California, Santa Cruz, 1976.

Barrera Caraza, Estanislao, *Prostitucion en Jalapa: Estudio de Algunos Socioeconomicos*, Tesis in Antropologia, Universidad Veracruzana, Jalapa, Veracruz, Mexico, 1974.

"Barristers Urge Non-Victim Crime Citation Program Here," *The Recorder*, October 23, 1974.

Barth, Gunther, *Bitter Strength: A History of the Chinese in the United States, 1850-1870* (Cambridge: Harvard University Press, 1964).

Basserman, Lujo, trans. by James Cleugh, *The Oldest Profession: A History of Prostitution* (New York: Stein and Day, 1968).

Bateman, A. J., "Intrasexual Selection in Drosophila," *Heredity*, 2 (1948), pp. 349-68.

Bauer, Bernard, "All Johns Are the Same As Long As They Have the Cash," *San Jose Mercury News*, November 11, 1979.

(de) Beauvoir, Simone, *The Second Sex* (New York: Vintage, 1974).

Beck, Robert (Iceberg Slim), *Pimp: The Story of My Life* (Los Angeles: Holloway House, 1969).

Becker, Gary S., "Crime and Punishment: An Economic Approach," *Journal of Political Economy*, 76 (March/April 1968), pp. 169-217.

Beebe, Lucius M., "Sincere Sinning of the One Sound State," *Saturday Review*, October 20, 1962, pp. 48-49, 63.

Bell, Ernest A., ed., *War on the White Slave Trade* (Chicago: Charles C. Thompson, 1909).

Bellamy, John, *Crime and Public Order in England in the Later Middle Ages* (London: Routledge & Kegan Paul, 1973).

Benjamin, Harry, "Prostitution," in Albert Ellis and Albert Abarbanel, eds., *The Encyclopedia of Sexual Behavior* (New York: Jason Aronson, 1973), pp. 869-82.

Benjamin, Harry, and Albert Ellis, "An Objective Examination of Prostitution," *International Journal of Sexology*, 8 (1954), pp. 101-05.

Benjamin, Harry, and R. E. L. Masters, *Prostitution and Morality: A Definitive Report on the Prostitute in Contemporary Society and an Analysis of the Causes and Effects of the Suppression of Prostitution* (New York: Julian Press, 1964).

Binderman, Murray B., Dennis Wepman and Ronald B. Newman, "A Portrait of 'The Life'," *Urban Life*, 4 (July 1975), pp. 213-25.

Black, D. J., and A. J. Reiss, Jr., "Patterns of Behavior in Police and Citizen Transactions," in *Studies in Crime and Law Enforcement in Metropolitan Areas, Vol. II, Sec. 1, President's Commission on Law Enforcement and the Administration of Justice* (Washington, D.C.: Government Printing Office, 1967).

Blackburn, George M., and Sherman L. Richards, "The Prostitutes and Gamblers of Virginia City, Nevada: 1870," *Pacific Historical Review*, 48 (May 1979), pp. 239-58.

Blanch, Lesley, *The Game of Hearts: Harriette Wilson's Memoirs* (New York: Simon and Schuster, 1955).

Bloch, Iwan, *120 Days of Sodom* (New York: Falstaff Press, 1934).

Boles, Jacqueline, and Albeno P. Garbin, "The Strip Club and Stripper—Customer Patterns of Interaction," in Clifton D. Bryant, ed., *Sexual Deviancy in Social Context* (New York: New Viewpoints, 1977), pp. 111-23.

Boles, Jacqueline, and Charlotte Tatro, "Legal and Extra-Legal Methods of Controlling Female Prostitution: A Cross-Cultural Comparison," *International Journal of Comparative and Applied Criminal Justice*, 2 (Spring 1978), pp. 71-85.

Bondeson, Ulla, "Argot Knowledge as an Indicator of Criminal Socialization," in Nils Christie, ed., *Scandinavian Studies in Criminology*, 2 (Oslo: Universitets Forlaget, 1968), pp. 73-107.

Borelli, Siegfried, and Willy Starck, *Die Prostitution als psychologisches Problem* (Berlin: Springer, 1957).

Borrell, Clive, and Brian Cashinella, *Crime in Britain Today* (London: Routledge & Kegan Paul, 1975).

Bowden, Martyn John, "The Dynamics of City Growth: An Historical Geography of the San Francisco Central District, 1850-1931," unpublished Ph.D., University of California, Berkeley, 1967.

Bradley, Donald S., Jacqueline Boles and Christopher Jones, "From Mistress to Hooker: 40 Years of Cartoon Humor in Men's Magazines," unpublished ms., 1979.

Brassaï, Gyula Halász, trans. by Richard Miller, *The Secret Paris of the 30s* (New York: Pantheon, 1976).

Bridenbaugh, Carol, *Cities in Revolt* (New York: Alfred A. Knopf, 1968).

Broderick, Alan H., *Little China: The Annamese Lands* (London: Oxford University Press, 1942).

Brokhin, Yuri, *Hustling on Gorky Street* (New York: Dial Press, 1975).

"Brothel Remains a Hot Spot: Neighbors Help Rebuild After Fire Strikes," *Daily Illini* (University of Illinois at Urbana—Champaign), December 13, 1979.

Broughton, Philip S., *Prostitution and the War*, Public Affairs Pamphlet No. 65 (New York: Public Affairs Committee, 1942).

Brown, Edmund Gerald, ed., *Prostitution* (Scrapbook on prostitution in San Francisco prepared when editor was District Attorney of San Francisco County, c. 1937).

Brownmiller, Susan, *Against Our Will: Men, Women and Rape* (New York: Bantam Books, 1976).

Brunhart, Kay England, Bob Congdon and Tom Teply, "Minority Report of Anchorage Committee to Study Prostitution," unpublished ms., May 17, 1976.

Bryan, James H., "Apprenticeships in Prostitution," in John H. Gagnon and William Simon, eds. *Sexual Deviance* (New York: Harper & Row, 1967), pp. 146-64.

Bryant, Clifton D., and C. Eddie Palmer, "Massage Parlors and 'Hand Whores': Some Sociological Observations," *The Journal of Sex Research*, 11 (August 1975). pp. 227-41.

Bryant, Clifton D., and C. Eddie Palmer, "Tense Muscles and the Tender Touch: Massage Parlors, 'Hand Whores,' and the Subversion of Service," in Clifton D. Bryant, ed., *Sexual Deviancy in Social Context* (New York: New Viewpoints, 1977), pp. 131-45.

Bucchianeri, Virgil A., District Attorney, Storey County, Nevada, letter to author, 1973.

Bullough, Vern L., *The History of Prostitution* (New Hyde Park, New York: University Books, 1964).

Bullough, Vern L., "Streetwalking—Theory and Practice: A Social Science Study of a Masked Profession," *Saturday Review* (September 4, 1965), pp. 52-54.

Bullough, Vern L., "The American Brothel," *Medical Aspects of Human Sexuality*, 7 (April 1973), pp. 198-211.

Bullough, Vern L., *Sexual Variance in Society and History* (New York: John Wiley, 1976).

Bullough, Vern L., and Bonnie Bullough, *Prostitution: An Illustrated Social History* (New York: Crown Publishers, 1978).

Burford, E. J., *Bawds and Lodgings: A History of the London Bankside Brothels c. 100-1675* (London: Peter Owen, 1976).

Burgess, Ernest, and Paul Wallin, *Engagement and Marriage* (Chicago: J. B. Lippincott, 1953).

Burley, Nancy, "Mate Choice and Sexual Selection in the Pigeon, *Columba livia*," unpublished Ph.D., University of Texas, Austin, 1977.

Burnham, John C., "The Progressive Era Revolution in American Attitudes Toward Sex," *Journal of American History*, 59 (1973), pp. 885-908.

Burns, Jerry, "Freitas to Go Easy on Vice Cases," *San Francisco Chronicle,* January 6, 1976.

Butler, Josephine E., *Personal Reminiscences of a Great Crusade* (London: Horace & Sons, 1896).

Butterfield, Fox, "Love and Sex in China," *The New York Times Magazine*, January 13, 1980, pp. 15-17, 43-49.

"By Public Demand," *Time*, November 25, 1957.

California Bureau of Criminal Statistics (Sacramento: 1976).

Canada, *Report of the Royal Commission, The Status of Women in Canada* (Ottawa: Information Canada, 1970).

Canada, *Report on Sexual Offences* (Ottawa: Ministry of Supply and Services Canada, 1978).

Carmichael, Benjamin G., "Youth Crime in Urban Communities: A Descriptive Analysis of Street Hustlers and their Crimes," *Crime and Delinquency*, 21 (January 1975), pp. 139-48.

Carroll, Rick, "Life at an X-Rated Truck Stop," *San Francisco Chronicle*, May 16, 1977.

Carson City Municipal Code, 1973.

Castle, Robert M., "Ash Meadows: A Fly-In Brothel," in Jerry Jacobs, ed., *Deviance: Field Studies and Self-Disclosures* (Palo Alto, California: National Press, 1974), pp. 41-51.

Caugherty, Madeline, "The Principal of Harm, Prostitution," *Denver Law Review*, 51 (1974), pp. 235-62.

Chambers, C. D., R. K. Hinesley and M. Moldestad, "Narcotic Addiction in Females: A Race Comparison," *The International Journal of the Addictions*, 5 (1970), pp. 224-79.

Chambliss, William J., "A Sociological Analysis of the Law of Vagrancy," in R. Serge Denisoff and Charles H. McCaghy, eds., *Deviance, Conflict, and Criminality* (Chicago: Rand McNally, 1973), pp. 256-71.

Chandler, Beverly, "Prostitution Thrives in Berkeley," *Daily Californian*, December 2, 1974.

Chesser, Eustace, "Sex in Great Britain," in Albert Ellis and Albert Abarbanel, eds., *The Encyclopedia of Sexual Behavior* (New York: Jason Aronson, 1973), pp. 457-65.

Chicago, Vice Commission of Chicago, *The Social Evil in Chicago* (Chicago: The Vice Commission of Chicago, 1911).

"Child Prostitution Gravest Social Cancer in Brazil," *Austin American-Statesman*, November 28, 1974.

Choisy, Maryse, trans. by Lawrence G. Blochman, *A Month Among the Girls* (New York: Pyramid, 1960).

Christian, Chester C. "Some Sociological Implications of Government Venereal Disease Control," unpublished M.A., University of Texas, 1960.

Clark, C. S., *Of Toronto the Good* (Montreal: Toronto Publishing, 1898).

(von) Cleef, Monique, with William Waterman, *The House of Pain: The Strange World of Monique von Cleef, The Queen of Humiliation* (New York: Bantam Books, 1975).

Clinard, Marshall B., *Sociology of Deviant Behavior* (New York: Holt, Rinehart and Winston, 1963).

Clinard, Marshall B., and Daniel J. Abbott, *Crime in Developing Countries: A Comparative Perspective* (New York: John Wiley, 1973).

Cobb, Richard, *The Police and the People: French Popular Protest 1789-1820* (Oxford: 1970).

Cointre, Marie-Therese, *I, Marie-Therese: Memoirs of a Prostitute* (New York: Brussel and Brussel, 1966).

Coleman, Kate, "Carnal Knowledge: A Portrait of Four Hookers," in George Paul Csicsery, ed., *The Sex Industry* (New York: New American Library, 1973), pp. 1-21.

Commission de Police du Québec, *Le Crime Organisé et le Monde des Affaires* (Montreal: Editeur Officiel du Québec, 1977).

Connor, W., *Deviance in Soviet Society: Crime, Delinquency, and Alcoholism* (New York: Columbia University Press, 1969).

Cordelier, Jeanne, trans. by Harry Mathews, *The Life: Memoirs of a French Hooker* (New York: Viking Press, 1978).

Cousins, Sheila (pseudo.), *To Beg I Am Ashamed* (New York: Vanguard Press, 1938).

Cross, Harold H. U., *The Lust Market* (New York: Citadel Press, 1965).

(de) Crow, Karen, *Sexist Justice—How Legal Sexism Affects You* (New York: Random House, 1974).

Cullen, John F., "A Combat Zone Conviction," *Boston Sunday Globe*, November 28, 1976.

Cullen, Tom A., *The Prostitute's Padre: The Story of the Notorious Rector of Stiffkey* (London: Bodley Head, 1975).

David, Edward M., "Victimless Crimes—The Case for Continued Enforcement," *Journal of Police Science and Administration* 1 (March 1973), pp. 11-20.

David, Hunter, ed., *The New London Spy: A Discreet Guide to the City's Pleasures* (New York: David White, 1966).

Davis, Burke, *Our Incredible Civil War* (New York: Ballantine, 1974).

Davis, Katherine B., *Factors in the Sex Life of 2200 Women* (New York: Harper and Brothers, 1929).

Davis, Kingsley, "The Sociology of Prostitution," *American Sociological Review*, 2 (October 1937), pp. 744-55.

Davis, Kingsley, "Prostitution," in R. K. Merton and R. A. Nisbet, eds., *Contemporary Social Problems* (New York: Harcourt, Brace and World, 1961), pp. 262-90.

Davis, Nanette J., "The Prostitute: Developing a Deviant Identity," in James M. Henslin, ed., *Studies in the Sociology of Sex* (New York: Appleton-Century-Crofts, 1971), pp. 297-322.

Dawkins, Richard, *The Selfish Gene* (New York: Oxford University Press, 1976).

Day, Beth, *Sexual Life Between Blacks and Whites: The Roots of Racism* (New York: World Publishing, 1972).

"D. C. Prostitution Statute Not Limited to Solicitation," *Sexual Law Reporter*, 4 (January-March, 1978), p. 6.

Després, Armand, *La Prostitution en France* (Paris: Librairie J. B. Bailliere et Fils, 1883).

Dirasse, Laketch, "The Socioeconomic Position of Women in Addis Ababa: The Case of Prostitution," unpublished Ph.D., Boston University, 1978.

Directory to the Seraglios in New York, Philadelphia, Boston, and All Principal Cities in the Union, edited and compiled by a free lover (New York: 1859).

The Discreet Gentleman's Guide to the Pleasures of Europe (New York: Bantam Books, 1975).

" 'Discrimination' Defense Fails in Prostitution Cases," *Sexual Law Reporter*, 2 (March-April 1976), pp. 15, 23.

"Disneyland East," *Time*, May 6, 1966, pp. 29-30.

Dock, Lavinia L., *Hygiene and Morality* (New York: G. P. Putnam's Sons, 1910).

Doherty, Nancy, "The Prostitution Question," *Anchorage Daily News*, April 19, 1976.

"Do Police Look Other Way, Allow Prostitutes to Operate?," *The Times-Picayune*, (New Orleans) June 10, 1974.

Douglas County Ordinances.

Drago, Harry Sinclair, *Notorious Ladies of the Frontier*, Vols. I and II (New York: Ballantine, 1972).

Drake, St. Clair, and Horace R. Cayton, *Black Metropolis: A Study of Negro Life in a Northern City*, Vol. II (New York: Harcourt, Brace & World, 1962).

Draper, George, *San Francisco—Prostitution* (San Francisco: typescript, 1940).

Drew-Bear, Annette, "Cosmetics and Attitudes Toward Women in the Seventeenth Century," *Journal of Popular Culture*, 9 (Summer 1975), pp. 31-37.

Drummond, Isabel, *The Sex Paradox* (New York: G. P. Putnam's Sons, 1953).

Drzazga, John, *Sex Crimes and Their Legal Aspects* (Springfield, Illinois: Charles C. Thomas, 1960).

Ebbels, Gary, "Prostitution Law Unconstitutional," *Las Vegas Review-Journal*, November 25, 1975.

Edwards, Allen, and R. E. L. Masters, *The Cradle of Erotica* (New York: Julian Press, 1963).

Edwards, William M., Chief, Community Health Services, Division of Health, Department of Health, Welfare, and Rehabilitation, State of Nevada, letter to Lander County Commissioner, September 1972.

Egner, Robert E., ed., *Bertrand Russell's Best* (New York: New American Library, 1958).

Egyptian Government, *Report of the Commission of Enquiry into the Problem of Licensed Prostitution in Egypt* (Cairo: Government Press, 1935).

Ehrlich, Isaac, "Participation in Illegitimate Activities: A Theoretical and Empirical Investigation," *Journal of Political Economy*, 81 (May/June, 1973), pp. 521-65.

Elazar, Daniel J., *Cities of the Prairie* (New York: Basic Books, 1970).

"Eleven Oakland Motels Pledge to Keep Prostitutes Out," *San Francisco Examiner*, July 15, 1976.

Elko County Ordinance 1971-G.

Ellington, George (pseudonym), *The Women of New York or the Under-World of the Great City* (New York: Arno Press, 1972).

Elliott, Russell R., *History of Nevada* (Lincoln: University of Nebraska Press, 1973).

Ellis, Albert, "Introduction," in Albert Mol, *Memoirs of an Amsterdam Streetwalker: Conversations with Greta* (New York: Universal, 1964), pp. 7-23.

Ely County Ordinance.

Engels, Friedrich, *The Origin of the Family, Private Property and the State*, 4th ed. (New York: International, 1942).

Erickson, Bill, *Nevada Playmates: A Guide to the Cathouses*, 4th ed. (San Francisco: Bangkok, 1973).

Erikson, Kai, "Notes on the Sociology of Deviance," *Social Problems*, 9 (Spring 1962), pp. 307-14.

Erwin, Carol, and Floyd Miller, *The Orderly Disorderly House* (Garden City, New York: Doubleday, 1960).

Esmeralda County Ordinance No. 124.

Esselstyn, T. C., "Prostitution in the United States," *Annals of American Academy of Political and Social Science*, 376 (1968), pp. 123-35.

Evans, Ellen, *Teenage Street Girl* (New York: Belmont Tower, 1975).

Evans, R. J., "Prostitution, State and Society in Imperial Germany," *Past & Present*, 70 (February 1976), pp. 106-29).

Everett, Ray H., "The Failure of Segregation as a Protector of Innocent Womanhood," *Social Hygiene*, 5 (October 1919), pp. 521-31.

Exner, John E., et al., "Some Psychological Characteristics of Prostitutes," *Journal of Personality Assessment*, 41 (1977), pp. 474-85.

Exner, M. J., "Prostitution in Its Relation to the Army on the Mexican Border," *Social Hygiene*, 3 (January 1917), pp. 205-20.

Fabian, Robert, *London After Dark* (London: Naldrett Press, 1954).

Fallon City Ordinance.

Farrell, Barry, "Part-time Pimping," *Chic*, 1 (March 1977), pp. 27-28, 38, 93.

Farrington, D. P., S. G. Osborn and D. J. West, "The Persistence of Labeling Effects," *British Journal of Criminology*, 18 (July 1978), pp. 277-84.

Federal Bureau of Investigation, *Ten Years of Uniform Crime Reports, 1930-1939* (Washington, D.C.: Department of Justice, 1939).

Federal Bureau of Investigation, *Uniform Crime Reports: Crime in the United States* (Washington, D.C.: U.S. Government Printing Office, 1965-78).

Feldman, Egal, "Prostitution, the Alien Woman and the Progressive Imagination, 1910-1915," *American Quarterly*, 19 (Summer 1967), pp. 192-206.

Fields, Ann, "Residents Want Prostitutes Off West MacArthur," *Oakland Post*, May 12, 1976.

Fifth International Congress, *Suppression of the White Slave Traffic* (London: National Vigilance Association, 1913).

Flannery, Michael, "90% of Hooker Cases Dropped," *Chicago Sun-Times*, August 18, 1976.

Flexner, Abraham, *Prostitution in Europe* (New York: Century, 1914a).

Flexner, Abraham, "The Regulation of Prostitution in Europe," *Social Hygiene*, 1 (December 1914b), pp. 15-28.

Forbis, William H., *The Cowboys* (New York: Time-Life, 1973).

Forman, Robert E., *Black Ghettos, White Ghettos, and Slums* (Englewood Cliffs: Prentice-Hall, 1971).

Fosdick, Raymond B., *European Police Systems* (Montclair, New Jersey: Patterson Smith, 1969).

"Francia Inquieta Ante Una Posible Legalidad de la Prostitution," *La Nacion*, December 21, 1978.

Freed, Louis Franklin, *The Problem of European Prostitution in Johannesburg* (Johannesburg: Juta, 1949).

"Fresno Has Distinction," *Oakland Tribune*, July 14, 1975.

Fulbright, Caterine, "Topless for the Revolution/New York," in George Paul Csicsery, ed., *The Sex Industry* (New York: New American Library, 1973), pp. 105-15.

Gagnon, John H., "Prostitution," in David L. Sills, ed., *International Encyclopedia of the Social Sciences, Vol. 12* (New York: Macmillan & The Free Press, 1968), pp. 592-98.

Gagnon, John H., and William Simon, "Introduction: Deviant Behavior and Sexual Deviance," in John H. Gagnon and William Simon, eds., *Sexual Deviance* (New York: Harper & Row, 1967), pp. 1-12.

Galloping Horse (pseudo.), "Local Gossip," *Coyote Howls*, 4 (Winter 1977), p. 4.

Gallup, George H., ed., *The Gallup International Public Opinion Polls, Great Britain 1937-1975*, Vols. I & II (New York: Random House, 1976).

G.A.R. Sporting Guide (Louisville: Wentworth, 1895?).

Garvin, Glenn, and Linda Anthony, "Massage Parlors: Behind the Doors, Part I," *Austin American-Statesman*, February 12, 1977.

Garvin, Glenn, and Linda Anthony, "It's Fast, Easy Money, Part II," *Austin American-Statesman*, February 14, 1977.

Garvin, Glenn, and Linda Anthony, "Bizarre Customers Familiar, Part V," *Austin American-Statesman*, February 17, 1977.

Gebhard, Paul H., "Amsterdam Prostitution," unpublished ms. (on file, Indiana University Library for Sex Research, 1966a).

Gebhard, Paul H., "Hamburg Prostitution," unpublished ms. (on file, Indiana University Library for Sex Research, 1966b).

Gebhard, Paul H., "Misconceptions About Female Prostitutes," *Medical Aspects of Human Sexuality*, 3 (March 1969), pp. 24, 28-30.

Gebhard, Paul H., "Fetishism and Sadomasochism," in Martin S. Weinberg, ed., *Sex Research: Studies from the Kinsey Institute* (New York: Oxford University Press, 1976), pp. 156-66.

Geiger, H. Kent, *The Family in Soviet Russia* (Cambridge: Harvard University Press, 1968).

Geis, Gilbert, *Not the Law's Business?: An Examination of Homosexuality, Abortion, Prostitution, Narcotics, and Gambling in the United States* (Rockville, Maryland: National Institute of Mental Health, Publication No. 72-9132, 1972).

Gemme, Robert, "Aspets Economiques de la Prostitution a Montréal," unpublished ms., 1971.

Gentry, Curt, *The Madams of San Francisco: An Irreverent History of the City by the Golden Gate* (Garden City, New York: Doubleday, 1964).

George, B. J., "Legal, Medical and Psychiatric Considerations in Controlling Prostitution," *Michigan Law Review*, 60 (April 1962), pp. 717-60.

George, B. J., "Should Prostitution Be Legalized?—Viewpoints," *Medical Aspects of Human Sexuality*, 8 (April 1974), pp. 60, 62.

Gibson, Ian, *The English Vice: Beating, Sex and Shame in Victorian England and After* (London: Gerald Duckworth, 1978).

Gibson, Mary Sharon, "Urban Prostitution in Italy, 1860-1915: An Experiment in Social Control," unpublished Ph.D., Indiana University, 1979.

Gitchoff, G. Thomas, Joseph Ellenbogen and Elsie Ellenbogen, "Victimless Crimes: The Case Against Continued Enforcement," *Journal of Police Science and Administration*, 1 (1973), pp. 401-408.

Glover, Edward, *The Psycho-pathology of Prostitution* (London: Institute for the Scientific Treatment of Delinquency, 1945).

Goldman, Emma, *The Traffic in Women and Other Essays on Feminism* (New York: Times Change Press, 1970).

Goldman, Marion, "Prostitution and Virtue in Nevada," *Society*, 10 (November-December 1972), pp. 32-38.

Goldman, Marion, "Gold Diggers and Silver Miners: Prostitution and the Fabric of Social Life on the Comstock Lode," unpublished Ph.D., University of Chicago, 1977.

Goldstein, Paul J. "The Relationship Between Prostitution and Substance Use," unpublished Ph.D., Case Western Reserve University, 1978.

Goodman, Mike, and Jerry Cohen, "Hollywood—Rated X: A Sleazy Decline Into Vice," *San Francisco Chronicle*, June 6, 1977.

Gorner, Peter, "Prostitutes and Housewives Unite, Forming a Surprising Sisterhood," *Chicago Tribune*, April 18, 1977.

Gosling, John, and Douglas Warner, *The Shame of a City: An Inquiry into the Vice of London* (London: W. H. Allen, 1960).

Gould, George, "Does Your State Need New Social Hygiene Laws?" *Journal of Social Hygiene*, 28 (1942), pp. 536-47.

Grand Rapids, Michigan, *Report of the Investigations of the Vice Committee of Forty-One* (Grand Rapids: 1911).

Gray, James H., *Red Lights on the Prairies* (New York: New American Library, 1973).

Great Britain, Report of the Committee on Homosexual Offenses and Prostitution, *The Wolfenden Report* (London: Stein and Day, 1963).

Great Britain, *Report of the Working Party on Vagrancy and Street Offenses* (London: Her Majesty's Stationery Office, 1976).

Green, Jerry, *Photo Digest of Nevada Cat Houses* (Utopia, 1974).

Green, Robin, "Joe Conforte, Crusading Pimp: A Concerned Citizen's Fight to Keep Prostitutes Off the Streets of Nevada," in George Paul Csicsery, ed., *The Sex Industry* (New York: New American Library, 1973), pp. 38-53.

Greenland, Cyril, "Patterns of Prostitution Following the Wolfenden Report," *Criminal Law Quarterly*, 4 (August 1961), pp. 202-18.

Greenwald, Harold, *The Elegant Prostitute* (New York: Ballantine, 1970).

Greenwald, Harold, and Ruth Greenwald, eds., *The Sex-Life Letters* (New York: Bantam Books, 1973).

Grunt, J. A., and W. C. Young, "Psychological Modification of Fatigue Following Orgasm (Ejaculation) in the Male Guinea Pig," *Journal of Comparative and Physiological Psychology*, 45 (1952), pp. 508-10.

Gunther, John, *Inside Russia Today* (New York: Harper and Brothers, 1957).

Guyot, Yves, *La Prostitution* (Paris: G. Charpentier, 1883).

Haft, Marilyn G., "Hustling For Rights," *Civil Liberties Review*, 1 (Winter/Spring 1974), pp. 8-26.

Haft, Marilyn G., "Legal Arguments: Prostitution Laws and the Constitution," in Jennifer James et al., *The Politics of Prostitution* (Seattle: Social Research Associates, 1975), pp. 23-39.

Hall, Susan, *Ladies of the Night* (New York: Trident Press, 1973).

Halle, Fannina W., *Woman in Soviet Russia* (London: Routledge, 1933).

Halleck, Charles W., "Should Prostitution Be Legalized?—Viewpoints," *Medical Aspects of Human Sexuality*, 8 (April 1974), pp. 54, 60.

Haller, Mark H., "Urban Crime and Criminal Justice: The Chicago Case," *Journal of American History*, 57 (December 1970), pp. 619-35.

Haller, Mark H., "Organized Crime in Urban Society: Chicago in the Twentieth Century," *Journal of Social History*, 5 (Winter 1971-72), pp. 210-34.

Halphen, Andre, "Le Gouvernement Declare la Guerre a la Prostitution: Le grand coup de balai qui va depeupler les trottoirs de Paris," *Paris-presse-lintransigeant*, November 18, 1960.

"Hard-currency Girls: Hotel Prostitutes in Warsaw," *Time*, May 7, 1973.

Harrell, Beverly, *An Orderly House* (New York: Dell, 1975).

Harris, Eugene, *An Appeal for Social Purity in Negro Homes* (Nashville, Tennessee: 1898).

Harris, Sara, *They Sell Sex* (Greenwich, Connecticut: Fawcett, 1960).

Harris, Sara, and Lucy Freeman, *The Lords of Hell* (New York: Dell, 1967).

Hartford, Connecticut, *Report of the Hartford Vice Commission* (Hartford: 1913).

Hartmann, Grethe, *The Girls They Left Behind: An Investigation into the Various Aspects of the German Troops, Sexual Relations with Danish Subjects* (Copenhagen: Ejnar Munksgaard, 1946).

Haywood, A. K., "Vice and Drugs in Montreal," *Public Health Journal* (Toronto), 14 (January 1923), pp. 1-20.

Hearing Before the Committee on Military Affairs, House of Representatives, Seventy-Seventh Congress, H. R. 2475, March 11, 12, and 18, 1941, *To Prohibit Prostitution Within Reasonable Distance of Military and Naval Establishments* (Washington, D.C.: U.S. Government Printing Office, 1941).

Heizer, Robert F., and Alan F. Almquist, *The Other Californians* (Berkeley: University of California Press, 1971).

Henriques, Fernando, *Prostitution and Society: Prostitution in Europe and the Americas* (New York: Citadel Press, 1965).

Henriques, Fernando, *Modern Sexuality* (London: MacGibbon and Kee, 1968).

Henslin, James M., "Sex and Cabbies," in James M. Henslin, ed., *Studies in the Sociology of Sex* (New York: Appleton-Century-Crofts, 1971), pp. 193-223.

Heyl, Barbara S., *The Madam as Entrepreneur* (New Brunswick, New Jersey: Transaction, 1979).

Hilton, Diana Gray, "Turning-Out: A Study of Teenage Prostitution," unpublished M.A., University of Washington, 1971.

Hilton, George W., "The Prohibition of Prostitution: An Economic Analysis," unpublished ms., 1975.

Hirschfeld, Magnus, *Men and Women: The World Journey of a Sexologist* (New York: G. P. Putnam's Sons, 1935).

Hirschfeld, Magnus, *The Sexual History of the World War* (New York: Falstaff Press, 1937).

Hite, Shere, *The Hite Report: A Nationwide Study of Female Sexuality* (New York: MacMillan, 1976).

Holmes, Kay Ann, "Reflections by Gaslight: Prostitution in Another Age," *Issues in Criminology*, 7 (Winter 1972), pp. 83-101.

Hong, Lawrence K., William Darrough and Robert Duff, 'The Sensuous Rip-Off: Consumer Fraud Turns Blue," *Urban Life and Culture*, 3 (January 1975), pp. 464-70.

Honolulu, Hawaii, *Honolulu Social Survey, Report of Committee on the Social Evil* (Honolulu: Honolulu Star-Bulletin, 1914).

Hooker, Edith Houghton, *The Laws of Sex* (Boston: Gorham Press, 1921).

"Hooker Law 'Too Harsh' ", *Montreal Star*, March 21, 1979.

"Hookers and Their Johns—A Strange Mosaic," *The Detroit News*, February 5, 1979.

"Hookers Battle Plan for Floating Brothel," *Montreal Star*, January 16, 1978.

"How to Remember? How to Forget?," *Coyote Howls*, 5 (Spring 1978), p. 13.

Hufton, Oliven H., *The Poor of Eighteenth-Century France, 1750-1789* (Oxford: Clarendon Press, 1974).

Hunt, Morton M., *Sexual Behavior in the 1970's* (Chicago: Playboy Press, 1974).

Hurwood, Bernhardt J., *The Sensuous New Yorker* (New York: Award Books, 1973).

Ianni, Francis A. J., *Black Mafia: Ethnic Succession in Organized Crime* (New York: Pocket Books, 1975).

Idsoe, O., and T. Guthe, "The Rise and Fall of Treponematoses," *British Journal of Venereal Disease*, 43 (1967), pp. 227-41.

Iga, Mamoru, "Sociocultural Factors in Japanese Prostitution and the Prostitution Prevention Law," *Journal of Sex Research*, 4 (1968), pp. 127-46.

Illinois Crime Survey (Chicago: Illinois Association for Criminal Justice, 1929).

International Abolitionist Federation, "The World Situation with Regard to Prostitution," *Journal of Social Hygiene*, 35 (1949), pp. 170-76.

"Italy, Lost Distinction," *Time*, September 29, 1958.

"It's the Old Storyville Game, But Price of the Deal is Higher," *The Times-Picayune* (New Orleans), June 9, 1974.

Jackman, Norman R., Richard O'Toole and Gilbert Geis, "The Self-Image of the Prostitute," in John H. Gagnon and William Simon, eds., *Sexual Deviance* (New York: Harper & Row, 1967), pp. 133-46.

Jackson, Bruce, *In the Life: Versions of the Criminal Experience* (New York: New American Library, 1974).

Jackson, Norman, *Sexy Europe* (New York: Pinnacle Books, 1976).

James, George Wharton, *Chicago's Dark Places* (Minneapolis: Thomas J. Morrow, 1891).

James, Jennifer, *A Formal Analysis of Prostitution*, Final Report to the Division of Research, State Department of Social and Health Services, Olympia, Washington, 1971.

James, Jennifer, "Sweet Cream Ladies: An Introduction to Prostitute Taxonomy," *Western Canadian Journal of Anthropology*, 3 (1972a), pp. 102-118.

James, Jennifer, "Two Domains of Streetwalker Argot," *Anthropological Linguistics* (May 1972b), pp. 172-81.

James, Jennifer, "Prostitute-Pimp Relationships," *Medical Aspects of Human Sexuality*, 7 (November 1973a), pp. 147-49, 53, 55, 58-60, 62-63.

James, Jennifer, "The Law and Commercialized Sex," unpublished ms., 1973b.

James, Jennifer, "Mobility as an Adaptive Strategy," *Urban Anthropology*, 4 (1975a), pp. 349-64.

James, Jennifer, "The History of Prostitution Laws," in Jennifer James et al., *The Politics of Prostitution* (Seattle: Social Research Associates, 1975b), pp. 11-21.

James, Jennifer, "Prostitution and Addiction: An Interdisciplinary Approach," unpublished ms., 1975c.

James, Jennifer, "Motivations for Entrance into Prostitution," in Laura Grites, ed., *The Female Offender* (Lexington, Massachusetts: Lexington, 1976a), pp. 177-205.

James, Jennifer, "Prostitution Arguments for Change," in Sol Gordon and Roger W. Libby, eds., *Sexuality Today and Tomorrow: Contemporary Issues in Human Sexuality* (North Scituate, Massachusetts: Duxbury Press, 1976b), pp. 110-23.

James, Jennifer, and E. J. Burstin, Jr., "Prostitution in Seattle," *Washington State Bar News*, 25 (1971), pp. 5-8, 25-30.

James, Jennifer, and Jean Withers, "Introduction," in Jennifer James et al., *The Politics of Prostitution* (Seattle: Social Research Associates, 1975), pp. xv-xviii.

James, Jennifer, and Jane Meyerding, "Early Sexual Experience and Prostitution," *American Journal of Psychiatry*, 134 (December 1977a), pp. 1381-90.

James, Jennifer, and Jane Meyerding, "Prostitution: Normal Men and Deviant Women," unpublished ms., 1977b.

Janney, Edward O., *The White Slave Traffic in America* (Baltimore: Lord Baltimore Press, 1911).

Janus, Sam, Barbara Bess and Carol Saltus, *A Sexual Profile of Men in Power* (Englewood Cliffs: Prentice-Hall, 1977).

Jeffers, H. Paul, and Dick Levitan, *Sex in the Executive Suite* (New York: Berkley, 1973).

Jennings, M. Anne, "The Victim as Criminal: A Consideration of California's Prostitution Law," *California Law Review*, 64 (September 1976), pp. 1235-84.

Johnson, Bascom, "Moral Conditions in San Francisco and at the Panama-Pacific Exposition," *Social Hygiene*, 1 (June 1915), pp. 589-609.

Johnson, Bascom, "What Some Communities of the West and Southwest Have Done For the Restriction of Morals and Health of Soldiers and Sailors," *Social Hygiene*, 3 (October 1917), pp. 487-503.

Johnson, Bascom, "Facing an Old Problem: How American Communities are Dealing with Commercialized Prostitution," *Journal of Social Hygiene*, 21 (1935), pp. 24-31.

Johnson, Claudia D., "That Guilty Third Tier: Prostitution in Nineteenth-Century American Theaters," *American Quarterly,* 27 (December 1975), pp. 575-84.

Johnson, Robbie Davis, "Folklore and Women: A Social Interactional Analysis of the Folklore of a Texas Madam," *Journal of American Folklore*, 86 (July-September 1973), pp. 211-24.

Johnston, Harry H., *The Negro in the New World* (London: Methuen, 1910).

Jones, A. E., "The Law Versus Prostitution," *Criminal Law Review* (London) (October 1960), pp. 704-709.

Jones, J. Bruce, letter to the editor of the *San Francisco Examiner*, printed in *Coyote Howls*, 5 (Spring 1978), p. 9.

Kalm, Florence, "Antillean Prostitution: Step-Up or Put-Down?," paper presented at the American Anthropological Association Meeting, Brooklyn College, New York, 1975.

Kaplan, John, "The Edward G. Donley Memorial Lecture: Non-Victim Crime and the Regulation of Prostitution," *West Virginia Law Review*, 79 (1977), pp. 593-606.

Karp, David Allen, "Public Sexuality and Hiding Behavior: A Study of the Times Square Sexual Community," unpublished Ph.D., New York University, 1971.

Kaye, B. C., "Brothels with a Touch of Class: Europe's New 'Eros Centers'," *Sexology*, 40 (February 1974), pp. 11-15.

Kellen, Konrad, *The Coming Age of Woman Power* (New York: Peter H. Wyden, 1972).

Kelly, Mike, "Killeen Residents Battling: Prostitutes Keep on Walking," *Austin American-Statesman*, August 15, 1974.

Kent, Robert B., and Dennis J. Dingemans, "Prostitution and the Police: Patrolling the Stroll in Sacramento," *The Police Chief*, 44 (September 1977), pp. 64-65, 73.

Khalaf, Samir, *Prostitution in a Changing Society: A Sociological Survey of Legal Prostitution in Beirut* (Beirut: Khayats, 1965).

Kinsey, Alfred C., et al., *Sexual Behavior in the Human Male* (Philadelphia: W. B. Saunders, 1948).

Kinsey, Alfred C., et al., *Sexual Behavior in the Human Female* (Philadelphia: W. B. Saunders, 1953).

Kinsie, Paul M., "The Prostitution Racket Today," *Journal of Social Hygiene*, 27 (1941), pp. 327-34.

Kinsie, Paul M., "Sex Crimes and the Prostitution Racket," *Journal of Social Hygiene*, 36 (1950), pp. 250-52.

Kinsie, Paul M., "Prostitution—Then and Now," *Journal of Social Hygiene*, 39 (June 1953), pp. 241-48.

Kizer, Jean, "Woman Challenges City Prostitution Law," *Daily News-Miner* (Fairbanks, Alaska), June 31, 1975.

Kizer, Jean, "Prostitution Business is Booming," *Daily News-Miner* (Fairbanks, Alaska), July 10, 1975.

Kneeland, George J., *Commercialized Prostitution in New York City* (New York: Century, 1913).

Knox, Robert, *The Greatest of Our Social Evils: Prostitution as it Now Exists in London, Liverpool, Manchester, Glasgow, Edinburgh and Dublin* (London: H. Bailliere, 1857).

Kobler, John, *Capone: The Life and World of Al Capone* (Greenwich, Connecticut: Fawcett, 1972).

Koper, Peter, "The Complex Reality of the Street," *Washington Newsworks*, 19 (June 17-23, 1976), p. 6.

(von) Krafft-Ebing, Richard, *Psychopathia Sexualis* (New York: G. P. Putnam's Sons, 1965).

Kuttner, Robert E., "Poverty and Sex: Relationships in a 'Skid Row' Slum," *Sexual Behavior*, 1 (October 1971), pp. 5£-63.

La Croix, Paul (Pierre Dufour), trans. by Samuel Putnam, *History of Prostitution Among All the Peoples of the World, from the Most Remote Antiquity to the Present*, 3 Vols. (New York: Covici-Friede, 1931).

La Fave, Wayne R., *Arrest: The Decision to Take a Suspect into Custody* (Boston: Little, Brown, 1965).

Lancaster, Pennsylvania, *Vice Commission Report on Vice Conditions, 1913, 1915* (Lancaster: 1914-15).

Lander County Ordinance LC 6-72.

Lane, Del, "Hookers Were Happy Here, Part II," *Oakland Tribune*, July 14, 1975.

Lane, Del, "Why Not Legalize Prostitution?, Part III," *Oakland Tribune*, July 15, 1975.

Lane, Del, "Pimps Get Big Money, Part IV," *Oakland Tribune*, July 16, 1975.

Las Vegas Review-Journal, September 2, 1973.

Layton, Monique, *Prostitution in Vancouver (1973-1975)—Official and Unofficial Reports: A Report to the B.C. Police Commission* (Vancouver: University of British Columbia, 1975).

Layton, Monique, "Street Women and Their Verbal Transactions: Some Aspects of the Oral Culture of Female Prostitute Drug Addicts," unpublished Ph.D., University of British Columbia, 1978.

Layton, Monique, "The Ambiguities of the Law or the Streetwalker's Dilemma," *Chitty's Law Journal*, 27 (1979), pp. 109-20.

League of Nations, *Advisory Committee on Traffic in Women and Children, Minutes of the Third Session* (Geneva: 1924).

League of Nations, *Commission of Enquiry into Traffic in Women and Children in the East* (Geneva: 1932).

League of Nations, *Prevention of Prostitution: A Study of Measures Adopted or Under Consideration Particularly with Regard to Minors* (Geneva: 1943).

Lee, Lois, "From Conformity to Innovation: A Typology of Pimping Strategies," paper presented at Pacific Sociological Association Meeting, 1975.

(de) Leeuw, Hendrik, *Sinful Cities of the Western World* (New York: Citadel Press, 1934).

"Legalize Prostitution?" *Honolulu Star-Bulletin*, August 13, 1974.

Lemert, Edwin M., *Social Pathology* (New York: McGraw-Hill, 1951).

Lemert, Edwin M., "Prostitution," in Edward Sagarin and Donal E. J. MacNamara, eds., *Problems of Sex Behavior* (New York: Thomas Y. Crowell, 1968), pp. 68-109.

Lemert, Edwin M., *Human Deviance, Social Problems, and Social Control* (Englewood Cliffs: Prentice-Hall, 1972).

Leonard, Carol A., "Prostitution and Changing Norms in America," unpublished Ph.D., Syracuse University, 1979.

Leonard, Carol, and Isidor Walliman, "Prostitution in America: A Macro-Sociological Analysis," unpublished ms., 1980.

Lewinsohn, Richard, trans. by Alexander Mayce, *A History of Sexual Customs* (New York: Perennial Library, 1971).

Lewis, David, *Sexpionage: The Exploitation of Sex by Soviet Intelligence* (New York: Ballantine, 1977).

Lewis, Naphtali, and Meyer Reinhold, eds., *Roman Civilization*, 2 Vols. (New York: Harper and Row, 1966).

Lexington, Kentucky, *Vice Commission Report of the Vice Commission of Lexington, Kentucky*, 2nd. ed. (Lexington: J. L. Richardson, 1915).

Light, Ivan, "From Vice District to Tourist Attraction: The Moral Career of American Chinatowns, 1800-1940," *Pacific Historical Review*, 43 (August 1974), pp. 367-94.

Lincoln County Ordinance No. 1971-76.

Lindsey, Robert, "Combat Zone Violence Heard Across Nation," *Boston Herald American*, November 28, 1976.

Lindsey, Robert, "Out in Nevada, a New Attack on an Old Profession," *New York Times*, November 8, 1977.

Lipton, Carol, "Proposal on the Decriminalization of Prostitution," unpublished ms., 1977.

List of All the Sporting Ladies Who is Arrived from the Most Principle Towns in Great Britain and Ireland to Take Their Pleasure at Leith Races on Tuesday the 22nd of July 1777 (Edinburgh: 1777).

Liswood, Rebecca, "Why Do Married Men Visit Prostitutes? A Panel Discussion," *Medical Aspects of Human Sexuality*, 4 (1970), pp. 88, 93.

Little Rock, Arkansas, Vice Commission, *Report of the Little Rock Vice Commission* (Little Rock: 1913).

Longstreet, Stephen, *Sportin' House: A History of the New Orleans Sinners and the Birth of Jazz* (Los Angeles: Sherbourne Press, 1965).

Lorenzen, Edward, "Prostitution in Colon, Republic of Panama," unpublished ms., 1974.

Lowman, John, "Street Prostitution in Vancouver," unpublished ms., 1980.

Lubove, Roy, "The Progressive and the Prostitute," *The Historian*, 24 (May 1962), pp. 308-30.

Lyon County Ordinance No. 77.

MacNamara, Donal E. J., and Edward Sagarin, *Sex, Crime, and the Law* (New York: Free Press, 1977).

Mankoff, Allan H., *Mankoff's Lusty Europe* (New York: Pocket Books, 1974).

Marlowe, Kenneth, *Mr. Madam: Confessions of a Male Madam* (Los Angeles: Sherbourne Press, 1964).

Martinez, William T., and J. Rafael Centeno, "Sexuality and Its Watchdogs," unpublished ms., 1974.

Marx, Gary, "Undercover Cops: Creative Policing or Constitutional Threat?," *Civil Liberties Review*, 4 (July/August 1977), pp. 34-44.

Mathis, James L., "Why Do Married Men Visit Prostitutes? A Panel Discussion," *Medical Aspects of Human Sexuality*, 4 (1970), p. 97.

Matsumoto, Y. Scott, *Contemporary Japan* (Philadelphia: American Philosophical Society, 1960).

Mayer, Joseph, "The Passing of the Red Light District—Vice Investigations and Results," *Social Hygiene*, 4 (1918), pp. 197-209.

Mayer, Joseph, "Social Legislation and Vice Control," *Social Hygiene* 5 (1919), pp. 337-48.

McKay, John W., City and County of Honolulu, letter to Playboy Foundation, January 10, 1974.

Mead, Margaret, "Should Prostitution Be Legalized?," *Redbook*, 136 (April 1971), pp. 50, 53.

Megino, Gloria Rivera, "Prostitution and California Law," California Legislature, Senate Committee on Judiciary, unpublished ms., 1977.

Melody, G. F., "Chronic Pelvic Congestion in Prostitutes," *Medical Aspects of Human Sexuality*, 3 (November 1969), pp. 103-104.

Mercier, Debbie, "Prostitution in Canada: Three Possible Approaches," unpublished ms., 1979.

Miller, Max, *Holladay Street* (New York: New American Library, 1962).

Millett, Kate, *The Prostitution Papers: A Candid Dialogue* (New York: Avon, 1973).

Milman, Barbara, "New Rule for the Oldest Profession: Should We Change Our Prostitution Laws?", *Harvard Women's Law Journal* Spring 1980.

Milner, Christina, and Richard Milner, *Black Players: The Secret World of Black Pimps* (New York: Bantam Books, 1973).

Miner, Charles E., "Repression Versus Segregation in Chicago," *Journal of Social Hygiene*, 17 (1931), pp. 283-87.

Miner, Maude E., *Slavery of Prostitution: A Plea for Emancipation* (New York: Macmillan, 1916).

Minneapolis, Minnesota, Report of the Vice Commission of Minneapolis, *The Prostitute and the Social Reformer* (New York: Arno Press, 1974).

Mol, Albert, *Memoirs of an Amsterdam Streetwalker: Conversations with Greta* (New York: Universal, 1964).

Montreal, Committee of Sixteen, *Preliminary Report of an Unofficial Organization Upon the Vice Conditions in Montreal* (Montreal: 1918).

Morgan, Ted, "Little Ladies of the Night," *New York Times Magazine*, November 16, 1975, pp. 34-50.

Morrill, Mitch, "Sex for Sale," *Hollywood Press*, May 6, 1977.

Morris, Norval, and Gordon Hawkins, *The Honest Politicians Guide to Crime* (Chicago: University of Chicago Press, 1969).

Morrison, Majbritt, *Jungle West 11* (New York: Universal, 1967).

Moses, Ed, et al., "Majority Report of Anchorage Committee to Study Prostitution," unpublished ms., May 17, 1976.

Murtagh, John M., and Sara Harris, *Cast the First Stone* (New York: McGraw-Hill, 1957).

National Advisory Police Committee, *Techniques of Law Enforcement Against Prostitution* (Washington, D.C.: U.S. Government Printing Office, 1943).

National Public Opinion Research Institute, *The Japanese People Look at Prostitution* (Tokyo: 1952).

"National Tattle," *Coyote Howls*, 4 (Autumn 1977), p. 5.

Neckes, Marilyn, "Batelle: Prostitution Statistics—Women Incarcerated in the S. F. County Jail in 1975," handout, 1976.

Nevada Revised Statutes, 1971.

Nevada State Journal, March 22, 1973.

Newark, New Jersey, Citizen's Committee, *Report on the Social Evil Conditions of Newark, New Jersey, 1913-1914* (Newark: 1914).

New York City, Committee of Fourteen, *Department Store Investigation of the Subcommittee* (New York: 1915).

"New York Court Voids Prostitution Law," *Sexual Law Reporter*, 4 (July-September 1978), p. 42.

"No Bail for Prostitutes Without VD Check 'Absurd'," *Berkeley Daily Gazette*, March 26, 1975.

Noll, Roger G., ed., *Government and the Sports Business* (Washington, D.C.: The Brookings Institution, 1974).

Norden, Peter, trans. by J. Maxwell Brownjohn, *Madam Kitty* (New York: Ballantine, 1974).

North Carolina, Report by the North Carolina Organized Crime Prevention Council, *Organized Crime in North Carolina* (Raleigh: 1972).

O'Donnell, Michael J., and George M. Bicek, "The Massage Parlor Problem," *FBI Law Enforcement Bulletin*, 46 (June 1977), pp. 16-20.

Oman, Wally, and John Ensminger, "Investigatory Report on the Emeryville Police Department," unpublished report, 1974.

d'Orban, P. T., "Female Narcotic Addicts: A Follow-Up Study of Criminal and Addiction Careers," *British Medical Journal*, 10 (November 1973), pp. 345-47.

Orlando Task Force on Prostitution, "Legalization and Decriminalization Alternatives to Present Governmental Responses," unpublished report, July 1977.

Pallavicino, Ferrante, *The Whore's Rhetorick* (London: George Shell, 1683; reprinted by Ivan Obolensky, New York, 1961).

Palmquist, Al, with John Stone, *The Minnesota Connection* (New York: Warner, 1978).

Parent-Duchatelet, A. J. B., *De la Prostitution dans la Ville de Paris*, Vols. I & II (Paris: Chez J. B. Baillière, 1836).

Parent-Duchatelet, A. J. B., *De la Prostitution dans la Ville de Paris*, 2nd ed. (Paris: J. B. Bailière de Fils, 1857).

"Paris Reconsiders Brothels' Closings," *New York Times*, January 6, 1952.

Partridge, Burgo, *A History of Orgies* (New York: Bonanza, 1960).

Partridge, Eric, *A Dictionary of the Underworld* (New York: Bonanza, 1961).

Patterson, Edna B., Louise A. Ulph and Victor Goodwin, *Nevada's Northeast Frontier* (Sparks, Nevada: Western Printing, 1969).

Pearsall, Ronald, *The Worm in the Bud: The World of Victorian Sexuality* (Toronto: Macmillian, 1969).

Pearson, Michael, *The Age of Consent: Victorian Prostitution and Its Enemies* (Newton Abbot: David and Charles, 1972).

Perry, Mary Elizabeth, " 'Lost Women' in Early Modern Seville," *Feminist Studies*, 4 (February 1978), pp. 195-214.

Pershing County Ordinance No. 53.

Pfeiffer, Timothy N., "Social Hygiene and the War," *Social Hygiene*, 4 (April 1918), pp. 417-31.

Philadelphia, Vice Commission of Philadelphia, *A Report of Existing Conditions with Recommendations to the Honorable Rudolph Blakenburg, Mayor of Philadelphia* (Philadelphia: Vice Commission of Philadelphia, 1913).

Philpott, Thomas L., *The Slum and the Ghetto: Neighborhood Deterioration and Middle-Class Reform, Chicago, 1880-1930* (New York: Oxford University, 1978).

Pilpel, Harriet F., "Sex vs. the Law: A Study in Hypocrisy," in Ailon Shiloh, ed., *Studies in Human Sexual Behavior: The American Scene* (Springfield, Illinois: Charles C. Thomas, 1970), pp. 61-68.

Pivar, David J., *Purity Crusade, Sexual Morality and Social Control, 1868-1900* (Westport, Connecticut: Greenwood Press, 1973).

"PLAN: Prostitution Laws are Nonsense, Statement of the British Prostitutes Organisation," *Coyote Howls*, 4 (Autumn 1977), p. 10.

Plowcowe, Morris, *Sex and the Law* (Englewood Cliffs: Prentice-Hall, 1951).

Polatin, Phillip, "Why Do Married Men Visit Prostitutes? A Panel Discussion," *Medical Aspects of Human Sexuality*, 4 (1970), pp. 80, 84.

"Police 'Stymied' on Prostitution," *San Francisco Chronicle*, April 10, 1975.

Polsky, Ned, *Hustlers, Beats and Others* (New York: Anchor, 1969).

Pomeroy, Wardell B., "Some Aspects of Prostitution," *Journal of Sex Research*, 1 (November 1965), pp. 177-87.

Pomeroy, Wardell B., *Dr. Kinsey and the Institute for Sex Research* (New York: Harper & Row, 1972).

Portland Scribe, March 8-14, 1975.

Powell, Hickman, *Ninety Times Guilty* (New York: Harcourt, Brace, 1939).

"Power to Prostitute Women All Over the World," (From the English Collective of Prostitutes, May 1977), *Coyote Howls*, 4 (Autumn 1977), p. 10.

The President's Commission on Law Enforcement and Administration of Justice, Task Force on Assessment, *The Challenge of Crime in a Free Society* (Washington, D.C.: U.S. Government Printing Office, 1967).

The Pretty Women of Paris: Their Names and Addresses, Qualities and Faults, Being a Complete DIRECTORY; or Guide to Pleasure for Visitors to the Gay City (Paris?: Privately printed at the press of the Prefecture de Police, by members of the Principal Parisian Clubs, 1883).

Price, Granville, "A Sociological Study of a Segregated District," unpublished M.A., University of Texas, Austin, 1930.

Primov, George, and Carolynne Kieffer, "The Peruvian Brothel as Sexual Dispensary and Social Arena," *Archives of Sexual Behavior*, 6 (1977), pp. 245-53.

"Private Sex Decriminalized in Vermont," *Sexual Law Reporter*, 5 (January-March 1979), p. 9.

"A Prostitute Speaks," *Playboy*, 13 (April 1967), p. 52.

"Prostitutes Ignore Rehabilitation Plan," *Los Angeles Times*, November 20, 1971.

Prus, Robert C., and Steve Vassilakopoulos, "Desk Clerks and Hookers: Hustling in a 'Shady' Hotel," *Urban Life*, 8 (April 1979), pp. 52-71.

Quaife, G. R., *Wanton Wenches and Wayward Wives: Peasants and Illicit Sex in Early Seventeenth Century England* (New Brunswick, New Jersey: Rutgers University Press, 1979).

Quennel, Peter, ed., *London's Underworld* (London: Spring Books, 1950).

Raab, Selwyn, "Pimps Establish Recruiting Link to the Midwest," *New York Times*, October 30, 1977.

Rasmussen, Paul K., and Lauren L. Kuhn, "The New Masseuse: Play for Pay," *Urban Life*, 5 (October 1976), pp. 271-92.

Reasons, George, and Al Delugach, "The Law in Las Vegas: All-Powerful Sheriff Reigns Over a 'Big Brothel' System," *Honolulu Advertiser*, April 14, 1977.

Reckless, Walter C., *Vice in Chicago* (Chicago: University of Chicago Press, 1933).

Reckless, Walter C., "The Distribution of Commercialized Vice in the City: A Sociological Analysis," in George A. Theodorson, ed., *Studies in Human Ecology* (Evanston, Illinois: Row, Peterson, 1961), pp. 50-55.

" 'Red-Light' District for City Proposed," *St. Louis Post-Dispatch*, June 4, 1975.

Reid, Ed, and Ovid Demaris, *The Green Felt Jungle* (New York: Pocket Books, 1964).

Reitman, Ben L., *The Second Oldest Profession: A Study of the Prostitute's "Business Manager"* (London: Constable, 1936).

Reno Evening Gazette, August 30, 1971.

Reno Evening Gazette, October 9, 1971.

Reno Evening Gazette, May 20, 1972.

Report of the United States Interdepartmental Social Hygiene Board, for the Fiscal Year Ended June 30, 1922 (Washington, D.C.: Government Printing Office, 1922).

Reuss, L., *La Prostitution au Point de vue de L'Hygiène et de L'Administration en France et a L'Ètranger* (Paris: Librairie J. B. Bailliere et Fils, 1889).

Rheinstein, M., *Max Weber on Law in Economy and Society* (Cambridge: Harvard University Press, 1954).

Richardson, James F., *The New York Police: Colonial Times to 1901* (New York: Oxford University Press, 1970).

Riegel, Robert E., "Changing American Attitudes Towards Prostitution (1800-1920)," *Journal of the History of Ideas*, 29 (1968), pp. 437-52.

Roberts, W. Adolphe, *Havana: The Portrait of a City* (New York: Coward-McCann, 1953).

Roe, Clifford G., ed., *War on the White Slave Trade* (Chicago: Charles C. Thompson, 1909).

Roebuck, Julian, and Patrick McNamara, "Ficheras and Free-Lancers: Prostitution in a Mexican Border City," *Archives of Sexual Behavior*, 2 (1973), pp. 231-44.

Rolph, C. H., ed., *Women of the Streets: A Sociological Study of the Common Prostitute* (London: Secker & Warburg, 1955).

Rose, Al, *Storyville, New Orleans: Being An Authentic, Illustrated Account of the Notorious Red-Light District* (University: University of Alabama Press, 1974).

Rosen, Ruth, "The Lost Sisterhood: Prostitution During the Progressive Era," unpublished Ph.D. thesis, University of California, Berkeley, 1976.

Rosen, Ruth, and Sue Davidson, eds., *The Maimie Papers* (Old Westbury, New York: Feminist Press, 1977).

Rosenbleet, Charles, and Barbara J. Pariente, "The Prostitution of the Criminal Law," *American Criminal Law Review*, 11 (1973), pp. 373-427.

Rosenblum, Karen E., "Female Deviance and the Female Sex Role: A Preliminary Investigation," *British Journal of Sociology*, 26 (June 1975), pp. 169-85.

Rossi, Peter H., et al., "The Seriousness of Crimes: Normative Structure and Individual Differences," *American Sociological Review*, 39 (April 1974), pp. 224-37.

Rotenberg, Lori, "The Wayward Worker: Toronto's Prostitute at the Turn of the Century," in Janice Acton, Penny Goldsmith and Bonnie Shepard, eds., *Women at Work: Ontario 1850-1930* (Toronto: Canadian Women's Educational Press, 1974), pp. 33-69.

Runkel, David, "Decriminalization, Panel Urges,"*Philadelphia Bulletin*, June 8, 1976.

Russell, Daniel, "The Road House: A Study of Commercialized Amusements in the Environs of Chicago," unpublished M.A., University of Chicago, 1931.

Ryan, Michael, *Prostitution in London, with a Comparative View of that of Paris and New York* (London: H. Bailliere, 1839).

Sagarin, Edward, "Say Cabbie, Where's the Action in This Town?," in Leonard Gross, ed., *Sexual Behavior* (Flushing, New York: Spectrum, 1974), pp. 215-23.

Sagarin, Edward, and Donal E. J. MacNamara, "The Problem of Entrapment," in Richard C. Dahl and George E. Dix, *Crime Law and Justice Annual 1972* (Buffalo: Wm. S. Hein, 1972), pp. 358-80.

Sahlins, Marshal, *The Use and Abuse of Biology: An Anthropological Critique of Sociobiology* (Ann Arbor: University of Michigan Press, 1976).

Salutin, Marilyn, "Stripper Morality," in George Paul Csicsery, ed., *The Sex Industry* (New York: New American Library, 1973), pp. 134-52.

Sanders, Wiley B., ed., *Juvenile Offenders for a Thousand Years: Selected Readings from Anglo-Saxon Times to 1900* (Chapel Hill: University of North Carolina Press, 1970).

Sandford, Jeremy, *Prostitutes: Portraits of People in the Sexploitation Business* (London: Secker & Warburg, 1975).

San Francisco Committee on Crime, *A Report on Non-Victim Crime in San Francisco, Part II* (San Francisco: 1971).

San Francisco Vice Meeting, WAC Task Force (notes), October 26, 1976.

Sanger, William W., *The History of Prostitution: Its Extent, Causes and Effects Throughout the World* (New York: Eugenics, 1937).

Sanger, William W., "Prostitution," in Harry E. Wedeck, ed., *Pictorial History of Morals* (New York: Philosophical Library, 1963), pp. 179-92.

"Satellites," *Time*, May 20, 1957.

Scarlet, Iain, *The Professionals: Prostitutes and Their Clients* (London: Sidgwick & Jackson, 1972).

Scarlet, Iain, "Prostitution in London: The Wages of Sin, Part II," *Spectator*, 7594 (January 12, 1974), p. 38.

Scarlet, Iain, "Prostitution in London: The New Professionalism," Part III," *Spectator*, 7595 (January 19, 1974), pp. 70-71.

Scherzer, Norman J., "Interview with a VD Investigator," *Sexual Behavior*, 1 (June 1971), pp. 20-27.

Schimel, John L. "Why Do Married Men Visit Prostitutes? A Panel Discussion," *Medical Aspects of Human Sexuality*, 4 (1970), pp. 98, 101.

Schimel, John L., " 'Commentary' on Prostitute-Pimp Relationships, by Jennifer James," *Medical Aspects of Human Sexuality*, 7 (1973), pp. 162-63.

Schmid, Calvin F., and Stanton E. Schmid, *Crime in the State of Washington* (Olympia: Law and Justice Planning Office, Washington State Planning and Community Affairs Agency, 1972).

Schultz, Leroy G., "The Control of Prostitution in West Virginia: A Social Policy Analysis, 1977," unpublished report, 1977.

Schwartz, Kessel, "The Whorehouse and the Whore in Spanish American Fiction of the 1960s," *Journal of Interamerican Studies and World Affairs*, 15 (November 1973), pp. 472-87.

Scott, George Ryley, *A History of Prostitution from Antiquity to the Present Day* (New York: Medical Press of New York, 1954).

Scott, Joan W., and Louise A. Tilly, "Women's Work and the Family in Nineteenth Century Europe," *Comparative Studies in Society and History*, 17 (January 1975), pp. 36-64.

Semper Idem (pseudo.), *The "Blue Book": A Bibliographical Attempt to Describe the Guide Books to the Houses of Ill Fame in New Orleans as They were Published There* (New Orleans: privately printed, 1936).

"Send Them to Alcatraz," *Oakland Tribune*, July 15, 1975.

"Sex Gang Warfare," *Washington Post*, January 11, 1976.

"Sexual Solicitation—Free Speech," *Sexual Law Reporter*, 5 (January-March 1979), p. 7.

Shaw, David, "Rentagirl: A Look at Escort Agencies," in Clifton D. Bryant, ed., *Sexual Deviancy in Social Context* (New York: New Viewpoints, 1977), pp. 195-201.

Shaw, Otto L., "The 1946 Law in Paris," *British Journal of Delinquency*, 1 (October 1950), pp. 129-33.

Sheehy, Gail, "The Landlords of Hell's Bedroom," *New York*, November 20, 1972, pp. 67-80.

Sheehy, Gail, *Hustling: Prostitution in Our Wide-Open Society* (New York: Dell, 1974).

Sheppard, Nathaniel, "Private Morals of Public Aides Set Off Debate," *New York Times*, November 11, 1979.

Shoemaker, Donald J., "The Teeniest Trollops: 'Baby Pros,' 'Chickens,' and Child Prostitutes," in Clifton D. Bryant, ed., *Sexual Deviancy in Social Context* (New York: New Viewpoints, 1977), pp. 241-53.

Shumsky, Neil Larry, and Larry M. Springer, "San Francisco's Zone of Prostitution, 1880-1934," unpublished ms., 1979.

Silver, Carol Ruth, "What Price Prostitution?, Part I," *Barristers' Bailiwick*, 8 (February 1974), p. 1.

Silver, Carol Ruth, "What Price Prostitution?, Part II," *Barristers' Bailiwick*, 8 (March 1974), pp. 4, 7.

Silverman, Art, "Encounter Studio Rip-Off Exposed," *Berkeley Barb*, March 25-31, 1977.

Simmons, Ozzie G., "Anglo Americans and Mexican-Americans in South Texas: A Study in Dominant-Subordinate Group Relations," unpublished Ph.D. thesis, Harvard University, 1952.

Simons, G. L., *A Place for Pleasure: The History of the Brothel* (London: Harwood-Smart, 1975).

Sion, Abraham A., *Prostitution and the Law* (London: Faber and Faber, 1977).

Skipper, James K., Jr., and Charles M. McCaghy, "Stripteasing: A Sex-Oriented Occupation," in James M. Henslin, ed., *Studies in the Sociology of Sex* (New York: Appleton-Century-Crofts, 1971), pp. 275-96.

Skolnick, Jerome H., *Justice Without Trial*, 2nd ed. (New York: John Wiley, 1975).

Smith, Jim, and Bonnie Bullough, "Sexuality and the Severely Disabled Person," *American Journal of Nursing*, 75 (December 1975), pp. 2194-97.

Smothers, David, " 'Johns' Open Game for Vice Squads Using Decoy Prostitutes," *Houston Chronicle*, September 26, 1976.

Snapp, Tom, "Fairbanks Becomes Wild City, Prostitution Up 5,000 Percent," *The Pioneer: All-Alaska Weekly*, July 25, 1975.

Spear, Allan H., *Black Chicago: The Making of a Negro Ghetto, 1890-1920* (Chicago: University of Chicago Press, 1967).

Spence, Steve, "Honolulu Hookers . . . and the Courts," *Honolulu Star-Bulletin*, March 19, 1980.

The Sporting and Club House Directory, Chicago: Containing a Full and Complete List of All Strictly First Class Club and Sporting Houses (Chicago: Ross and St. Clair, 1889).

Stafford, Peter, *Sexual Behavior in the Communist World* (New York: Julian Press, 1967).

Stanford, Sally, *The Lady of the House: The Autobiography of Sally Stanford* (New York: G. P. Putnam's Sons, 1966).

Stein, Martha L., *Lovers, Friends, Slaves . . .: The Nine Male Sexual Types, Their Psycho-Sexual Transactions with Call Girls* (New York: Berkley, 1974).

Steiner, Shari, *The Female Factor: A Study of Women in Five European Societies* (New York: G. P. Putnam's Sons, 1977).

Stinchcombe, Arthur, "Institutions of Privacy in the Determination of Police Practice," *American Sociological Review*, 69 (1963), pp. 150-60.

St. James, Margo, "An Embarassment to the Patriachry," *International Coyote Howls*, 3 (Summer 1976), pp. 1-2, 4.

Stokes, Henry Scott, " 'Sex Package Tours' are Protected in Japan," *New York Times*, August 5, 1979.

Stone, Erica, "The Topless-Bottomless B-Girl Hustle," in George Paul Csicsery, ed., *The Sex Industry* (New York: New American Library, 1973), pp. 116-33.

Stopp, G. Harry, Jr., "The Distribution of Massage Parlors in the Nation's Capital," *Journal of Popular Culture*, 11 (Spring 1978), pp. 989-97.

Storch, Robert D., "Police Control of Street Prostitution in Victorian London," in David H. Bayley, ed., *Police and Society* (Beverly Hills: Sage, 1977), pp. 49-72.

Strom, Fredric A., *Zoning Control of Sex Businesses* (New York: Clark Boardman, 1977).

Stuckey, Johanna, "A Feminist Looks at Prostitution," in Benjamin Schlesinger, ed., *Sexual Behaviour in Canada: Patterns and Problems* (Toronto: University of Toronto Press, 1977), pp. 221-34.

Sweeney, Ester E., "News from the States and Communities," *Journal of Social Hygiene*, 34 (1948), pp. 433-37.

Swingler, Nicholas, "The Streetwalkers Return," *New Society*, 16 (January 1969), pp. 81-83.

Symanski, Richard, "Prostitution in Nevada," *Annals*, Association of American Geographers, 64 (September 1974), pp. 357-77.

Symons, Donald, *The Evolution of Human Sexuality* (New York: Oxford University Press, 1979).

Syracuse, Committee of Eighteen, *The Social Evil in Syracuse, Being the Report of an Investigation of the Moral Condition of the City Conducted by a Committee of Eighteen Citizens* (Syracuse: 1913).

Tabor, Pauline, *Pauline's* (Greenwich, Connecticut: Fawcett, 1973).

Tampa Prostitution Committee, "Minority Report for Decriminalization of Prostitution," unpublished report, c. 1976.

Tancer, Shoshana B., "La Quisqueyana: The Dominican Woman, 1940-1970," in Ann Pescatello, ed., *Female and Male in Latin America* (Pittsburgh: University of Pittsburgh Press, 1973), pp. 209-29.

Taylor, G. Rattray, *Sex in History* (London: Thames and Hudson, 1953).

Teresa de Gallo, Maria, and Heli Alzate, "Brothel Prostitution in Colombia," *Archives of Sexual Behavior*, 5 (1976), pp. 1-7.

Terman, Lewis, *Psychological Factors in Marital Happiness* (New York: McGraw-Hill, 1938).

Terrot, Charles, *Traffic in Innocents: The Shocking Story of White Slavery in England* (New York: E. P. Dutton, 1960).

Texier, Catherine, and Marie-Odile Vézina, *Profession: Prostitute* (Ottawa: Editions Libre Expression, 1978).

Thomas, H. "Prostitution in Great Britain Today," *Social Defense*, 8 (October 1972), pp. 14-26.

Thornton, Robert Y., "Organized Crime in the Field of Prostitution," *Journal of Criminal Law, Criminology and Police Science*, 46 (March-April 1956), pp. 775-79.

Thran, Earnhard W., Douglas County (Nevada) Clerk and Treasurer, letter to author, 1973.

Time, October 10, 1960.

Tower, Philo, *Slavery Unmasked* (Rochester: 1856).

Toynbee, Polly, "Love for Sale," *Manchester Guardian Weekly*, 119, October 15, 1978.

Trivers, Robert L., "Parental Investment and Sexual Selection," in B. Campbell, ed., *Sexual Selection and the Descent of Man, 1871-1971* (Chicago: Aldine, 1972), pp. 136-79.

"Trouble Along 'Combat Zone' ," *San Francisco Chronicle*, December 9, 1976.

Trudgill, Eric, *Madonnas and Magdalens* (New York: Holmes & Meier, 1976).

Turner, Graham, "Scotland and the Wolfenden Report: A Unique Special Investigation," *The Scotsman* (Edinburgh, Scotland: 1959).

Ullerstam, Lars, *The Sexual Minorities* (Stockholm: 1966).

United Nations, *Study on Traffic in Persons and Prostitution* (New York: United Nations, Department of Economic and Social Affairs, 1959).

United States, Bureau of the Census, *Historical Statistics of the United States: Colonial Times to 1957* (Washington, D.C.: Government Printing Office, 1960).

United States, Bureau of the Census, *Characteristics of the Population: California, Part I* (Washington, D.C.: U.S. Government Printing Office, 1973).

United States, Bureau of the Census, *Statistical Abstract of the United States: 1979* (Washington, D.C.: U.S. Government Printing Office, 1979).

Van Gelder, Lindsy, "She's Pretty: That's All the Massage Parlors Ask," in George Paul Csicsery, ed., *The Sex Industry* (New York: New American Library, 1973), pp. 94-104.

Vaz, Edmund W., "Metropolitan Taxi-Driver: His Work and Self-Conception," unpublished M.A., McGill University, 1955.

Velarde, Albert J., "Becoming Prostituted," *British Journal of Criminology*, 15 (1976), pp. 251-63.

"Victoire vs. Ferdon," *San Francisco Bay Guardian*, October 31, 1975.

Vintras, A., *On the Repressive Measures Adopted in Paris Compared with the Uncontrolled Prostitution of London and New York* (London: Robert Hardwicke, 1867).

Vogliotti, Gabriel R., *The Girls of Nevada* (Secaucus, New Jersey: Citadel Press, 1975).

Vorenberg, Elizabeth, and James Vorenberg, "The Biggest Pimp of All," *Atlantic*, 239 (January 1977), pp. 27-38.

Wade, Daniel E., "Prostitution and the Law: Emerging Attacks on a 'Woman's Crime,' " *UMKC Law Review*, 43 (1975), pp. 413-28.

Wagner, Roland Richard, "Virtue Against Vice: A Study of Moral Reformers and Prostitution in the Progressive Era," unpublished Ph.D. thesis, University of Wisconsin, 1971.

Wald, Matthew L., "Therapy Association Combats Current 'Massage' Connotation," *New York Times*, August 12, 1979.

Waldberg, Patrick, trans. by Helen R. Lane, *Eros in La Belle Epoque* (New York: Grove Press, 1969).

Walker, Nigel, *Crime and Punishment in Britain* (Edinburgh: Edinburgh University Press, 1965).

Wallach, David, *The New Geishas* (Berkeley: Ten Speed Press, 1973).

Walton, William, *Paris: From the Earliest Period to the Present Day*, Vol. I (Philadelphia: George Barrie & Son, 1899).

Ward, Francis, "Porn, Crime Lessened by 'Detroit Ordinance,' " *Honolulu Advertiser*, July 18, 1977.

Warren, John, Jr., *Thirty Years' Battle with Crime* (New York: Arno Press and the New York Times, 1970).

Washburn, Charles, *Come Into My Parlor: A Biography of the Aristocratic Everleigh Sisters of Chicago* (New York: Knickerbocker, 1934).

Washoe County Ordinance No. 137.

Waterman, Willoughby C., "Prostitution and Its Repression in New York City, 1900-1931," unpublished Ph.D. thesis, Columbia University, 1932.

Wells Emergency Ordinance No. 24.

Wells, John Warren, *Tricks of the Trade* (New York: New American Library, 1970).

Wendt, Lloyd and Herman Kogan, *Lords of the Levee: The Story of Bathhouse John and Hinky Dink* (Indianapolis: 1943).

White Pine County Code 1971.

White, W. Wallace, *Caring for the Environment: My Work with Public Health and Reclamation in Nevada* (Reno: University of Nevada Press, 1970).

Wilcox, R. R., "Prostitution and Venereal Disease," *British Journal of Venereal Disease*, 38 (1962), pp. 37-42.

Williams, Robert H., *Vice Squad* (New York: Thomas Y. Crowell, 1973).

Wilson, J. R., R. E. Kuehn and R. A. Beach, "Modification in the Sexual Behavior of Male Rats Produced by Changing the Stimulus Female," *Journal of Comparative and Physiological Psychology*, 56 (1963), pp. 636-44.

Wilson, Paul, *The Sexual Dilemma* (St. Lucia, Queensland: University of Queensland Press, 1971).

Wilson, Robert A., ed., *Playboy's Book of Forbidden Words* (Chicago: Playboy Press, 1974).

Winick, Charles, "Clients' Perceptions of Prostitutes and of Themselves," *International Journal of Psychiatry*, 8 (1962), pp. 289-97.

Winick, Charles, " 'Commentary' on Prostitute-Pimp Relationships, by Jennifer James," *Medical Aspects of Human Sexuality*, 7 (November 1973), pp. 160, 162.

Winick, Charles and Paul M. Kinsie, *The Lively Commerce: Prostitution in the United States* (Chicago: Quadrangle, 1972).

Winnemucca Municipal Code 1973.

Winter, Marcel, *Prostitution in Australia* (Balgowlah, New South Wales: Purtaboi, 1976).

Wisconsin Legislative Committee, *Report and Recommendation of the Wisconsin Legislative Committee to Investigate the White Slave Traffic and Kindred Subjects* (Madison: 1914).

Witness 1: Japan, "Prostitution," in Diana E. H. Russell and Nicole van de Ven, eds., *Crimes Against Women: Proceedings of the International Tribunal* (Millbrae, California: Les Femmes, 1976), pp. 175-77.

Witness 2: Korea, "Prostitution," in Diana E. H. Russell and Nicole van de Ven, eds., *Crimes Against Women: Proceedings of the International Tribunal* (Millbrae, California: Les Femmes, 1976), pp. 177-79.

"Women Blast Hooker Law," *Montreal Star*, March 26, 1979.

Women Endorsing Decriminalization, "Prostitution: A Non-Victim Crime?," *Issues in Criminology*, 8 (Fall 1973), pp. 137-62.

Women That Pass the Night: Reminiscences of the Parisian Queens of Prostitution (Paris: Charles Carrington, 1906).

Women's Jail Study Group, "Facts on Prostitution in San Francisco," unpublished ms., 1976.

Woolston, Howard B., *Prostitution in the United States* (New York: Century, 1921).

Wunsch, James L., "Prostitution and Public Policy: From Regulation to Suppression, 1858-1920," unpublished Ph.D., University of Chicago, 1976.

Yondorf, Barbara, "Prostitution in Washington State," Testimony before the Subcommittee on Social Concerns, Washington House Commerce Committee, ms., October 17, 1975.

Yondorf, Barbara, "Prostitution as a Legal Activity: The West German Experience," *Policy Analysis*, 5 (Fall 1979), pp. 417-33.

Young, Wayland, "Prostitution," in John H. Gagnon and William Simon, eds., *Sexual Deviance* (New York: Harper & Row, 1967), pp. 105-33.

Bibliography
for the Appendix

Adriani, N., and Albert C. Kruyt, *[The Bareé-speaking Toradja of Central Celebes (The East Toradja)]* 2nd vol., 2nd ed. (Amsterdam: N. V. Noord-Hollandsche Vitgevers Maatschappij, 1951).

Alexander, Richard D., "The Evolution of Social Behavior," *Annual Review of Ecology and Systematics*, 5 (1974), pp. 325-383.

Bahrein, *Administrative Report for the Years 1926-1937* (n.p.: 1937).

Bailes, Sylvia, "Slavery in Arabia," unpublished paper, Philadelphia, Institute for Israel and the Middle East of the Dropsie College for Hebrew and Cognate Learning, 1952.

Balandier, Georges, *[Contemporary Sociology of Black Africa: Social Changes in Gabon and the Congo]* (Paris: Presses Universitaires de France, 1955).

Bancroft-Hunt, Norman, and Werner Forman, *People of the Totem* (New York: G. P. Putnam's Sons, 1979).

Barnes, John A., *Marriage in a Changing Society: A Study in Structural Change Among the Fort Jameson Ngoni* (London: Oxford University, 1951).

Basedow, Herbert, *The Australian Aboriginal* (Adelaide: F. W. Preece, 1925).

Beals, Ralph L., *Cherán: A Sierra Tarascan Village* (Washington, D.C.: Smithsonian Institution, 1946).

Bennett, Albert L., "Ethnographic Notes on the Fang," *Journal of the Anthropological Institute of Great Britain and Ireland*, 29 (1899), pp. 66-88.

Bennett, Wendell C., and Robert M. Zingg, *The Tarahumara: An Indian Tribe of Northern Mexico* (Chicago: University of Chicago, 1935).

Berndt, Ronald W., and Catherine H. Berndt, *Arnhem Land, Its History and Its People* (Melbourne: F. W. Cheshire, 1954).

Bertram, Brian C. R., "Kin Selection in Lions and in Evolution," in P. P. G. Bateson and R. A. Hinde, eds., *Growing Points in Ethnology* (Cambridge: Cambridge University, 1976), pp. 281-301.

Bogoraz-Tan, Vladimir G., *The Chukchee*, 2 vols. (Leiden: E. J. Brill, 1904-1909).

Bouroncle-Carreón, Alfonso, "[Contribution to the Study of the Aymara]" *América Indígena*, 24 (1964), pp. 129-169, 233-269.

Breton, Raymond, and Armand de la Paix, *[An Account of the Island of Guadeloupe]*, ed., Joseph Rennard, *Les Caraïbes, La Guadeloupe, 1635-1656* (Paris: Librairie Générale et Internationale, 1929).

Brettes, Joseph de, "[The Arhuaco-Cagaba Indians: Replies to the Sociological and Ethnographic Questionnaire of the Société d'Anthropologie]," *Société d'Anthropologie de Paris, Bulletins et Mémoires*, 5 (1903), pp. 318-57.

Broderick, Alan H., *Little China: The Annamese Lands* (London: Oxford University, 1942).

Brownmiller, Susan, *Against Our Will: Men, Women and Rape* (New York: Bantam, 1976).

Burgesse, J. Allan, "The Woman and the Child Among the Lac-St-Jean Montagnais," *Primative Man*, 17 (1944), pp. 1-18.

Chabot, Hendrik T., *[Kinship, Status and Sex in South Celebes]* (Groningen: J. B. Wolters, 1950).

Chao, Chéng-hsin, "Ping-chiao-tsun as a Social Laboratory: The Process of Social Cooperation in the Solution of Similar and Common Problems of the Population of a Peiping Suburban Village," *Yenching Journal of Social Studies*, 4 (1948), pp. 121-153.

Chewings, Charles, *Back in the Stone Age: The Natives of Central Australia* (Sydney: Angus and Robertson, 1936).

Christian, John L., *Modern Burma, A Survey of Political and Economic Development* (Berkeley: University of California, 1942).

Cline, Walter B., *Notes on the People of Siwah and El Garah in the Libyan Desert* (Menasha, Wisconsin: George Banta, 1936).

Cline, Walter B., et al., The Sinkaietk or Southern Okanagon of Washington (Menasha, Wisconsin: George Banta, 1938).

Cohen, Ronald, *The Structure of Kanuri Society*, unpublished Ph.D., University of Wisconsin, 1960.

Cohen, Yehudi, "The Sociology of Commercialized Prostitution in Okinawa," *Social Forces*, 37 (December 1958), pp. 160-168.

Colson, Elizabeth, *The Social Consequences of Resettlement: The Impact of the Kariba Resettlement Upon the Gwembe Tonga* (Manchester: Manchester University, 1971).

Conzemius, Eduard, *Ethnographical Survey of the Miskito and Sumu Indians of Honduras and Nicaragua* (Washington, D.C.: Smithsonian Institution, 1932).

Cook, William A., *Through the Wilderness of Brazil by Horse, Canoe and Float* (New York: American Tract Society, 1909).

Cornell University, Department of Far Eastern Studies, India Program, *India: Sociological Background* (New Haven: Human Relations Area Files, 1956).

Covarrubias, Miguel, *Island of Bali* (New York: Knopf, 1938).

Coxe, William, *Account of the Russian Discoveries Between Asia and America, To Which are Added, the Conquest of Siberia, and the History of the Transactions and Commerce Between Russia and China* (London: Cadell and Davies, 1804).

Crowder, Michael, "The Revolution," in *Pagans and Politicians* (London: Hutchinson, 1959), pp. 44-74.

Czekanowski, Jan, *[Investigations in the Area Between the Nile and the Congo, 1st Vol.: Ethnography, the Interlacustrine Region of Mpororo and Ruanda]* (Leipzig: Klinkhardt and Biermann, 1917).

Czekanowski, Jan, *[Researches in the Region Between the Nile and the Congo]*, 2nd Vol. (Leipzig: Klinkhardt and Biermann, 1924).

Damm, Hans, et al., *[The Central Carolines, Part II: Ifaluk, Aurepik, Faraulip, Sorol, Mog-Mog]* (Hamburg: Friederichsen, De Gruyter, 1938).

Davenport, William, "Red-feather Money," *Scientific American*, 206 (1962), pp. 94-104.

Dawkins, R., and T. R. Carlisle, "Parental Investment, Mate Desertion and a Fallacy," *Nature*, 262 (1976), pp. 131-133.

Dawkins, R. and John R. Krebs, "Animal Signals: Information or Manipulation," in J. R. Krebs and N. B. Davies, eds., *Behavioural Ecology: An Evolutionary Approach* (Sunderland, Mass.: Sinauer Associates, 1978), pp. 282-315.

Dickson, Harold R. P., *The Arab of the Desert: A Glimpse into Badawin Life in Kuwait and Saudi Arabia*, 2nd Ed. (London: Allen and Unwin, 1951).

Dim Delobsom, A. A., *[The Empire of the Mogho Naba: Customs of the Mossi of Upper Volta]* (Paris: Domat-Montchrestien, 1932).

Djamour, Judith, *Malay Kinship and Marriage in Singapore* (London: Athlone, University of London, 1959).

Dorsey, George A., and James R. Murie, *Notes on Skidi Pawnee Society* (New York: American Museum of Natural History, 1914).

Drucker, Philip, *The Northern and Central Nootkan Tribes* (Washington, D.C.: Government Printing Office, 1951).

DuBois, Cora, *The People of Alor: A Social-Psychological Study of an East Indian Island* (Minneapolis: University of Minnesota, 1944).

Dubois, J. A., trans. by Henry K. Beauchamp, *Hindu Manners, Customs and Ceremonies*, 3rd ed. (Oxford: Clarendon, 1906).

Dundas, Charles, "The Organization and Laws of Some Bantu Tribes in East Africa," *Journal of the Royal Anthropological Institute of Great Britain and Ireland*, 45 (1915), pp. 234-306.

East, Rupert, ed., *Akiga's Story: The Tiv Tribe as Seen by One of its Members* (London: Oxford University, 1939).

Eckhardt, Kenneth W., "Exchange Theory and Sexual Permissiveness," *Behavior Science Notes*, 6 (1971), pp. 1-18.

Erdland, August, *[The Marshall Islanders: Life and Customs, Thought and Religion of a South Seas People]* (Münster i.w.: Aschendorff, 1914).

Erlich, Vera St., *Family in Transition: A Study of 300 Yugoslav Villages* (Princeton: Princeton University, 1966).

Evans-Pritchard, Edward E., "Witchcraft (Mangu) Among the A-Zande," *Sudan Notes and Records*, 12 (1929), pp. 163-249.

Faron, Louis C., *Mapuche Social Structure: Institutional Reintegration in a Patrilineal Society of Central Chile* (Urbana: University of Illinois, 1961).

Ferrars, Max, and Bertha Ferrars, *Burma*, 2nd ed. (London: Low, Marston, 1901).

Field, Margaret J., *Search for Security: An Ethnopsychiatric Study of Rural Ghana* (New York: W. W. Norton, 1970).

Firth, Rosemary, *Housekeeping Among Malay Peasants* (London: London School of Economics and Political Science, 1943).

Fock, Niels, "Mataco Marriage," *Folk*, 5 (1963), pp. 91-101.

Fried, Morton H., *Fabric of Chinese Society: A Study of the Social Life of a Chinese County Seat* (New York: Praeger, 1953).

Furness, William H., *The Island of Stone Money: Uap of the Carolines* (Philadelphia: Lippincott, 1910).

Gallin, Bernard, and Hsin Hsing, *Taiwan: A Chinese Village in Change* (Berkeley: University of California, 1966).

Gamble, David P., *The Wolof of Senegambia, Together with Notes on the Lebu and the Serer* (London: International African Institute, 1957).

Garcilaso de la Vega, el Inca, *First Part of the Royal Commentaries of the Incas*, 2 Vols. (London: Hakluyt Society, 1869-1871).

Glacken, Clarence, *Studies of Okinawan Village Life* (Washington, D.C.: Pacific Science Board, National Research Council, 1953).

Glubb, John B., "The Sulubba and Other Ignoble Tribes of Southwestern Asia," *General Series in Anthropology*, 10 (1943), pp. 14-17.

Gluckman, Max, "The Lozi of Barotseland in Northwestern Rhodesia," in E. Colson and Max Gluckman, eds., *Seven Tribes of British Central Africa* (Manchester: Manchester University, 1959), pp. 1-93.

Gluckman, Max, *The Ideas in Barotse Jurisprudence* (Manchester: Manchester University, 1972).

Goldstein, Melvyn C., "Fraternal Polyandry and Fertility in a High Himalayan Valley in Northwest Nepal," *Human Ecology*, 4 (1976), pp. 223-233.

Gorer, Geoffrey, "Book One: Senegalese," *Africa Dances: A Book About West African Negroes* (London: Faber and Faber, 1935), pp. 25-39.

Gorer, Geoffrey, *Himalayan Village: An Account of the Lepchas of Sikkim* (London: M. Joseph, 1938).

Gourou, Pierre, *Les Paysans du Delta Tonkinois* (Paris: Les Éditions d'Art et d'Histoire, 1936).

Grad, Andrew J., *Formosa Today: An Analysis of the Economic Development and Strategic Importance of Japan's Tropical Colony* (New York: International Secretariat, Institute of Pacific Relations, 1942).

Graebner, Fritz, "[Ethnography of the Santa Cruz Islands]," *Ethnologica*, 1 (1909), pp. 71-184.

Griffis, William E., *Corea: The Hermit Nation* (New York: Charles Scribner's Sons, 1882).

Guérin and Bernard, "[The Aborigines of the Island of Formosa]," *Société de Géographie (Paris), Bulletin*, 5 (1868), pp. 542-548.

Gutierrez de Pineda, Virginia, *[Social Organization in La Guajira]* (Bogota: 1950).

Halpern, Joel M., *A Serbian Village* (New York: Columbia University, 1958).

Harrison, William, *Harrison's Description of England in Shakespeare's Youth* (London: N. Triibner, 1881).

Hart, Charles W. M., and Arnold R. Pilling, *The Tiwi of North Australia* (New York: Holt, 1960).

Hartung, John, "On Natural Selection and the Inheritance of Wealth," *Current Anthropology*, 17 (1976), pp. 607-622.

Heckewelder, John G. E., *An Account of the History, Manners, and Customs of the Indian Nations, Who Once Inhabited Pennsylvania and the Neighboring States* (Philadelphia: Abraham Small for the American Philosophical Society, 1819).

Herskovits, Melville J., *Life in a Haitian Valley* (New York: Alfred A. Knopf, 1937).

Herskovits, Melville J., and Frances S. Herskovits, *Rebel Destiny: Among the Bush Negroes of Dutch Guiana* (New York: McGraw-Hill, 1934).

Heyworth-Dunne, James, *Al-Yemen: A General Social, Political and Economic Survey* (Cairo: Renaissance Bookshop, 1952).

Hilger, M. Inez, *Arapaho Child Life and Its Cultural Background* (Washington, D.C.: U.S. Government Printing Office, 1952).

Hollis, Alfred C., *The Masai: Their Language and Folklore* (Oxford: Clarendon, 1905).

Honigmann, John J., *Culture and Ethos of Kaska Society* (New Haven: Yale University, 1949).

Howell, P. P., "Observations on the Shilluk of the Upper Nile. Customary Law: Marriage and the Violation of Rights in Women," *Africa*, 23 (1953), pp. 94-109.

Hrdy, Sarah Blaffer, *The Langurs of Abu* (Cambridge, Mass.: Harvard University, 1977).

Hulbert, Homer B., *The Passing of Korea* (New York: Doubleday, 1906).

Hulstaert, Gustabe-E., *[Marriage Among the Nkundu]* (Bruxelles: G. van Campenhout, 1928).

Hurault, Jean, *[The Boni Refugee Blacks of French Guiana]* (Dakar: Institut Francais d'Afrique Noire, 1961).

Irons, William, "Cultural and Biological Success," in Napoleon A. Chagnon and William Irons, eds., *Evolutionary Biology and Human Social Behavior: An Anthropological Perspective* (North Scituate, Mass.: Duxbury, 1979), pp. 257-272.

Itkonen, Toivo I., *[The Lapps in Finland up to 1945]*, Vol. I (Porvoo, Helsinki: Werner Söderström Osakeyhtio, 1948).

Iyer, Lik Anatha K., "The Sudras of Cochin" in: *The Cochin Tribes and Castes*, Vol. 2 (Madras: Higginbotham, 1912), pp. 1-102.

Jenness, Diamond, *The Life of Copper Eskimos* (Ottawa: F. A. Acland, 1922).

Jones, Dorothy M., "A Study of Social and Economic Problems in Unalaska, an Aleut Village," unpublished Ph.D., University of California, Berkeley, 1969.

Jones, Livingston F., *A Study of the Thlingets of Alaska* (New York: Revell, 1914).

Kahn, Morton C., *Djuka: The Bush Negroes of Dutch Guiana* (New York: Viking, 1931).

Karve, Irawati, "Kinship Organization in India," (Poona: Deccan College Monograph Series, 1953).

Kaufmann, Hans, "[The Aven, A Contribution to the Study of the Bushmen]" *Mitteilungen aus den Deutschen Schützgebieten*, 23 (1910), pp. 135-160.

Kerr, Madeline, *Personality and Conflict in Jamaica* (Liverpool: University Press, 1952).

Knapp, Frances, and Rheta L. Childe, *The Thlinkets of Southeastern Alaska* (Chicago: Stone and Kimball, 1896).

Koch, Gerd, *[The South Seas—Yesterday and Today. Cultural Change Among the Tongans and an Attempt to Interpret This Development]* (Braunschweig: Albert Limbach, 1955).

Krämer, Augustin, *Truk* (Hamburg: Friederichsen, De Gruyter, 1932).

Krämer, Augustin, and Hans Nevermann, *[Ralik-Ratak (Marshall Islands)]* (Hamburg: Friederichsen, De Gruyter, 1938).

Krause, Aurel, trans. by Erna Gunther, *The Tlingit Indians: Results of A Trip to the Northwest Coast of America and the Bering Straits* (Seattle: University of Washington, 1956).

Krause, Fritz, *In the Wilderness of Brazil: Report and Results of the Leipzig Araguaia Expedition of 1908* (Leipzig: R. Voigtländers, 1911).

Kulp, Daniel H., *Country Life in South China* (New York: Bureau of Teachers, Teachers College, Columbia University, 1925).

Kurland, Jeffrey A., "Paternity, Mother's Brother, and Human Sociality," in Napoleon A. Chagnon and Williams Irons, eds., *Evolutionary Biology and Human Social Behavior: An Anthropological Perspective* (North Scituate, Mass.: Duxbury, 1979), pp. 145-180.

LaBarre, Weston, *The Aymara Indians of the Lake Titicaca Plateau, Bolivia* (Menasha, Wisconsin: American Anthropological Association, 1948).

Lagae, C.-R., *[The Azande or Niam-Niam . . . Zande Organization, Religious and Magical Beliefs, Familial Customs]* (Bruxelles: Vromant, 1926).

Lambrecht, Francis, *The Mayawyaw Ritual, Parts 1-5* (Washington, D.C.: Catholic Anthropological Conference, 1932-1941).

Lamson, Herbert D., *Social Pathology in China* (Shanghai: Commercial Press, 1934).

Lang, Olga, *Chinese Family and Society* (New Haven: Yale University, 1946).

Latcham, Richard E., "Ethnology of the Araucanos," *Journal of the Royal Anthropological Institute of Great Britain and Ireland,* 39 (1909), pp. 334-370.

Lattimore, Owen, *Manchuria: Cradle of Conflict* (New York: Macmillan, 1935).

Lattimore, Owen, *Pivot of Asia: Sinkiang and the Inner Asian Frontiers of China and Russia* (Boston: Little, Brown, 1950).

Leakey, Louis S. B., *Mau Mau and the Kikuyu* (London: Methuen, 1953).

Leighton, Dorothea C., and Clyde Kluckhohn, *Children of the People* (Cambridge, Mass.: Harvard University, 1947).

Levy, Marion J., *The Family Revolution in Modern China* (Cambridge, Mass.: Harvard University, 1949).

Lewis, Ioan M., *Marriage and the Family in Northern Somaliland* (Kampala: East African Institute of Social Research, 1962).

Lewis, Naphtali, and Meyer Reinhold, eds., *Roman Civilization,* 2 Vols. (New York: Harper and Row, 1966).

Lewis, Oscar, *Life in a Mexican Village: Tepoztlan Restudied* (Urbana: University of Illinois, 1951).

Lingenfelten, Sherwood G., "Political Leadership and Cultural Change in Yap," unpublished Ph.D., University of Pittsburgh, 1971.

Lips, Julius E., *Nas Kapi Law: Law and Order in a Hunting Society* (Philadelphia: American Philosophical Society, 1947).

Little, Kenneth L., *The Mende of Sierra Leone: A West African People in Transition* (London: Routledge & Kegan Paul, 1951).

Lodge, Olive, *Peasant Life in Jugoslavia* (London: Seeley, Service, 1942).

Logan, J. R., "Plan for a Volunteer Police in the Muda Districts, Province Wellesley, Submitted to Government by the late J. R. Logan in 1867," *Journal of the Royal Asiatic Society, Straits Branch,* 16 (1886), pp. 173-202.

Ma, Ho-t-ien, trans. by John De Francis, *Chinese Agent in Mongolia* (Baltimore: Johns Hopkins, 1949).

Maiskii, I., *[Contemporary Mongolia]* (Irkutsk: Gosudarstvennoe Izdatel'stov, Irkutskoe Otdelenie, 1921).

Malcolm, James P., *Anecdotes of the Manners and Customs of London During the Eighteenth Century,* 2nd ed. (London: Longman, Hurst, Rees and Orme, 1810).

Malinowski, Bronislaw, *The Sexual Life of Savages in Northwestern Melanesia,* Vols. I and II (New York: Horace Liveright, 1929).

Maretzki, Thomas W., and Hatsumi Maretzki, "Taira: An Okinawan Village," in Beatrice B. Whiting, ed., *Six Cultures: Studies of Child Rearing* (New York: John Wiley and Sons, 1963) pp. 1-13, 363-539.

Massé, Henri, *[Persian Beliefs and Customs]*, 2 Vols. (Paris: Librairie Orientale et Américaine, 1938).

Masters, William M., "Rowanduz: A Kurdish Administrative and Mercantile Center," unpublished Ph.D., University of Michigan, 1953.

McIlwraith, Thomas F., *The Bella Coola Indians*, Vol. I (Toronto: University of Toronto, 1948).

Mead, Margaret, *Growing Up in New Guinea: A Comparative Study of Primitive Education* (New York: Morrow, 1930).

Mead, Margaret, "The Manus of the Admiralty Islands," in Margaret Mead, ed., *Cooperation and Competition Among Primitive Peoples* (New York: McGraw-Hill, 1937), pp. 210-39.

Merker, Meritz, *[The Masai: Ethnographic Monograph of An East African Semite People]*, 2nd ed. (Berlin: Dietrich Reimer, 1910).

Messing, Simon D., "The Highland-Plateau Amhara of Ethiopia," unpublished Ph.D., University of Pennsylvania, 1957.

Modi, Jivanji J., "The Pundits of Kashmir," *Journal of the Anthropological Society of Bombay*, 10 (1913/1916), pp. 461-485.

Moose, J. Robert, *Village Life in Korea* (Nashville: Publishing House of the Methodist Episcopal Church, 1911).

Mukherjea, Charulal, *The Santals*, 2nd ed. (Calcutta: A. Mukherjee, 1962).

Murdock, George P., *Social Structure* (New York: Free Press, 1965).

Murphy, Rhoads, *Shanghai, Key to Modern China* (Cambridge, Mass.: Harvard University, 1953).

Murphy, Robert F., and Buell Quain, *The Trumai Indians of Central Brazil* (Locust Valley: J. J. Agustin, 1955).

Nimuendajú, Curt, ed., Robert H. Lowie, *The Eastern Timbira* (Berkeley: University of California, 1946).

Orians, Gordon H., "On the Evolution of Mating Systems in Birds and Mammals," *The American Naturalist*, 103 (1969), pp. 589-603.

Park, Willard Z., "Tribes of the Sierra Nevada de Santa Marta, Colombia," in Julian H. Steward, ed., *Handbook of South American Indians*, Vol. II (Washington, D.C.: Government Printing Office, 1946), pp. 865-886.

Parker, G. A., "Sperm Competition and its Evolutionary Consequences in the Insects," *Biological Reviews*, 45 (1970), pp. 525-568.

Paulme, Denise, *[Social Organization of the Dogon (French Sudan)]* (Paris: Editions Domat-Montchrestien, F. Loviton, 1940).

Pelc, Hynek J., *Organization of the Public Health Services in Czechoslovakia* (Geneva: League of Nations, 1925).

Pelleschi, Juan, "Los Indios Matacos y su Lengua," *Instituto Geográfico Argentino, Boletín*, 17 (1896), pp. 559-622; 18 (1896), pp. 173-350.

Peter, Prince of Greece and Denmark, *A Study of Polyandry* (The Hague: Mouton, 1963).

Petrullo, Vincenzo, *The Yaruros of the Capanaparo River, Venezuela* (Washington, D.C.: Government Printing Office, 1939).

Pilsudski, Bronislaw, "[Pregnancy, Birth and Miscarriage among the Inhabitants of Sakhalin Island (Gilyak and Ainu)]," *Anthropos*, 5 (1910), pp. 756-774.

Pitts, Forrest R., et al., *Post-war Okinawa* (Washington, D.C.: National Research Council, Pacific Science Board, 1955).

Ploss, Herman Heinrich, Max Bartels and Paul Bartels, *Woman: An Historical Gynecological and Anthropological Compendium*, Vol. II (London: William Heinemann Ltd., 1935).

Preuss, Konrad T., *[Journey of Exploration to the Cagaba]* (St. Gabriel-Mödling bei Wien: Administration des "Anthropos," 1926).

Pumphrey, M. E. C., "The Shilluk Tribe," *Sudan Notes and Records*, 24 (1941), pp. 1-45.

Reichard, Gladys A., *Navaho Religion: A Study of Symbolism* (New York: Bollingen Foundation, 1950).

Reinach, Lucien de, *[Laos]* (Paris: A. Charles, Librairie-Éditeur, 1901).

Richards, Audrey I., *Land, Labour and Diet in Northern Rhodesia: An Economic Study of the Bemba Tribe* (Oxford: Oxford University, 1939).

Roscoe, John, *The Baganda: An Account of Their Native Customs and Beliefs* (London: Macmillan, 1911).

Rosman, Abraham, "Social Structure and Acculturation among the Kanuri of Northern Nigeria," unpublished Ph.D., Yale University, 1962.

Sahagún, Bernardino de, *Florentine Codex: General History of the Things of New Spain, Book 12—The Conquest of Mexico*, trans. by Arthur J. O. Anderson and Charles E. Dibble (Santa Fe: School of American Research and University of Utah, 1955).

Sanders, Irwin T., *Rainbow in the Rick: The People of Rural Greece* (Cambridge, Mass.: Harvard University, 1962).

Sarychev, Gavriil A., *Account of a Voyage of Discovery to the Northeast of Siberia, the Frozen Ocean, and the North-East Sea*, Vol. II (London: Richard Phillips, 1806).

Schlegel, Alice, *Male Dominance and Female Autonomy: Domestic Authority in Matrilineal Societies* (New Haven: Human Relations Area Files, 1972).

Schulze, Louis, "The Aborigines of the Upper and Middle Finke River: Their Habits and Customs, with Introductory Notes on the Physical and Natural History Features of the Country," *Royal Society of South Australia, Transactions and Proceedings and Report*, 14 (1891), pp. 210-246.

Schwarz, Franz X. Von, "[Way of Life, Customs and Habits of the Sedentary Population of Turkestan]," in *Turkestan, die Wiege der Indogermanischen Völker* (Freiburg im Breisgau, Herdersche Verlagsbuchhandlung, 1900).

Sen, Probhat K., *Land and Peoples of the Andamans* (Calcutta: Post-Graduate Book Mart, 1962).

Senfft, Arno, "[The Legal Customs of the Yap Natives]," *Globus*, 91 (1907), pp. 139-143, 149-153, 171-175.

Shirokogorov, Sergieĭ Mikhaĭlovĭch, *Social Organization of the Manchus: A Study of the Manchu Clan Organization* (Shanghai: 1924).

Slaski, J., "The Luapula Peoples," in Wilfred Whiteley and J. Slaski, *Bemba and Related Peoples of Northern Rhodesia and Peoples of the Lower Luapula Valley* (London: International African Institute, 1951), pp. 77-100.

Smith, Edwin W., and Andrew M. Dale, *The Ila-speaking Peoples of Northern Rhodesia*, Vol. II (London: Macmillan, 1920).

Smith, Mary F., *Baba of Karo: A Woman of the Muslim Hausa* (London: Faber and Faber, 1954).

Smith, Michael G., *The Economy of Hausa Communities of Zaria* (London: Her Majesty's Stationery Office, 1955).

Smith, Michael G., "The Hausa of Northern Nigeria," in James L. Gibbs, Jr., ed., *Peoples of Africa* (New York: Holt, Rinehart and Winston, 1965), pp. 119-155.

Smith, Watson, and John M. Roberts, *Zuni Law: A Field of Values* (Cambridge, Mass.: Harvard University, 1954).

Smithson, Carma L., *The Havasupai Woman* (Salt Lake City: University of Utah, 1959).

Speiser, Felix, "[Ethnological Data on the Santa Cruz Islands]," *Ethnologica*, 2 (1916), pp. 153-214.

Spiro, Melford E., "Ifaluk: A South Sea Culture," unpublished ms.—Washington, D.C., coordinated investigation of Micronesian Anthropology, Pacific Science Board, National Research Council, 1949.

Srinivas, Mysore N., *Religion and Society Among the Coorgs of South India* (Oxford: Clarendon, 1952).

Stanford University, China Program, *East China* (New Haven: Human Relations Area Files, 1956a).

Stanford University, China Project, *North China* (New Haven: Human Relations Area Files, 1956b).

Stanford University, China Project, *Taiwan (Formosa)*, 2 Vols. (New Haven: Human Relations Area Files, 1956c).

Stannus, Hugh S., "The Wayao of Nyasaland," *Harvard African Studies*, 3 (1922), pp. 229-372.

Steggerda, Morris, *Maya Indians of Yucatan* (Washington, D.C.: Carnegie Institution of Washington, 1941).

Steward, Julian H., et al., *The People of Puerto Rico: A Study in Social Anthropology* (Urbana: University of Illinois, 1956).

Stirling, A. Paul, *Turkish Village* (London: Weidenfeld and Nicolson, 1965).

Stout, David B., *San Blas Cuna Acculturation: An Introduction* (New York: Viking Fund, 1947).

Stow, John, *A Survey of London*, Vol. II (Oxford: Clarendon, 1971).

Suggs, Robert C., "Marquessan Sexual Behavior," unpublished ms.—New Haven, Human Relations Area Files, 1963.

Sutlive, Vinson H., "From Longhouse to Pasar: Urbanization in Sarawak, East Malaysia," unpublished Ph.D., University of Pittsburgh, 1972.

Sverdrup, Harald U., *[With the People of the Tundra]* (Oslo: Gyldendal Norsk Forlag, 1938).

Swanton, John R., "Social Organization and Social Usages of the Indians of the Creek Confederacy," *U.S. Bureau of American Ethnology, Annual Report*, 42 (1924/1925), pp. 23-472, 859-900.

Symons, Donald, *The Evolution of Human Sexuality* (New York: Oxford University, 1979).

Tessmann, Günter, *[The Fang Peoples: An Ethnographic Monograph on a West African Negro Group]*, Vol. II (Berlin: Ernst Wasmuth A.-G., 1913).

Textor, Robert B., *A Cross-Cultural Summary* (New Haven: Human Relations Area Files, 1967).

Thomas, Elizabeth M., *The Harmless People* (New York: Knopf, 1959).

Thompson, Virginia M., *French Indo-China* (New York: Macmillan, 1937).

Thompson, Virginia M., *Thailand, The New Siam* (New York: Macmillan, 1941).

Titiev, Mischa, *Araucanian Culture in Transition* (Ann Arbor: University of Michigan, 1951).

Titiev, Mischa, *The Hopi Indians of Old Oraibi: Change and Continuity* (Ann Arbor: University of Michigan, 1972).

Trézenem, Édouard, "[Ethnographic Notes on the Fan Tribes of the Middle Ogooué (Gabon)], *Société des Africanistes*, 6 (1936), pp. 65-93.

Trivers, Robert L., "Parental Investment and Sexual Selection," in B. Campbell, ed., *Sexual Selection and the Descent of Man, 1871-1971* (Chicago: Aldine, 1972), pp. 136-179.

Turnbull, Colin M., *The Mbuti Pygmies: An Ethnographic Survey* (New York: American Museum of Natural History, 1965).

Turner, Victor W., *The Lozi Peoples of North-western Rhodesia* (London: International African Institute, 1952).

Underhill, Ruth M., *Papago Indian Religion* (New York: Columbia University, 1946).

Valkenburgh, Richard F. van, "Navaho Common Law III: Etiquette-Hospitality-Justice," *Museum of Northern Arizona, Museum Notes*, 10 (1938), pp. 39-45.

Vinci, Miguel, trans. by James Cadell, *Red Cloth and Green Forest* (London: Hutchinson, 1959).

Voegelin, Erminie W., *Culture Element Distributions: XX, Northeast California* (Berkeley: University of California, 1942).

Wagley, Charles, *The Social and Religious Life of a Guatemalan Village* (Menasha, Wisconsin.: American Anthropological Association, 1949).

Washington (State) University, Far Eastern and Russian Institute, *A Regional Handbook on the Inner Mongolia Autonomous Region* (New Haven: Human Relations Area Files, 1956).

Whited, Stephen, *Report on Indians Taxed and Indians Not Taxed in the United States (except Alaska), at the Eleventh Census: 1890* (Washington D.C.: Government Printing Office, 1894), pp. 137-146.

Williams-Hunt, P. D. R., *An Introduction to the Malayan Aborigines* (Kuala Lumpur: Government Press, 1952).

Wilson, E. O., *Sociobiology: The New Synthesis* (Cambridge, Mass.: Belknap, 1975).

Wissler, Clark, *The Social Life of the Blackfoot Indians* (New York: American Museum of Natural History, 1911).

Wolf, Arthur P., "Marriage and Adoption in a Hokkien Village," unpublished Ph.D., Cornell University, 1965.

Worthington, E. E., *Middle East Science* (London: His Majesty's Stationery Office, 1946).

Wyndham, Richard, *The Gentle Savage: A Sudanese Journey in the Province of Bahr-el-Ghazal, Commonly Called "The Bog"* (New York: William Morrow, 1936).

Yang, Ching-kun, *The Chinese Family in the Communist Revolution* (Cambridge, Mass.: Center for International Studies, Massachusetts Institute of Technology, 1954).

Zimmerman, Carle C., and Phra Chedt Valdhyakara, "A Demographic Study of Eight Oriental Villages Yet Largely Untouched by Western Culture," *Metron*, 2 (1934), pp. 179-198.

Index

Index to Argot